D0233201

A Life of
Bishop John A. T. Robinson

BAXTER

A LIFE OF

Bishop John A.T. Robinson

Scholar, Pastor, Prophet

ERIC JAMES

COLLINS
8 Grafton Street, London WI
1987

William Collins Sons & Co. Ltd
London · Glasgow · Sydney · Auckland
Toronto · Johannesburg

Acknowledgements

To the signatories of letters, for their permission to quote them;

to the Central Board of Finance of the Church of England for permission to quote passages from the Church Assembly Report of Proceedings;

to the Registrar of the Convocation of Canterbury for permission to quote passages from the Record of Proceedings of the Convocation of Canterbury;

to Faber and Faber Ltd., for permission to quote from *Four Quartets*, T. S. Eliot Collected Poems 1909–1962: *For the Time Being*, W. H. Auden: *A Christmas Oratorio*; and from *Markings* by Dag Hammarskjöld translated by W. H. Auden and Leif Sjoberg;

to Sir Henry Fisher, the Executor of Lord Fisher of Lambeth and Lady Fisher, for permission to quote their letters;

to the Estate of Sir Osbert Lancaster for permission to reproduce a cartoon;

to A. R. Mowbray and Co. Ltd., SCM Press Ltd., and to *Sunday Mirror* to quote at length from the published works of Bishop John A. T. Robinson;

to *Time and Tide* for permission to quote a letter of Miss Valerie Pitt;

to Trog (Wally Fawkes) for permission to reproduce a cartoon.

BRITISH LIBRARY CATALOGUING IN PUBLICATION DATA

James, Eric
A life of Bishop John A. T. Robinson:
scholar, pastor, prophet.
1. Robinson, John A. T. 2. Church of
England—Bishops—Biography 3. Bishops
—England—Biography
I. Title
283'.092'4   BX5199.R722

ISBN 0-00-217366-2

First published 1987
© Eric James 1987

Set in Linotron Ehrhardt by
Rowland Phototypesetting Ltd
Bury St Edmunds, Suffolk
Made and printed in Great Britain by
William Collins Sons & Co. Ltd, Glasgow

For Ruth

Contents

Illustrations

Preface

It was in September 1977 that Bishop John Robinson asked me to be his literary executor. It seemed a somewhat pretentious title for what it then involved. He would phone me before he went away on a long journey, and tell me where his will was, and in what state – and where – his latest writings were. He would phone again as soon as he got back to report his safe return. It was at the end of May 1983 that he phoned one day and, after listening to my troubles for quite a time, said: 'Well, now I have some news for you: I have inoperable cancer.' My role and responsibility assumed then a sudden importance I had hoped it would never need to be given.

I describe towards the end of the biography how, shortly before he died, John said: 'Your job is to see that, if anyone should want to write a biography of me, it's the right person who does it.' He paused, and then added: 'But Ruth and I want you to know that most of all we should like you to do it.' I was much moved, and said I felt honoured by the invitation; but immediately dismissed the idea that I should write the biography myself and began to think of others who might.

It was only after John's death – he had also made it clear that he wanted me to preach at his Memorial Service in the Chapel of Trinity College, Cambridge – that I began fully to realize the degree of confidence he (and, I must add, his wife Ruth) had placed in me, and that there was much to be said for simply trusting their judgment. In that same conversation about the possibility of a biography John had also said: 'You know me best,' which I discovered he had also written in his 'Suggestions for Memorial Service'. It was a complete surprise to me. Obviously Ruth knew him best. Could it be true, I asked myself, that I knew John better than any other of his friends? I was also bound to ask: Did anyone ever really know John?

I first met John one afternoon in 1957 when he was Dean of Clare

College, Cambridge, and I was Chaplain of Trinity. He had heard that I loved his uncle Forbes' book of *Letters to His Friends*, and had asked me round to see whether I was interested in preparing a new edition. I found John absorbed at his desk. Only with difficulty did he detach himself and transfer his attention to me. The meeting was uneasy, awkward and brief. To my surprise, within hours Ruth was on the phone. John, she said, had been very pleased with our meeting and wanted me to come to supper with the family. Around the supper table John seemed to me a different man. My first evening with the Robinsons was sheer delight.

In the next nearly thirty years I had many such meals at the Robinsons' table. When John left Cambridge for South London I left with him to serve in the same diocese and, as Vicar of St George's, Camberwell and Warden of the Trinity College Mission, was in his area of episcopal care and shared in much of his pioneering work. When he returned to Cambridge to be Dean of Trinity, the fact that I had been Chaplain there served only to strengthen the bond between us. He was always the most loyal of friends.

The realization of John's confidence in me made me willing to write his biography. But questions remained. It was clear to me that a theologian of distinction should in due course write a book on The Theology of John Robinson: Richard McBrien's *The Church in the Thought of Bishop John Robinson* is a superb beginning. It was important that John's biography should not trespass in that land more than was necessary. Yet the life of a theologian is bound to be inextricably entwined with his theology; and the biographer of a theologian cannot possibly write his life and avoid his work. (The function of a theologian is often, of course, to 'distinguish without dividing' the Person and the Work.) In John's case most people would only want to read his life because of his work.

There was also the biographer's inescapable problem. A publisher's contract is a comfort, but sometimes that comfort vanishes, leaving only paralysis, when you find you have been asked to write about a hundred thousand words. There were, for instance, over four thousand letters to John in response to *Honest to God*. How do you put the river of a life like John's into a bottle? There is also all that arises from that crucial question: 'Did anyone ever really know John?' A biography is a creative work of reconstruction – not least by selection – 'Selection is interpretation'. The biographer is bound to go on asking: Is my portrait a likeness? Have I shown sufficient sympathy? Or too much? Are the shadows too dark? Have I got him right? Or wrong? Sargent said that every time he painted a portrait he lost a friend. With a posthumous portrait that possibility is, alas, removed. But such was John's friendship that his biographer need have no doubt of his subject's understanding and forgiveness.

Writing John's biography has given me a great deal of pleasure. I think he must have known it would. I think of it as a kind of present for me. But it would not have been possible without Ruth's co-operation, which has been total (and at times, undoubtedly, very costly) – and the family's and many friends'. The paragraphs on John at Arncliffe, for instance, would have been impossible without Janet Taylor. I am also particularly indebted to Professor Donald M. MacKinnon who specially undertook for me an evaluation of John's thesis *Thou Who Art*. Many of those who have helped are named in the text, but there was simply no room for all the contributions, which were so willingly made and were vital to the background of the biography. I must also thank Christian Action (of which John was a much valued sponsor) whose council has generously encouraged our indefatigable secretary Jane Spurr to wrestle with mountains of John's papers and to type my manuscript.

Writing the life of a friend who has died only recently is also painful – but it was not only John's death that was painful. Often it felt intrusive – like going into a friend's inner sanctum and rummaging through the contents when you've been given the run of the house when they were suddenly called away – and this was especially true when I was working in his study at Arncliffe, sitting in his chair and at his desk. I had to remind myself again and again that John had asked me to do what I was doing. It was sad, too, to have the last word, when so often I longed to hear – as I so often had – John's comment on what I had written. He could, and would, have told me if and when I had got him wrong.

I am glad it never occurred to me when John was alive that I 'knew him best'. It has helped to deliver me from feeling now that I could ever give the *whole* truth about him. John will remain – however many biographies of him are written and however long or short they may be – a mystery. And could it be otherwise in someone whose favourite verse was from Gerard Manley Hopkins' poem *The Wreck of the Deutschland*, which he first read at Marlborough: he chose the volume as a school prize; and in his last years caused the verse to be set in the additional prayers in the manual for Holy Communion prepared for Trinity College Chapel:

> Thou mastering me
> God! giver of breath and bread;
> World's strand, sway of the sea;
> Lord of the living and dead;
> Thou has bound bones and veins in me, fastened me
> flesh,
> And after it, almost unmade, what with dread,
> Thy doing; and dost thou touch me afresh?
> Over again I feel thy finger and find thee.

To me, those words encompass much of the mystery of John.

Michaelmas Day 1986   ERIC JAMES

I

Inherited Blessing

On 19 December 1917 Arthur William Robinson, Canon of Canterbury, wrote to Mary Beatrice Moore, a VAD nurse lodging in Camberwell:

The Precincts, Canterbury

Dear Miss Moore

You told me, I think, that your engagement at the Hospital will end in February. My old friend Dr Mason encourages me to think that you have as yet made no other, and further that you may be willing to consider the suggestion which I am now going to make. It is that you should come and share my life and work here at Canterbury. I deeply need such help and companionship as, I believe, you could give: and I hope that I am capable of returning a full measure of gladdest affection. Our knowledge of one another is not great, but it has existed for a good while, and you are perfectly familiar with the conditions of life here. I will add no more than this, a hope and prayer that we may both be guided in a matter which to me, at all events, is of very vital concern.

Yours most sincerely
Arthur W. Robinson.

Miss Moore, who, when she began to read the letter, had thought it was an invitation to join a committee, replied at once:

70 Camberwell Grove, SE5
December 21st 1917

Dear Dr Robinson

Your letter came today and has taken me so by surprise – I feel I hardly know how I can answer except by asking if you will give me time to think.

It is such a great thing to come upon suddenly and I do feel it very overwhelming for, in many thoughts and wonderings about the future, I had never thought of this. If only I felt able to give what you ask. It was strange your letter coming today, for I had this very morning gone up to see Matron to 'give notice' and came home feeling free to make fresh plans, to find your message waiting for me.

I do appreciate it and thank you for it. But it means so much for us both and life here is very strenuous just now with little time for quiet thought. My time at King's is up on Jan 28th. May I have this time to try and get to know what I ought to do?

Always yours very sincerely
Beatrice Moore.

Canon Robinson decided not to let the grass grow under his – or her feet, and replied by return:

The Precincts, Canterbury
December 23 1917

My dear Miss Moore

Your waited-for letter has reached me this morning, and I hasten to thank you for it. Of course, I must give you time, as long as you will: but as soon as you see your way to say 'yes', you must let me know! And might we not meet to talk over the matter. I would gladly come to London as soon as Christmas is over.

Let me add a few things that it may help you to consider. The idea is not quite so new to me as it is to you. For years I have known that my work rightly kept me from any other than a single life. After a year in Canterbury I begin to see as clearly that the old restriction does not hold, and to feel a great need of the companionship and blessing that marriage might bring. I have always been a sufferer through weakness of eyesight, and my working powers are painfully soon overtaxed when I am alone. Moreover I know that there are parts of my being that need to be developed, and can only be developed in fellowship of the closest kind.

Forgive the seeming egotism. I can only say these things to show you how really I should hope to give as well as to get. As to our ages, the Frenchman said that a man should marry a woman ½ his own age + 7 years!

I shall be 62 in January – the 19th – so that my wife ought to be 38. I daresay you are not far from it!

With more thanks and hopes,
Yours most sincerely
Arthur W. Robinson.

On Christmas Day 1917 Miss Moore penned her reply:

70 Camberwell Grove, SE5

My dear Dr Robinson

Please do come, for writing goes such a little way – I do thank you so gratefully for your letter, it has helped so much. There is so much I wish I could tell you, and perhaps some day I shall be able to, of what I have been taught in these very few days so that looking back they seem like weeks – and I feel there is no need to wait longer, and that I should not wait longer before telling you I am ready. It is so utterly different to what I expected to be told to do, that I just didn't recognise it at all at first – but to-day I did, and can only *very thankfully* try and obey. I know I mustn't write more tonight. It has been a very long day with no time to myself after the hour in Chapel this morning from 6 to 7, and it is now well after midnight.

Will you tell me when you can come? My hours are very limited and dreadfully strict! But it is generally possible to change round with one of the other nurses if you know beforehand. I have one precious ½ day (afternoon) in the week – generally Friday – but even this might be altered for urgent reasons. Would you be staying in London or just coming up for the day?

By the way – I am afraid I am just 3 weeks too old for I shall be 38 on the 29th!

Yours in all true sincerity
Beatrice Moore.

During the time of their engagement Arthur took Beatrice to the family home at Eastbourne to meet his blind and aged mother. 'Mother, I've brought Beatrice to see you,' he said, as Beatrice stood by her bed. 'Is she suitable?' his mother asked, 'Yes, Mother,' said Arthur very solemnly. 'Quite suitable.'

The marriage took place on Easter Tuesday, 2 April 1918, in the chapel of the eastern crypt of Canterbury Cathedral. Randall Davidson, Archbishop of Canterbury, conducted the service and gave an address; Armitage, Arthur's brother, celebrated the Holy Communion. On Trinity Sunday, 15 June 1919 there was great rejoicing in the Precincts when a son, John Arthur Thomas, was born. A month later Arthur conducted the baptism 'in the presence of a large crowd,' he wrote, 'including 1 Bishop 1 Dean 2 Archdeacons and 2 other Canons. So I think all was duly performed.'

A second son, Edward Armitage, arrived on 11 May 1921; and a daughter, Mary Cecilia, on 22 May 1924.

The children lived their first years in the Precincts close to the Cathedral, with a gate that opened on to the grass of its grounds. They took their first steps amid the sightseers come with guide-books and the latest of the seven-century line of pilgrims to Canterbury.

Beatrice was glad to be taking a full part again in the life of the Cathedral she had first come to love when, in the last years of his life, her father, like her husband, served it as a residentiary canon. For seven years there was 'Nannie' to help her with the children – even when they took a house at West Runton for their memorably happy family holidays. The children virtually lived in the nursery, but were occasionally taken downstairs. Nurse Parris, who had been brought in to help Nannie when the children were ill, wrote a description of their life, accompanied by a photograph of the children, for *Nursery World*:

> Our day nursery is a large airy room with two big windows looking on to the garden; the floor is covered with brown linoleum and washable rugs, and the walls are papered with blue wallpaper. A big cupboard holds the toys and on a wooden table stand the farmyard treasures, trees, houses, farms and animals of every description. On either side of the room is a camp bed, where the two little boys sleep. The two brothers are devoted to each other. One of their favourite games is to engage in a fight. One becomes an Israelite, the other a Philistine, and I often have to be Goliath. Day begins with cries from the children of 'Open your eyes, Nannie'. Then we have a game in bed or tell our dreams. Next comes the cold baths at 8 a.m., and after a good rub down, toothbrush parade and physical exercises, we are ready for breakfast – at 8.30. John then goes to school. He loves his lessons and is most upset if he has to stay away.

Arthur was an erudite and much loved man – who probably could not boil an egg. He was a calm and gentle father who, like John in later years, could never lose his temper. Yet to John he 'always looked like King Agrippa in *Struwelpeter*, with a great long beard . . . I imagined he'd put us all in the ink pot'. When Aunt Bessie brought some bricks with a Bible story on each side, and on one side a murderous looking Abraham sacrificing Isaac on the altar, John's mother recalled him pointing and saying 'Da-da'! Eventually John went away to preparatory school. Towards the end of his first term, in his weekly letter home on 2 December 1928 he asked anxious questions: 'What is the result of the X-raying?' 'Is Dada better now?' But there is no letter for the next weekend for, suddenly, on 7 December his father died, and Master John Robinson is listed as one of the chief mourners at the funeral in the Cathedral. It was conducted by the Dean, George Bell (his wife was Cecilia's godmother), who was to become such a significant figure in John's life.

It is curious that in John's next letter home, only five days after the funeral – he had been sent back to school immediately for the end of term – he simply writes with no reference at all to his father's death or the funeral:

Wellesley House, Broadstairs
December 16th 1928

Dear Mama

Last night we had a feast and had a lovely time with crackers and all sorts of things. I had one helping of soup, one of turkey, one trifull, and one of jelley. We had other things like tangerines and lemonade. Some that was left over we had for lunch today.

Did you have snow in Canterbury? We had a little here on Thursday and Friday.

I am top in form again this week. All the form are down again now [after chicken-pox], except the two that are at home. There is a sort of Magazine that the first form have edited called 'The Currant Bun'. There was a puzzle in it which most of the school went in for. I came out 2nd of the school, I think I am going to get a prize for it. The work prize-giving is tomorrow night. Am I going by train or car on Tuesday? I must stop now because the bell has gone long ago.

Lots of love and kisses from John.

John's only recorded remark immediately after his father's death was: 'We don't have to be quiet any more.' But that his father died when John was only nine years old is undoubtedly one of the most significant facts of his life.

'I was born and bred under the shadow of Canterbury Cathedral,' wrote John in *The Roots of a Radical*. 'My father and my mother's father were Canons there, and if you are an Anglican, you can't get much nearer than that to the heart of the establishment.' But the chapter of autobiography containing that paragraph is headed 'A Large Room'. 'Thou hast set my feet in a large room' (Ps. 31:8) was a favourite verse of his father's, which early in his life John knew to be profoundly true. Canterbury to John was much more than 'the heart of the establishment'. The rambling Romanesque and Gothic arches of the Cathedral; the stone shipped from Caen; Augustine, Alcuin and Alphege – and Thomas à Becket (after whom John had been given his third name) – all spoke to him of the *Una Sancta Ecclesia Catholica*, the 'Holy Catholic Church, the mother of all who bear the name of Christ'. It was through his father and mother in his earliest years that John first entered this 'large room'. His father, he wrote, was 'essentially a man of inclusiveness rather than of exclusiveness or party faction'. John loved to quote from one of his father's books, *The Holy Spirit and the Individual*: 'Large souls do not try to impose themselves upon us . . . In their presence we spread, and feel strangely at home.'

Arthur Robinson had been a priest of the Church of England of remarkable distinction. He was born in 1856 in his father's vicarage in the village of Keynsham, Somerset, the son of parents whose family had settled in Ireland for several generations: the Revd George and Henrietta Cecilia Robinson. Arthur went to Bristol Grammar School until his father moved to a poor parish at Everton, Liverpool, and sent him to Liverpool College. At Cambridge he gained a 'First' in Theology at Jesus College; but because of his bad eyesight he dictated his papers to his brother John. In 1879 he was ordained as a curate to his father at St Augustine's, Liverpool.

Arthur was the second son of a family of thirteen children – eight sons and five daughters – but after the death in the same year of his father and his oldest brother George the task of bringing up the large family fell heavily upon him. For three years he was rector of the village of East Shefford in Berkshire, and for four vicar of Bilton, Harrogate, until in 1888, still in his early thirties, he joined the College of Mission Clergy established by Archbishop Benson in London at the city church of All Hallows, Barking-by-the-Tower. In this work, with which he was connected for thirty years, twenty-one of them as vicar and warden of the college, he had an unrivalled experience of conducting parish missions and clergy retreats, not only at home but in Australia, New Zealand, South Africa and Canada; not surprisingly therefore during the First World War Archbishop Davidson chose him to lead the National Mission of Repentance and Hope. While still vicar of All Hallows he was appointed to be one of the prestigious 'Six-Preachers' of Canterbury Cathedral, where he first set eyes on his future wife, and where in 1916 the archbishop made him a canon residentiary.

Arthur Robinson was no mean scholar; he was a DD of Cambridge and in 1907 a candidate for the Lady Margaret's Professorship of Divinity there. A disciple of Frederick Denison Maurice, he was widely read in science and philosophy and the author of a dozen books, one of which, *The Personal Life of the Clergy*, was reissued in 1980 with a preface by John and a revised title: *The Personal Life of the Christian*. But it was his father's last work, *The New Learning and the Old Faith*, to which John particularly warmed. Bishop George Appleton, who well remembers John's father lecturing, has written: 'Arthur Robinson would have felt that his son John was a "chip off the old block",' and adds: 'It looks as if spiritual chromosomes are transmissible.'

Few men have been more conscious of their roots than John

Robinson, witness *The Roots of a Radical*. He was aware that, largely unwittingly, he had been shaped by the influence of his father whom he never really knew; but it was not only his father's influence of which he gradually became conscious but that of his twelve uncles and aunts and of all his 'English family Robinson'. He was a descendant of the Robinsons of Rokeby; and the first Lord Rokeby, Dr Richard Robinson, had been translated to the archbishopric of Armagh. There were also the Forbes family of his paternal grandmother and the Moore and Mackenzie families of his mother.

Arthur's mother lived on to the ripe age of ninety-two, to see him married but not to see her grandson John. Of her eight sons six were ordained, two of whom were missionaries in Africa, where another two became a missionary doctor and a missionary schoolmaster. Of her five daughters one married a parson, two became deaconesses, and one was among the first women to read theology at Oxford. Only one son, Edward, reacted against the evangelical piety of his home.

The most famous son and the 'most complex and cantankerous' was Armitage. After a brilliant academic career at Cambridge he produced what is arguably the greatest commentary on the Epistle to the Ephesians, and became Dean of Westminster and subsequently Dean of Wells. In the 1920s he was one of the representatives of the Church of England at Malines, at the Conversations between the Church of England and the Church of Rome. (John wore as his episcopal ring that given to Armitage by Lord Halifax on this occasion and inscribed: *Malines. Amicus amico*. In 1976 he attended at Malines the celebration of the fiftieth anniversary of the death of Cardinal Mercier, the host of the Conversations.)

Armitage's brother John – with the same initials – got a 'First' in Theology at Christ's College, Cambridge the same year as Armitage, and died on the Niger, after a pioneer ministry and beginning the first translation of the New Testament into Hausa. He was followed there by his brother Charles, who completed the first dictionary of the Hausa language and spent his later years as editorial secretary of the Anglican missionary society, the Society for the Propagation of the Gospel.

Another brother, Forbes, the eleventh of the thirteen children, appropriately figures in a volume called *Great Christians*, published fifty years ago. Forbes won more university prizes than all his brothers and succeeded Armitage as Dean of Christ's College, Cambridge. He was no less a scholar than Armitage, in Coptic and in the philosophy of religion, but it was not so much for his scholarship that he was

remembered as for the remarkable influence he exercised over undergraduates through friendship steeped in prayer. He died in 1904 aged
thirty-seven and his posthumous *Letters to His Friends*, published by his
brother Charles, was treasured by his nephew John as 'one of the
spiritual classics of the 20th century'. John caused a new edition to be
published in 1961, re-named *Forbes Robinson: Disciple of Love* (it was
edited by Michael Manktelow – now Bishop of Basingstoke – one of
Forbes' successors as Chaplain of Christ's). John maintained, and with
good reason, for it had been suggested to him by Canon Charles Raven,
former Dean of Emmanuel, Master of Christ's and Vice-Chancellor of
the University, that the Cambridge system of college chaplaincy which
has now spread to many another university was inspired by the example of
Forbes' pastoral work as Chaplain of Emmanuel and Dean of Christ's.

John would not want his aunts forgotten. Cecilia, like Forbes, died
tragically early of tuberculosis but not before she had written a
pioneering study of *The Ministry of Deaconesses*, with a remarkable width
and depth of learning in church history and liturgy. Elizabeth Mary
('Bessie') wrote the life of Head Deaconess Gilmore, the founder of
their work in South London. Florence was engaged in pastoral work
and wrote the life of her brother Charles.

John's father would speak of 'inherited blessing'; and this descended
from John's mother as well as his father. Beatrice's father, Edward
Moore, gained four 'Firsts' and was elected to a Fellowship of The
Queen's College, Oxford. He was in the first rank of Dante scholars.
For forty-nine years from the age of twenty-nine he was Principal of
St Edmund Hall, Oxford and was made a canon of Canterbury in
1903, where he was active in the chapter till his death in 1916.

John had a special respect and affection for his uncle Alfred, Edward
Alfred Livingstone Moore, his grandfather's son by his first marriage.
He was a CMS missionary who gained a 'First' at Oriel before he went
out to South India to take charge of the CMS college at Kottayam. He
was consecrated Bishop of Travancore and Cochin on 25 February
1925. He did much to stimulate the medical and educational work of
the diocese as well as its evangelism. He ordained the first two
clergymen from the backward-class community. Alfred, like the
Robinson uncles, exemplified for John the Robinson family motto,
which had been instilled into him from his earliest years: *non nobis
solum, sed toti mundo nati*: 'Not for ourselves alone but for the whole
world are we born.'

2

School and University

The death of her husband brought Beatrice face to face with immediate and inescapable decisions. The breadwinner of the family had been taken away. The house in the Precincts which they had inhabited for more than ten years had soon to be vacated for the successor to Arthur's canonry. There were friends, at the Cathedral and elsewhere, and relatives. The children's godparents assumed an increased importance. But Beatrice was now a mother who must make provision for herself and her brood of three intelligent children: John aged nine; Edward, seven; and Cecilia, four.

Beatrice had already proved both her ability to adapt to changed circumstances and her capabilities. She was born in St Edmund Hall where there had been a retinue of half a dozen servants. She had lived in Germany for some of the years of her education – she had received no formal education. She had moved to Canterbury with her parents in 1903; and when, within three years, her mother had died, as the only unmarried daughter she had managed her father's household. In Canterbury at 'Meister Omers', the canonical residence of her father, there were two parlour-maids, two housemaids, a cook, a kitchen-maid, a gardener and a coachman. After her father died Beatrice had become a wartime nurse at King's College Hospital, London, living in the lodgings where she had received Arthur's proposal of marriage; and had looked after Arthur and the children for a whole decade. She was a woman of discipline and devotion. Before marrying Arthur she had had thoughts of joining the Community of St Mary the Virgin, Wantage. She had received his proposal as a 'call of God to this holy estate'; and it was with renewed dedication that she now set about providing a home for her young family.

Beatrice was not without means, but a vast expenditure on the children's education was now out of the question. She wrote

immediately to the headmaster of Wellesley House seeking some reduction in John's fees, only to have her request refused. After two terms
therefore he was taken away and sent to Oaklands Court, a much less
expensive establishment. The move was a disaster. The headmaster
even forgot the day of the Marlborough scholarship examination
until all but too late. John managed to catch up with the last possible
train – at another station. But failing the examination had revealed what
the school had failed to teach; and again John was moved, to Bright-
lands at Newnham-on-Severn. But there, with little time before
re-sitting the scholarship, he lost all interest in his work. His mentors –
and his mother – were in despair. Next term however he came back to
life and achieved by the skin of his teeth a foundation scholarship for
the sons of the clergy, to Marlborough. He was sixteenth out of sixteen.

In the first months of anxiety over John's education Beatrice had also
been grappling with her other main problem: somewhere to live.
Canterbury, she decided, was home; and in July 1929 she moved with
the children to Cherries, a family house near St Martin's with an acre of
garden and a not too distant view of the Cathedral.

John settled happily at Marlborough. His reports were somewhat
monotonous: 'Knows how to use his memory . . . a scholarly mind . . .
can write clearly . . . uses his imagination . . . reached a high standard
. . . hard to beat his work . . . best scholar in the set . . . excellent . . .
conscientious . . . expecting him to do very well.' But in the Lent Term
1936 there was an important warning: 'He must not let his work make
him a recluse,' wrote his housemaster. 'I should like to see him mix
more.' His first letters home however recorded one area of signal – and
enduring – failure: 'This afternoon we were given temporary places in
the chapel and had our voices tried, but as I was on completely the
wrong note all the time (as usual) I was *not* put in the choir!!' Otherwise
his letters were much like other schoolboys' letters, concerned with
position in form, exams and games; pens, watches and foreign stamps;
visits, half-terms, ends of terms and holidays; plays and chapel – and,
not least, the provision of cherry cake.

John's career at Marlborough was certainly not brilliant in any way.
Basil Garnons Williams who taught him classics in the Upper Sixth
(and later became headmaster of Berkhamsted School) regarded him
as a late-developer. He describes him as 'a rather immature boy,
though not in a silly way', and would 'never have predicted any
particularly noteworthy future for him'.

In the vacations John invariably returned to Canterbury, which meant home and the cathedral to the Robinsons. It also meant cricket. In Oxford Beatrice had been taken to the Parks by her father to watch the university matches. In Canterbury the Cricket Week each year became for him – and for her and thus for all the children – a kind of secular Holy Week, with Frank Woolley, L. E. G. Ames and other Kent cricketers as the holy ones. Their scores and strokes were meticulously recorded and analysed by 'spiders'. At Marlborough John produced what was virtually his first book, an analysis of the career of L. E. G. Ames, occupying 150 pages. To the last years of her life Beatrice took her place in the pavilion enclosure at Canterbury. To the end of his life watching cricket in general was a favourite pastime of John's, and following the fortunes of Kent in particular. He was not an outstanding cricketer; at Marlborough and Cambridge he watched and played. He could have been very much better had his priorities not lain elsewhere. His sister Cecilia, however, was to become a great cricketer – the pride of the family when she played for England in 1958 and made a century at Adelaide on her second tour of Australia.

It was at Marlborough that theology first captured John's imagination. In 1937 the young and vigorous newly appointed school chaplain, Ronnie Howard (later headmaster of Hurstpierpoint), started a Religious Discussion Society and introduced John, in the upper sixth, to Berdyaev and *The Destiny of Man*, a copy of which he bought with the Council Divinity Prize. The book defeated him on first reading, but the great issues it tackled, its breadth of background and the profundity of mind of its author fascinated him. With the divinity prize he also bought volumes of poetry: Hopkins, Housman and Eliot.

John took to the idea of ordination much as he took to theology. There was no dramatic decision. He could not remember a time when it did not seem right for him to follow in his father's, and so many of his uncles', footsteps.

At 5.45 p.m. on 15 December 1937 B. L. Manning, the senior tutor of Jesus College, Cambridge – John's father's old college – sent a telegram to John at Marlborough: 'Awarded Rustat exhibition £40 titular value congratulations.' An hour after he received it John telegraphed his mother the good news. Beatrice's pencilled calculations on the back of a letter from the Master of Jesus make it clear that the news did not solve all her problems:

	£	s	d
Rustat Ex.	40	0	0
Ordination Fund	60	0	0
Leaving Ex.	40	0	0
Miss White	30	0	0
Self	50	0	0
	220	0	0
Estimated Expenses	240	0	0

Beatrice had moved to a flat in Chiswick in September 1936 in order to provide a home for Cecilia when she started as a day girl at St Paul's Girls' School at Brook Green, and for John and Edward in the vacations; but no tenant could be found for Cherries in Canterbury, on which Beatrice had pinned her hopes of financing the children's education. Mercifully Jesus College was generous and agreed to give John £80 for his first year in college. Further relief came to Beatrice from another quarter. Uncle Alfred, retiring from his episcopate in South India to be Vicar of Horspath in Oxfordshire, invited his half-sister to keep house for him and make it the family home. It was an opportune invitation, and Beatrice readily accepted.

October 1938 was not the easiest month for a young man to go up to Cambridge. It was the morrow of Munich. Within six months Prague would be occupied. But for the country – and for Cambridge – it was 'business as usual'. In his first term John coxed the sixth Jesus boat – he coxed one of the lower boats throughout his time at Jesus – and attended his first Roosters' dinner with Sir Arthur Quiller-Couch ('Q') responding to one of the toasts. In his first long vacation in 1939, just before the outbreak of war, John went to the Student Christian Movement Conference at Swanwick. Twenty-five years later he was to write in *The New Reformation?*: 'I reckon that my theological education began when I was plunged in at the deep end with Reinhold Niebuhr at the SCM Conference at Swanwick . . . I think I can say that I learned more theology which has subsequently been of vital concern to me as a Christian in the world from SCM than I ever did from the University Faculty.' John shared a tent with David Cartwright, who after Cambridge was to be with him in Bristol and to be a lifelong friend. (David became Bishop of Southampton just after John died.)

In October 1939 John had to register for National Service. He expected to be called up at any moment, and one day was actually notified that he must report, only for it to be cancelled because he was an ordinand and therefore in a reserved occupation. Others also were in the same limbo, which was hardly conducive to work. His results in the Classics Tripos Part I were in fact disappointing. He managed only a 2.1. Yet nobody but John himself doubted he was a first class scholar. He began carefully to monitor his reading – a practice he continued all his life – strictly recording all the books he read each term and vacation, dividing them into LL for very long; L for long; ML for medium long; MS for medium short, and S for short. Thus in 1940 he read forty books and in 1941 seventy-six. Nothing so clearly reveals the width and depth of his reading as a list of the books he read in a term or a vacation. During the long vacation 1940, for instance, at the height of the Battle of Britain, he read:

  L *St Clair Donaldson*, Dimont and Batty
  S *Do the State and Nation belong to God or the Devil?* Reinhold Niebuhr
  S *Why the Church is not Pacifist*, Reinhold Niebuhr
ML *The Price of Leadership*, Middleton Murry
  L *The Failure of a Mission*, Nevile Henderson
MS *W. G. Grace*, Bernard Darwin
MS *The Essentials of Democracy*, A. D. Lindsay
  L *The Road to Endor*, E. H. Jones
ML *Christians in a World at War*, Edwyn Bevan
MS *Christianity and Justice*, O. C. Quick
  L *An Introduction to Philosophy*, Jacques Maritain
ML *Law and Love*, T. E. Jessop
  S *Nietsche or Christ?* C. F. Rogers
MS *The Village on the Hill*, J. Maarten
  S *Reinhold Niebuhr: An Introduction*, David Paton
  S *Creed or Chaos?* Dorothy L. Sayers
  S *Christianity and Communism*, Essays
  S *Christianity and Civilisation*, Arnold Toynbee
  S *The Spiritual Issues of the War* W. H. Elliott
LL *Guide to the Philosophy of Morals and Politics*, C. E. M. Joad
  L *The Destiny of Man*, Nicholas Berdyaev
  L *Great Contemporaries*, W. S. Churchill
  L *Oliver Cromwell*, John Buchan
ML *Locke, Berkeley and Hume*, Morris
  L *A History of the Early Church*, J. W. C. Wand
MS *The Rudiments of Criticism*, Greening-Lamborn
  L *Introduction to the Philosophy of Religion*, J. Caird
  L *Studies in Christian Philosophy*, W. R. Matthews

LL	1	Theology	15
L	10	Philosophy	5
ML	4	Biography	4
MS	5	Politics	2
S	8	Literature	1
		Fiction	1
28			28

After Dunkirk it seemed the war might go on for years. John worked hard. The one friend who shared a lecture course with him on philosophical theology in the autumn of 1940 soon had to leave for the RAF and was killed in the first mass raid over Cologne. The resulting one-to-one relationship with his lecturer H. C. L. Heywood (later Provost of Southwell) proved productive, for it was he who introduced John to Martin Buber's dull-brown paperback, *I and Thou*, whetting his curiosity with the remark that he would find it very difficult, that it would be useless for the Tripos, but that it might transform *him*. John had his academic reward in 1942. It particularly pleased him that he won the Burney Prize exactly fifty years after his uncle Forbes had won it; and the Burney Studentship for 1942–3. His subject was 'Kant's Ethics and the Christian Moral Ideal', for which he steeped himself in Kant and the freedom, autonomy and integrity of the personal. Alexander Ewing, his examiner for the Prize, wrote to him: 'It was a very good piece of work indeed.' John was awarded the only 'First' that year in the Theological Tripos in the Philosophy of Religion and Christian ethics. At Michaelmas 1941 he had gone into residence at Westcott House where B. K. Cunningham was still the wise and revered Principal. 'Do not lose the human touch, John, or become too "distant",' wrote B.K. when he sent him his congratulations on his 'First'.

John was not only working hard at his studies. He was president of the Student Christian Movement in Cambridge 1942–3, and gave it lively leadership. It introduced him to a wide range of people in the Church: Algy Robertson and Denis Marsh of the Franciscans, C. S. Lewis, Charles Williams, Franz Hildebrandt, J. S. Whale, Charles Raven and others. In his role as president of the SCM he had one of his first brushes with ecclesiastical authority, when Edward Wynne, then Bishop of Ely, refused to allow the woman president of the Presbyterian Society in Cambridge to take her turn as head of one of the denominational groups in conducting the Sunday evening service for the SCM in St Andrew the Great, Cambridge. John caused a greater stir by praying for 'our enemies' at the Leper Chapel outside Cambridge, of which he was the Westcott House 'bishop', and mentioning Adolf Hitler by name! Feelings were outraged; objections were lodged; opinions in Westcott were divided – and John was of course genuinely surprised by the furore. B.K. said that praying for our enemies was right, but this was not the right way to do it in wartime. B.K. loved John, and was much more perplexed when he objected to tipping the college servants at the end of term!

There is little doubt that John made his mark at Westcott. He was recognized as an outstanding student though socially somewhat immature. He was always the centre of a ferment of ideas, with which not all agreed. Some were irked that a student should seem sometimes to be taking upon himself the role of a teacher. He loved argument, discussion and debate, and questioning assumptions. It was those who knew him best who liked him best. At his own suggestion he lived for the Michaelmas term 1942 with the Presbyterians in Westminster College. At the end of term he made the proposal to the principal, W. A. L. Elmslie, that a 'Union Theological College' be formed from all the existing theological colleges in Cambridge. It was perhaps the first of John's many prophetic proposals, for even today there is only a limited *federation* of Cambridge theological colleges. It was at this time John became one of the comparatively few juniors invited to join C. H. Dodd's seminar. In this exalted company John was understandably a rather solitary brooding figure, of few words, and those mostly enquiring or critical. In the Lent term 1944 he was 'sheriff' (senior student) at Westcott. B.K. had departed and Peter de Denne May was acting principal. He records in the Westcott House Record Book that John was 'efficient and surprisingly self-effacing'.

In John's Westcott years a meeting of Christian pacifists and non-pacifists, called the Cloister Group, was held regularly at the Master's Lodge, Christ's College under the joint leadership of William Temple and Charles Raven, the Master of Christ's. It was particularly through his membership of this group that John came to know William Temple, who became Archbishop of Canterbury early in 1942; and he was devoted to him and greatly influenced by him. Temple had known John's father; and Armitage Robinson had helped Temple with his difficulties concerning the Virgin birth and the bodily resurrection of our Lord, which for a time had impeded his ordination. Temple had the reputation of being so kindly in his judgment of men that he accepted a number of people for ordination who should probably never have been ordained. But even John was somewhat shaken when, at one of Temple's visits to Christ's, John told him he wanted to be ordained and Temple simply said: 'Right. Let me know when you are ready.' End of interview!

In June 1943 Trinity College had elected John to the Stanton Studentship for 1943–4. F. R. Tennant, aged and very shy but able to understand others who were shy, was the Fellow of Trinity who saw John about the work he wanted to do; and Professor H. H. Farmer was appointed his supervisor. The degree committee accepted as the subject of the dissertation on which John was to work – which in due course he would successfully submit for his PhD – 'The notion of personality and its relation to Christian theology, with particular reference to the contemporary "I – thou" philosophy, and the doctrine of the Trinity and the Person of Christ.' It is sad that the dissertation, entitled 'Thou Who Art', a conscious counter to E. L. Mascall's Thomist work *He Who Is: A Study in Traditional Theism*, was never published and therefore not widely read. Professor Farmer had no doubt that it should be. Professor John Baillie, John's examiner, judged it to be the best PhD ever to have come his way. But it is over 600 typed pages; 160,000 words. Professor Donald MacKinnon, reading it forty years after it was written, describes it as a 'very impressive work'. It was undoubtedly the foundation of much of John's future theological writing. The dissertation required of course a considerable amount of preparatory reading. In 1942 John read fifty-four books of philosophy and theology; in 1943 forty-four; in 1944, when the dissertation was being written up, twelve. Barth, Brunner, Berdyaev, Kierkegaard, Heim, MacMurray and others, all made their contribution; but at the heart of John's thinking was Martin Buber's 'medium small' but seminal volume *I and Thou*.

More than anyone else in Britain Farmer had integrated the insights of the 'I – thou' philosophy with the biblical doctrines of God and man; and it was under Farmer's guiding hand that John explored both the history and the implications of this tradition of thought for how one could speak of personality in God, rather than of God as "a Person". C. C. J. Webb's Gifford Lectures of 1918, *God and Personality*, also played a decisive part in shaping John's mind.

The heart of all talk about personality [John wrote] is the reality of a certain quality of relatedness, of being encountered and drawn out by the grace and claim of the 'Thou'. This is the centre-point, the existential reality, which has to be given expression. And the need to speak of 'God' derives from the awareness that in and through and under every finite 'Thou' comes, if we are open to it, the grace and claim of an eternal, unconditional 'Thou' who cannot finally be evaded by being turned into an 'It'. This was the reality which the language of 'the personality of God' was trying to represent.

In his dissertation John was beginning his work as a theologian as he meant to go on: questioning accepted doctrine, stripping away, getting to the heart, reinterpreting, constantly pushing out, being stretched, never resting content. He was, in Barth's great phrase, 'taking rational trouble over the mystery'.

John was to a fault a rational man; but at the beginning of 1944 an event was to occur in his life which would ground and test all he had been writing in the depths of his personal experience. In January 1944 Ruth Grace was a nineteen-year-old undergraduate in her second year at Newnham. She had come up to Cambridge from war-scarred Liverpool to read Modern Languages, after a promising school career at Holly Lodge High School, Liverpool. During the Christmas vacation her father, a clerk in a tea merchant's office, had died of tuberculosis; as had his father and sister before him. Since the beginning of term Ruth had been confined to bed with a feverish cold. The last thing she felt like was attending a theological discussion. But the college SCM group was holding its first meeting of term and the Cambridge past president John Robinson – to Ruth he was just a name – was coming to lead the group on C. S. Lewis' *The Problem of Pain*. Only *esprit de corps* got Ruth to the meeting. What most struck her about John that evening was what often struck many others on first meeting him, what seemed to be his rather odd mannerisms: his continuous nervous shifting about in his chair; the way he champed his teeth when he laughed and above all his penetrating and grating voice. But she went to the group again the next week! This time, and not for the last time, she endlessly (and fruitlessly) argued with him about time and free will.

Ruth was infuriated when, at a meeting a few weeks later to which she had taken some mending to do at the discussion, which was the general custom, seeing her needle and cotton John threw her a leather glove with a split seam and said: 'While you're at it, you could do this.'

After a protest she did what she was asked – and recognized later it had been a secret tentative language of offering and acceptance. Ruth went with others to tea with John at Westcott that term, and they corresponded during the vacation. John was studying that vacation at St Deiniol's Library, Hawarden under Alec Vidler (later Dean of King's College, Cambridge), and came over for the day to pay his first visit to Ruth's Anfield home. That day John and Ruth first held hands – on a Liverpool tram. On the first Sunday evening of term she caught sight of him at the Great St Mary's service, and on the way out felt his hand on her shoulder. In the next few weeks, they spent an increasing amount of time together, bicycling out into the country to pick oxlips, cowslips and bluebells; John always loved picking flowers for indoors. On the evening of Saturday 13 May Ruth was going to the Cambridge Music Club concert, as was her custom, and was surprised when John asked to come too; it was not an easy evening for a non-music-lover like him. She was embarrassed by his audible shuffling in his seat and his drumming his fingers on the arm of the chair in time with the music. She only too thankfully agreed when at the interval he said, 'I think we have had enough, don't you?' and invited her back to Westcott for a cup of tea. In fact John had had a particular reason for being fidgety that evening, for it was then and there that he suddenly asked Ruth whether she loved him enough to marry him. Ruth knew at once what she must reply: that of course she loved John enough to marry him; that it was right for her to do so; and that nothing else would do. That was so in spite of the fact that he seemed to her a somewhat gauche person with odd mannerisms; that he had that very evening caused her embarrassment; that he did not share her consuming interest in music; that she was a very young nineteen-year-old, less than two years out of school, who had been encouraged, not least by her headmistress, in the assumption that she had a successful academic career ahead of her; that she had also the vague idea that having once established herself in a profession she might then turn her mind to marriage and a family. And there was the fact that during the latter years of her father's illness her mother had been the breadwinner of the family, and Ruth wanted to make some contribution to the family purse.

But the basis of marriage for Ruth, as for John, was already there in the tenderness and trust with which the exploration of each other's world had been made in the few weeks of their courtship. In the terms of John's dissertation – and of Buber's *I and Thou* – John and Ruth knew themselves to be in the profoundest sense the other's 'Thou', totally and gladly vulnerable to each other. It was this tenderness, so surprising and humbling for Ruth to find in one who could sometimes appear to be brash and insensitive, that enabled her to respond – as Beatrice had responded to Arthur's sudden proposal – with her own 'I am ready', from which there could be no going back.

From January 1943 to August 1945 John kept a journal, with intermittent rather than consecutive daily entries. Many pages of the journal provide clues to his innermost thoughts during this crucial period of his life, but none more than his entry on 26 March 1944:

Mar. 26 Passion Sunday Tonight God has spoken to me forcibly, though not through the word spoken from the pulpit, but battling against it, shouting through it, invading my soul and assuring me of His presence, so often forgotten and doubted. It seemed to come just out of the blue and disconnected with any 'Church context'. But many spiritual forces must have been gathering only to break out tonight – this morning's eucharist, Passion Sunday and its hymns – it is also B.K.'s birthday and JWTT's priesting. When it came, the experience had about it that double quality of absolute sweetness, fruition, repose and of absolute demand, searching and condemning and exhausting – which I have so often written about and never completely experienced. Oh, there is not that sharp break between ἀγάπη and ἔρως of which Nygren speaks! There is a fundamental similarity of structure between love of God and love of a woman. This other, this 'Thou' can never be regarded as a 'piece' of my world, to be used for my own fruition and the fulfilment of my being. There is a severe limitation of the ego, resulting in the highest degree of unselfishness of which man is capable. The 'other' constitutes the sole end of my being, the sole spring of my action – which is pure listening. It is not a question of self-fulfilment to a certain limit and self-sacrifice thereafter or of self-sacrifice first rewarded by self-fulfilment. The utter infinitude of fulfilment is present only in the total constriction upon self-will which respect for the inviolability of the other's personality means. *Cui servire est regnare.* That is true of God and of a woman. The marriage relationship is not the antithesis of the God relationship; rather, as the Bible says, the one is the type of the other. ἔρως is not opposed to ἀγάπη as something selfish and self-centred – even in its prototypal sexual form.

Yet the love of a woman and of God are not simply to be equated. When the two are set together, the former becomes utterly subordinate. Neither the fulfilment nor the demand is ultimately absolute – the claim of the finite Thou may not be averted by any other finite consideration, but beside the infinite it is nothing. That is to say, though the two loves are in form identical, in content they are very different and may be mutually exclusive.

On 3 June John wrote in his journal: 'Visit to Little Gidding with Ruth . . .' On 17 June he recorded a dream which, with good reason, he judged to be of some significance. Its most obvious interpretation however – with Ruth 'in the house' and 'part of me for ever' – seems either to have eluded John or to have been too obvious to warrant comment; or perhaps to have been too hard for him to accept at the conscious level:

> This morning I woke up early with the dream that Mother had just died. Seldom have I dreamt anything quite so vivid. She died very peacefully in her bed and the nurse and I closed her eye-lids and composed her for burial. Yet on waking never for one moment did I believe that she had actually died in reality. There was none of that nightmare feeling when you battle with yourself for the blessed realisation that it was only a dream. No, I *knew* it wasn't true, and this allowed it to speak to me in quietness. My first reaction was one of penitence. To think that I owed her so much and loved her so deeply and showed it and told her so little! But thanks be the God who has spoken to me in time and allowed me opportunity to make amends. May he grant that I do not throw it away.
>
> Ruth was in the house at the time. It was a great consolation to me to know that I had still got her and that together we would live out a holier life and more truly thankful life than I would alone. But her presence also made me realise in a way I had never felt before what it really must have been like for Mother to have Father, and how she must have missed him in a way that we could never make up and did little to try. Once more God grant that this revelation may not be useless, but may accomplish that whereunto Thou sentest it.
>
> Oh the peace and joy and quiet confidence I derive from the fact that Ruth is part of me for ever! How little I knew of her when I committed my life to her. *Gott sei Dank* that it has turned out like this. Little can be more awful than to discover after you have hopelessly fallen in love with someone that after all she will not do, and to have to tell both yourself and her that. Thank God who has spared me that and given me absolute joy and certainty more than I ever thought to hope for.

In his dream, since it is before John's marriage to Ruth, he not surprisingly idealizes his future wife; but the dream also foreshadows the burdens he will ask Ruth to bear in the years ahead. Without a father John's relationship with his mother was particularly close and the dream, which clearly illustrates the mother-wife transition every married man has to make in some way, indicated also the particular demands the transition made on John.

During that summer Ruth stayed several times with John's family at Horspath Vicarage and in September John went to stay with Ruth in Liverpool. Hardly had he arrived when on 22 September the telegram came from his mother: 'Uncle Alfred died this morning. Can you come?' When Ruth saw him off on the train at Lime Street she was overcome by the extent of John's grief. Through the train window she watched him sobbing, the tears pouring down his face. She was never to see John cry again.

Only a month later William Temple died. John wrote in his journal: 'Tonight I feel it just like when Uncle Alfred died – never before has the death of a public figure seemed to me such a real personal bereavement.' The loss for John of William Temple and of his Uncle Alfred was clearly the more painful and intense because he had been from such an early age without a father; indeed his bereavement at their deaths may well have been the expression of a grief suppressed at the time of his father's death. So it was that on Tuesday, 31 October 1944 John – having jumped the special train from London 'composed entirely of first-class carriages and stiff with every VIP you could think of' – returned to Canterbury – thanks to the Archbishop's Chaplain, Ian White-Thomson (later Dean of Canterbury) – and sat in the Choir for the funeral of the Archbishop: 'one of the most moving occasions I can recall'.

Although he never doubted he should, and would, be ordained, the experience he recorded in his journal on 26 March 1944 clarified and confirmed his vocation. An even greater clarity and conviction came through another experience recorded on 28 November that year. Indeed this experience foreshadows not only his ordination but, for instance, what he would feel called to do twenty years later, when with a sense of divine imperative he wrote *Honest to God*:

November 28th   cf. Mar 26 of this year. Again it has come, with the same constricting and exhausting effect that makes you want to clutch your head and bite your lips. It is impossible to analyse – but the author of Psalm 139 knew it – 'Thou hast laid thine hand upon me'. It is being locked and chained by the claim of another, yet in such a way that one's own freedom and responsibility and the sense of decisiveness are, so far from being destroyed, almost painfully accentuated. It is the situation of

Isaiah and Samuel – the situation of listening passively for a divine command which is also actively the most decisive choice.

This is the end of a Quiet Day. I have been reading S. K.'s *Training in Christianity*. Seldom has anything affected me so powerfully. There is that in K. and Buber and Barth and Brunner and Baillie and Farmer and Unamuno and the rest which seems to strike a chord deeper down in me than anything else – it is this which, though often satisfying only the intellect (but that fully) induces and is finally verified by such experiences as tonight's and my deepest experiences of the meaning of love. If these be not real then nothing is.

It is this experience of a really *existential* theology which leaves me so completely unsatisfied by the approved (esp. Catholic) techniques of meditation. The assumption is that for a quiet day or Chapel meditation you should select something entirely different from your ordinary study reading. This is just disastrous. It means that your devotion becomes untheological and pi and your theology barren, critical and unexistential. The results are obvious enough. The ideal book is one that it is impossible to decide whether it should go into the ordinary or the devotional library. These are practically non-existent – Kierkegaard is one of the very few authors who would begin to qualify. I can honestly say that I should have read *Training in Christianity* today whether it had been a Quiet Day or not: therein lies half the value of the reading.

It is no little source of suffering and straitening to feel that in writers such as K., Buber, Unamuno is the truth, and truth which is shouting at me with a Divine imperative to pass it on; to know too that such truth by its very nature is such that it can only be communicated in the infinite subjectivity of becoming in its transmission, no longer theirs but *mine*; and yet to know myself to be one who is by nature a 'systematic' doctrinal 'it' theologian, by whom as such such truth is incommunicable!

On the eve of the anniversary of their first meeting, 19 January 1945, John wrote in his journal: 'As Ruth said tonight, "The old year ends." What a year! *Gott sei Dank.*' But they were both well aware that what the new year held was all unknown.

John's mother was having to move once more now that Horspath Vicarage could no longer be home. (The army had occupied Cherries during the war. It might now be released; but in what condition?)

In Canterbury a 'pharaoh had arisen which knew not Joseph', and John would sometime have to see him about his future. Geoffrey Fisher would be enthroned as Archbishop of Canterbury in mid-April.

Ruth still had her finals ahead of her that summer. Although she was engaged to John, according to the extraordinary rules of the Church of

England at that time they would not be allowed to be married for nearly three years – until a year after John had been ordained priest, which would be a year after he had been ordained deacon; and as yet there was no certainty where – or when – that was to be, though it was assumed it would be in the autumn of that year.

Suddenly, by way of the seventy-eight-year-old Dr Tennant, came the possibility for John of becoming Assistant Professor in the Philosophy of Religion at Swarthmore College, Pennsylvania. 'Quite a young man' was wanted, 'equipped to teach courses dealing with the philosophy of religion, the history of religion, and Christian thought . . . who has also a good grounding in general philosophy.' It was in some ways tailor-made and therefore could not be rejected out of hand. But it precipitated a host of questions. It was 'in the first instance for a short period of time, and then, if it turned out mutually acceptable, for an indefinitely long period of time.'

Here, clearly, was John's first crisis of decision. Should he even contemplate going indefinitely to the USA? (In January 1945 there was still 'a war on'.) Was he meant primarily to be an academic? Now he was engaged Ruth's future was as important as his: had he not written in his journal 'This other, this "Thou" can never be regarded as a "piece" of my world, to be used for my own fruition and the fulfilment of my being'? But had he not also written: 'The claim of the finite "Thou" may not be averted by any other finite consideration, but beside the infinite it is nothing'? Could the claim of the infinite be concealed within this admittedly tempting and flattering offer that was now on his plate?

John was perplexed, and took his problem to his Principal at Westcott, Billy Greer (later Bishop of Manchester). Wisely Greer sent him to George Bell, by then Bishop of Chichester, who had befriended the family from his days as Dean of Canterbury. (Had William Temple still been Archbishop, undoubtedly John would have gone to see him.) John made his visit to Bell at Chichester in the blackout on 16 February 1945. It was a crucial conversation. Bell had no doubt that John – the product of preparatory school, public school and Cambridge – should go to a parish rather than straight to an academic appointment. 'He knew that I would respect his advice', said John in one of his last sermons, 'and I have never regretted it.' Bell's advice echoed insights John had already received from his reading – and hearing – of Niebuhr, Temple, Vidler, Buber and others. He was as clear as Bell that his vocation was to be a Christian theologian. He also believed his theology must be earthed in experience of the world. (That was not to say he must never be a theologian in a university; John would never imagine a university was not 'in the world'.) After giving his unhurried time to John, the bishop returned to his desk until ten o'clock. Then he said, 'Now I'm going to read you some modern poetry.'

With George Bell's counsel, the next step became clear: ordination to the diaconate in a down-to-earth part of God's world. Ruth was greatly relieved at the decision. John arranged to see the suffragan bishop of Dover, Alfred Rose – in charge at Canterbury until the archbishop was enthroned – about a possible parish in the Canterbury diocese. The bishop had in mind Buckland-in-Dover for John.

On 15 May however there occurred one of the most momentous meetings in John's life. Mervyn Stockwood, then Vicar of St Matthew Moorfields, Bristol came to Westcott House to conduct a Quiet Day. At the end of it John, characteristically taking the initiative, asked him whether he could come to him as his curate. Mervyn did not immediately agree but invited John to Bristol for a weekend. There Mervyn walked him along the Avon, showed him the parish – consisting mainly of unskilled workers, dockers and railwaymen and their families, a warm-hearted people living still in a neighbourhood ripe for slum clearance – and took him into a pub in the parish, leaving him in the bar to fend for himself. Afterwards Mervyn asked the publican what he had made of John. The publican said he was 'champion'. John secured from the new archbishop his release from his obligations to Canterbury and it was soon signed and sealed that John should be ordained that Michaelmas to serve at St Matthew Moorfields.

Ruth's Cambridge career was crowned with success. She gained a 'First' in the Modern Language Tripos in Spanish and French. Her tutor at Newnham had hoped she would go on to qualify for university teaching. She decided however not take up the offer of a fourth year at Newnham but to take a teaching post in Liverpool. It was time, she felt, to provide a little for her mother – who during her husband's illness and since his death had worked as a Prudential insurance agent – and to begin to prepare for her marriage to John.

So John went off to Bristol eager to begin his ordained ministry, while Ruth returned rather reluctantly to Liverpool, home and school.

3

The Bristol Years

John was ordained deacon by Bishop C. S. Woodward at the Michaelmas ordination on Sunday, 23 September 1945. The hymn at the communion was 'O thou who camest from above', which would be sung at John's ordination to the priesthood, at his marriage, at all the family baptisms, at his consecration and at his funeral, thanksgiving eucharist and memorial service. He received, of course, many letters sending good wishes and assuring him of prayer. His Dean at Jesus College, Cambridge, Percy Gardner-Smith, wrote:

I hope Moorfields is not a purely working-class district, for your gifts and attainments would find more scope in a parish where there were a good many educated people. The theory, popular among the heads of theological colleges, that only cottagers have souls, that the upper classes ought to be neglected, and that to associate with educated people is unworthy of the zeal of a young clergyman, seems to me great nonsense. In a town parish you will find your time pretty well occupied, often with little things; but I hope you will still be able to open a book occasionally and perchance to write. You may find preaching a tax. It comes harder to the scholar and thinker than to the mass-produced product of the seminary. To the latter it is easy just to say a few words.

But to the man who feels that there is a lot to be said and he ought to be able to say it, even the preparation of quite short addresses involves serious labour. At any rate, it ought to. The Church has suffered grievously from the possessors of the gift of the gab, men who find it so easy to talk and so difficult to say anything. Your own difficulty may be to maintain a reasonable brevity. No doubt you have thought it all out and decided what your aim is to be. To me it seems that the next 50 years will be a period of increasing doctrinal fluidity and the task of the Church is to secure continuity. There is much in traditional Christianity which is not acceptable to the present generation, and it is the business of our future leaders to pour the old wine into new bottles. The shape and size of those bottles constitutes the problem of the age.

John preached his first sermon at the 'People's Service' at 6.30 p.m. on 14 October on 'Blessed is he who shall not be offended in me' (Luke 7:23). (There was Parish Communion on a Sunday morning and the People's Service in the evening.) The Parish Leaflet for that month gives a good indication of the kind of church to which John was now attached. Holy Communion: Tuesdays, Wednesdays and Fridays. Sir Richard Acland, Bt (founder of the Common Wealth Party) was the preacher at the Harvest Festival Evensong at the beginning of the month. Pastor Franz Hildebrandt, the curate, before he became a refugee, to Pastor Niemoller in Berlin, was to be the conductor of the parish weekend conference the week after the ordination. The Parish Communion was to be broadcast the following Sunday for 'the second time in the history of broadcasting'. Once a month there was a spiritual healing service. The children's festival service was to be conducted by the Boy Bishop. *Gaslight* was to be performed in the parish hall on three weekday nights. The St Matthew's skittles team had been re-started. There was the vicar's careful explanation of 'Why do you ring the Angelus?' and on 'How you should address a clergyman' – not 'Father' but 'Mr' – though John must always be called 'Dr' Robinson, a title Mervyn Stockwood liked, but which was to create some confusion in the minds of the simpler members of the congregation; at least one old lady was to ask the curate if he would mind having a look at her varicose veins.

John's diaries add to the picture – Rover Scouts, teaching, whist drive, beetle drive, cathechism party, old people's party, neighbourhood brains trust, scouts' dance, cider supper, Blundell's School – John was Blundell's School missioner (St Saviour's mission church in the parish was sponsored by Blundell's public school in Tiverton, Devon). The pages of the diary are, of course, mostly full of visits to individual parishioners.

To start with John did not find it easy to adapt his university experience to this totally different world, but he proved himself perfectly capable of adapting. He was immediately part not only of a parish staff but of the Redfield United Front – the ecumenical team initiated by Mervyn Stockwood in 1941 with a dozen full-time members of staff: two incumbents, assistant clergy, an Anglican woman worker, the ministers of three Methodist churches, a Baptist church and a Congregational church, youth leaders and a leader of a community house. The team met each Tuesday morning under Mervyn's chairmanship for Holy Communion at St Matthew's, breakfast and a two-hour team-meeting. Although only Anglican priests celebrated the communion all the team received the sacrament. The team was as much concerned with the care of the surrounding community, young and old – and with the political life of the area – as with co-operation between churches.

Things had turned out less happily for Ruth since her return to Liverpool. Cut off from John and so much of his new life in Bristol except for the occasional weekend, and with the same prospect ahead for at least another year; severed also from her Cambridge academic interests and confined to teaching elementary French grammar to third division pupils, her spirits plummeted. A visit to the doctor in December however revealed a tubercular lesion of the lung; and she was immediately ordered to bed for some months. Her mother's work made it impossible for her to look after her at home. John suggested Ruth should go to Canterbury and be looked after by his mother – Beatrice had recently moved back into Cherries; Edward was at Oxford, and Cecilia was teaching in South London. Beatrice welcomed Ruth warmly, and she stayed with her till she was given the all-clear by her doctors the following August. The very close relationship between Ruth and Beatrice dates from this time. Before ever she was married she felt herself one of the family. It was recommended that Ruth should not return to Liverpool but should spend some time in Switzerland. Through Max Williman, an Old Catholic friend of Mervyn Stockwood's, arrangements were made for her – after John's priesting – to live for some months *au pair* with a colleague with three children, in Trimbach, a village not far from Basle, and to look after the children.

John was ordained priest by the new Bishop of Bristol, George Cockin, in Bristol Cathedral on Sunday, 22 September 1946. He celebrated the Holy Communion for the first time at 8.30 a.m. on the Tuesday morning. A few days later Ruth had to leave for Switzerland.

At the Advent ordination that year Ralph Scrine was ordained deacon and shared lodgings with John in a house two miles from the church up a steep hill, the home of Irene and Ethel Blackmore. They were a kindly couple, proud of their descent from John Wesley, lifelong spinsters, devoted choir members and possessed of an unshakeable conviction that fried potato is an essential ingredient of the British breakfast. Rene took up the stair-carpet, as she thought John's heavy tread was wearing it out, and would then regularly repaint the stair-boards with chocolate-brown paint. On Christmas eve John looked into Ralph's room to say that it was his custom to read the Prologue to St John's Gospel in Greek that evening and to ask whether Ralph would like to join him. They read it together, and then got on their bicycles to go to midnight mass. It was dark and freezing and there was ice on the road. Throughout the journey downhill John continued to share with Ralph his current thoughts on the Greek text of the Johannine Prologue. The inclement weather, the hill, and Ralph's apprehension as a deacon about what might go on at his first midnight mass somewhat diminished his ability to profit from all that John was saying.

Some weeks later Ralph contracted tonsillitis, which led eventually to tonsillectomy. He was in bed with a temperature of 104, wondering why the pattern on the wallpaper appeared so contorted, when John appeared. 'I'm awfully sorry you're not feeling well, Ralph,' he said. There followed a very long silence, which eventually John broke: 'Would you like me to give you a game of chess?' he asked.

John's sermons at St Matthew's were sometimes at this stage in content above the heads and in length beyond the endurance of the congregation, but were mostly listened to attentively and frequently aroused discussion. Perhaps the most provocative was delivered at a local Methodist church during the week of Prayer for Unity. John was no stranger there; it was part of the team. He chose to deal with the redemptive work of God in Jesus: how God deals with evil that good may come; and illustrated his argument with a reference to the Methodist use of unfermented wine at communion. As they considered alcohol an evil it might be more appropriate, he suggested, for them to use fermented wine since the purpose of a sacrament is to express the redemption of all that is sinful. The Methodist minister Donald Rose remarked that it was a 'pretty conceit'. John was concerned but unrepentant. (Would he not at the end of his life preach on 'God in Cancer'?) John's kindliness and sense of logic would however on occasions lead him into places where few other men would go. During his vicar's absence on holiday, when the Mothers' Union had booked a coach for an outing all had been arranged with great precision including the seating. When two late-comers wishing to join the outing appealed to John, he re-arranged the whole seating plan without further consultation, and was completely mystified by the expressions of outrage.

During his curacy John would often take a group of young people pot-holing in the Mendips. John Norsworthy, who had first met him as a fellow undergraduate when he, John Robinson, was commandant of the camp of the Cambridge Fruiting Campaign, and who remained a close friend for the rest of his life, was surprised to receive a sudden summons in the summer of 1946 to help John to run the St Matthew's Scout camp. He could not reach Bristol in time to travel to Blagdon and the Mendips in the Scout coach and had to follow on a few hours later by bus. He remembers heaving his kit-bag off the bus, having the probable camp site pointed out by the friendly conductor, and trudging up to a field in which there were signs of a camp about to be started. Two tents were half up, and baggage was piled upon the grass. One Scout, wearing full uniform and holding a pole, was standing about in a bored manner. John Norsworthy himself must now continue the account of what followed:

> 'Where is everyone?' I asked the Bristol lad.
> 'You're to come with me,' he replied, 'I've been told to wait here for you and to take you to the Scout-master.'
> 'But where is he?' I enquired somewhat apprehensively.
> 'He's gone pot-holing and is stuck. They can't get him out.'
> We reached the mouth of the cave, to find a milling crowd of unoccupied, disorganised Scouts.
> I called into the cave, 'What do you want me to do to help?'
> 'Don't worry about me,' came the answer, 'Some farmers are going to pull me out when they've brought a suitable rope. You just get the camp started!'
> So, with a crowd of lively youngsters of whom I knew not one, I had to return to the camp, start the fires, cook lunch, have the tents put up and the equipment properly sorted, organise the sleeping – without any knowledge of supplies, conditions, or the basic plans – and I didn't receive much help from those lads. John turned up, freed, at about 5 p.m. I was too exhausted to question his order of priorities. Two days later John gave each Scout two shillings and told them all to amuse themselves for the day, whilst we set off to walk to Wells.

Pot-holing became a favourite pastime for John. It was an obvious way of getting alongside the young people and the Mendips were fairly close at hand. In the 1940s it was a primitive occupation compared with today – no helmets, wet suits, nylon ropes. The Scouts used head-lamps made from cycle lamps. There were no plans of caverns and no rescue arrangements. The news that the curate was 'stuck' was transmitted back to Moorfields in no time – and that he was reading the day's mail underground and keeping his toes warm with a candle! John's pot-holing was not without its anxieties for the mothers of the Scouts or indeed for Ruth. John once told Ruth, to her horror, that if he was uncertain of the safety of a route his method was to 'send down the smallest boy first to report on conditions'. Rene Blackmore's complaint was the condition of John's clothes after expeditions. No amount of washing would entirely remove the red Mendip mud, and her washing line disgraced her before her neighbours.

There is, of course, something almost of the absurd about John the Pot-holer, but it is a view essential to the whole picture. If John was humorous – or even absurd – he was usually serious at the same time. What may also seem fanciful to the point of absurdity – but again it cannot be omitted – is the question: was there some subconscious connection between John's underground exploration of the Mendips and his particular attraction to the image of 'depth', for example his delight in Paul Tillich's sermon 'The Depth of Existence', which was published while he was Chaplain of Wells Theological College in 1949. In *Honest to God* he was to write of his experience:

> I did what I have never done before or since: I simply read Tillich's sermon, in place of an address of my own, to the students I was then teaching. I do not remember looking at the words again till I came to write this, but they formed one of the streams below the surface that were to collect into the underground river of which I have since become conscious . . .

Ruth's absence in Switzerland meant that John would write to her most days and she to him. It was in the course of this correspondence over some months that they hit upon the idea of being married in Switzerland. John's curate's pay was a pittance. They had little money for a large reception or a honeymoon abroad. John was in any case bringing the St Matthew's youth group to Switzerland in six months time. Why not get married then? But it was easier said than done. Nobody seemed to have any experience of two foreigners marrying under Swiss law. The arrangements which seemed simple to John from the safe distance of England were a nightmare of complexity for Ruth. Indeed it proved impossible to arrange the legal ceremony for 15 April 1942, the day that was agreed for the church ceremony in Zurich. So eventually John and Ruth were married twice, five days apart. On 10 April they presented themselves with their two Swiss witnesses at the appropriate office in Basle. The official, seeing John's clerical collar, said in German that he presumed there was no need to impress on them the seriousness of what they were now undertaking and asked whether John was now ready to make the promises. John said 'Ja' and waited for the formal words, only to find he had said the only 'Ja' necessary. (John said afterwards that if he had known he would have said it less casually!) During the next five days they stayed with the Willimans, each evening rehearsing Max in the Anglican marriage service and communion service, and leaving out words like 'propitiation', which he simply could not pronounce! On the morning of the 15th a taxi duly arrived at the Willimans. John had his rucksack with him. Ruth had her rucksack in one hand and a bridal posy in the other. The rucksacks were deposited at the hotel where there was to be a family lunch, and Edward (best man) and Cecilia (bridesmaid) were picked up and taken to the church, where Max was soon solemnly declaring John and Ruth man and wife – which he had no legal right to do – and Old Catholics from Switzerland and Anglicans from Canterbury, Liverpool and Bristol were all singing 'O thou who camest from above'. After the reception Beatrice, Cecilia and Edward went off to the holiday Ruth had planned for them at Weggis, and her mother and her brother Richard for theirs at Lucerne, while the bridal couple spent their honeymoon partly on Lake Lugano and partly on Lake Maggiore, afterwards visiting the family in Trimbach. It was 10 May when, after brief stays at Cherries and in Liverpool, Ruth and John returned to Bristol.

For a few months Ruth and John, Ralph Scrine and Mr Cornish, an RSPCC inspector, were all part of the Summerhill Road, East Bristol household presided over by the Misses Blackmore. Rene and Ethel were kindly folk and it was a happy set-up. These were still post-war days of rationing. Rene did the cooking while Ethel spent much time trying to get hold of anything 'off the ration'. John and Ruth had a room at the top of the house. The question of a more permanent home was, of course, important. In August 1947 Mervyn Stockwood let them have his flat above the corner wine shop while he was away on holiday. It was there Ruth did her first housekeeping. But when they learnt that they were to expect their first child the next February the situation became urgent. John showed his characteristic initiative. The next door parish of St Leonard's was vacant and the vicarage empty. John, having consulted his vicar, wrote to Bishop Cockin suggesting that he and

Ruth move into the vicarage during the interregnum and that David Cartwright, his friend at Cambridge, should be offered the living. He wrote to David saying that he was 'just the sort of person the place wants' but that the vicarage would be too large, and suggested that the Robinsons should be their 'squatters'. It was one of John's 'eminently reasonable' and 'obvious' solutions. And, like so many of them, it worked! David was appointed and stayed in the diocese twenty-five years; and by the time Mervyn returned from holiday John was moving the Robinsons' few possessions into St Leonard's Vicarage, on a pram inherited from one of the Methodist ministers. The parish was aghast to see the curate pushing his belongings on a pram at such an indelicately early stage in his wife's pregnancy, but to John it was the 'obvious' thing to do.

Furniture at this time was still rationed and John and Ruth had none of their own. The Polish 'Utility' furniture John purchased at this time became his proud possession and was still in his rooms at Trinity at the end of his life. John's aunt Florence – the last of the thirteen Robinsons – was making her final move into a home nearby in Somerset; and thereby his uncle Armitage's desk joined the Polish 'Utility'. David and Elsie Cartwright arrived early in 1948; both the wives were very pregnant. The Robinsons lived separately from the Cartwrights; but there was much communication and the ménage was a happy one.

John was out visiting in the parish when at 5 p.m. on 20 February 1948 Ruth had to take herself off in the ambulance to Southmead Hospital, the other side of Bristol. At 11.40 p.m. their first child Stephen was born. John, unwilling to take advantage of his 'dog-collar', and knowing that all had gone well, busied himself at his desk the next morning spreading the good news, and paid his first visit to his wife and their newborn son at visiting time, 3 p.m. Ruth's joy that a man had been born into the world was somewhat diminished by the fact that she had not seen her husband for twenty-four hours at that crucial time.

Three months later Elsie Cartwright went into hospital and three days later was still in labour. David was overcome by anxiety. John told him Elsie was in the best possible hands and that his best way of helping was to get on with his parish work – as he would have done himself. John was a man of deep feeling but emotions that did not respond to reason were neither admitted in himself nor easily understood in others. A son was born safely to the Cartwrights by Caesarean section, and so by May 1948 there were two babies in the vicarage. John believed that crying babies were best taken care of at the far end of the garden – and said so.

John's three years at Moorfields were crucial to the whole of his ministry. Brian Weston, one of the Scouts who had chiselled at the rock-face to help John make his pot-holing escape, remembers, forty years on, his arrival at St Matthew's:

> high-browed, fresh-faced, a quiff of black hair, incredibly young look-ing, and with a high-pitched, nervous laugh. In retrospect, the cultural shock for him must have been enormous. The question for us was: would this young man, who looked so different and who intellectually seemed so superior, fit in? A sympathetic congregation warmed to someone with obviously still a lot to learn about the world. His stint with the Scouts was not a success: anyone less like a practical back-woodsman would be difficult to find. But, as always, he approached it in a most cheerful way – I don't recall him ever giving up and he took all the jokes at his expense in a most good humoured way.

By the time John left Bristol, he had had his first two substantial theological articles published in *Theology* – the first on 'Agape and Eros' (48: 1945) and the second – on 'The Temptations' (50: 1947). (The second would later be included in *Twelve New Testament Studies*.) It was clear he had learnt much about the working-class world and about relating to less intellectual people. He was notably kind to lonely and distressed people. He had proved himself as senior as well as junior curate. He was now a husband and a father – with a second child on the way. Part of the credit for John's maturing must go to Ruth, who was more practical and down-to-earth and at this stage somewhat more mature than John; though one of John's closest friends believed that John and his mother were also 'moulding' a malleable Ruth, who understandably wanted very much to fit in with the 'Robinson tradi-tion'. But without doubt it was Mervyn Stockwood who at this stage was the major influence upon John, teaching him his 'craft' as a priest. Mervyn said in his sermon at the Southwark Cathedral Thanksgiving Service for John:

> Like all curates he was asked to submit his sermons to me, and occasionally I suggested that he should use the language of the *Daily Mirror* or indeed of the *News of the World* rather than that of *The Times* or *The Observer*. He kept us on our theological toes. He provoked intelligent

argument. He was a dedicated pastor. In short, he was the curate for whom a vicar prays although rarely gets. He and his wife, Ruth, were much loved in the parish.

A hand-written fragment – a note from the vicar – survives from one St Matthew's occasion, presumably passed to John, the preacher: 'Sir Walter Monckton is in the congregation – so no reference to the Government!!!' In his Southwark Cathedral sermon Mervyn regaled the congregation with a reminiscence of John the curate:

> We had a splendid character in the congregation called Charlie Hodder, an ex-railwayman. He was a rough-and-ready man of enormous girth. He was, among other things, an excellent dancer. He had two places of worship which he visited each day of the week: St Matthew's and the Dove and Crown. On Sundays he went morning and evening to both. In an early sermon, while John was still a deacon, he spoke of 'the eschaton entering history'. Later in the week Charlie said to me, 'What was Dr Robinson on about last Sunday – eskimos and history?' For some time after, when John sent me his sermons to look at and I came across an abstruse sentence, I would write over it in red pencil, 'What *will* this mean to Charlie Hodder?' This became a much loved joke between us, and often when later we sat through dreary debates in the Diocesan Conference or the General Synod, he would pass me a note 'What *does* this mean to Charlie Hodder?'

It was under Mervyn's influence that John worked out a Socialist response to the social realities of East Bristol. Some said that Mervyn seemed to 'get hold of' John – a son without a father – and that in the special relationship of curate to vicar, he was much less independent than he would be in later years. But one thing is certain: there could have been few better places than St Matthew's, and few better people than Mervyn Stockwood, to train John at the beginning of his ministry. Not surprisingly John never looked back to his Bristol days with anything but gratitude and affection.

4

The Wells Years

The Cathedral at Wells is only twenty miles from Bristol. Uncle Armitage had been its Dean from 1911 to 1933. Now, only fifteen years later, John was invited by the Principal, Kenneth Haworth (later Dean of Salisbury) to be Chaplain to the Theological College, which had been attached to the Cathedral since 1841, and to lecture in New Testament and ethics. John had no doubt he should accept. It was a creative appointment – for John and his family and for the College. He had often been over to Wells, sometimes to lecture. (His paternal grandfather had been an incumbent in the diocese as Vicar of Keynsham.) After the Cathedral itself some of the most striking buildings in the environs were those provided in the fourteenth century for the deputies to the canons: Vicars Close. Much of the life of the College went on in the buildings of this ancient Close – the houses, the hall and the chapel. For the next three years 14 Vicars Close was to be home for John and Ruth and the children, and to be open house to members of the College whenever they should want to drop in. John's study commanded a view of the whole length of the Close, with its dozen or more tall stone chimneys each side, dating from 1470.

Catherine, a sister for Stephen, was born in the February after the Robinsons moved into the Close. At the age of ten months she was seriously ill with a digestive disorder and was admitted to the children's hospital in Bristol. A fortnight later she was sent home, since the only remedy was an operation considered too dangerous for such a small child to undergo. John conducted a laying-on-of-hands service in the presence of members of the college in the small chapel in the Close. A month later under X-ray the condition had disappeared.

After his Bristol days John went to Wells with a sense of mission. It was a College with a very strong tradition. It was somewhat ingrown. It had had for a considerable time a succession of principals and staff who were themselves 'Wells men'. It had probably not had a scholar of John's calibre on its staff since R. H. Lightfoot was successively vice-principal and principal of the College at the end of the First World War. Most of the immediate post-war students were not particularly adventurous theologically. Comparatively few had done any previous theological study, and owing to the war most, understandably, found it difficult to get back to their books. In his booklist John had noted with some satisfaction that in his three Bristol years as a curate he had read fifty theological books, twenty on politics, seven on philosophy and thirty others.

Inevitably the presence on the staff of a scholar with such a powerful mind as John's – and particularly in his more youthful years an unwillingness or an inability to 'temper the wind to the shorn lamb' and a tendency sometimes to dismiss or ignore other opinions – soon involved some strain in staff relations. Kenneth Skelton, then priest-vicar of the Cathedral and lecturer at the College, describes how: 'Staff meetings tended to be polarised, with the Vice-Principal, Deryck Hutchinson, and I sitting as heavily as we could on one end of the see-saw, to balance John, with Principal Haworth, to change the metaphor, holding the ring with an amiable impartiality.' Kenneth Skelton and his wife Phyllis, and John and Ruth, who were neighbours in Vicars Close, remained good friends through thirty and more years. Kenneth, who became first Bishop of Matabeleland and later Bishop of Lichfield, insists that the position he took in the staff 'polarisation' was 'not from any rooted opposition to John's stimulating presentation of new ideas, but in order to preserve a balance'.

It was not only the staff which was polarised. Kenneth Haworth must have anticipated something of the division within the College when he invited John. He would surely have known not only John's intellectual capacity and willingness to explore new and radical ideas, but his strong experience of community in Moorfields, that parish's particular re-sponse to the industrial world and the world of the city, and the importance John now attached to worship in the context of the Liturgical Movement. In the opinion of Kenneth Skelton, Vicars Close and the 'Wells system' did not encourage much community living and thus the college tended not to share its concerns at any great depth. Much of John's thought was based on orthodox biblical theology. The more conventional students were indignant, however, not only that he also introduced them to Bultmann, Brunner, Bonhoeffer, Jeremias and

Tillich, but that when his turn came round for preaching the weekly Compline address, instead of preaching his own thoughts, he should read them the address on 'The Depth of Existence' (already referred to) from Tillich's *The Shaking of the Foundations*, which had just been published.

In rural Wells John succeeded in persuading the staff that the 'college visit' should be to Bishop Leslie Hunter's Sheffield. The students and staff stayed all over the city, visited steel works and met the Sheffield Industrial Mission and the remarkable diocesan missioner to industry Ted Wickham, later Bishop of Middleton. John himself displayed on that visit a sure 'homing instinct', staying with Alan Ecclestone, Vicar of Darnall, so as to see this man of deep spirituality and radical ideas at work in the setting of his own parish. As a result of this college visit one student who had intended to work in the south of England when he was ordained changed his mind at the very last moment and went to work in Sheffield.

Soon after his arrival John discovered the existence of the Wells Parliament, a political debating society in the town which met on Friday evenings, and persuaded the Principal to move the Compline address to Thursday, in order that students could be encouraged to participate, for John found unacceptable the principle that (in the words of the College Statutes) the students should 'refrain from entering much into society'. John maintained that he did not know what a 'devotional' address was, and would not want to produce one. His Compline addresses were therefore invariably provocative, and instead of being succeeded by a 'holy silence' had part, at least, of the College sitting up into the small hours arguing furiously. (He also persuaded the Principal to move the beginning of the August term a week later so that he could get to the Canterbury Cricket Week!)

John was undoubtedly irked and irritated by what with some justification he considered to be the remoteness of Wells from the 'real' world, and feared that it would produce only inward-looking clergy. During part of his time there R. H. Malden was Dean of the Cathedral, a classical scholar and historian whose caustic conservatism is reflected in a series of brilliant Crockford Prefaces (twenty-two of which were collected in *The Editor Looks Back*) and in his *The English Church and Nation*. Malden, who always went about in top hat and frock-coat, was irate when, during the 1950 election campaign, he learnt that John was stumping Somerset in a red tie, speaking on Labour Party platforms.

Kenneth Haworth remembers slipping in at the back of a meeting which John was addressing or chairing. Malden was succeeded as dean by F. P. Harton, author of *The Elements of the Spiritual Life*, whose views were also very different from John's. The other cathedral clergy, though not necessarily thinking on the same lines as Harton, were equally disturbed by what were reported to be the views of the College Chaplain. The story was spread abroad that during the election campaign, students, inspired by J.A.T.R., had joined in the campaign on behalf of their own political preferences, and that one of them encountering Dr Bradfield, Bishop of Bath and Wells, on voting day, had asked him: 'Are you going to vote, my Lord?' and not waiting for an answer had added: 'Oh, but I had forgotten: lunatics and peers cannot vote'; having also forgotten, or not realized, that the bishop was not yet a member of the House of Lords.

The simple fact was that the Cathedral, College, town and surrounding villages were overwhelmingly and staunchly conservative, and John was not. Put more positively: it was a vital part of John's work at Wells to stir up the students on behalf of the Kingdom, and this he did. John Alford, the College tutor (later Archdeacon of Halifax), remembers John saying in a Compline address: 'When the Bomb goes off, some of you will sail up into the sky still clutching your Bicknell', a textbook on the Thirty-nine Articles then heavily relied on by many Church of England theological students for whatever success they might achieve in examinations.

What John believed was for him a matter of both personal experience and scholarship. In the post-war years the conventional personal piety of both Catholics and Evangelicals needed to be challenged. John's questioning critical mind was brought to bear upon the relation between 'the Body of Christ, the Church, and the body of this world, the body politic'. He was the moving spirit behind a course of lectures delivered by the staff on the doctrine of the atonement, on the basis of fresh study of original documents. He examined critically and rationally the assumptions most of his students – and staff – had inherited about personal prayer and devotion; about membership of the Church, and the relation of the Church to the Kingdom, and how all this was to be worked out in worship – not least in the worship of their theological college. He made everyone think, with awkward questions and provocative statements. He once said, for instance, that he did not believe in praying for guidance. You should pray after a decision rather than before it. It was a statement calculated – consciously or unconsciously – to irritate the conventionally pious. After John had given a Compline address on the text 'Though we have known Christ after the flesh, yet now we know him no more' in which he cast doubt upon the validity of a personal devotion to Jesus, Kenneth Skelton felt it incumbent upon him to devote his next Compline address to redressing the balance. John hated most of the medieval hymns in the *English Hymnal*, which by Kenneth's choice were used with unfailing regularity.

During those years at Wells John was already raising with the students the issues which he would later write about – not least in *Honest to God*. The heated debates went on unceasingly throughout his time there.

For many of the post-war students, most of whom had had far more experience of the world than John, for they had been through the war as combatants, the opportunity of a period of withdrawal and recuperation was doubly welcome, and indeed very necessary to their full development. John, although recognizing the need for what Max Warren called 'periods of transfiguration', of 'withdrawal with intent to return', and valuing times of 'retreat', was always quick to condemn the too easy identification of the place and time of withdrawal with 'the Holy' – not least because for him temperamentally the characteristic way to 'the Holy' was not through withdrawal but through involvement. John of course needed time for uninterrupted study but he could concentrate wherever he was and be oblivious to what was going on around him. His most significant thoughts did not come to him by going away from the scene or the subject. (Mervyn Stockwood once insisted that John and his fellow-curate Patrick Fedden should go away on retreat to the Cowley Fathers at Oxford. When they arrived they were told by the guest master what devotions they should attend and who would be in charge of them. After supper in silence they met outside the house for a clandestine consultation. Next morning they repaired to a nearby hostelry, where they remained until – much refreshed by reading, walking and what the hostelry had to offer – it was time for them to return. Their vicar was not amused.) John never accepted that a theological college should by virtue of that fact be an evident place of withdrawal. To that extent he never accepted Wells.

John soon made his mark on the villages surrounding Wells, mostly by preaching in their churches. He could not talk now without interesting his hearers. But it was not long before he was influencing a wider world than Wells. One of the Compline addresses he gave in November 1949 was printed the next year in *Theology* and, ten years later, in his *On Being the Church in the World*. It concerned 'The house church and the parish church'. He called it later 'a theological kite', but it was a superb example of his work. It was both New Testament theology and pastoral theology. It was also prophetic. At the time Ernest Southcott's parish of Halton, Leeds (which John was to visit in due course), and his ministry based primarily on the house church – which 'Ernie' would describe in his book *The Parish Comes Alive* – were unknown to John. The address was relevant to the theological students both at the College and in their future ministries:

> The house Church is *itself* the Church, the Church in the basement, in the smallest possible unit of Christian existence, whether it be among the dockers at Corinth or theological students at Wells. Indeed, a theological college (and particularly this one with its house structure) so far from being 'above' this sort of thing, would seem to be one of the most obvious places in which to start trying to live out what it means. One has in such an institution a relative independence, and can count, one presumes, on a tolerably high level of theological awareness. And it might be hoped from a centre such as this to contribute by experiment quite a lot to the kind of liturgy appropriate to this basement level of Christian living (though, of course, it would be very different liturgy from that suitable, say, for a group of dockers).

The article was not simply theory. It was based not least on John's Bristol experience. It reads as well today as it did thirty-five years ago and says things which still need to be heard. Kenneth Skelton describes how he received the address.

> As the College's history lecturer, I felt bound to challenge what I felt was a failure to answer the reasonable question why, if the House Church was not a 'purely temporary expedient', or 'simply an evangelistic weapon', but 'a theologically necessary part of the life of the body', it had apparently so completely disappeared between the end of the 1st Century and the middle of the 20th; and I remember being secretly delighted when I dug out a quotation from John's uncle Armitage making this very point, and was able to quote it in a lecture the following week! Even so, it is significant that 'house-churches', if not always in the form that John – or the New Testament – envisaged, have become quite an accepted part of the Anglican scene – even if Canon B40 severely restricts them.

In 1950 John's first book appeared: *In the End God . . . ; A Study of the Christian Doctrine of the Last Things.* There was material in it which represented John's earliest essay into the field of theology and must first have been penned in 1942 or 1943. The book went into a second impression and was made a paperback nearly twenty years after its first publication. John wrote in that edition: 'I wondered as I read it after an interval in which so much water had passed under the bridge how much of it I could make my own today. I was surprised. In one sense, I could never write it now. In another I found I wanted to alter remarkably little. I did not wish to withdraw anything of substance I had said.' Professor C. F. D. Moule wrote only recently: 'I have often been tempted to call it John's best book. When I first read it, I thought it said superbly much that needed to be said about eschatology.' The first paragraph of the book is John at his most stimulating:

Nowhere, over the field of Christian doctrine, is the gulf between the Biblical viewpoint and the outlook of modern secularism so yawning as in the matter of eschatology. The whole New Testament prospect of a return of Christ, accompanied by the transformation of this world-order, a general resurrection, a final judgement, and the vindication of the sovereignty of God over heaven and earth, is regarded by the scientific humanist of the 20th Century as frankly fantastic. The Biblical narratives of the Last Things seem to him as incredible as the Biblical narratives of the First Things appeared to his grandfather a century ago. Or, rather, they are more incredible. For, whereas, the Genesis stories, reinterpreted, could, it was found, be harmonised with the evolutionary picture, the Second Advent and its accompaniments appear to the modern a simple contradiction of all his presumptions about the future of the world, immediate or remote. And yet, despite its incompatibility with the modern outlook the Biblical view of the Last Things, unlike that of the First, has hardly stirred a ripple of controversy. The entire Christian eschatological scheme has simply been silently dismissed without even so much as a serious protest from within the ecclesiastical camp. This could only have happened if the Church's doctrine at this point had become not merely incredible, but irrelevant.

This is John writing as he spoke. He puts to you the baffling question and carries you along with his determination to get to the bottom of it.

In the End God made Wells Theological College proud of John. Of course he had had his devoted followers in and out of the College before ever it was published, and it is clear that his influence on the students at Wells was profound and is still being felt today. John Alford writes:

John made men think about the nature of vocation, and in particular of their own vocation. There were a number who left the College because of his influence on their sense of vocation, and it is understandable that it caused a great deal of worry in some quarters. But these were not men being destroyed. He strengthened and changed their vocational perceptions. The trouble was that some of them were among the stronger people, whom we could not afford to lose to the ministry. Other members of staff had to do a good deal of rescue work among men going through spiritual and intellectual crises as a result of John's activities in and out of the lecture room and chapel.

He concludes:

I am inclined to think that in fact the force of his personality and mind was too much for so small a community as a college of 45 men, and the radicalism of his politics and theology were too much for the conservatism of the small town and the villages.

Let Robert Gibson, now Vicar of Halifax, speak for the students at Wells to whom John was Chaplain:

I well remember the first time that I met John – as a shy student, visiting with a view to joining the College. A somewhat awkward conversation ensued, in which the only meeting point seemed to be a common love of cricket; and I went away wondering what sort of a man the Chaplain really was. I was soon to learn.

I came from a home in which a deep but simple and perhaps naive approach to the faith was taken for granted. John was a catalyst, providing the necessary stimulus to enable me to widen and deepen my understanding of the faith, which has played its part in my ministry ever since.

At Wells, he and his family were so much part of College life. I remember with particular gratitude the lectures he gave us on Pauline theology – which he eventually wrote up as the SCM study *The Body* – and sharing in the debates of what came to be called the 'Kingdom' Group, in the Upper Room of the Chantry Chapel at the end of Vicars Close – with the emphasis on the central importance of a faith to live by, related to the world of today. These undoubtedly inspired me to seek work in Industrial Mission in South London, and have remained with me throughout the course of my ministry.

I am thankful for the glimpse of that great vision which John shared with us all at Wells.

There appeared in *Theology* in June 1952 an article by John: 'The Theological College in a Changing World'. There was another in

December 1958: 'The Teaching of Theology for the Ministry'. Although in them John was being wise after his not uneventful three years at Wells, it is safe to say that few of the thoughts in those articles had not already occurred to him and had not been expressed by him while he was there. What he wrote in them he wrote with conviction – he had originally intended to include them in *On Being the Church in the World*. In the first article in 1952 John wrote prophetically:

> It seems to not a few that the only hope for the Church of England, economically as well as evangelistically, is to recognise without further delay, and ·to act on the recognition, that the coming pattern of its ministry is bound to be largely non-professional, in the sense that its priesthood will consist in great proportion of men working in secular jobs at every level, both manual and administrative . . . Though working priests would take their proper part in the corporate Sunday worship of the parish community, their prime day-to-day responsibility would be their 'house-church' in the street, block, the factory, the office, or the school where they were living or working . . . For the training of such a non-professional ministry, the existing theological college set-up would be virtually irrelevant. For it is essential that it must be done *without* taking men out of the jobs and milieu in which they are. The experience of the trade unions in training their leadership through night classes, summer schools, Ruskin College, etc. should give the Church something to work on.

In the second article, which was concerned with the academic 'high-fliers', John wrote: 'It is absurd that the country should be dotted with small colleges, inadequately staffed with semi-trained and underpaid men, however devoted, to give teaching in academic theology which could much better be given at university centres.' He believed these 'high-fliers' reading theology should also during their theological college training 'spend stretches of time in groups working in parishes and in secular jobs, and that their studies of doctrine, ethics, worship and the like should be allowed to develop directly out of these real-life situations and the questions they throw up, under the qualified guidance of men who were theologically involved in them.'

John formed as many lasting friendships at Wells as anywhere in his ministry. They were formed most often with John and Ruth together; for when students had finished a supervision with John – or were waiting for one – they could pop into the kitchen for coffee or tea with Ruth. The kitchen with the two young children was the centre of the

Robinson home. A domestic fragment of those days is embedded in the pages of *But That I Can't Believe!* John had discovered that all the spring bulbs had been trampled underfoot. The likely culprits – 'my Stephen' and Christopher, Kenneth Skelton's son – were assembled. The Skeltons' cat Mou was present as an observer. The inquest began. John records the conversation:

> MYSELF: '???!!'
> CHRISTOPHER: 'Ste'en done it!'
> STEPHEN: 'Mou done it!'

'Adam and Eve and the serpent!' – in the shade of the Cathedral at Wells.

5

The Clare Years

The appointment of John Robinson as Dean of Clare College, Cambridge was at the suggestion and warm recommendation of Michael Ramsey, later, of course, Archbishop of Canterbury, but in 1951 Regius Professor of Divinity in the University of Cambridge. The Revd C. F. D. Moule had resigned the Deanship on his appointment as Lady Margaret's Professor of Divinity in the University. 'Charlie' Moule had known John in his undergraduate days, and as a graduate when he was doing his PhD, and would be there as a Fellow to welcome John back to Cambridge and befriend him in all the thirty and more years that remained to him.

There is a world of difference between being chaplain to a theological college of less than fifty students and dean of a Cambridge college. John, brought up in the shadow of the Cathedral at Canterbury, was almost too familiar with the life of an English cathedral close for his responsibilities at Wells ever to have seemed to him awesome. But Clare was different. He had only to look towards the College across the lawn of King's; or to stand by the parapet, surmounted by great stone balls, on Clare's most lovely bridge over the Cam, and look beyond the copper beech to the seventeen bays of the Clare buildings fronting the river; or to enter via the porter's lodge and wend his way through the courts of the College to the octagonal ante-chapel and the Chapel itself, to be aware of the greatly increased dimensions of his responsibilities. After the beginning of term there would be nearly four hundred young men milling about the College – members not only of the College but of every faculty in the University; and in Hall he would be dining most evenings with some of the thirty or so Fellows of the College, men of eminence and distinction in many walks of life. Up to now there had been a gad-fly quality about John in his insistent questioning of entrenched positions and his willingness to take unfashionable views seriously. It was a quality which would always be particularly attractive to students and would remain one of his best gifts; but Clare needed more than a gad-fly when they invited John to be their Dean of Chapel, and the crucial question was what more he had it in him to be.

Predecessors are not always the best judges of their successors, but there can be little doubt in this instance that 'Charlie' Moule is the best person to answer that question. He writes:

> When John arrived back in Cambridge, he was friendly (instantly so with me and others who worked closely with him) but shy. I recall his preparing an undergraduate for Confirmation and finding it so difficult to 'get through' to him that he invited me to sit in on the classes and run them jointly with him, by way of breaking the ice – though I doubt if I succeeded. Still less, I fancy, did he cut much ice with most of the Fellows, since he hadn't much small talk (which academics value more than they are reputed or would admit to) and was too shy to be instantly or easily approachable. A perceptive Senior Tutor, who recognised John's real worth, spoke of first-year undergraduates encountering him and either bouncing off or sticking. Many did stick; and, so far as I remember, he really began to 'take off' as a result of his lead in worship. This is well, if over modestly, described in *Liturgy Coming to Life*. In my time as Dean, the furnishings of the 18th century Chapel were Victorian – a huge altar standing against the east wall, with heavy frontals and an inferior brass eagle-lectern, and brass altar-rails. John soon made radical changes, and successfully enlisted the good will and co-operation of the Master and Fellows, many of whom scarcely ever came to Chapel but cared about the aesthetics. He did what I hadn't the courage to do – throw the eagle out. More radically, he scrapped the brass rails, in favour of a rail-less sanctuary, and the Victorian altar (which meant discontinuing the use of huge silver candlesticks given by Bishop Terrick at the consecration of the Chapel), and had a pleasing, smallish refectory-type table made. With artistic advice from appropriate Fellows, and with the Finance Committee's blessing, he chose a beautiful old-gold velvet cloth to cover this altar for all seasons. In addition to Terrick's candlesticks, we had also been using two exquisite 17th century silver-gilt candlesticks, and a totally incongruous brass Victorian cross. The candlesticks were now matched by a new cross specially designed in silver-gilt and wood – again, with help and guidance from Fellows. Concealed vertical strip-lights were installed to pick up its high-lights. The traditional Communion plate – apart from a stunning 17th century gold cup, so vast and heavy that it was not normally practicable to use it – was a rather unworthy and far too small chalice and paten. John gained the College's approval for

having a new and lovely silver chalice designed (echoing something from the style of the candlesticks, without slavish imitation) with paten to match. Two beautiful wooden lecterns were designed by a distinguished craftsman Lough Pendred, to serve for lessons and sermon. Thus the Chapel was given a light touch, with the natural beauty of good functional objects.

But behind these material changes was a clear theology, and out of it arose what can only be called a genuinely theological revival of worship. John translated into an idiom appropriate to the context the main thrust of the Parish and People movement. *Liturgy Coming to Life* describes how his intelligent ordering of the way the Eucharist was done, so as to make it genuinely congregational, and his thoughtful sermons, enlisted an overwhelming response from undergraduates, who not only came to Eucharistic worship in larger numbers than in my deanship, but took a genuinely active and intelligent part in the worship and carried its meaning out into daily life. One vacation, John led a team from the College to help do some amateur rebuilding and rehabilitation on a derelict site in Ernie Southcott's parish in Leeds and I remember one undergraduate (now a distinguished consultant surgeon) mixing cement and intoning like a mantra, as he pushed his shovel into a heap of cement, 'The thrust of the sacred into the secular'.

Another instance of John's lead in social work was when the Fens were flooded in 1953, and volunteers were called for to fill sand-bags to make an emergency dyke. There was a good contingent from Clare. That day the whole day's work was swept away at nightfall by the pressure of water building up.

A typescript draft of a companion to the Eucharist was tried for a Long Vacation period of residence, during which time it was discussed, improved and subjected to the scrutiny of people like Professor E. C. Ratcliff. When it had reached a 'steady state' it was printed (exquisitely by the Cambridge University Press under the guidance of the Secretary to the Syndics, R. J. L. Kingsford, who was a Fellow of Clare) and became the celebrated manual, in demand all over the world. The extraordinary thing was that what it presented was Cranmer's 1662 rite, as pure and virtually uncontaminated as could be found anywhere in the country. What brought it vividly alive was the intelligent use of action, such as the Offertory procession – with specially baked loaves and wine from the College cellars – and interpretative marginalia – brief and restrained, but sufficient to point to the theology of the action. The bringing of the unconsecrated bread left over to the Chapel breakfast after the service, and the use, with it, of the prayer from the *Didache* as a grace – 'As this bread that is broken was scattered as grain upon the mountains and, gathered together, became one; so let thy Church be gathered from the ends of the earth into thy Kingdom' – made the link with the secular world explicit.

John had the imagination to take the Chaplain (first, Denis Wakeling, then 'Bill' Skelton) and me to a day or two of Retreat (e.g. at Madingley Hall) before the start of a new academical year, which enabled us to pray and think together about plans and policy. He was at that time much influenced by books from the French Catholic Liturgical Movement (e.g. the Abbé Michonneau) and one or other of these formed a focus for the Retreat. It may have been in part from this inspiration that 'staircase churches' came into being, as described in *Liturgy Coming to Life*: 'The committee . . . recommended that, except on saints' days, the normal and proper place for weekday celebrations was at the level, not of the College as a whole, but of the house Church. But this proposal, though it actually commanded a majority in the Chapel Meeting, was too revolutionary a step to push through.' The decisive bar to pushing it through was strenuous agitation by one deeply sincere but extreme Anglo-Catholic undergraduate, who so passionately believed it wrong to celebrate the Eucharist in an unconsecrated building that he threatened to appeal to the Archbishop against the proposal. The matter was brought to the level of College Council, uncomprehending though the Fellows were. The remarkable thing is that the undergraduate was subsequently completely converted to the idea, and became an enthusiastic advocate of the house Communion. This speaks of John's remarkable loyalty to democratic principles even when he felt strongly the urge to push ahead regardless. In fact it must be said that from first to last, in all he wanted to do, John deeply involved undergraduates and Fellows.

John's pastoral concern was unremitting. He and Ruth did a great deal, together or singly, for individuals. Speaking for myself, very early in his time as Dean I had to go into St Bartholomew's Hospital for drastic and radical surgery, and John imaginatively arranged, entirely on his own initiative, to have a Eucharist in the Chapel on the day I went to London, including a quiet and undemonstrative laying-on-of-hands by him with prayer and blessing. He let it be known among Fellows, and I was deeply touched by the fact that a Fellow who normally never came to Communion came on this occasion.

John claimed to be tone-deaf, and took little part in the Chapel or College music. He joined in the mounting disapproval of the bad old system of drawing untrained choir-boys from the town – a practice mercifully long since abolished.

He was always fair to the CICCU (Cambridge Inter-Collegiate Christian Union), and gave them a welcome and reasonable look-in in the choice of preachers. The worshipping community was a happy one.

He adored talking theology, and was given to staying in College to a late hour, talking, talking – often with me. I remember Bishop Evered Lunt asking whether John was being fair to his family. But he loved his home, and it was always a delight to visit it, even if there were sometimes 'children crises'. When Stephen was disobedient, there was the alarming ritual of John's counting, 'One – two – three . . .' in his harshest voice. I can't remember Stephen's ever not caving in before the dire eschaton, and I never found out, any more than he did, what it would have been. Perhaps John didn't know.

He overworked. On one occasion during term the doctor ordered him away for a rest. Taking me with him, we set off in an Austin Seven for the Peak District. Only a mile or two outside Cambridge we had a puncture and at the same moment a drowning thunderstorm burst over us. In the Peak District we went for glorious walks, talking theology all the time, John pressing a corporate, liturgical and political theology with which I was always far more in accord than I think he ever imagined.

John and I always swopped whatever we happened to be writing, and I think we reckoned that any piece that got by the other's scrutiny had a chance of surviving when it got into print. We lived across the landing from each other, and were always in and out of each other's dens. I read *The Body* before it was published.

I don't know that John would count as a 'popular Dean', in the sense of taking a lot of trouble to display interest in what the chaps were doing. He enjoyed cricket, and played a light-hearted part himself; but I don't recall his being specially assiduous on the tow-path or touch line. He was a 'theological Dean' if you like, and won respect by his integrity, courage and concern for those in need. The undergraduates registered their affection at his farewell by giving him his pectoral cross – even if most of them had little idea what a big person he was. By the all too early time of his leaving Clare, he had gained a lot in confidence and had won universal respect in the College and the University, where he was a popular University Lecturer, and among his pastoral colleagues in other Colleges.

Denis Wakeling (later Bishop of Southwell) who was Chaplain when John arrived at Clare says: 'John came into Clare like a whirlwind . . . his sermons at the College Eucharist changed my whole thinking and the trend of my ministry.' The 'theological Dean' won respect not least for his books that were published while he was at Clare.

John's second book, *The Body: A Study of Pauline Theology*, was published in 1952 and has been reprinted six times. It is a small book of less than a hundred pages, written for the student and the intelligent reader, but was recognized by scholars all over the world as a little masterpiece. It encapsulates a big subject in a small space. The choice of subject confirmed John as a pastor-theologian, for the book was read as much by parish clergy as by students. He writes:

> Paul starts, as we do, from the fact that man is bound up in a vast solidarity of historical existence which denies him freedom to control his own destiny or achieve his true end. This is the 'body' of sin and death, in which he is involved at every level of his being, physical, political and even cosmic. The great corporations of modern society are expressions of this all-embracing solidarity. The temptation of Western man is to seek salvation by exalting the individual *against* such collectives or by seeking withdrawal from the body of socio-historical existence. Paul saw that the Christian gospel is very different. For the body is not simply evil: it is made by God and for God. Solidarity is the divinely ordained structure in which personal life is to be lived. Man's freedom does not lie in the fact that he is not bound, nor his individuality in the fact that he is not social. Both derive from an unconditional and inalienable responsibility to God, which is not denied by the solidarities of the body and can indeed be discharged only in and through them. Christians should be the last people to be found clinging to the wrecks of an atomic individualism, which has no foundation in the Bible. For their hope does not lie in escape from collectivism: it lies in the resurrection of the body – that is to say, in the redemption, transfiguration, and ultimate supersession of one solidarity by another. That is Paul's gospel of the new corporeity of the Body of Christ, which itself depends on the redemptive act wrought by Jesus in the body of His flesh through death. One could say without exaggeration that the concept of the body forms the keystone of Paul's theology.

In 1954 John contributed an important essay on 'Kingdom, Church and Ministry', to the influential book, *The Historic Episcopate*, edited by Kenneth Carey, then Principal of Westcott House, later Bishop of Edinburgh. It was in this essay that John made one of his most memorable statements: 'Just as the New Testament bids us have as high a doctrine of the ministry as we like, as long as our doctrine of the Church is higher, so it commands us have as high a doctrine of the Church as we may, provided our doctrine of the Kingdom is higher.'

John's third book also appeared during his time at Clare. *Jesus and His Coming: The Emergence of a Doctrine* was published in 1957. (It was given a second edition in 1979.) John was particularly pleased with a letter from Gabriel Hebert of the Society of the Sacred Mission, Kelham, who said he was 'delighted with it'. He wrote:

> There is above all the exposure of Albert Schweitzer's fatal error in assuming that our Lord's eschatological message was therefore an apocalyptic message. His message was 'The Kingdom of God is upon you' (NEB); it meant the fulfilment of God's purpose announced by the prophets, the breaking-in of the Kingdom in His mighty works and mighty words, the supreme Crisis, taking form in His mission.

Others thought that, for all John's brilliance, it over-simplified. *Jesus and His Coming* originally formed the William Belden Noble Lectures delivered at Harvard in 1955. And so began John's 'in journeyings often'.

It was not easy for a married man with four young children – Elizabeth Clare ('Buffy') was born in January 1952 and Judith in November 1954 – to balance the call of the world Church and the call of his own family. The family motto and his whole upbringing made John give considerable weight to the former. There was a third call – self-fulfilment – to be recognized; and of course a fourth – self-indulgence. In February 1954 John was invited by Norman Goodall, secretary of the International Missionary Council, to visit 'one of the theological colleges in the lands of the younger churches' – in Africa, India or Japan. All that year John worked at the details of a visit to the Episcopal Seminary, Tokyo and other seminaries in Japan, and had all but committed himself. It was likely he would be away from early April to the end of September 1955. But at the end of January 1955, he wrote to Dr Goodall:

> From the start I felt that in the abstract this was a call that I ought not to refuse. Its importance was clear, and it seemed that unless anything obviously prevented me I should go. It became evident that nothing was likely to stand in my way from the point of view of the College or University and the whole question then came back to my wife in what I now realise was an unfair form. Once I had made up my mind independently that I ought to go then it was obvious that anything she said about family commitments was bound to appear in the light of deflecting me from my duty, and it was evident that whatever decision I made she was going to be equally unhappy.
>
> I see now that this was to put her in an intolerable position and the decision that this was a job I ought to do was not one that could be taken in the abstract – with family ties simply coming in afterwards. I feel that in

this job as in any other missionary job here or abroad one has got to ask from the beginning: Is this the sort of assignment that a married man with four young children can undertake while being loyal to his existing commitments as a husband and father?

I believe that the situation today may make the answer different from what it was for a middle-class family, say, in the twenties or thirties. Today the reserves are so much thinner. Certainly in our case, and I imagine it is not untypical, there are no unemployed relatives on to whom children can be drafted in an emergency, boarding schools are out of the question, and domestic help is so much a matter of hand to mouth. If everything went entirely without a hitch then I think it might be managed. But this is a supposition that one can't really make, and if anything goes wrong or anyone gets ill I really don't see there is any second line on which to fall back.

My wife and I have talked the matter out thoroughly and she is perfectly ready to 'go it alone' if I decide that, all things considered, I should still go. In ten years time perhaps such an assignment would.be within the realm of practicability, but I have reluctantly concluded that it would be wrong to undertake it now.

But the question would not go away. On 5 May 1955 Dr George A. Buttrick wrote on behalf of President Nathan Pusey of Harvard – and on the prompting of Bishop George Bell – to invite John to give the Noble Lectures in December. Within days there followed an invitation from Dr Henry Van Dusen and Dr John Knox for John to give two lectures at Union Theological Seminary in New York. By June he was also invited to do a term's teaching at the Harvard Divinity School. The proposal – at Dr Charles Taylor's invitation – was that John should live at the Episcopal Theological School, Boston and that Ruth should join him for the last four weeks.

On the day Dr Buttrick despatched his invitation Stephen Robinson was seven, Catherine six, Buffy three, and Judith not yet six months. The obvious question was whether and with whom the children could be left. But there was an equally important underlying question. In Bristol and Wells Ruth had been able to share John's life. The home was within the College. At Cambridge John worked for the most part in Clare. He would come home for tea, be there for the children's bathtime and bedtime, and go back to College to dine and do more work. 'Once he was sent up to the bathroom to bath us,' Buffy remembers. 'I can see him reading with one eye and watching us with the other. We didn't often have what felt like his undivided attention.'

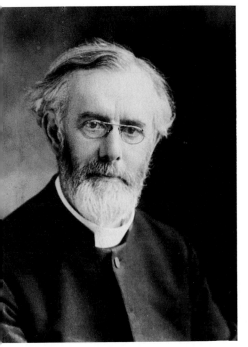

John's father, Arthur Robinson, Canon of Canterbury

John's mother, Beatrice, with the infant John

The eight year old John with his family

John on leaving Marlborough

ABOVE LEFT AND RIGHT: Ruth and John at the time
of their engagement

ABOVE CENTRE: On honeymoon in the Tessin, Switzerland

Weekends, which most 'secular' dons would delight in at home, required the presence of the Dean in Chapel or in College about his pastoral business. Undergraduates might come out for a meal with John and Ruth and be glad of 'a bit of home' with the Robinsons – at 'Etheldreda' in Chesterton Road, their first home in Cambridge, and later at 76 Milton Road. But both houses were some distance from the College; and four young children were in any case a full-time occupation for Ruth. A Cambridge College by its very constitution was a domestic set-up, a second home – for a man. However kind and friendly the college, a don's wife could feel from time to time excluded, out on a limb, and alone – even though invited into the Ladies' Annexe, so to speak, of an essentially male club. There were of course the vacations; but John was already in demand as a speaker and preacher and felt it a duty to give what help he could to those who asked. Cambridge always seemed a place of privilege and heightened John's sense of duty to help those in less privileged places. ('Not for ourselves alone . . .') It was important for John and Ruth somehow to get more time together. But how?

Together they made the decision that John should leave for the USA at the end of September 1955 and that Ruth should join him for the last week in November – leaving the children with kind and trusted friends at 76 Milton Road – and that they should return together a week before Christmas. It was no easy decision, particularly for Ruth, but it meant that she was present with John at the Noble Lectures and with him made friends in the US who became friends for life.

Whenever John went to the US (or any other country) he was assiduous in looking up his English friends who were there. Jeremy Bray (now Dr Jeremy Bray, M.P. for Motherwell and Wishaw), who had been a graduate student at Clare from 1952 to 1955 (and whose wife Elizabeth had attended John's lectures in the Divinity Faculty), went to Harvard as Choate Fellow for 1955–6 and well remembers both the delight of meeting John there and the not uncharacteristic incident that ensued: 'We met John outside the Memorial Church on our first Sunday. Our eldest daughter, Margaret, was then a toddler, in a push-chair. John looked at this bundle and asked, "How old is it?" When Elizabeth said, with due haughtiness, "*She* is fifteen months," John compounded his villainy by saying, "An unpleasant age."' Nevertheless the friendship between Jeremy and his wife and John and Ruth became one of the most important in John's life.

In 1958 he was back again in the US from the beginning of March to mid-June. He had been invited to deliver the Reinicker Lectures at the Episcopal Theological Seminary at Richmond, Virginia, and also to be visiting professor for a term at Union Theological Seminary, Richmond. Once in the U.S. John was a compulsive traveller, and on this journey lectured or preached at Memphis, Yale, Harvard and Princeton, before Ruth arrived with Stephen and Catherine in mid-May. They accompanied him to New York, Washington, D.C. and to the University of Utah, before they had a week's holiday together in Yellowstone National Park (during which a brown bear found its way into the back of their parked car!). Then there was more lecturing for him in Cleveland, Rochester, Lexington and Concord before their return.

John took as his subject for the Reinicker Lectures 'Matter, Power and Liturgy'. (These lectures were published as a chapter of *On Being the Church in the World*.) It was indeed worldly theology – *about* the world (the Bomb, for instance, and Race), and *for* people living in the world. It was biblical theology. It was about how 'we may begin to unite politics and prayer, and prayer with a concern for "men where they are"'. In January 1958 CND had been founded. In his second lecture on 'Power' John said:

> The Campaign for Nuclear Disarmament, which has been written off in America (as well as by much of the English Press) as pacifist, leftist, Labourite, Communist (or whatever the current or the local slur word may be), represents, I believe, a much more profound reappraisal than anything I detect going on in public over here in the States. I am sure such a reappraisal will also be forced upon you. But under the smart of the *sputnik* I fear it will take a long time. For the effect of this last has been to retrench all the most conventional and monolithic attitudes to power . . . If Aesop had lived today he might have written a fable about the bee, who one day became conscious of the fact that he could not use his sting except in the act of dying.

Most of the third lecture, on 'Liturgy', is to be found in *Liturgy Coming to Life*, which remains one of John's most effective books, not least because it is simple personal testimony – to a conversion:

> When I was at my theological college there was no subject that seemed to me so remote from any living concern for the Gospel and its relevance to the modern world than what was taught and examined as 'liturgiology' . . . In the parish to which I subsequently went as a curate I was to receive an entirely new vision; for here the Parish Communion formed the

centre and power-house of everything that was done in the week, both within the life of the Christian congregation and in the world outside. It was this vision that was decisive . . . It was then for the first time that I saw the essential connection between liturgy and evangelism . . . It was not liturgical reform for its own sake or in isolation from the rest of the life of the worshipping, witnessing and healing Community . . . The sharing of Bread . . . must be continued socially – and thence economically and politically . . . Holy Communion is the great workshop of the new world . . . Liturgy is at its heart social action, the point where this world is taken and consecrated, broken and restored for God and his Kingdom, and where the Church itself is renewed as the agent of the Christian revolution.

No one would normally expect a Cambridge college chapel to have great relevance, let alone be a dynamic example, to the world outside. But what went on at Clare inspired many a parish, as 'Charlie' Moule has said, all over the world; and *Liturgy Coming to Life* remains today one of the best manuals on worship for the intelligent layman.

John did most of the work on his *Twelve New Testament Studies* (1962) at Clare. (A third impression was published in 1984.) He used the material for many lectures in Cambridge and elsewhere. Their clarity of analysis was again widely acknowledged, and the way he handled several problems of detail, well-known to scholars, freshly and lucidly. Two pages in fact consist simply of a scholar's footnote – in which John shows the paucity of evidence for rivalry in early Christianity from sects attached to the name of John the Baptist. It was nevertheless an important footnote which subsequent writers could not ignore. But the *Studies* were pre-eminently pastoral scholarship – helping the parish clergy most of all, in, for instance, their preaching on the parable of the Sheep and the Goats, and the Temptations, and with their concern with the New Testament doctrine of baptism.

It was not surprising therefore that Geoffrey Fisher, Archbishop of Canterbury, should in 1953 have made John one of his Examining Chaplains, and in 1958 should invite him to become one of the Six-Preachers of Canterbury Cathedral, an office established by Henry VIII now involving only a sermon a year. John's mother, who was nearing her seventy-ninth birthday, was particularly delighted. She wrote:

> I can't tell you how it pleases me to think that the Archbishop has given you this appointment and how kindly he expresses himself! Here is yet another way in which you follow your Father, and I like to remember that

it was on an occasion of his coming to stay with my Father and me for one of his Six-Preacher's sermons that I first came into personal contact with him. I can see his tall figure now as he came through the gallery door into the drawing room as I wrestled with a boiling tea kettle, and 'Chief', my deerhound, whose welcome to visitors was unpleasantly violent. How I shall look forward to your visits and seeing and hearing you in the Cathedral pulpit.

As 'Charlie' Moule implied, John grew in stature at Clare – though F. A. Simpson, by then a septuagenarian Fellow of Trinity, would always refer to John as 'Unreliable Robinson' (partly because Simpson always took care of the sound of an epithet and let the sense take care of itself; and partly to echo 'Prosperity Robinson' the nineteenth-century politician, but chiefly as a back-handed tribute to John's flashes of insight, not all of which he deemed of equal illumination). Certainly John's rationality could still lead him into brushes with the absurd. One vacation, just as he had gone away to lecture, the editor of the *Cambridge Daily News* 'phoned Ruth. An advert, he said, had been submitted for the 'Wanted' column, in the name of Dr John Robinson: 'For Sale: Electric Razor, or Exchange Lawnmower.' The editor thought it might be an undergraduate hoax and wanted Dr Robinson's confirmation. Ruth could only say that she knew John had acquired a new razor and had talked of getting a lawnmower. That evening when John 'phoned Ruth, he said in response to her enquiry that he had intended to insert two advertisements, but when he heard the cost he thought he would put them in together. 'It's obvious what it means,' he said, and was quite uncomprehending as to why anyone should find it at all odd. Soon after however the 'Odd-Ads' column of the *Daily Mirror* reprinted the advertisement, illustrating it with a cartoon showing a man with a minuscule lawnmower mowing his outsize beard.

John's growth in stature was recognized in ways formal and informal. He was appointed Assistant Lecturer in Divinity to the University in 1953 and Lecturer in 1954. That year Dr Alec Vidler, Dean of Windsor, who had been conducting since 1938 what he had called the 'Windsor Correspondence', a privately circulated quarterly letter from him to which kindred minds could contribute, asked John to be the future collator of the Correspondence – thenceforth to be called the 'Cambridge Correspondence'. It was really a way of trying out ideas and sharing experiences that were not ripe for publication and might never be. When John took it over, there were nearly fifty correspondents. It was clearly valuable to people all over the world – such as Martin Jarrett-Kerr, CR in Johannesburg, Mrs Reinhold Niebuhr in New York, Tony Dumper in Malaya, Fred Welbourn and Dennis Payne in Makerere, Leonard Schiff in Bangalore, Stanley Booth-Clibborn in Nairobi – as well as to people in universities and parishes in England. In the Correspondence, John was able to explode (in December 1956) about, for instance, Suez:

> Rarely, one has got the impression, have the mass of people in this country had their heads so complacently in the sand. It was shock enough to realise that, after the first dazed uneasiness, most people had not really been shaken to any degree by the Suez intervention. One imagined a wave of revulsion such as swept over the country after the Hoare-Laval deal. But within a week most people were preparing to justify it by results. And now there is such a concerted effort to pretend that the results have justified it and proclaim a famous victory that one despairs of any political maturity in the country . . . I found myself dismayed and shattered by political events to a degree that I seldom if ever remember before. I feel it has destroyed the only basis upon which Britain could hope to exercise leadership in our post-war situation and that it has finally finished us as a great power more effectively than Hitler ever did.

Although a College will be proud of a Dean whose books receive recognition and acclaim in academic circles, it will also expect from him faithfulness in his day-to-day duties; and the time he may spend – for good reason – away from the college and university (on, say, sabbatical and as a visiting professor) in no way diminishes that expectation. There is no doubt that in his eight years as Dean of Clare John was 'found faithful'. When, for instance, the kitchen manager's wife was dying of cancer, it was John he most wanted to visit her. Each beginning of term the Dean and the Chaplain together sent every member of the College a printed College Letter. Each of the two dozen letters John sent were substantial, introducing the carefully chosen preachers for the term, for example Trevor Huddleston, George MacLeod, Alec Vidler and so on, commenting on, say, the Billy Graham Mission to the University or some other subject the Dean and Chaplain believed should be at the forefront of an undergraduate's mind, for instance, 'How to confront the question of vocation'. Clare in those days knew it was pastorally well served.

In January 1955 an event had occurred which was ultimately to alter the whole course of John's life. Mervyn Stockwood – still Vicar of St

Matthew Moorfields after a ministry there lasting nineteen years –
accepted the invitation to be Vicar of Great St Mary's, Cambridge. As
the Revd F. A. Simpson said four years later, in the sermon he
preached at Mervyn's consecration as Bishop of Southwark:

> We had seen, in a little more than three years, our University Church of
> Gt St Mary's raised up from the very earth to be all, or almost all, that
> such a church could be. And when, with that work so recent, so
> manifestly important, so still precariously poised, they came to us saying,
> 'Knowest thou the Lord will take away thy prophet from thy head today?'
> it was as much as some of us could do at first to answer, 'Yea, I know it,
> hold ye your peace.'

Mervyn's ministry at Great St Mary's had indeed been remarkable.
The congregation which averaged about two hundred in his first year as
vicar became over a thousand in his last year. Mervyn and John saw a
good deal of each other in the years between. 'Uncle' Mervyn would
drop in at 76 Milton Road, and tell the children bedtime stories. Ruth
would take the family regularly to Parish Communion at Great St
Mary's. It was in the first week of November 1958 that the Prime
Minister, Harold Macmillan, asked Mervyn to let his name go forward
to the Queen for nomination to the bishopric of Southwark. It was not
immediately clear to Mervyn that he should. The following Sunday he
asked several of his friends to come together for a late night meeting in
the rooms of Hugh Montefiore, Dean of Caius (later Bishop of
Birmingham), to help him make up his mind. It was a unique occasion.
John was one of those who attended.

All except Kenneth Carey, then Principal of Westcott House, were
clear that Mervyn should go to Southwark. Little did John realize the
consequences to himself of the advice to which he was party. But at the
beginning of December, having signified his willingness to go, Mervyn
told John that the incumbent Bishop of Woolwich, the Rt Revd R. W.
Stannard, had informed the retiring Bishop of Southwark, Bertram
Simpson, of his intention to resign. Mervyn said that he wanted John to
succeed him. It was not of course easy for Mervyn, who had needed
some persuading that it was right for himself to leave Cambridge, now
to maintain that it was right for John also to leave. And whereas the
Archbishop was quite clear that Mervyn should go to Southwark he was
equally clear that John should not. There were also close friends in
Cambridge who believed John should stay. As one of John's closest

friends, as well as Lady Margaret's Professor, none could put the case more strongly than 'Charlie' Moule – and none did. 'Charlie' felt John still had a lot to give both in Clare and in the University, and that he was young to be shutting the door on all that.

When John told Ruth of the invitation her immediate reaction was: 'Ridiculous!' But the more they talked it over together the more it seemed right to accept. To John it was not as if he was being asked to forsake his vocation as a theologian. Quite the reverse. Even in 1944 at Westcott House he had felt it 'no little sense of suffering and straightening' to know himself to be by nature both a 'systematic' theologian and someone who had a 'Divine Imperative' to pass on and communicate truth which he had made his own. The truth and vision he had received at Bristol he knew he could not have received at Cambridge. His experience at Wells – spelt out in his article in *Theology* on 'The Theological College in a Changing World' – had made him profoundly unhappy that this was the way to 'Do Theology Today'. Much of his writing at Clare, not least his most recent lectures, the Reinecker Lectures delivered but a few months before Mervyn extended his invitation, made explicit what he felt to be the heart of his vocation. He might have entitled it 'On being a theologian for the Church in the world'.

In January, John went to see the retiring Bishop of Woolwich.

Mervyn Stockwood had already spelt out to the Archbishop his reasons for wanting to appoint John as his suffragan:

I want as Bishop of Woolwich a man (i) who understands what I am trying to do (ii) who has the intellectual competence and theological knowledge to advise me (iii) who is accustomed to the teaching of ordinands (iv) who, in addition to his special concerns and experimental work, will diligently carry out the normal pastoral and routine duties of a suffragan bishop. At Southwark, there is a strong team at the centre. I have already established a happy relationship with most of them and I know they will be a great help to me. But they are essentially conventional Churchmen. I use the word 'conventional' in no unkindly sense, but to describe an attitude. But in addition to the six men I want a seventh who, while realising the importance of the conventional approach in large areas of the diocese, will appreciate the need for a new approach in places like Rotherhithe and Bermondsey. I must have somebody to whom I can talk, with whom I can discuss and argue, and on whom I can rely. It would be unfortunate if I felt I had to keep this part of my episcopate to myself. Moreover being made as I am, I can always work best when I can put my mind against another man's mind.

On 19 February the Archbishop of Canterbury wrote to Mervyn Stockwood:

My dear Stockwood

I have consulted the Archbishop of York [Ramsey] and Thirkill [Master of Clare] about your proposal for Woolwich, and I find that in fact the Archbishop of York has discussed the thing directly with Robinson. I could, no doubt, ask the advice of other people, but as on the whole what the Archbishop and Thirkill say bears out my own feelings, I think perhaps I ought to write straight away. What I have to say will, I am afraid, run counter to your own clearly seen and clearly desired wishes, but I think what I say does merit your earnest consideration.

As the Archbishop of York has no doubt made known to Robinson he recognises that you are desperately keen to carry through, under the best possible auspices a frontal attack at the heart of an immense problem, and that for this project you wish to have a man with Robinson's own clear mind and theological weight and uninhibited courage.

But on the other side are a number of weighty considerations. Your own work for the Church would be fatally damaged if you became known as a man of one idea only, and I think there would be some danger of giving that idea if you brought in as your Suffragan one chosen entirely to give additional backing to a particular project of your own. If the frontal attack is to be made you have the freedom and the resources which any other Diocesan Bishop has for making that frontal attack. It might well be thought that you were rather unfairly weighting your own ideas if you brought in a young man already wedded to them as a Suffragan of the Diocese.

To do so might be unwise for you: it might be fatally bad for Robinson. As the Archbishop has told him the job you want him for is only a fraction of the whole responsibilities of a Suffragan Bishop. If he came he would have identified himself at the start with a particular project which however important is still limited in scope. What you and the Diocese and everybody else must ask is a quite general question regarding the whole work of the Church and its whole manpower and resources: is it right at this moment to choose Robinson for the office and work of a Suffragan Bishop in its full status of episcopal responsibility. Here four things seem important:

(a) Robinson is only 40. Sometimes it is right to choose a young man, but there is a certain gravitas needed, and perhaps particularly needed for a Suffragan, since he has to rely not on his powers of jurisdiction but entirely on his powers of personal discretion and weight with his brethren. One would have to be sure that in all the manifold calls upon a

Suffragan Bishop, Robinson's qualifications are so certain as to justify his being picked out to be a Bishop so soon.

(b) And then, is it good for him at the age of 40 to turn to the highly specialised and in many ways very limited and constricted responsibilities of a Bishop? I should have thought that in any case he ought to have longer experience in which to measure his abilities against the tasks of the Church so as to be better equipped to bring experience to bear on what would be episcopal office for the rest of his life.

(c) There is, of course, the other question whether it is right for him to be taken away from academic work, whether in Cambridge or in Manchester[1] at this moment. I should have thought that again in his total contribution to the Church there was a further contribution which he ought to make in academic life with all its bearing on stimulating thought and giving theology some commanding power. I should have thought again that he needed it for himself as well as for the contribution he can give.

(d) With all this in mind I come to the simple question whether he is now sufficiently developed in the personal gravitas needed for the office of a Bishop. I think Thirkill is right in saying that although he has grown he is still immature: whether because he travels faster than other people in his thinking or not, he is not always tactful and occasionally is unconsciously harsh and brusque. Thirkill adds that he is barely 40: he has an exceptionally creative mind: he ought for the sake of scholarship to give more years in its service, and in the end he will be in a better position to tackle the office and work of a Bishop.

I have only a nodding acquaintance with Robinson but all the things which Thirkill says bear out my own strong impression that in due time he will be fitted quite admirably as a Bishop with the courage and far sightedness needed, but at present he has not got the well founded personal weight to make his appointment acceptable in the Diocese, or is yet adequate to the manifold calls upon a Bishop. And, as I hinted above, I think it would be bad for him, as well as unwise for you, that he should come to the office of a Bishop as your adherent to be plunged into a particular enterprise. Let the enterprise go forward but I think you must be prepared to embark on it relying on the general resources of a Diocese: and in choosing your Suffragan Bishop you should choose one, if possible, not already wedded to you or to your outlook, but able in the Diocese to be in the fullest sense all things to all men as a pastor. For remember that the chief work of a Suffragan is to be a pastor, to do for

---

[1] There was some possibility John would be offered a vacant professorial appointment in biblical studies in the University of Manchester. In the event the offer was not made.

the clergy what the Diocesan Bishop has not time to do: sometimes his most valuable service is to make up for his diocesan's shortcomings rather than to say ditto to them!

Well, I have tried to express as clearly as I can what is really a general feeling, understood by the Archbishop of York and Thirkill, that this is not really the right solution. I do hope, therefore, that you will think again before choosing your two names.

> Yours sincerely
> Geoffrey Cantuar.

On 7 March Mervyn wrote to the Archbishop:

I have thought a great deal about the vacancy at Woolwich and I have most carefully considered the points in your letter. While I realise the strength of your arguments against the nomination of John Robinson, I am inclined to think – though I have not yet decided – that, on balance, there are slightly more arguments on the other side.

Robinson has been to Manchester and no doubt he is turning things over in his mind; whether or not he will be offered the professorship remains to be seen.

He would, I know, like to discuss the position with you, and I told him I would ask you whether you would see him. I am doing it this way because I thought it might be breaking protocol if Robinson were to write to you directly about a suffragan bishopric, unless the diocesan-to-be wrote to you first.

You will remember that I said in my previous letter that while his qualifications might be deficient in some respects, the total score might be as good as I could reasonably expect of any candidate. So I will say no more, at this stage, on the personal issue. What concerns me more is the sort of job Robinson ought to be doing in the general interests of the Church. I am trying to be objective about this and keeping my mind as open as possible; and so is Robinson – that is why he wants to see you, so that you can put all the arguments to him, pro and contra, and help him to sort them out.

As I see it the basic argument is this:

Case against Robinson going to Woolwich
There are many priests of experience who could become Bishop of Woolwich. Why take a chap who is doing a first-class job in the theological faculty at Cambridge? Moreover if he were to be offered the professorship at Manchester he would fill the chair with distinction. Theologians like Robinson are much too thin on the ground as it is; it would be a serious blow to the Church if he were removed from theological work. And if he were to become a suffragan bishop it would

be a misuse of his abilities. Why not leave him at Cambridge or Manchester for ten years and then, when he has made his contribution in the theological field, put him on the Bench?

Case for Robinson going to Woolwich

What is wanted in the new Bishop of Woolwich is a man who, while capable of doing his routine duties in his stride, will have the mind and theological grip to tackle experimentally a situation which is probably the major problem that confronts the Church in Europe. While it would be unwise to make a blue-print, it is obvious that if cautious experiments are to be made much will depend on the theological foundations that are laid. Good intentions and vague aspirations are not enough. There must be a man in charge, under the diocesan bishop, who really 'knows his stuff' and can keep the experiment within the limits of Biblical theology and the doctrinal boundaries of the Church of England. Nobody knows what the outcome may be; it may be a failure, on the other hand, it may open up all sorts of possibilities.

In my judgement few men are as well qualified as Robinson to take charge of such work. He is a theologian; at the same time he is a practical man who has his feet firmly on the earth. And the situation which would confront him in the particular part of the diocese of Southwark that would be his special care would give him the opportunity to apply his academic knowledge to an urgent need.

What is the alternative?

If Robinson does not come to me, what is the alternative? I can think of three or four people who might be valuable colleagues at the ordinary level, but I can think of nobody who has the particular qualifications for which I am looking.

David Stephens[1] and others have put forward the name of Ernie Southcott of Leeds. I admire Southcott, but I doubt if he has the theological competence for this particular work. Moreover he is, by nature, so intense I should, for temperamental reasons, find it difficult to work with him. And I think he might overwhelm the clergy.

Conclusion

And that, Your Grace, is the position as I see it. But you, with your vastly greater experience and insight, will see things that I do not see. And you are in a position, which I am not, to see the overall picture. So before I commit myself I should be most grateful if you would see Robinson and put to him the position as you see it. If, after discussion, both you and he feel that he should stay in academic work I shall be satisfied. But if you come to the conclusion that there is something to be said for my

[1] Secretary for Appointments to the Prime Minister 1955–61.

view-point it will help me considerably in making up my mind about the nomination.

Geoffrey Fisher saw John on 19 March and wrote to Mervyn on the same day:

(i) I think for a time longer he ought to put his undoubted abilities to the theological life of Cambridge. (ii) I am not satisfied that there is any final reason why you and the diocese should have his services at the moment. (iii) There is John Robinson himself. He is only thirty-nine. Is it right to bring him at this stage of his experience and activity into the machine of ecclesiastical and episcopal authority? I told him all that, and I added that having said it I should be perfectly content, and that he and you should judge as best you can. Having given him my own advice I have done all that is proper for me to do.

John returned to Cambridge and saw Mervyn immediately. Mervyn wrote to John the next day:

My dear John

Thank you for letting me know the gist of your conversation with the Archbishop. I have had a letter from him in which he frankly sets out the points you mentioned.

I recognise the strength of his arguments against you going to Woolwich, and, with one exception, would not wish to make any comments. Here is the exception:

Let me give you an illustration. Since my appointment to Southwark, I have asked the suffragans to keep me informed of any incumbents who might be in particular need. In December I was told of a priest whose wife was dying of cancer. We have corresponded regularly and a fortnight ago the wife died. Although I have not met the man I was impressed by his letters: he was obviously a man of deep spiritual understanding.

When I was in London yesterday I had a word with one of the diocesan authorities and asked him how many people attended the church of this man. The answer was shattering – two. (That at any rate was the number present on recent occasions when this particular diocesan official took a Sunday service.)

This is probably an extreme illustration but it will help you to understand what is in my mind when I say that in some parts of the diocese we must work out a new pattern if the Church is to come to life.

Here is my problem. The incumbent in question appears to be a faithful parson, intelligent and devout. Presumably he has had the customary academic preparation. But what is the result of all this? He has learnt theology but circumstances are such that he appears to be unable to work theologically.

If you continue in the academic sphere you will give ordinands their theological equipment. But what will they do with it? If they go to some parts of England, it will bear fruit; in other parts it won't.

As I see it you must decide whether you want to continue teaching theology at Cambridge to people who may, or may not be able to implement it in their parishes; or whether you feel called to devote your abilities and energies to that section in English life in which theology means next to nothing.

As I hope you realise, I have spent a part of my ministry in a setting in which the orthodox pattern of work bears fruit so I will not question your decision if you feel you should remain within that pattern for the time being. I am sure you will continue to make a considerable contribution. If, however, you think you are called by God to devote yourself to this other pattern, I shall be pleased to submit your name to the Queen for nomination to the bishopric of Woolwich. While you are trying to make up your mind I am sure you will carefully consider the points that have been put to you by the Archbishop. I am particularly anxious that he shall not think that I have been bringing unfair pressures upon you. I can only repeat that if you think you should stay in Cambridge I shall accept your decision without question – and with respect.

> My love to you both.
> Yours ever.
> Mervyn.

PS I have sent a copy of this letter to the Archbishop.

The Archbishop was to fly to Japan on the following Wednesday, 25 March. John and Ruth had been wrestling with Woolwich for nearly four months. It was time now to decide. John wrote to Mervyn on the Tuesday in Holy Week:

I write to confirm what I said to you over the telephone, that after a good deal of thought and advice I have decided to accept your very kind and indeed overwhelming proposal that you should submit my name to the Queen for the bishopric of Woolwich. It has been one of the most difficult decisions of my life but having made it, both Ruth and I feel convinced that it is right. I suppose the thing that finally weighed down the scales on this side was the recognition that, however important it might be to keep the theological bridge-head open at the Cambridge end, at the other end it virtually did not exist at all. There must be something into which ideas and people from this end can engage if any traffic is to take place.

Mervyn, after 'phoning the Archbishop with the news, wrote at once to John:

> My dear John
> I need hardly say how delighted I am to have your letter. I always look back to your curacy at St Matthew's as the most constructive period in my ministry there; and I am quite sure that with you at my side in Southwark I shall be able to do things which if left to myself I could never do. And of course it will be delightful to have Ruth and the children close at hand . . .
>
> Yours ever
Mervyn.

Ruth was not only entirely with John in his decision. From her point of view the move promised more of a share in John's ministry, and the prospect that he would again be able to operate from their own home was a source of joy.

John wrote to the Archbishop so that he had a letter waiting for him on his return from Japan:

> After much wrestling with the problem I have expressed my willingness to let Mervyn Stockwood put my name forward for Woolwich. I have taken this decision not without a great deal of heart searching, and no one is more conscious than I of the considerations which you and others put forward on the other side. I could heartily have wished that the choice had not been put before me so soon. But I have come to feel that this particular challenge is one that I could not duck. At some point a bridge has to be made whereby ideas of theology and ministry which have validity in a place like Cambridge can have impact on the situation of the Church in industrial society and vice versa; and, rightly or wrongly, I have become persuaded that I should pull up from here and allow myself to be used, if I can be, in response to such a specific request. So I hope perhaps that I may claim the backing and good-will which you very generously promised whichever way the decision came out, and which I have valued so much throughout my ministry.
>
> Though I should not expect to start the work in Woolwich till September, it would make things very much easier at this end if the appointment could now be announced, if that is what seems good to everyone concerned, with as little delay as possible. I should like to be able to inform the College and University as early in May as it is

practicable, as they must set about finding a successor for me. May I thank you again for the time and help you gave me when you were so pressed before your departure?

Yours sincerely
John A. T. Robinson.

But the Archbishop was not able to act so quickly. He wrote to John three days after the consecration of Mervyn Stockwood as Bishop of Southwark:

Lambeth Palace, SE1
4th May 1959

My dear Robinson
I have now got back to letters, and have read yours of the 24th, and I also had a word with the Bishop of Southwark the other day. I fully accept the decision to which you and he have come. In due course I will take the necessary action.

You ask that your appointment might possibly be announced early in May. I am afraid that is quite impossible; there has to be a petition of a formal kind; that I have to send to the Prime Minister. The Prime Minister in due course submits it to Buckingham Palace; again in due course it comes back from Buckingham Palace to the Prime Minister, and then he notifies me of the final assent.

I cannot hurry that process, but I will see that it is started.

Yours sincerely
Geoffrey Cantuar.

The process was by no means a formality. On 12 May the Bishop of Southwark was informed by No. 10 that the appointment was held up because the Prime Minister wished to discuss it with the Archbishop of Canterbury who would not be available until the last week of May. Mervyn wrote that day:

My dear John
I think I am running into some difficulty with Downing Street, but I intend to put up a fight. There may, however, be delay.

Love,
Mervyn.

It was nearly a month therefore before the process resulted in the letter from the Prime Minister informing John of the Queen's approval of the appointment. It was made public on Tuesday, 2 June 1959.

The announcement was of course followed by many letters of congratulation. Most of the Cambridge letters bemoaned the loss to New Testament scholarship; some were almost letters of protest. Canon E. C. Ratcliff, Regius Professor of Divinity, wrote:

> First, let me offer my congratulations on your elevation. You could not do otherwise than go. It must have been a difficult decision, because, if you leave learning for Woolwich, you really leave it for good. But you will now be able to apply your learning instead of hoping that someone else may do so! And it will be exciting and proper that you should help in the experiments in 'bishoping' which Southwark Diocese is soon to see. Second, let me say what, I admit, came into my mind first. Your going will be a great blow to the Divinity Faculty. Even if your successor is stimulating, he cannot be so in the very particular and personal way in which you have stimulated both colleagues and pupils. You will go (and I know that here I speak for the Faculty as a whole and not only for the Board) with our best wishes, though not without our regrets; and you will take with you our gratitude.

Percival Gardner-Smith, formerly Dean of Jesus, just retiring after ten years as President of the College, wrote to John (as he had at his ordination):

> I hasten to offer my congratulations on your elevation. In his declining years (if he ever did decline) Foakes Jackson found consolation in the varied achievements of his pupils, and to a lesser extent I do the same. I wish you every blessing, and do not doubt that it is only the first step.
>
> Having said that I must add that I greatly regret your decision. There is no difficulty in finding bishops, but the Church is lamentably short of scholars – not least in Cambridge – and in time this will have a serious effect. When I read your last book I felt that you would make a great contribution, and now you will spend your life taking confirmations and dedicating church bells. I am sure you will do it very well, but I think you were Stockwood's curate long enough.

It had been a great sadness to John that George Bell, Bishop of Chichester, had died only the previous October in the first days of his retirement; had he lived, John would undoubtedly have consulted him about his future; but his widow wrote John a letter full of practical help:

> Dear John
> I do rejoice greatly to think that you and your wife are going to help Bishop Mervyn in the big task that lies ahead. It must have been a very hard decision to make, and your friends must stir up their prayers for you

in this big task. Your mother has just been to lunch and encourages me to write and ask if some of my husband's episcopal things may be of help to you. He was, roughly, 5 ft 8½–9 in height. I enclose a list of things which you might find useful and which I should be very glad to hand over to you if you could ever wear them. I would send one garment for you to try, or you could come and inspect and try on when you are down here.

1 Purple evening dress coat and cassock and belt
1 Purple cassock and cap
1 (very old) black chimere (satin)
1 scarlet chimere (cloth)
2 black silk scarves
1 pr. red wrist bands
1 robe case

I would love to think of them being in use.

Yours very sincerely,
Henrietta Bell.

John was particularly glad to have the 'mantle' of Bell fall upon him and accepted this offer with alacrity. He used the robe case with pride and affection until his life's end, only putting sticking plaster over the silvered and embossed 'Bishop of Chichester' and writing on it 'Bishop of Woolwich'.

There was one other reach-me-down item of clothing, for Bishop Stephen Neill (formerly Bishop of Tinnevelly in south India) with his letter of congratulation told John he had brought him Uncle Alfred's episcopal scarlet chimere 'in splendid condition, being made of almost indestructible material, such as is very hard to come by in this post-war world'.

There was little time for farewells at Clare, for the term ended only three weeks after the announcement of John's appointment. (Clare would in fact be saying farewell not only to John but to the Revd F. S. Skelton, DFC and bar, DSO and bar, who had been Chaplain of Clare alongside John for seven of his eight years, and who after term ended decided to go to Southwark with him, as Rector of Bermondsey.) 'Charlie' Moule has already recorded the gift of John's pectoral cross from members of Clare.

Let two Clare men speak a final word on his time there. First, a Fellow when John was Dean, Bill Wedderburn (now Lord Wedderburn of Charlton, Cassel Professor of Commercial Law at the London School of Economics; University of London):

Soon after I became a Fellow of Clare College, John came as Dean. It was an odd time –'non-political', yet the beginning of new intellectual inquiry.

John wanted to get to know the Fellows and students not just in the usual social manner (though he and Ruth played that role) but as people. He also made no bones about his progressive social and political attitudes – a breath of fresh air, for Clare under Henry Thirkill (Tutor and Master, the 'power' in the College since the 1920s) was a pleasant but rather stuffy place. The one thing John was *not* was stuffy. Moreover, if his whinnying giggle sometimes annoyed one, his wish to know what one was thinking never had the appearance of any intrusion into privacy. It was impossible not to respond to him as someone of strong beliefs but genuine wish to pursue truth wherever it led.

At that time the nature and extent of belief in Christianity became a central point of interest in Cambridge. We had our first visit by Billy Graham's crusade and circus. John had decided soon after his arrival that he wanted to know where his colleagues stood. At that time we had the privilege of port (free port!) up in the Combination Room after dinner in Hall. John made a point of initiating discussions which brought out our positions on religious belief. When he saw the range of opinion – and the low level of 'turn-out' of Fellows at Chapel – he proposed that we adjourn on evenings convenient to as many Fellows as possible for sustained and serious discussion.

I remember the first of these vividly, if only because those of us who were 'non-believers' were amazed to find ourselves in a large majority among the dozen or so Fellows who came to it. It was in Charlie Moule's rooms. I suppose we represented almost all the possible positions – John Gilmour (then Director of the Botanical Garden, bibliophile and savant) nearest to a traditional atheist stance, the rest of us bearing marks of unreconstructed logical positivism or less rigorous agnosticism. I recall the contrast between Charlie Moule's responses and John's. He was not at all perturbed by any of the positions (though I would not say that he gave the impression of being deeply read in, say, Oxford linguistic philosophy – very influential at that time, of course). The interpretation of Christianity with which we were faced was, for some of us, new – an odd mixture of simplicity and sophistication. When I read John's *Honest to God* later, it was very familiar. Nor was John particularly downcast when the evening revealed that less than a handful of these Fellows could account themselves Christians in any way at all. You certainly did not get the feeling from him that this condemned you to everlasting fire. For many of us, that evening led to an important development. John Gilmour and I already knew that some Fellows and graduates in King's wanted to initiate some kind of forum for those who wished to meet in a positively secular context. Shortly afterwards, therefore, we founded the Cambridge Humanists. We often told John later that he was the real founder, because without his initiatives, which led the un-Godly Fellows in Clare to know one another, we doubted whether we would have acted as we did. I think he took a certain pride in this, in so far as he may have felt that, if we could not be converted, at least we were now spending more time asking about the nature of our own beliefs and philosophies.

My other main field of co-operation with John, apart from being colleagues in the College, was sometime later, when he took a leading role in activities about South Africa. We raised a Fund, and founded some scholarships, as part of our campaign against apartheid. You never had to ask twice where he would stand on an issue like that.

John was a better 'College man' than I was; yet his leaving Cambridge to go back into the wider work of the Church was no surprise to anyone who knew him.

Now one of John's students must again stand for all: Anthony Moore, who after he was ordained in 1961 served in Southwark all the years that John was Bishop of Woolwich, and is now Team Vicar of Dorchester:

My dear John
It would be extremely ungrateful of me if I were to leave Cambridge without expressing, in a very inadequate way, my deep sense of gratitude for all the help you have given me over the last four years.

You know as well as I how much many of us owe to you for being allowed to experience the wonderful joy of being part of the Christian fellowship in Clare. It has all been said before, not least in the Chapel letter. But I know what a reality it has been in my own life, and in the stair-case groups I have seen people grow spiritually almost week by week. And we all know the strengthening power of the Clare Sunday 8 a.m. service. Patrick Peacey still writes of it in glowing terms to me, from his lonely outpost in Kenya.

Bonhoeffer in *Life Together* says 'in this world the uplifting experience of genuine Christian community can be no more than a pious extra' – a not very comforting thought . . . At Clare I have lived in a Spirit-filled community, for which I thank God. It is difficult for me to imagine Clare Chapel and yourself apart, for they have seemed synonymous . . . I think that at least a few of us have some conception of what it must have meant for you to decide to retire from the academic world. It does not look as though that 'magnum opus' will now materialise.

You have a tremendous task in front of you, and the prayers of myself and of all of us will be with you.

6

The Woolwich Years

John and Ruth and the four children (and Dangle the cat) moved to South London, to 17 Manor Way, Blackheath, on 6 August 1959. They drove ahead of the removal van and had lunch at the Welcome Inn cafe in Blackheath village.

Stephen would soon be going to his preparatory school at Hastings. Catherine was transferring from the Perse School at Cambridge to Blackheath Junior. Buffy, who hated leaving Cambridge and cried much of the way to Blackheath, would be going to the local primary school. Judith was not yet at school.

Both John and Ruth were determined to get behind them all the business of settling in before the consecration on 29 September, Michaelmas Day, so that together they could immediately begin to get to know the clergy and their families, deanery by deanery. Once the house was straight Ruth set to work on the large garden. She remembers being driven indoors once or twice with migraine but there was no other sign of what was to befall her.

On Thursday, 17 September, in the early evening, she was in her bedroom preparing to go to the theatre, to *My Fair Lady*, with Edward, John's brother, who was on furlough from Africa. There was a meeting going on in the house downstairs. It was Buffy, aged seven, who discovered her groaning and trying to call for help, but virtually unconscious, on the bedroom floor. She was taken first to Lewisham Hospital. Next day she was transferred to the Atkinson Morley Hospital at Wimbledon. The first X-ray was inconclusive. The following Monday a second X-ray revealed no tumour – which had been suspected – but that Ruth had had a subarachnoid brain haemorrhage, and that she had a fifty-fifty chance of survival. After a week she was transferred to Hither Green Hospital where she remained until she was released from hospital in November.

The anxiety for John, so few days before his consecration, was of course huge. Domestically his mother, his sister Cecilia, and 'auntie' Nan – Ruth's former headmistress at Holly Lodge High School, Liverpool – came to the rescue. John of course went to the hospital each day. Ruth's memories of those weeks – apart from the pain, which gradually decreased – were of trying to eat her meals with the plate balanced on her chest (she was not allowed to lift her head off the pillow); of waving to the children through the window of the ward; and of John arriving in his cassock, her clean 'nightie' under his arm. 'Why should I want to wrap it up?' he asked characteristically.

John had to abandon any thoughts of a long time of quiet preparation for his consecration – he managed one day at St Christopher's College, Blackheath. Rosamond Fisher, the wife of the Archbishop of Canterbury, kindly asked John's sister to come and stay with the children at the Old Palace, Canterbury, when John stayed there with the Fishers the night before the consecration.

John called in to see Ruth at Hither Green Hospital on his way to Canterbury and left her the order of service. She was able to read it while the service was taking place, opening one eye at a time for a few seconds. It was the first time she had managed to read anything since she had been admitted to hospital.

There could have been no cathedral more appropriate than Canterbury for John's consecration. Yet with Ruth absent, and still not out of the wood, some element of pathos was always present in the proceedings and a wondering what the future might hold. Faith and foreboding were met together. Throughout the service people's eyes kept moving across to where the four children aged eleven, ten, seven and four had their seats with John's mother, sister and brother. Faith was radiantly present in the hymns and the prayers – not least in 'O thou who camest from above'. And when – after the new Bishop of Mauritius, Alan Rogers, had been consecrated – John knelt before the Archbishop, a dozen assisting bishops, encircling John, stretched forth their hands and laid them on him, the whole congregation was united in prayer for him – and for Ruth.

On their way back from Canterbury John and Mervyn called into Hither Green Hospital to see Ruth. It was her first sight of John wearing his purple stock and pectoral cross. Next day she received a memorable letter from Mrs Fisher:

Lambeth Palace
September 29th 1959
Your John's great day

My dear Mrs Robinson

I feel I must write and tell you how very good and sweet the children have been, both as visitors and as members of the congregation at the great service. Everyone is tremendously impressed by their charming be-haviour – no showing off, no whining(!) no awkward shyness and yet no awkward precocity either. I think you and John are wonderful parents.

We were very sad that you had to miss this occasion (I deliberately avoid the word 'experience' because you are not missing *that* at the deep and lasting level). The service was full of praise and of angels. I *knew* the Presence of Christ and knew that His life was being poured out upon the two Bishops.

John looked very full of faith, indeed his whole attitude in the face of his disappointment about your absence and its cause was a great witness to the power of Christ in his life.

I hope you will be the first person to receive God's blessing through his Bishop hands.

Yours affect.
Rosamond Fisher

John Norsworthy wrote a letter which gave Ruth hardly less delight:

I must say how well the children behaved. To me the ritualistic high-light of the whole ceremony was not the mere movements of the archiepis-copal entourage so much as the regal exit of Buffy during the Com-munion. It is a pity that the Queen has ceased to have Presentations. Buffy would have scored a hit at one. She walked through the Presbytery smiling in the most superior, well-meant manner upon all, her head moving from left to right, and every now and then, a nod being granted to someone (I was a lucky one) singled out for particular recognition: rather in the manner of a bishop bestowing his pontifical blessing upon the cowering faithful . . .

After his consecration, in spite of Ruth's illness John immediately got down to work. The Bishop of Woolwich was responsible under the Bishop of Southwark for the episcopal oversight of the eastern part of the diocese of Southwark – the deaneries abutting on to the South Bank of the Thames: Lewisham, containing thirty-two parishes; Greenwich, twenty-nine; Bermondsey and Southwark, twenty-three; and further in from the Thames, Camberwell and Dulwich, twenty parishes. This was a heavy load of over a hundred mainly inner city parishes, most of which had considerable problems. But the Bishop of Woolwich also had within his oversight another forty-eight parishes in the south of the diocese: Sutton deanery, fifteen; Caterham, eighteen; Godstone, fifteen. These 152 parishes in all had full-time staff of about three hundred clergy, deaconesses and lay-workers. It was a daunting responsibility.

John did not come entirely 'green' to his work, for not only had his Bristol days prepared him but he had learnt something of Southwark as Dean of Clare. The College had had a mission in Rotherhithe – in the deanery of Bermondsey – since 1885. (Clare was also patron of the ancient church of St Mary, Rotherhithe.) Each year while John was Dean he had visited Rotherhithe with Clare undergraduates and stayed in the parish. John Pirie, Clare missioner most of the time John was Dean of Clare, but from 1956 to 1971 Vicar of St John's, Larcom Street, Walworth, looked forward to John's coming as bishop for he 'always made me feel as if I was his equal'.

On his first Sunday morning in the diocese John celebrated the Holy Communion in the great Doric church of St Alfege, Greenwich, designed by Nicholas Hawksmoor but wrecked, like so many other inner London churches, in the blitz during the Second World War. It was harvest festival and John preached there again in the evening. Next morning there was a staff meeting at Bishop's House, Streatham. Mervyn Stockwood, the diocesan coat-of-arms emblazoned on the high back of his chair, presided from behind his desk. Around the bishop's study with John sat the Bishop of Kingston (William Gilpin); the Archdeacon of Kingston (Percy Robb); the Archdeacon of Lewisham (Laurie Brown – later Bishop of Birmingham); the Archdeacon of Southwark (Haviland Sands); the Provost of Southwark (George Reindorp – later Bishop of Salisbury), and Gordon Davies, Canon Missioner (later Archdeacon of Lewisham). Bishop's staff meeting once a month for the next ten years would be one of John's most important engagements covering, as it did, appointments, the personal problems of the clergy and their families, and future plans and policies.

That evening John was again with Mervyn, at the induction of Eric James as Vicar of St George's, Camberwell, another huge Doric church built in 1824 to seat 1,750 people. John was there not only to see how an induction should be conducted: for much of the time that he was Dean of Clare Eric had been Chaplain of Trinity, and St George's,

Camberwell was the Trinity College Mission. Their friendship had begun from Eric's interest in the published collection of John's uncle Forbes' *Letters to His Friends* and was to continue until John's life's end. There was a third reason for his presence that evening. Mervyn Stockwood's thoughts on the shape of a Southwark ordination course were understandably somewhat imprecise when he arrived in Southwark; but in his enthronement address in May 1959 he had promised 'a cautious experiment with regard to the training of ordina-tion candidates and their subsequent employment', and at his first Diocesan Conference the next month he announced:

> I have appointed the Revd Eric James, Chaplain of Trinity College, Cambridge, to be Vicar of St George's, Camberwell. He will, I hope, bring with him half a dozen graduates who will earn their living by day in industry and at night will go ahead with their theological studies, and in this connection, the new Bishop of Woolwich will be of great assistance. When these men have reached ordination level, they may become curates in the ordinary way, or they may feel that they can be of greater use if they remain where they are and discover their way to a new pattern of priesthood. I am fully alive to the dangers of this scheme, but I am prepared to take risks, in order that we shall do something to get alongside that large section of our society which has little or nothing to do with the Church.

Glad as Eric had been to hear that his bishop was ready to take risks in setting up an ordination course, and ready as Eric was to give all possible help to the setting up of such a course, he was clear that it would be folly to devote himself to the course before he had really addressed the problems of the large urban parish to which he had committed himself. The decision was therefore taken to base the scheme elsewhere, and later that month the Bishop of Southwark spoke of the possibility of 'a new type of theological training with its centre at the Cathedral'. John made the preparation of such a scheme a top priority for his first year in the diocese. He worked with astonishing speed and application, so that by the following January he was able to present his first draft of the Training Scheme to the bishop's staff meeting. It meant not only thinking out the syllabus of the course, but all the academic, pastoral and devotional requirements, the selection procedures and the financial and administrative arrangements. Ama-zingly by March 1960 the scheme had the backing of the Central Advisory Council for the Ministry (the forerunner of the present

Advisory Council for the Church's Ministry). It built on the course of lectures which for several years had been provided at Southwark Cathedral Chapter House in association with the University of London Extra-Mural Department and the City Literary Institute. Besides the lectures two evenings a week there was to be a weekend once a month and a fortnight's summer school each year.

At the beginning of the scheme John was in general charge; George Reindorp the Provost was responsible for pastoralia; Canon Fenton Morley (later Dean of Salisbury) was in charge of the academic side; and Canon Gordon Davies saw to the devotional training. One crucially important appointment was made from outside the diocese. Stanley Evans, Vicar of Holy Trinity, Dalston, was appointed Chancellor of the Cathedral and Director of Training. John wrote of Stanley (when he was tragically killed in a road accident in 1965):

> He was a man of metal they seldom make nowadays, and of whom the Church and the country have only a few. His make-up was one in equal measure of conviction, courage and compassion. Valiant for truth as a Christian Socialist, and friend of the Soviet Union, he endured privation in the ecclesiastical wilderness for many years. No patron was prepared to offer him a benefice for twenty years after his ordination; yet he had gifts possessed by few of his contemporaries. He was a great preacher and a true pastor . . . Stanley was one of the rare polymaths of the modern world . . . There was no one for whose integrity of mind I had greater respect. He could have run the entire Southwark Ordination Course and Post-Ordination Training Scheme single handed. Unsparing of himself and uncompromising in his standards, he was essentially a man of hard centre – and often of hard edges as well; but within was a person of deep compassion and warm affection.

Without Stanley Evans the ordination course could never have got off the ground. John worked unbelievably hard at the scheme but his other duties demanded that someone should be appointed to be virtually principal whom he could trust and to whom he could delegate.

The scheme of ordination training was offered as a possible form of preparation for ordination to three classes of men:

1 Men in established jobs who wished to become ordained to a full-time ministry, but who for family or financial reasons found it impossible or impracticable to go away for a full residential course at a theological college.

2 Men in established jobs who wished to become ordained but to

exercise their ministry within the sphere in which they were already working.

3   Younger graduate ordinands who felt the need to do at least part of their training in the context of the industrial world in which they hoped later to work.

The Bishop of Southwark made public the details of the scheme in his presidential address at the Southwark Diocesan Conference in June 1960. The *Church Times* welcomed it as a 'heroic attempt to remedy an exceptional situation'. Archbishop Fisher wrote to the Bishop of Southwark: 'I think it is a wholly admirable adventure and we shall all learn much from it.' Within a couple of months more than ninety enquiries had been received from interested persons, of whom sixty sent in application forms; and thirty – the maximum that could then be taken – started in September 1960 on the first of the three-year courses: a year almost to the day since John was consecrated Bishop of Woolwich. He would have liked the course to be ecumenical from the start and to train women as well as men, and laity as well as those to be ordained; but he was persuaded to be content for the time being with what he, primarily, had pioneered, a 'theological college without walls'.

Paradoxically he soon began to concern himself with a building for the course: Wychcroft, a large house near Blechingley, Surrey, in the south of the diocese, had suddenly become available. It would eventually accommodate thirty people. John saw Wychcroft not only as a base for the Southwark Ordination Course but as a training centre for the laity, and for the post-ordination training of the clergy. By the end of 1961 Douglas Rhymes had been appointed Warden of this Diocesan Training Centre, Director of Lay Training for the Diocese and Canon Residentiary and Librarian of the Cathedral; and John Hayward the artist had transformed the chapel (formerly a badminton court) not least by providing a central altar and a striking painting of 'Christ the Worker, Triumphant'. John preached a characteristic sermon ('To equip God's people for the work of ministry, to the building up of the body of Christ') at the dedication of the training centre on 2 February 1962.

Without Wychcroft the Southwark Ordination Course (and the diocese) would certainly not be the same. For twenty-five years now it has been used by the Course for its weekends and summer schools.

But the Ordination Course and the training centre were only two of John's concerns in these first months and years as a bishop. He gave strong support, for instance, to the South London Industrial Mission. Its present secure base for ministry at Christ Church, Blackfriars was due primarily to his vision; and he brought Peter Challen (whom he had taught at Clare) from Sheffield to be its imaginative Senior Industrial Chaplain and Rector of Christ Church.

John felt particularly privileged to give the first of the Stafford Cripps Memorial Lectures in St Paul's Cathedral within three weeks of his consecration. Sir Stafford – Ambassador to Moscow in 1940, Chancellor of the Exchequer in 1947 – had been MP for Bristol East and on most Sundays when he was in Bristol used to attend St Matthew Moorfields. John's lecture on 'The Christian Society and This World: The Biblical Teaching' was published in *On Being the Church in the World* in 1960.

Ruth came out of hospital on 6 November 1959. At first the world seemed to move too fast for her. When she ventured up to the West End to do some Christmas shopping she had to escape from the store, overwhelmed. It would be unreasonable to expect to emerge entirely unscathed from a severe brain haemorrhage such as Ruth had suffered. In the years ahead she would often feel the world was overwhelming and that she could only cope given more space. Nevertheless as soon as she could she bravely took on the role of chauffeuse for evening engagements; suffragan bishops do not merit chaplains or chauffeurs. She would cook the supper, serve out, pack the robe case, get herself ready, and look out the best route while she swallowed her own meal. She and John would generally have to leave at about seven for the confirmation or induction or whatever the engagement that evening might be; so the last thing Ruth did was to say good-night to the younger ones in bed. John would look over his sermon on the way. After handing him over to the churchwarden Ruth would park the car and hope to get into the church unrecognized, so that she could sit at the back and recover during the service to be ready for the 'bun-fight' in the parish hall. She managed to keep up this routine until one day Judith's 'Do you *have* to go out this evening?' made her decide that 'enough was enough', and that it was more important to stay at home unless there was a particular reason for her going with John.

In June 1960 a conference was held at Keble College, Oxford which was to be of considerable importance for the future of the Church of England. Over 130 clergy and leading laymen took part. John chaired the conference and made a major contribution to it. His address was published in *New Ways with the Ministry*. It was entitled 'Taking the Lid off the Church's Ministry' – to release 'the potential that is at present stopped up'. He drew attention to three inhibiting 'lines'. First the professional line, which reserved the ordained ministry to those who derive their living from it. Secondly the clergy line: 'the distinction between clergy and laity is neither fundamental nor native to the life of the Church'. Thirdly the sex line: 'Let us face the fact frankly that the Church has not yet become the body in which there is "neither male nor female".'

The conference had originated with a group of clergymen in the Birmingham diocese, mainly men ordained since the Second World War, who issued a statement on the Reform of the Church of England. It called for more efficient use of men and money in the Church's ministry. The statement was widely distributed in the English dioceses, not least by John through the Cambridge Correspondence; and it was clear from the response that there were many in support. Nicolas Stacey, who was chaplain to the Bishop of Birmingham when he did much of the preparatory work for the conference, had become Rector of Woolwich by the time it took place and proved a most dynamic secretary. At the conference, a proposal of Lt Col. Hubert Madge that it should press in the Church Assembly for a review of the payment, deployment and conditions of service of the ordained ministry was greeted with enthusiasm, and Colonel Madge himself was urged to bring the matter before the Assembly. This was in fact the genesis of the significant Paul Report, for it was not many months before Colonel Madge's motion was carried in the Assembly and the sociologist Dr Leslie Paul was asked by CACTM 'to make a fact-finding inquiry and submit a report to them'. It was to take two years intensive work.

The motion of Colonel Madge was not the only outcome of the Keble conference. A permanent organisation, the Keble Conference Group, with supporters in every diocese was formed under John's chairmanship, and the Revd Timothy Beaumont (now the Revd Lord Beaumont of Whitley) agreed to act as secretary. It was realized that the group must take the structures of the Church seriously, not least the Church Assembly. John himself (among many others) therefore stood as a candidate in the election, which was imminent at the time of the Conference, and was elected a Proctor for the Clergy of the Diocese of Southwark in the Convocation of Canterbury. In the early 1960s, before the advent of the General Synod of the Church of England, election as a Proctor in Convocation meant attending both the entirely clerical Convocation and the Church Assembly, a body in which clergy and laity met together. The proceedings of Convocation were exceedingly formal. The House of Bishops (the Upper House) and the House of Clergy (the Lower House) met and discussed, clad in their Convocation robes even at the height of summer. (John, as a suffragan bishop elected to Convocation by the clergy of Southwark, had to wear purple cassock, doctoral hood, black preaching scarf and white preaching bands.) The subject which took up most time when John was elected – the re-formulation of the Church's Canon Law – which was very important in the eyes of the Archbishop of Canterbury (and the older generation of Proctors), was uncongenial in the extreme to John and to many of the younger clergy elected at that time. John decided nevertheless to make his maiden speech in Convocation the proposal of an amendment to one of the new canons. The canon in question would allow a Reader to administer the cup at Holy Communion. It seemed to many innocuous enough; but John believed there were matters of principle at stake.

John was always listened to attentively and with respect both by the Assembly and Convocation. He was careful to speak less frequently than some – he would often furnish his friends with 'ammunition' for their speeches. But if he pleased some of his auditors he irritated others. There was indeed something about his phrases which sometimes suggested he intended – consciously or unconsciously – to irritate them. His grating voice would become rather more grating. He rarely attempted to woo either the Assembly or Convocation. He would often speak with some asperity. It was usually the voice of protest and of someone who was convinced he was right and simply could not see how any intelligent person could think otherwise. The phrases of his first speech to Convocation on 17 January 1961 were therefore not entirely uncharacteristic:

> It is highly desirable to destroy any idea that there is a particular *mystique* attached to administering the Bread as opposed to the Cup . . . Clearly it would be premature to consider the question of a woman administering the Cup when a deaconess has not yet received such permission. But I hope we will not deliberately write in the sex line for ever . . . No academic training or examination whatever is needed for handing a man a cup! And to limit this to Readers, merely shows the existing state of theological confusion – and above all inbred clericalism – that we must

have someone to do it who looks as nearly as possible like a clergyman. I
am glad to say we are beginning to break through the crust of clericalism
– which is imposed just as much by the laity and by the lay Readers as by
the clergy . . .

The Rules of Procedure of Convocation particularly irked John. The
Minutes record:

> The Rt Revd J. A. T. Robinson PhD, on a point of order asked whether
> he might have permission to move his amendment.
>
> The President: We have no notice of your amendment and the question
> will arise whether you have leave to put it at all.
>
> The Rt Revd J. A. T. Robinson PhD, added that this was what he was
> requesting.

The Minutes do not begin to capture John's exasperation. But he had
not laboured in vain. The final form of the canon in question bore the
mark of John's intervention: 'No person shall distribute the Holy
Sacrament of the Lord's Supper to the people unless he shall have been
ordained . . . or unless he has been specially authorised to do so by the
Bishop.'

In the next session John spoke on a more secular subject, capital
punishment. He first reminded the Lower House that, three years
before, the Episcopal Church in the USA had passed a resolution
recording its opposition to capital punishment. His second point was
equally telling:

> The Old Testament had frequently been quoted, but he had heard no
> reference to what the Old Testament treated as the archetypal murder,
> that of Abel by Cain, and the climax of that very profound story, that if
> anyone slew Cain vengeance would be taken on him sevenfold and that
> 'the Lord set a mark upon Cain, lest any finding him should kill him'.
> They still talked of 'the mark of Cain' branding a man as a murderer, but
> they did not remember that it had been a saving mark to protect him from
> the retribution of society. What society did today in taking life was
> precisely what the Almighty had felt unable to bear in the case of Cain . . .
> The death sentence said, in effect, 'There is nothing more that we can do
> with this man; for his own sake or for society's sake we must put an end to
> his life. He is strictly speaking unredeemable; we can only put him away.'
> The Christian faith said 'There is no man who is unredeemable; in
> Christ all men can be raised above the level of mere human nature and
> given the capacity to become the sons of God' . . . He had resolved not to
> rest until this blot had been removed from our national life. He was

convinced that it would be removed; the only question was whether the Church would be in the forefront of those who sought to remove it or whether, as so often in these matters, it would be seen to be dragging its feet.

At the same session John spoke in the debate on 'Ought suicide to be a crime?' The Minutes record:

> It seemed to him to be entirely right that the Committee had continued to regard suicide as a sin and indeed as a grievous sin, but he regretted that nowhere did the Report correct the impression given that the sin was primarily that of the suicide himself . . . It seemed to him very much more often that it was an offence of society against the individual.
>
> Time and again after a suicide one was left with a feeling of repentance and remorse. There was always a feeling of 'if only', a failure of knowledge, a failure of understanding, of sympathy, of love, that was immediately poignant to those who were nearest and dearest to him because he had taken his life, but there was also a failure deep in our whole social order . . .

John made his maiden speech to the Church Assembly in the debate in November 1962 on the Report on *Gender and Ministry*. While he welcomed the Report, he criticized it:

> because it did not put the finger on the real deterrent to the recruitment of an adequate supply of women for the work of the Church. It hardly referred in the sociological section to the major change in their society, the almost fantastic explosion in the opportunities now open to women in the secular world, especially in responsible jobs demanding high professional qualifications and carrying equal pay. It was in this field that the Church fell so pathetically behind. The nub of the problem was their failure to give women real responsibility, with good conditions and security of employment . . . He heard one of the people concerned in the production of this Report say, discussing the placing of women students, 'Of course when it actually came to the point I should advise her to go into teaching, where she will have the chance in due course of becoming the head of a department in a fully professional way. . . .' The failure to face this question of real responsibility was sterilising almost all their efforts on behalf of women, and having an insidious effect on the integrity and honesty of the whole Church . . .

What John had to say almost invariably provoked thought and disturbed his hearers. In his maiden speeches he began as he meant to go on.

It was not only in his speaking but in his writing that John was becoming nationally known in the Church. *On Being the Church in the World*, a collection of his essays and addresses of the past decade, was published in 1960 and went through three editions. It included, not least, two articles on intercommunion: one, 'Intercommunion and Concelebration', printed in the *Ecumenical Review* in April 1957; and another on 'Episcopacy and Intercommunion' from *Theology* (October 1959). John would also write an article in March 1962 for *Prism*, on 'The Church of England and Intercommunion' which would be published as the second *Prism Pamphlet*. Oliver Tomkins, then Bishop of Bristol, the chairman of the Inter-Communion Commission, would refer several years later in the Church Assembly, in June 1968, to 'the writings of the Bishop of Woolwich, who was a member of the Commission' which suggested that 'the tradition of concelebration might have relevance to our divisions at the eucharist'. When John wrote on intercommunion, he was not simply writing theory:

> The spiritual and theological conditions of intercommunion can properly be stated only by holding *together* the two great Pauline principles that on the one hand, if we eat and drink with no sense of the Body we eat and drink judgement to ourselves (1 Cor. 11:29), and, on the other, that it is because of the one loaf that we who are many are one Body (1. Cor. 10:17) . . . it is necessary to emphasise the implications of St Paul's second great truth. It has indeed been hidden from English eyes very largely by the sad failure at this point of the Authorised Version, which renders scarcely comprehensibly 'For we being many are one bread and one body' . . . The RSV and the NEB however bring out quite clearly the *causal* relationship, that it is *because* of the one loaf that we are one Body – which Paul goes on to underline in the second half of the verse: 'For we all partake of the one loaf.' But the truth of this does not rest upon a single text. It has been confirmed for me beyond dispute by the experience of having seen it happen in a situation in a Cambridge college chapel . . . It was the Communion that made of us a single ecumenical community.

In 1961 *Bishops*, a volume of essays edited by Glyn Simon, Bishop of Llandaff, was published by Faith Press. John's contribution, 'A New Model of Episcopacy', was evidence of how creatively he was harnessing his gifts as a theologian to his new work and situation:

> I am convinced as I argued in my contribution to *The Historic Episcopate* that episcopacy belongs to the *fullness* of the Church, in the sense that the

The curate with his vicar, Mervyn Stockwood, at
St Matthew Moorfields, Bristol

The Dean of Clare with his wife and family – Judith,
Stephen, Catherine and Buffy

Archbishop Fisher and the newly consecrated
Bishop of Woolwich

Church will never be fully one, catholic and apostolic until its episcope is unified in the historic episcopate . . . But three streams in the life of the contemporary church could give that episcopate purer expression. *The revival of biblical theology* is forcing us both to a higher and a humbler understanding of the office of a bishop in the Church of God . . . *The ecumenical movement* frankly recognises that the episcope of the Church cannot be confined to one man. Episcope, like priesthood and ministry, is a function of the whole Church . . . *The liturgical movement* has reminded us that the bishop is the *persona* of the local church and its link with the universal church.

John pleads for an extension of team ministry at the episcopal level to make suffragan bishops more genuinely local:

There is no return to the small independent unit . . . the Church can get nowhere by 'pocket bishops' . . . An episcopal Church is not merely a Church that 'has bishops'. It is a Church that takes *episcope*, the *episcope* of Christ, seriously at every level . . . Less than ever can one be content to be a bishop in the Church of England representing simply that section of Christendom according to whose Use one was consecrated. For a bishop, wherever he is, is called to represent the wholeness of the catholic Church to its divided parts, to be the creative force of its coming unity.

What John wrote he illustrated in detail from his own new hard-earned experience in Southwark as he gradually got to know the deaneries, parishes and people – the work he had made his first priority. The scholar, pastor and prophet in John were all helping him to understand and interpret his function and role as a bishop in the Church of God.

When John's first year as Bishop of Woolwich came to a close he was still a relatively unknown person outside the Church. He had simply got on with his job. But on 7 September 1960 he received a letter which was in due course to make him notorious:

Rubinstein, Nash & Co. Solicitors
5 & 6 Raymond Buildings
Gray's Inn, WC1

My Lord
Lady Chatterley's Lover
Your name has been suggested to me since I am preparing the defence of my clients, Penguin Books Limited, in relation to the Summons issued against them for their publication of the above book, as an expert who might be prepared to give evidence in support of my clients.

I enclose a copy of a letter which was prepared for circulation a few weeks ago. Since then we have reason to believe that the trial will take place before a Jury at the Old Bailey within the month following 11th October next. Although the decision as to the witnesses to be called to give evidence will, of course, only be taken by Counsel at a later stage, I know that my clients would particularly appreciate it if you were prepared to express your opinion on the lines indicated in the enclosed form of letter, and if it were favourable to their intended publication.

May I hear from you as soon as you have been able to consider the matter? If you have not had an opportunity to read the book I will at once arrange for a copy to be sent to you. If you already know it and are willing to help Penguin Books, then I would like to prepare a proof of your evidence as soon as possible. For this purpose I should particularly like to see you to discuss the matter within the next week or two and would greatly appreciate it if your Secretary would telephone me and give me an appointment to call on you.

> I remain
> your obedient servant
> Michael B. Rubinstein.

The copy letter enclosed, further spelt out the purpose of the first letter:

Lady Chatterley's Lover

We are concerned for Penguin Books Limited, who, as you may know from advance announcements in the Press, have prepared for publication on the 25th August 1960 an unexpurgated edition of this important novel by D. H. Lawrence, to complete their issue of all his novels this year – the 75th Anniversary of his birth and 30th of his death.

Our Clients urgently need to know the measure of support which they may hope to receive from experts to defend any proceedings under the Obscene Publications Act 1959.

Under the Act, which has not previously been invoked since it came into operation, the test of obscenity is stated to be that 'an article shall be deemed to be obscene if its effect . . . is, if taken as a whole, such as to tend to deprave and corrupt persons who are likely, having regard to all relevant circumstances, to read, see or hear the matter contained or embodied in it'.

For the first time, however, the Act provides that a person shall not be convicted of the offence of publishing an obscene article and an order for forfeiture shall not be made 'if it is proved that the publication of the article in question is justified as being for the public good on the ground that it is in the interests of science, literature, art or learning, or of other objects of general concern'. Further, 'the opinion of experts as to the literary, artistic, scientific or other merits of an article may be admitted in any proceedings under this Act either to establish or to negative the said ground'.

Our Clients had decided to publish the first unexpurgated edition of *Lady Chatterley's Lover* to appear in this country because they do not regard it as obscene, and because they do regard its publication as of particular importance 'for the public good' to vindicate D. H. Lawrence's integrity and non-pornographic intent in writing it, and to enable his significance in English literature to be properly appraised in this country, on his whole output, for the first time.

They have given us your name as an expert whose opinion might be relevant to the available defence under the Act referred to above. We should be very grateful if you would let us hear from you in early reply to this letter whether you favour the publication of *Lady Chatterley's Lover* as 'for the public good', and if so, whether you would be willing to give evidence in any proceedings, if required. In addition, it would be extremely helpful to us at this stage to have a brief summary (not more than, say, 200 words) of the grounds which in your view justify its publication as being 'for the public good'. You will, we feel sure, appreciate that a decision as to whom our Clients should call in any proceedings depends on factors and circumstances which cannot be known now, and on the advice of Counsel at the time.

John wrote back the next day:

Dear Mr Rubinstein

I shall be happy to try and help you over *Lady Chatterley's Lover*. Naturally I cannot commit myself to anything until I have read it, but if you can arrange for a copy to be sent to me I will do so as soon as I can. I find the prosecution of this book very difficult to understand.

Yours sincerely
John Woolwich.

The following day John received a letter from the one Anglican theologian who could justly claim to be an expert on the writings of D. H. Lawrence: Father Martin Jarrett-Kerr of the Community of the Resurrection:

Dear John

You will know that Messrs Penguin Books are hoping to issue the unexpurgated edition of D. H. Lawrence's *Lady Chatterley's Lover* but that this is dependent on their winning a Court case.

I have been asked my own opinion, as an 'expert' in the matter; and if I support publication of the book, I may have to give evidence in the case. (I should, of course, have to make it clear that I do so as an individual, and not as representing anybody.)

My personal view is that

(i) *Lady Chatterley* is not an 'obscene' book, in the sense of that word as defined by the present law, though portions of it could, taken out of context, give the impression of obscenity.

(ii) The free circulation of the book would in the long run help to deliver it from the misuse of it which at present results from its being banned, and being therefore sought out and read for the wrong purposes.

(iii) It is important, not only for the sake of Lawrence's memory, but for the public good, to realise that Lawrence's general teaching about sex was healthy and valuable: that he was a profoundly serious, as well as great, novelist. So long as the book is banned, it is hard to convince people of this.

(iv) It is questionable whether the standards of 'purity' or 'decency' by which the ban on the book has hitherto been maintained are in fact necessarily Christian. At least, standards of this sort vary considerably in different parts of Christendom.

You may not agree with any or all of these judgements. But I should very much value your own opinion on the following questions – for my information only, and of course confidential:

(a) Do you consider the book 'obscene', and if not, would you be happy to see it, in a paper-back edition, obtainable at c. 5/- on any book-stall – for your children (if any) to read?

(b) Whatever your answer to (a), do you think that harm would be done to the Church if a priest of the Church appeared to testify in favour of publication? That is to say, do you think that the kind of publicity such an appearance might be given in the 'gutter press', plus the general uncertainty of standards in the general public, dictates extreme caution in the matter?

(c) If your answer to (b) is 'Yes', do you think, on the other hand, that the Church's reputation might suffer, among the educated, by being accused of 'suppression', 'puritanism', 'insensitiveness to great literature' etc.?

Sorry to trouble you in the midst of a busy life, but the matter may have considerable repercussions in the social and religious life of Gt Britain.

Yours sincerely,
Martin Jarrett-Kerr, CR.

On 10 September John received the copy of the unexpurgated edition of *Lady Chatterley's Lover* which Michael Rubinstein had arranged should be sent to him. On the 13th he wrote to Michael Rubinstein:

Dear Mr Rubinstein

I have now read *Lady Chatterley's Lover* and am deeply grateful for having been given the chance of doing so.

I enclose comments which express my reaction to it. If you wish to see me to arrange anything further, perhaps you would give me a ring.

Yours sincerely,
John Woolwich.

It had taken John three days to make up his mind. In fact he had to make up his mind about more than one question. First he had to decide whether the action against the book was – as he at first thought – 'an incredible piece of folly and misjudgment' or – as he in fact concluded – that it was a 'real crime'. Secondly he had to decide not only whether he was in favour of support being given to the defence, but whether he *as a bishop of the Church of God* should speak in the book's defence. (The Bishop of Southwark had made it clear that, as far as he was concerned, John was free to speak.) Loyalty to the truth was fundamental to John. One of his favourite remarks – said most often with incredulity – was 'But it's obvious!' Once something had become obvious to *him* he had to proclaim it and defend it. The defending it was often a matter of justice – in this case both to Lawrence and to the true nature of sex. To John the question was not so much: should he take part in the case; but, why was it that more people in his position would *not* take part in it when asked?

Many people would have steered clear of the publicity involved. But John had not sought it. He was in a group which the Master of the Temple, 'Dick' Milford, had called together to study questions of sexual ethics. Milford was priest and preacher to many judges and barristers. Among his published works was a booklet on *The Philosophy of Sex*. He had been vicar of the University Church, Oxford for nine years. As Canon and Chancellor of Lincoln Cathedral he had had much responsibility for the theological college. He had already agreed, at the request of Joan Rubinstein, a member of the group (and partner and cousin of Michael Rubinstein) to appear as a witness for the defence. All the group including Sir John Lawrence, Canon George Appleton (later Archbishop of Perth) and Canon Edward Carpenter (later Dean of Westminster) strongly encouraged John to appear; hence Michael Rubinstein's letter of invitation to him.

Many people would have steered clear not simply of publicity in general but in particular that of a 'sex' case such as the trial of *Lady Chatterley* was almost bound to involve through the media. But John saw the occasion as a real opportunity to get across to the world the truth about sex as Christians, he believed, should see it. Many people could not have appeared in such a 'sex' case because inevitably what they said would be tested by their own sexual 'record'. They would be literally too guilty to appear. Others could not have appeared for fear of implicating, or appearing to implicate, in other ways their own sexuality. Such a consideration would not have occurred to John. There was an extraordinary innocence about him. He saw no reason to fear his sexuality, and the sexual aspect of the case held no threat for him.

John was free – released – to concentrate on what he saw to be the main questions of truth and justice. In the three days he had had to make up his mind both he and Ruth had read the book. They agreed that Lawrence's intention was honest – to put sex in the context of tender human relationship – which is precisely *not* the intention of those who exploit sex and detach it from any profound human relating. John was always delighted when people actually took note of what he said and thought it important. Again there was something almost childlike about his attitude to publicity. He loved being 'at the centre' and being 'involved'. But it would be cruelly unjust to him to say that he got involved in the *Lady Chatterley* case *for* the publicity. He felt the Church's standing in society – or lack of it – very deeply. It mattered to him that the Church should speak out on certain subjects – not least on the Christian understanding of sex. His 'I – Thou' thesis, which he had worked at in 1943/4, and which had at first been an intellectual perception, had been earthed and deepened when he fell in love with Ruth (and had been taken deeper still in and through their marriage). But his experience of the human 'I – Thou' had earthed and deepened his experience of the transcendent 'I – Thou'. Once again the truth was shouting at him 'with a Divine imperative to pass it on' – the truth that 'sex is something sacred, in a real sense an act of holy communion'.

It was John, the author of *The Body*, who had decided to appear at the Old Bailey. He agreed wholeheartedly with Fr Jarrett-Kerr that:

> Christians owe a debt to Lawrence for insisting again and again that man is not without a body, and expresses himself as man not without a body

. . . The Christian should know that sex involves three surrenders. First, there is the surrender of the self to the other (the man to the wife, the wife to the man). Then, and this is the most easily evaded, there is the surrender of the mind, of the thinking, conscious self, to the instinctive self, in fact, to the body. And finally, there is the surrender of these two surrenders to God – to God who (so to speak) thought it all up, whose idea it was, who established the process.

The intellectual, rational John had particular reason to insist that the Christian doctrine of sex is, as Lawrence said, more than 'sex in the head'; and to believe that 'unless Christian preaching is a preaching to the whole man, which includes man's instinctual, bodily, and archetypal self, then it is partial and maimed'. John had written on the theology of *The Body*; now he was to proclaim it, not from the housetops but from the witness box of the Old Bailey, to an audience of several million.

On 22 September John met Michael Rubinstein and by the 26th had sent the 'draft Proof of Evidence' to him. Michael Rubinstein 'further modified it, very little' and sent him the retyped copy for his final approval on the 28th. It reached John on the first anniversary of his consecration.

It is important to set out the evidence in full:

I was born in 1919. I was educated at Marlborough and Jesus College, Cambridge, where I gained a Degree in Classics, a 1st in Theology and a Doctorate in Philosophy. In 1945 I was ordained, and until 1948 I was Curate in Bristol. Between 1948–1951 I was Chaplain at Wells Theological College. 1951–1959 I was Dean of Clare College, Cambridge and Lecturer in New Testament in the University Faculty of Divinity. I was consecrated Bishop of Woolwich in 1959 and elected a Proctor in the Convocation of Canterbury in 1960. I have published a number of books on New Testament subjects – Christian Doctrine and practical theology and numerous articles for learned journals. I have a great deal of experience in teaching and ministering to University students. I am married and have a boy of 12 and three younger daughters.

I am not a literary expert but I read *Sons and Lovers* this summer holidays and decided that I must read more of D. H. Lawrence's works whenever I had time to do so. Since then my wife and I have been doing this. I was, therefore, glad when I had the opportunity to read *Lady Chatterley's Lover*.

I am, of course, concerned very closely with human relations and the relations between men and women are an extremely important aspect of them. For this reason I am concerned not only at the relevance of Christian theology to such relations in the world and in our society today, but also with the impact of every form of expression – films, television and broadcasting, newspapers, and advertising posters as well as books.

I have considered this edition of *Lady Chatterley's Lover* as a whole in the circumstances of its proposed publication as a paper-back book. In this form it will appear on book-stalls not only with established classics such as the *Decameron* and Chaucer which have previously been condemned as obscene, but also with many crude novels deliberately intended to portray sex as degrading. I believe that *Lady Chatterley's Lover* should be made available to the English public as Lawrence wrote it, along with the rest of his works. I do not believe either its intention or effect to be to 'deprave and corrupt'.

Archbishop William Temple once said that Christians do not make jokes about sex for the same reason that they do not make jokes about Holy Communion – not because it is dirty, but because it is sacred. Lawrence did not share the Christian valuation of sex, but he was always straining to portray it as something sacred, in a real sense as an act of holy communion. For him flesh was completely sacramental of spirit, and his description of sex which in this book is of a piece with his extraordinary sensitivity to the whole organic life of nature is not obscene, unless sex itself is obscene. There may be lapses of taste as he seeks to speak of things for which conventional 'purity' has left only the language of the gutter. But there is a beauty and delicacy and emotional purity in his total approach which is liberating rather than degrading. Though it is describing an adulterous relationship, it is not advocating adultery or promiscuity. I would agree that it does not represent a balanced picture of the whole marriage relationship, but there is nothing that could give any encouragement to sexual perversion. But the point at issue is that it describes an intimate human relationship (even if it is unsatisfactory) with complete artistic integrity. It is concerned to insist that sex is not sordid; and any expurgations are by implication saying it is.

I believe that Christians in particular should read this book, if only because Lawrence believed passionately and with much justification that they have killed and denied the natural goodness of creation at this point.

Before reading the book, I judged the action against it to be an incredible piece of folly and misjudgment. I am now convinced that it is a real crime. In an age when sex is commercialized on all sides, it is monstrous that the State should officially proceed against one of the few authors who have stood out against its prostitution and perversion. By dragging this book through the courts, the prosecution has ensured that it is given the maximum publicity (with the implication, I believe wrongly, that it is a dirty book) in the most undesirable circles, circles whose only interest in literature is dirt. I believe that instead of proceeding against authors of established literary merit, it would be much more profitable to devise means of restraining book-sellers who deliberately flaunt any kind of books for their sex-appeal (e.g. Chaucer's *Canterbury Tales* labelled 'For adults only').

Lady *Chatterley's Lover* is, of course, a thoroughly adult piece of writing; but in due course I would much rather my children read it than that they should take their valuation of sex from the current exploitation of it which the Government shows itself so strangely powerless or unwilling to curb. I would not try to prevent my children from reading *Lady Chatterley's Lover* when they were old enough to appreciate it, and my wife and I have in fact talked about it with the two older ones.

The trial of *Lady Chatterley* began in Court No. 1 at the Old Bailey on Thursday, 20 October. Mr Griffith-Jones, senior Treasury Counsel at the time (later His Honour Judge Griffiths-Jones), opened the case for the prosecution; and Mr Gerald Gardiner, QC (later a distinguished Lord Chancellor) opened the case for the defence. (The whole case was published in a Penguin Special edited by C. H. Rolph in 1961.) Mr Justice Byrne decided the jury should read the book in a special room within the Old Bailey. The last juryman finished the book in three days, and on Thursday, 27 October, Mr Gardiner began calling his witnesses. First Graham Hough, Lecturer in English and Fellow of Christ's College, Cambridge. Then Helen Gardner, Reader in Renaissance English Literature at Oxford. Next came Joan Bennett, Lecturer in English at Cambridge University and Fellow of Girton College. Dame Rebecca West was the first of the witnesses whose name was well known to all the jury. The next witness was the Bishop of Woolwich.

'What, if any, are the ethical merits of this book?' asked Mr Gardiner; but before the bishop could answer a dispute arose as to whether ethical qualifications were relevant. Mr Justice Byrne eventually admitted they were, so John went ahead with his answer. The judge interrupted to make a note when John said that 'what Lawrence is trying to do is to portray the sex relationship as something essentially sacred' and went on to quote Archbishop William Temple – as he had done in his draft Proof of Evidence.

'Would you make any difference,' Mr Gardiner asked, 'between the merits . . . of the book as it is and those of the book as it would be if the description of sexual intercourse and all four-letter words were expurgated from it?'

'I think the whole effect of that,' said John, 'would be to suggest that what Lawrence was doing was something sordid in putting it before the public, if these things were eliminated.'

Mr Gardiner then said, 'It has been suggested that the book places upon a pedestal promiscuous and adulterous intercourse.'

John replied: 'It is not dealing with intercourse for its own sake, and it is not dealing with sexual promiscuity. If the Jury read the last two pages, there is a most moving advocacy of chastity and the remark "How can men want wearisomely to philander?" and I think that is Lawrence's whole approach to the subject, and that the effect of this book is against rather than for promiscuity.'

In his cross-examination after lunch Mr Griffith-Jones turned again to the question of ethics.

'Marriage is another aspect of ethics, is it not?'

'Certainly,' replied John.

'This book doesn't help much in educating anybody into a correct view about that particular aspect of ethics?'

'Naturally,' said John, 'it is not a treatise on marriage. What it does, though, is, I think, to make it obvious he is not against the marriage relationship. On the contrary, he is concerned with establishing a permanent, genuine, spiritual relationship between persons.'

'Bishop,' said Mr Griffith-Jones unexpectedly, 'I don't want to be offensive to you, but you are not here to make speeches. Just try and answer my question. "Yes" or "No", if you can.'

'With respect,' said Mr Gardiner at once, 'the witness *has* answered the question.'

Mr Griffith-Jones went back to his first question: 'Are you asking the Jury to accept that this book is a valuable work on ethics?'

'It depends on what you mean by a valuable work on ethics,' John replied.

'A work of instructional value,' Mr Griffith-Jones added by way of elucidation.

'As I said,' John insisted, 'it doesn't set out to be a treatise on ethics.'

'I am not asking you what it sets out to be; I am asking you to apply your mind to my question and answer it if you can "Yes" or "No". Are you suggesting this book is of instructional value upon the subject of ethics?'

'No,' replied John. 'I would not say it was of instructional value upon the subject of ethics.'

'As you read the book,' interposed Mr Justice Byrne, 'does it portray the life of an immoral woman?'

'It portrays the life of a woman in an immoral relationship,' John answered, 'in so far as adultery is an immoral relationship. I would not say it was intended in any way to exalt immorality.'

(The phrase 'in so far as' was understood by most people in Court to mean 'inasmuch as').

Mr Gardiner put a few further questions to John in re-examination.

'Is this a book which in your view Christians ought to read?'

'Yes, I think it is,' he replied, 'because I think what Lawrence was trying to do . . .'

That answer supplied a banner headline for the evening papers 'CHRISTIANS SHOULD READ LADY C. Bishop: "Essentially something sacred".'

From this time onwards John was the *notorious* Bishop of Woolwich. Indeed the very next morning the Robinson family woke up to find a line of press cars outside the house, and on the Sunday following the press pursued them to church. In Sussex the twelve-year-old Stephen Robinson in his last year at preparatory school, proud that his father had hit the headlines, was left in no doubt of his mentors' disapproval of the cause of his father's notoriety.

There were more than thirty witnesses for the defence besides John, including Richard Hoggart, C. V. Wedgwood, E. M. Forster, Roy Jenkins, Norman St John-Stevas, C. Day-Lewis, Dilys Powell and the Master of the Temple. Others such as T. S. Eliot and Fr Jarrett-Kerr, CR who had consented to be witnesses for the defence were not called.

In the closing speech for the defence, on the fifth day, Mr Gerald Gardiner reminded the jury of John's words: 'Clearly, Lawrence did not have a Christian valuation of sex, and the kind of sexual relationship depicted in the book is not one that I would necessarily regard as ideal, but what I think is clear is that what Lawrence is trying to do is to portray the sex relationship as something essentially *sacred*.'

'Where *are* we getting to?' asked the Judge expressively in his summing up. '*You* will consider. It is for you to *decide*. Reading that book do *you* find that it is a book in which the author is trying to portray sex in a real sense as something sacred, as an act of holy communion?'

It was 2.53 p.m. on 2 November, the sixth day, when the jury returned; it had been out for three hours.

'Members of the Jury,' said the Clerk, 'are you agreed upon your verdict?'

The usher motioned to the foreman to stand up.

'We are,' said the foreman.

'Do you find that Penguin Books Ltd are guilty or not guilty of publishing an obscene article?'

'NOT GUILTY,' said the foreman, loudly and firmly.

But his voice was all but drowned by an outburst of clapping, and what sounded scandalously like cheers, from the back of the court. The trial of *Lady Chatterley* was over. The trial of the Bishop of Woolwich was about to begin.

The very next day the Archbishop of Canterbury, Geoffrey Fisher, wrote to John:

> Lambeth Palace
> *3rd November 1960*
>
> My dear Bishop
> A short while ago I gave you a private hint which you did not welcome. I am now in the very embarrassing position of having to answer protests of distressed or indignant people at the evidence which you gave and at the fact of your giving evidence in the recent case. I cannot defend you, of course, at all. The distress you have caused to very many Christian people is so great that I think I must say something in public. I enclose a copy of what I propose to say at my Diocesan Conference on Saturday. I was preparing to say a good deal more, but in the end I made it as brief as I could without obscuring what I had to say.
>
> Yours sincerely,
> Geoffrey Cantuar.

Two days later the archbishop wrote a second letter:

> The Old Palace
> Canterbury
> *November 5th 1960*
>
> My dear Bishop
> I enclose a copy of what I actually said this morning to my Diocesan Conference. You will note some slight variations from and, I think, improvements upon my first version. That I wrote in manuscript early last Wednesday morning and left behind me. Since then I had no opportunity to look at it again till Friday evening and again this morning.

Thus you got really a first draft only for which I am sorry as I always like to revise and re-revise anything I send out. But this time the pressure of other things has been intense.

Yours sincerely,
Geoffrey Cantuar.

The Archbishop had actually said to his Diocesan Conference:

I think it is my duty to refer to two aspects of the recent book trial.

First, I would say that the law is concerned with facts when they are available as evidence and with legal rights. In this case the law was concerned with the legal rights of authors and publishers and potential readers of their books. The law is a very clumsy instrument for dealing with matters of moral discretion. Thus the law regrets adultery but does not say it is illegal: the law does not like the prostitutes looking for business in public, and tries to drive them out of sight: but it expresses no legal disapproval of fornication. It is an extremely clumsy instrument for deciding what is and what is not obscene.

In this recent case the Judge clearly indicated a number of very grave considerations of a moral kind with which in fact the law is not equipped to deal. For all moral questions are really pastoral questions and can only be satisfactorily solved by those whose first concern is not with rights but with duties, duties to God and to one's neighbour. Many kinds of obscenity which constantly appear in print and circulate widely may be lawful in the eyes of the law. But they may yet be very inexpedient to the point of scandal to those whose primary concern is with the pastoral care of people.

That brings me to the second aspect which, in view of questions addressed to me by many people, I think I must deal with. The Bishop of Woolwich had full right to appear as a witness on the point of law involved. But to do so would obviously cause confusion in many people's minds between his individual right of judgment and the discharge of his pastoral duties. Inevitably anything he said would be regarded as said by a Bishop whose chief official concern is to give pastoral advice to the people committed to his charge, and particularly in these moral questions to teachers and parents upon whom such a heavy burden of responsibility lies. Anyone must know that in this sexually self-conscious and chaotic age, to speak pastoral wisdom in public on particular questions is extremely dangerous. The Bishop exposed himself to this danger. The Christian fact is that adultery whether in fact or in lustful longing is always a sin, and at present a very prominent, even all pervasive sin. The good pastor will teach his people to avoid both the fact of and the desire for sex experience of an adulterous kind and of fornication also, from the plain undeviating teaching of the Bible, both Old and New Testament. That is the short way there: and the pastor will not encourage his people to travel by all the side roads and tortuous windings and muddy lanes of the long way round.

In my judgement, the Bishop was mistaken to think that he could take part in this trial without becoming a stumbling block and a cause of offence to many ordinary Christians, and I think I ought to say so here where I am above all a pastor among you and by my office your chief pastor.

John's mother wrote to him from Canterbury on 7 November:

Yesterday evening I went to borrow something from my very good neighbour, Miss Jackman – she is, too, a member of the Diocesan Conference – and I would like to tell you what she said she wanted me to know – that the Archbishop made his criticism of you *very* quietly and in such a kind voice – no sign whatever of evil feeling! She felt sure we would like to hear this from one who heard it. She was particularly impressed by his manner and voice. How good to hear this after the head-lines in the Sunday papers 'Archbp. Furious'. It was also soothing to read the simple accurate report of it in today's *Times*.

All my love and trust,
Mother.

John wrote to the Archbishop on 8 November:

My dear Archbishop

Thank you for your two letters. I appreciate very much the trouble you have taken to supply me with the full text of what you said at Canterbury, and for the very restrained tone of it. I am deeply sorry if I have caused you embarrassment. I have no desire to enter into public controversy on the subject, and I have given the press no handle whatever. I feel, however, that I ought to explain my action and try to mitigate some of the misunderstandings that have been aroused by it. I am therefore proposing to write a considered article, to set the matter in perspective as I see it, in next Sunday's *Observer*. I trust it will be the least explosive form in which to say what I feel on the subject. I enclose a draft of it. You will see that I have deliberately avoided any direct reference to your Grace's statement.

I hope I have made it clear that I fully appreciate and share the dangers to which you refer. But I am still persuaded that there is another side to the matter. I am sorry that your words 'I cannot defend you, of course, at all' seem to rule out any appreciation that this has been a very delicate and difficult decision which I certainly did not enter into lightly or unadvisedly. Where the prophetic witness of the Church is concerned, I imagine there will always be honest and sincere division between Christians at every level. The letters I have received certainly bear this out.

It has taken me a little time to decide what if anything I should do. Hence the delay in answering, which I hope has not appeared discourteous.

Yours sincerely,
John Woolwich.

The Archbishop immediately replied:

Lambeth Palace
9th November 1960

My dear Bishop

I have had no time to do more than glance at your letter and at the first paragraph or two of your script. Nor shall I have any time for the rest of today. Perhaps it might help if I just said this much. There are two matters under consideration: one your views on the book, the other your action in becoming a witness.

I have expressed no views of my own on the book or on your views on the book, and of course you can go on expressing your views quite freely in appropriate directions, but I was alarmed when I just saw in your letter that in your article you were not going to make any direct reference to my statement.

Inevitably readers of the *Observer* will think that your article on your views is in some way a comment on my statement on your actions, unless you clearly distinguish between the two. I would say, therefore, that if you publish your article it is your bounden duty to refer to my statement in such manner as you consider appropriate.

If I might make a suggestion as to what might be appropriate, I would say this: My comment was that your action was bound to cause confusion and distress to many engaged in the pastoral work of the Church, and to many of those whose pastoral care is committed to us. There is no disputing that fact, and if you made clear that you had caused confusion and distress on the pastoral side, and that I as Archbishop had only done my duty in drawing attention to the fact, your article would then be clear and would not add to the confusion.

I did just note at the beginning that you said that some other distinguished ecclesiastics had been willing to join with you in the witness box. I hope that you might add, in order to get a right balance, that it is known certainly to me and probably to you, that some other distinguished ecclesiastics (and, I might add, at least one distinguished headmaster) had declined an invitation to give evidence. It is this pastoral question that is important; indeed, I think somewhere in your opening paragraphs you said that under the conditions of the witness box you were unable to say all that you wanted to say. No doubt it was partly consideration of that fact which deterred some others from giving evidence.

Yours sincerely,
Geoffrey Cantuar.

John began his *Observer* article 'Why I gave evidence', which was published on 13 November, with an apology:

First I wish to acknowledge respectfully that the Archbishop of Canterbury has very rightly drawn public attention to some of the pastoral questions involved, and I wish to express my great regret that by giving evidence I unwittingly caused confusion and distress to many of my fellow Christians.

It is important to note that John was *not* saying that he regretted appearing at the trial. Indeed in an article, 'Farewell to the Sixties', published in *The Observer* on 28 September 1969 (and later in his *Christian Freedom in a Permissive Society*, he wrote – perhaps with some exaggeration in view of his earlier *Observer* article – 'I have no regrets whatever for my part in this crucial case.' In 'Why I gave evidence' he continues:

I believe it will be seen in twenty years time, if it is not clear already, that the fact that churchmen were prepared to add their testimony to the massive weight of responsible witnesses who appeared at this trial will have done far more for the public image of the Church in the eyes of the intelligent non-Christian (and indeed of the intelligent Christian) than any damage that may have been caused by my seeming (however absurdly) to commend adultery.

John explains how he came to be involved and says:

Within the narrow restrictions imposed by the rules of evidence, I was not permitted in court to say many of the things I should have wished to say. I was confined, very strictly, to speaking on 'the literary, artistic, scientific, or other merits' of the book. I did not say, and would never say (as I have since been quoted), that '*all* Christians should read this book'.

He went on: 'Only too many of the letters I have received reveal that otherwise devout and moral persons (and by no means all my correspondents could be so described!) still think that sex is disgusting, and that any book which portrays the sexual relationship is *ipso facto* undesirable.'

John then gave a particularly telling quotation from a former Archbishop of Canterbury, Cosmo Gordon Lang (still remembered by many for his broadcast at the time of the abdication of Edward VIII), who in addressing the London Diocesan Council for Rescue Work on 4 April 1930 had said:

> I would rather have all the risks which come from free discussion of sex than the great risks we run by a conspiracy of silence . . . I notice how silence has given place to complete and free discussion. In my judgment this is a great improvement. In the old days silence drove one of the necessary natural instincts within. Nowadays people recognise sex as one of the great fundamental questions of human society, and all thoughtful Christians and citizens ought to take their part in discussing the great problems with which it deals . . . We want to liberate the sex impulse from the impression that it is always to be surrounded by negative warnings and restraints, and to place it in its rightful place among the great creative and formative things.

John stated: 'I am fully aware that the pastoral problem remains . . .' but went on: 'I believe there is more involved in this issue than the immediate pastoral problem of protecting individuals. The Church has a prophetic as well as a pastoral task.'

He then quoted a letter he had received from 'the Headmaster of a well-known Christian Public School' (Douglas Graham of Dean Close School, Cheltenham, a school 'in the Evangelical Tradition'): 'I am delighted to see that you are giving witness on behalf of the publishers of *Lady Chatterley's Lover*. I read it as a young man and found it vastly liberating and not at all pornographic. Thank you very much. The boys here are sure to read it and I am busy thinking out a series of talks on it.'

Although John had no regrets whatever about his part in the case – except that he had unwittingly but unavoidably 'caused confusion and distress to many of my fellow Christians' – he had considerable regrets about the way the press had handled it.

He had said: 'I think Lawrence tried to portray this relation as in a real sense an act of holy communion', and had specifically stated in court that 'holy communion' in this context was to be spelt in the lower case. Of the dailies the *Daily Mail* and *Evening Standard* got it right; *The*

Times, *Daily Telegraph*, *Daily Mirror*, *Daily Herald*, *Evening News*, *Yorkshire Post* and *The Scotsman* got it wrong.

He had said: 'Sex is not just a means of using people.' The *Daily Sketch* alone had got that right. *The Times* had 'a means of union'; *The Daily Express* and *Yorkshire Post* had 'a means of unions'.

He had said: 'I would not say that it was intended to exalt immorality.' The *Daily Sketch* got this right: *The Times* had 'absolve immorality'.

It was of course John who was used to using words carefully and precisely expecting the professionals of the press, particularly *The Times*, to do the same. He was of course expecting a great deal. (Some said that he had uttered the words 'lower case, of course' almost under his breath.)

John's collection of the articles concerned with his appearance at the trial published in papers and journals, of the letters that filled the correspondence columns and of the hundreds of letters that were sent to him privately, would make a book in themselves. There can be little profit to truth in simply adding up the letters for and against; but perhaps it is significant that John himself only received two letters from clergy in the diocese against his appearance in court and what he had said. Perhaps some profit to truth may be found – a quarter of a century later – in a selection of half a dozen letters written at the time.

John Doherty was curate-in-charge of Crowhurst, Surrey in John's part of the diocese of Southwark. He was seventy-six and had spent many of his years of ministry with the Mission to Seamen:

> From the age of about nineteen years I have opposed to the best of my ability that which you defended in Court recently. If, presumably after invoking the Name of a pure God, your statements expressed your ideas of the truth, the whole truth, and nothing but the truth, upon the particular subject then under discussion, it seems but fair on my part to tell you that we are in opposite camps.
>
> Very much in turmoil
Yours sincerely,
J. W. Doherty.

Alan Ecclestone, Vicar of Holy Trinity, Darnall, Sheffield was fifty-six; he had gained a 'First' in both the History tripos and the English tripos at Cambridge:

> I expect you have been inundated with letters recently, but may I add this brief note just to tell you how grateful we are to you for all that you said

in the Lady Chatterley case. It badly needed saying and you said it admirably, and we are thankful for your courage and discernment. In a world where so few believe in the Incarnation or really believe that the body is holy, you have made a brave stand which gives heart to the rest of us. (It was incidentally a triumph for the British jury system.) But don't let prelates get you down. 'The dogs are on us, but we will not die.'

Miss Valerie Pitt, a member of the General Synod, who said she was wholly in sympathy with her bishop (the Bishop of Woolwich) on few subjects, nevertheless wrote to the editor of *Time and Tide* on 12 November 1960:

Sir
I attach a copy of a letter which I have sent to the Archbishop of Canterbury:

Your Grace, I would like some further guidance on your remarks on the Bishop of Woolwich's remarks on *Lady Chatterley's Lover*. You are reported as saying that the Bishop would be interpreted as giving advice to teachers and parents as their pastor. Your own remarks, you say, were pastoral, and it is a fair deduction to suppose that they were addressed to teachers and parents. Now I am a teacher of literature and I confess that your remarks confuse me. Perhaps you will enlighten me.
1   Am I to understand that I must never introduce my pupils to any literature in which one or more of the characters commit adultery or fornication, or which is likely to show sexual desire and fulfilment as enjoyable?
2   What am I to do about those novels and plays which treat of murder, pride, avarice and cruelty?
3   When I have finished bowdlerising English literature, will your Grace advise me about my conscientious scruples as a scholar?
4   Will you tell me where I can find another job?
5   Will you tell me why it is so iniquitous to write about adultery, but not apparently to oppress the poor, to lie on political issues, to make money out of other people's needs, to deny the doctrines of the Christian Faith, and yet to remain a minister in the Church? Your Grace has been a Bishop for an uncommonly long time. I do not notice that vehemence in condemnation of these sins as I find in your utterances on adultery.
6   Will you tell me just how those of us who live and work with this generation of non-Christian intelligentsia are going to re-make the bridge of understanding between the Church and them which we so carefully build, and which you so often throw down. *Lady Chatterley* is, in fact, the high point, the major literary expression of the post-Christian

humanist insistence on the vitality and value of personal relations. There could be few judgments more insensitive than a treatment of it as no more than a novel about adultery. It is like saying that *Hamlet* and *Oedipus Rex* are about incest and murder. It is our business as Christians, not to say that these pagan values are worthless, but that there is more to humanity than that. Your Grace's persistently negative attitude to these questions makes it nearly impossible for the rest of us to say that Christianity does not deny, it includes all the values of humanism.

I should then be very glad if you will perhaps draw your mind away from the consciences of the parish tea party, and attend to the problems of those of us who actually have to deal with and teach young people, most of whom, you may believe me, have already read things a great deal less desirable than D. H. Lawrence.

> I am Your Grace's obedient
> Valerie Pitt.

A groups of Cambridge theologians wrote thus to *The Times*:

We regret that on one of the infrequent occasions when a bishop has caught the ear of the nation in a manner befitting a spokesman of the National Church he should have been publicly rebuked by the Archbishop of Canterbury.

> Yours faithfully,
> G. W. H. Lampe

G. W. H. Lampe
(Ely Professor of Divinity, University of Cambridge and Canon and Librarian of Ely Cathedral)

Donald MacKinnon
(Norris-Hulse Professor of Divinity, University of Cambridge and Fellow of Corpus Christi College)

Hugh Montefiore
(Canon Theologian of Coventry and Fellow and Dean of Gonville and Caius College, Cambridge)

Alec Vidler
(Fellow and Dean of King's College, Cambridge)

H. A. Williams
(Fellow and Lecturer, Dean of Chapel and Tutor, Trinity College, Cambridge)

John Burnaby (Regius Professor of Divinity in the University of Cambridge 1952–8, Fellow of Trinity College, Cambridge 1915–78 and Dean of Chapel 1945–58) wrote to John:

I had hoped that your article in the *Observer* would clear up some ambiguities and perhaps misrepresentations in the published accounts of your evidence in the Lady Chatterley case. But I was disappointed. Your main point seemed to be that while Christians should not expect to find the sanctity of marriage upheld by Lawrence, they can learn much from him about the sacredness of sex.

To me the opposite seems at least nearer the truth. If it is the case that Lawrence detested promiscuity and showed his detestation of it in all his writings including this one, then *pro tanto* he is a defender of marriage itself if not an opponent of divorce. Whereas the 'sacredness' which he is said to give to sex is (to my mind) an entirely different thing from the sacredness which it should possess for the Christian. To us, sex should be sacred as a gift of God, though not the highest gift; it is sacred as life is sacred, as the body is sacred, as nature is sacred. To Lawrence, if I am not mistaken, the sexual act *is* the religious act *par excellence*: the phallus is the supreme sacrament. The only point in the deplorable *Church Times* leader with which I found myself in agreement was its description of Lawrence's attitude to sex as pagan; and I see in your reply of last week that you admit the paganism. I can hardly distinguish between his religion and that of the Canaanite high places. In effect, what is Lady C. to her lover but a qedesha? If Hosea's Gomer was that, the terrible thing for him was surely not that she had betrayed *him* but that she had become priestess of a cult that set up a false god in place of the true one. And that is what Lawrence's 'serious treatment of sex' seems to me to have done.

I should add, however, that Alan Ker, a sensible Christian layman (and Fellow of this College), who admires Lawrence as novelist more than I do, and has read Lady C. as I have not, is amazed that anyone should feel that this particular book tends to uphold the 'sacredness' of sex. And he thinks that the sheer animality of its presentation of the male approach to the female is at least as likely to make a girl reader react with disgust against the whole business of sexuality, as to give her a 'saner and cleaner' attitude towards it. In his opinion, the whole affair has been bedevilled by a natural and proper eagerness to repudiate the notion of sex as something dirty or shameful – to such an extent that 'enlightened' parsons as well as men of letters have lost their heads and talked nonsense about Lady C. in consequence.

Of course, none of this makes any difference to the rightness of the jury's verdict: suppressing is not the way to deal with conscientious paganism. But it does give still greater cause to deplore the gratuitous advertising of sexual paganism by the trial and its result.

You will probably think both me and A.K. mistaken; and I would not have bothered you with such a letter if you had not had enough encouragement and sympathy from Cambridge to keep you going. But I wanted to get the thing off my chest without sacrificing the distinction of *not* having written to the Press! Anyhow, I know how weary of the controversy you must be, and I am quite honest in saying that I hope you will *not* allow further time to be taken from your proper work in order to answer me.

'Joe' Fison, Vicar of Great St Mary's, Cambridge, who was to become Bishop of Salisbury, wrote:

> I have been meaning to write to you all the week. Irene and I immensely admired your courage in speaking out as you did in the *Lady Chatterley* case, and we are so very sad at all the hullabaloo which has followed. This must have been frightful for you. I do hope you are bearing up. I ought to be honest and add that I personally didn't feel absolutely happy about all the extracts I read of your evidence. I feel that if only the relationship described had been within marriage, it could have been easier for me to go all the way with you. Nevertheless the great point I have been feeling the whole of the past year has been that what we all need is to have reverence for something that is holy – not belief in God or Christ, but reverence for something holy seems to be the crux – and the point you made seemed to me splendidly to emphasize is the point that the place where a sense of such reverence might begin in every life is sex. If only I had read the book 20 or 30 years ago, I believe it might have saved me from all sorts of things. At the same time I don't feel I want it going the rounds of the schools, and it now certainly will. But perhaps that's a hang-over from the past in my case. What I would like – and I really wrote this to you last week before the Archbishop's intervention (which I'm very sad about) – would be a prosecution and condemnation of books etc. etc. that are undoubtedly obscene – and that soon – so that everyone can see that a line has to be drawn.
>
> God bless you all and strengthen you, and we both send our love to you all.

Whether he liked it or not, in addition to the general controversy over *Lady Chatterley's Lover* John had stirred up one of his own within the Church. Happily it was a field day for the cartoonists as well as for the article and letter writers. Osbert Lancaster in *The Daily Express*, had 'Maudie Littlehampton' saying: 'It's an odd thing, but now one *knows* that it's profoundly moral and packed with deep spiritual significance, a lot of the old world charm seems to have gone.'

On the Sunday following John's appearance in court he was taking a confirmation at St George's, Camberwell. Millie Best was a member of the congregation who had lived much of her life in a wheel-chair after paralysis at an early age. She was a Cockney of indomitable spirit. As the bishop walked up the centre aisle before the service, in purple cassock with his episcopal crook in his hand, Millie turned round and with a broad grin – and in a voice that the rest of the congregation were delighted to hear – said: 'Well! If it ain't Lady Chatterley's Lover 'imself!!' No one enjoyed the remark more than John.

In *The Roots of a Radical* John describes himself at the time of his appearance at the 'Lady Chatterley' trial as a 'green young bishop'. Six years after the trial, in a submission to the Advisory Committee of the Episcopal Church of the USA,[1] set up to try to bring some wisdom out of the unhappy attempt to arraign James A. Pike, then Bishop of California, for heresy, John wrote of the:

> additional responsibility which it seems to me that a bishop should reasonably be expected to show . . . He will be the more aware that his lightest word is liable to be taken up – and distorted – by the public media. The inordinate attention paid to what he says – which is largely a secular phenomenon – derives almost entirely from his office, and his utterances and actions will therefore appear, particularly outside the Church, but also to embarrassed faithful within, to commit many others than himself. This means that he must exercise special prudence and imagination (though ultimately how things will be taken up is beyond his control and often beyond anyone's imagination). And he will have the theological responsibility, not only of being as well read and well informed as his time and capacity allow, but of being careful to insist when he is speaking with the authority of his office and when he is not. But in the last analysis the responsibility of the bishop in doctrine is different only in degree, not in kind, from that of any other baptized Christian, just as the responsibility of the priest in politics differs from that of the laity only in degree, not in kind.

It may be said that this was John being wise after the event (of *Honest to God* as well as *Lady Chatterley's Lover*), but there is no evidence that this was *not* what he believed when he appeared at the Old Bailey.

Twenty-five years after the event Michael Rubinstein, asked to give his considered judgment on the significance of the case, and of John's evidence in particular, replied:

---

[1] Published in its Report, *Theological Freedom and Social Responsibility* (Seabury Press 1967), repr. in *Christian Freedom in a Permissive Society*, pp. 126–7.

2 Raymond Buildings
Grays Inn   WC1R 5BZ
8th October 1985

In his *Observer* article in 1969 and the subsequent SCM publication of *Christian Freedom in a Permissive Society* in 1970, Dr Robinson referred to the *Lady Chatterley* trial as 'crucial'. Crucial for what, I wonder now. He might have thought the trial crucial for the subsequent freedom of literature from censorship on the ground of supposed obscenity, leaving 'literature', 'censorship' and 'obscenity' for each reader's individual definition. My surmise is that he would rather have had in mind 'crucial for the exposure of hypocrisy on the subject of obscene publications', however 'obscene' might be defined in that context.

My clear impression is that Dr Robinson's invariable concern was to be honest to himself, under his determination to be Honest to God. It was his integrity, not vanity I believe, which impelled him to appear as a witness at the trial, even if he would thereby cause 'confusion and distress' to many of his fellow Christians – the 'embarrassed faithful within the Church'. He will have known that the sword of truth often brings not peace but confusion, distress and embarrassment. The trial illuminated so many dark corners that its eventual impact on society was impossible to predict and is even now impossible to comprehend. Perhaps it has been exaggerated – the verdict may only have signalled changes which had already occurred in society's attitudes to the supposed 'obscene' elements in Lawrence's novel; or to the matter of freedom to publish writings about those elements without risk of criminal prosecution.

In the event, it seems likely that how people think and what they say and write and what they read about behaviour, in the realm of sex, are interwoven with their own sexual behaviour patterns, so that no distinct trend of cause and effect can be discerned however these attitudes and activities are analysed. Each witness at the trial contributed no more than a reflection on a few assorted aspects of the whole subject. Love, tenderness, lust and adultery (between the gamekeeper, a crippled victim of the Great War and his Lady – the Class implications seemed to underpin the Prosecution's venom) as well as the famous words, fast losing their magical power over men, were flashed before the wide-eared members of the jury. Then through the avid media, members of the public were entertained or shocked with the daily news of the revelations of those expert witnesses. The most sensational of all was the evidence of the Bishop of Woolwich when he was reported as suggesting that Lawrence tried to portray 'the sex relation . . . as in a real sense an act of holy communion' – his murmured addendum, 'lower case, of course' ignored because unheard, or because its significance was simply not appreciated.

Anyone who was a literate adult in 1960 asked now to name a witness at the trial would recall the Bishop and, I should think, none other – not Rebecca West, E. M. Forster, Roy Jenkins, Norman St John-Stevas or even Sir Allen Lane himself. It does not follow that the verdict turned on Dr Robinson's evidence, but his presence as a witness undoubtedly added to the respectability of the Defence, beyond the scope of two Canons and a parish priest.

In 1982, Dr Robinson wrote to me of his view then of the influence of the trial and the verdict on society: 'I think things are wildly encouraging, but there is a tremendous barrier to break.' Not wildly encouraging in 1982, surely? I had forgotten his idiom and mis-read his handwriting of course – 'mildly', not 'wildly'.

A lecture tour in the United States always had a special attraction for John. On 17 June 1961 he flew to Washington, D.C. to begin a six weeks tour, spending the first weekend with the Revd Al Shands, whose young church then gathered for worship each Sunday in Hogate's sea-food restaurant on the bank of the Potomac – 'St Hogate's' as it was known! Al and John had been friends since Al had come to Cambridge in 1956 to study the Liturgical Movement in England and on the Continent – a study which resulted in his book *The Liturgical Movement and the Local Church*. From Washington John went on to lecture at the University of the South, Sewanee, Tennessee – hopping over the hills from Chattanooga in a four-seater plane, sitting with the pilot and taking the controls for some of the time. Then he flew to New York and on to the Episcopal Theological School at Boston; then to Philadelphia and Detroit – to the Detroit Industrial Mission; then to Cleveland and Dayton, Ohio; and finally to Stanford University, California and to the Church Divinity School of the Pacific.

John found such tours immensely rewarding. At most places there would be friends he was looking forward to seeing again and who would look after him: a parish priest such as Al Shands in Washington or Scott Paradise in Detroit Industrial Mission; a New Testament scholar, John Knox, or the theologian Charles Taylor. John gave out a great deal on such tours but was stimulated, renewed and refreshed by them. In New York he preached at Columbia University on 'The Mastery of Time'. (The sermon was published in *Christian Freedom in a Permissive Society*.) The problem of time and 'busy-ness' was obviously occupying his mind. It is more a retreat address than a sermon, John at his most meditative:

> A car should always be charging its battery as it runs. If it simply uses up without putting back, it has to go into dock to be re-charged. It is not a sign that we are running particularly well if we are constantly needing to go into dock . . . Jesus is never recorded as taking a holiday. He retired for the purposes of his mission, not from it . . . He was busier than anyone, the multitudes were always at him – yet he had time, for everything and everyone. He was never hurried, or harassed, or too busy . . .

It is not surprising that John was pondering the subject of 'busy-ness' nor that after two such exacting years his body should now begin to protest. He had been maintaining a punishing timetable. The uproar the *Lady Chatterley* trial had caused – and the opprobrium – were taxing enough (though John had a remarkable ability to shrug off such things, almost as though he did not feel them). It was in late autumn 1961 bending to put on his socks that he had the first signs of the trouble with his back which was to be with him, on and off, for the rest of his life. At first he was inclined to dismiss it as lumbago and struggled on for several days, sitting whenever he could during services; but a procession round a church finally put him to bed and the doctor ordered a complete rest.

John spent Christmas that year in bed; the family Christmas dinner was eaten round a table in his bedroom. He began to hold meetings round his bed and licensings; indeed any of his duties he could do from his bed, he did. The back showed no signs of improvement by the new year and he began visits by ambulance to the noted orthopaedic physician Dr James Cyriax at St Thomas's Hospital – mainly for injections. It was this treatment which finally put John on his feet again and by the end of February the diary was as full as it had ever been. His last visit to Dr Cyriax that year was in April.

While John was lying flat on his back in bed he found it a strain on his eyes to read, so Ruth read aloud to him Tillich's *The Shaking of the Foundations*. They discussed as they read, and it was from these discussions that the idea of a book emerged, which would eventually become *Honest to God*. John had of course begun to think many of the thoughts that are in *Honest to God* many years before he went to Southwark – when writing his thesis '*Thou Who Art*' at Cambridge, as a

curate in Bristol, as chaplain at Wells and as Dean of Clare. Nevertheless it is virtually certain that John would not have written what he wrote
in *Honest to God* or in the way he did but for the particular pressures
upon him as a bishop in South London in 1962.

Inner South London in the 1960s was in many respects little different
from what it is today, though the population has now shrunk considerably and unemployment has of course greatly increased. The basic
inequalities of life were much as they are now. There was the same
Suburban Captivity of the Churches (to use the title of Gibson Winter's
book John bought in the USA in 1961) evidenced in church attendance
(or the lack of it). Even in the small congregations of the inner city the
middle classes were much over-represented. The black – mainly West
Indian – migration into London was at its height. Above all there was
the all but total alienation of the urban working class from the
institutional church. John was aware that in Southwark he was ex-
periencing *The Secular City*, to use another great title of the time (by
Harvey G. Cox, 1965), as he had never experienced it before, not even
in Bristol, and in complete contrast to the religious 'boom' he had come
from in Cambridge.

In his first confirmation address in Southwark John had said: 'You
are coming into active membership of the church at a time when great
things are afoot. I believe that in England we may be at a turning of the
tide. Indeed, in Cambridge, where I have recently come from, I am
convinced that the tide has already turned.' But within weeks he knew
that the religious situation in Cambridge was seriously misleading. In
inner Southwark a number of the clergy – and those some of the best –
were 'burnt out cases' most of all because of the alienation of the
surrounding working-class population. The Church so often seemed
to the people an irrelevance. John quickly knew himself to be a bishop
in a church which must 'sing the Lord's song in a strange land'. There
were those in the church – high and low – who managed to ignore
society and adopt an 'ark' approach: what went on in the ark was all
important. John knew that was often a form of suicide – or of being
'burnt out' without recognizing it.

John was soon aware of the need of a 'New Reformation'. A year
after *Honest to God* he would write a book with that title. But however
much the Church needed reformation in its liturgy and in its structures, however inappropriate so many of the church buildings were for
their purpose, it was clear to John that the first and fundamental

question which needed interpreting afresh to the people of the world which now surrounded him was the question of God himself. Many of those inside 'the ark' might not – and did not – see it that way; but to John this truth was shouting at him, and shouting again 'with a Divine imperative to pass it on'.

John decided to send a copy of the manuscript of what he had written to several of his friends, and to ask them to come to supper, bringing with them their answers to three questions. First, should what he had written be published? Secondly, if it should be published, what amendments did they suggest? Thirdly, what should the book be called?

The supper was held on the evening of Friday, 29 June 1962. The new Archbishop of Canterbury (Michael Ramsey was enthroned in 1961) was invited and sent a copy of the manuscript. Understandably he was too busy to accept and had not the time to read the manuscript but sent warm good wishes. The others invited were Timothy Beaumont, Secretary of the Keble Conference Group and editor of the radical Anglican monthly *Prism*; David Edwards, a former Fellow of All Souls College, Oxford, then editor of SCM Press, now Provost of Southwark; The Revd Eric James; Dennis Nineham, then Professor of Divinity, University of London, and now Professor of Theology, University of Bristol; The Revd Al Shands, and Canon Max Warren (a 'First' in History and Theology at Cambridge who had been General Secretary of the Church Missionary Society since 1942 and was shortly to become a Canon of Westminster).

David Edwards was invited as prospective publisher. SCM Press had already published several of John's books and David had told him he wanted to publish a series of 'five-shilling SCM paper-backs – like Pelican books', and had asked him whether he had anything to contribute. John had mentioned a 'general' kind of little book he had been writing, and sent him the manuscript.

Al Shands, who had recently arrived from Washington, and would be staying the night with John and Ruth, remembers John tossing the manuscript at him as soon as he arrived that afternoon and saying: 'Read this before supper.' Al rushed upstairs and managed to get through half of it before the other guests started to arrive.

After a great deal of talk over supper everyone agreed that what John had written should be published without drastic amendment. Dennis Nineham particularly remembers Ruth's eagerness and enthusiasm for the project. It was in fact Ruth who suggested the title *Honest to God*. John at first thought it too flippant but David Edwards pounced on it and said: 'No. That's it!'

Al Shands well remembers John's last remark of the evening: 'When it's published, I hope you will come to visit me on some theological Devil's Island!'

John did not only consult the members of the supper party. He circulated other copies of the manuscript before it was printed, and later several uncorrected proofs. One who received the latter was Dr John Wren-Lewis, a young industrial scientist and lay theologian whose pungent criticisms of the contemporary religious scene in articles and broadcasts had attracted John's attention. John had first got in touch with him only a week after his back had confined him to bed; but the references to him in *Honest to God* make clear what a powerful contribution he had made to John's recent thinking, and it is not surprising that John sent him an uncorrected proof – on which he made a number of detailed comments.

In the calm before the storm that was to follow *Honest to God*, John broadcast a BBC talk, 'On Being a Radical' (published in *The Listener*, 21 February 1963 and subsequently in *Christian Freedom in a Permissive Society*), in which he succeeded in defining an important aspect of his stance in life:

> The reformist overhauls the institution and titivates the orthodoxy; and in this way everything is enabled to go on smoothly, and the revolution is averted. [For the revolutionary, on the other hand] the institution is rotten, the orthodoxy stinks and enslaves. The entire structure must be changed if man is to be free . . . The radical must be a man of roots. The revolutionary may be déraciné, but not the radical. And that is partly why in our rootless world there are so few genuine radicals. Reformism, too, requires of necessity no depth of root, merely a feel for tradition: hence it can continue to flourish where men have lost their integrity. If the Establishment can thereby be preserved, it may be expedient that one man should die for the people. For man, after all, is made for the Sabbath.
>
> The roots of the radical, moreover, must go deep enough to provide the security from which to question, even to the fundamentals. No one can be a radical who is uncertain of his tenure – intellectually, morally, or culturally. Only the man who knows he cannot lose what the Sabbath stands for can afford to criticize it radically. Faith alone can dare to doubt – to the depths.

For the same reason a radical is necessarily a man of passion. He is jealous for the truth, the root-meaning, of what the institution has corrupted. He cannot be content to snipe from the sidelines. To be a radical means involvement, commitment. True, it means travelling light, being prepared to laugh at the institution one loves. And therefore he welcomes genuine satire and enjoys seeing the Establishment taken off. For irony is very near to faith – as it was for the Old Testament prophets. But always underneath there is a certain intensity and controlled fire. He has the salt of good humour – but the salt that savours and stings. The radical is an 'insider' – yet always a bad party-member, an unsafe churchman. He is continually questioning the shibboleths, re-examining the orthodoxies. And he will have a disconcerting habit of finding himself closer to those whose integrity he respects than to those whose conclusions he shares ... Such an attitude to living [John maintained] is dependent upon having roots that reach very deep. For myself [he said] I doubt if I could sustain it unless I were a Christian: for God is for me the 'depth' of love, as indeed of all reality, and it is in Christ that love is given its definition and power. But I have the utmost respect for the integrity of the radical humanist. Or perhaps it would be truer to say that, because I am a Christian, I *am* a radical humanist. For that, I believe, is the quality and direction of life to which Jesus referred when he said that the Sabbath was made for man, and when he summoned his disciples to be salt to the world. But it would not be fair to equate the Christian outlook with the radical, to suggest that all Christians should be radicals any more than that all radicals should be Christian. For radicalism is simply *an* attitude of mind and its relevance is to some extent a matter of degree. There are some situations to which the reformist response is appropriate, others which demand the revolutionary. The radical cannot claim to have the whole truth. To remember that should help to keep him humble – for the besetting sin of the radical is self-righteousness, as complacency is of the reformist and ruthlessness of the revolutionary. Nevertheless, I believe that the radical temper is a uniquely precious element in our cultural inheritance. I have no doubt that the other two are needed – and I find myself embracing each at times. But, if I had to choose, I would rather rest my reputation, for what it is worth, on being a radical.

David Edwards, like John himself, was well aware that *Honest to God* would be controversial – it was he who had therefore suggested that John should consult Archbishop Ramsey; but David never foresaw the size of the controversy which was to follow publication, not least because what was said in *Honest to God* contained little that was surprising to those who were familiar with the writings of Bonhoeffer, Bultmann, and Tillich. So SCM printed only six thousand copies, with two thousand for the USA publishers, Westminster Press, a Presbyterian publishing firm which, like SCM Press, went in for serious theology not sensationalism.

There were two factors the effect of which it was difficult, even impossible, for a publisher to calculate. First, it was a bishop who had written *Honest to God*. Secondly, this particular bishop had been known since November 1960, two years and five months before the publication of *Honest to God*, as 'The Lady Chatterley Bishop'. From November 1960, as we have said, John was notorious. But there was a third factor. Ivan Yates, the responsible and respected political correspondent of *The Observer*, who had a deep and devoted interest in the Church of England and its leading personalities, was asked by his editor at the last minute to suggest a feature. Ivan had been a friend of David Edwards' since Oxford and David had mentioned the forthcoming book to him. It was arranged that on 17 March 1963 John should sum up his book in an article. But the headline 'Our Image of God Must Go' was added by *The Observer*. When it was suggested it struck John as negative and arrogant and he resisted it. But under pressure of time, and with nothing convincing to propose in its place, he eventually concurred. Journalistically it was a good title, as events were to show. But superficially it suggested the episcopal author was an atheist – superficially: for it is surely legitimate for a bishop or any other Christian to feel that 'our image of God must go', in order that a truer knowledge of God may be received and communicated; prophets and mystics without number have said so. But as well as leaving a destructive impression, it also had the effect of shifting the centre of gravity of the subsequent debate.

19 March 1963, the publication day of *Honest to God*, was undoubtedly a watershed in John's life. As Ruth confirmed: 'Life was never the same afterwards!' As a result of *Honest to God*, for instance, John received over four thousand letters; and replied personally to most of them.

The book with its powerful cover-photograph of the German sculptor Wilhelm Lehmbruck's 'Seated Youth 1918', reminiscent of Rodin's 'Thinker', immediately became the centre of a huge controversy: TV programmes, broadcasts, cartoons, articles, letters, reviews, sermons. It sold out its first edition on the day of publication. On

Maundy Thursday that year Kathleen Downham, assistant editor of SCM Press, stood silently watching bowler-hatted men at the central W. H. Smith bookstall on Waterloo station, queuing for copies. What had John said to cause such an explosion? The book is still in print to answer that question. It has sold over a million copies and is translated into seventeen languages.

John himself summed up what he had written in an article, 'Why I wrote it', in the *Sunday Mirror* on 7 April 1963, less than three weeks after the publication of *Honest to God*.

Some years ago Mr Gaitskell proposed revising the famous Clause Four of the Labour Party's constitution (on nationalization).

Those who opposed him dubbed it all 'theology' – theoretical statements about things that make no practical difference. Such is the name that 'theology' has gained. But suddenly that image seems to have changed.

Up till now the Press took notice of clergymen only if they spoke on morals or politics. What they said on God and the Gospel was ignored. Archbishop William Temple constantly complained of this. But now 'God' is news!

My book seems to have touched people at a point where truth really matters to them. And of that I am glad – even if it has meant some pain. For God is to be found at the point where things really do matter to us.

What drove me to write my book was that this is simply not true for most people. What matters to them most in life seems to have nothing to do with 'God'; and God has no connection with what really concerns them day by day.

At best he seems to come in only at the edges of life. He is out there somewhere as a sort of long-stop – at death, or to turn to in tragedy (either to pray to or blame).

The traditional imagery of God simply succeeds, I believe, in making him remote for millions of men today.

What I want to do is not to deny God in any sense, but to put him back into the middle of life – where Jesus showed us he belongs.

For the Christian God is not remote. He is involved; he is implicated. If Jesus Christ means anything, he means that God belongs to this world.

So let's start not from a heavenly Being, whose very existence many would doubt. Let's start from what actually is most real to people in everyday life – and find God there.

What is most real to you? What matters most for you? Is it money, and what money can buy?

I doubt it, deep down. For you know that you 'can't take it with you'. And seldom does it bring real happiness.

Is it love? That's a good deal nearer, because it has to do with persons not things.

But what is love? Sex? Sex is a marvellous part of it. But sex by itself can leave people deeply unsatisfied. Remember Marilyn Monroe?

We all need, more than anything else, to love and be loved. That's what the psychologists tell us. But by that they mean we need to be *accepted* as persons, as whole persons for our own sake. And this is what true love does. It accepts people, without any strings, simply for what they are. It gives them worth. It 'makes their lives'.

That is precisely what we see Jesus doing in the Gospels, making and re-making men's lives, bringing meaning back to them.

In him we see love at work, in a way that the world has never seen before or since.

And that's why the New Testament sees God at work in him – for God is love. In the Cross that love comes out to the uttermost. 'There's love for you!' says Calvary.

And in the Resurrection we see that not even death was able to destroy its power to transform and heal. Love still came out top.

The Christian is the man who believes in *that* love as the last word for his life.

It is quite simply for him the ultimate reality: it is God.

The universe, like a human being, is not built merely to a mathematical formula. It's only love that gives you the deepest clue to it.

'It's love that makes the world go round'. That's what all Christians have always said. But so often they have *pictured* it in a way that makes it difficult for modern man to see it.

They have spoken as though what makes the world go round were an old man in the sky, a supernatural Person.

Of course, they don't take that literally. It helps only to make God easier to *imagine*. But it can also hinder.

Perhaps a comparison will show what I mean. The ancient Greeks thought of the earth being upheld on the shoulders of a superman called Atlas. That was their way of saying that it doesn't support itself in space.

We also know that it doesn't. For us it is held in orbit by the sun's gravitational pull.

The ancient myth was saying something true. But such language today would not convey the truth to modern man. It would be much more likely to conceal it.

So with Christian truth. The reality is that in Jesus we see the clue to all life. To say that he was the Son of a supernatural Being sent to earth from heaven may help to bring this home.

But for others it may take it out of their world altogether – so that the events of Christmas and Holy Week seem to belong to a religious fairy story. If the traditional way of putting it makes Christ real for you – the most real thing in the world – well and good. I don't want to destroy anyone's imagery of God. I wrote my book for those who have increasingly come to feel that it makes him unreal and remote.

I tried simply to be honest about what God means to me – in the second half of the twentieth century. The hundreds of letters I have received, particularly from the younger generation, inside the Church and out of it, have convinced me that I may have rung a bell for others too. For that I can only be humbly thankful.

For I want God to be as real for our modern secular, scientific world as he ever was for the 'ages of faith'.

It undoubtedly hurt John that the Archbishop of Canterbury for whom he had great respect (whom indeed he had attempted to consult) should have said, in John's opinion unjustly, in an interview on television on Sunday, 1 April – without in any way consulting him in the intervening twelve days since publication – that his book caricatured the ordinary Christian's view of God, and continued:

> I think he is right when he is trying to find whether some new mode of the image of God may be going to help some of the people who are right outside Christianity and the Church. But it is utterly wrong and misleading to denounce the imagery of God held by Christian men, women and children: imagery that they have got from Jesus himself, the image of God the Father in Heaven, and to say that we can't have any new thought until it is all swept way.

It was of course important what attitude the Bishop of Southwark would take, as John's diocesan bishop; for he too was being bombarded with letters and was bound to be concerned, not least for churchmen in the diocese, clerical and lay, who were hurt and bewildered because they felt that a bishop to whom they looked for support was undermining what was precious to them, and had told them – quoting Tillich – 'Perhaps you must forget everything traditional that you have learned about God, perhaps even the word itself.'

The Bishop waited three weeks, then declared his hand in an article in the *Evening Standard*. He began with an apposite quotation from William Temple:

In times when new categories are being freely applied to the whole field of thought, it is difficult to avoid blunders in exposition; but I feel sure that it is better, with whatever friction, to try to bring forth things 'new and old' than to keep exclusively to the old; and I hope I may be able to take a small share in helping the Church to do this great thing.

Then Mervyn testified to his confidence in John: 'In each of the jobs he has done he has proved himself a faithful pastor, a fearless thinker and a dynamic Christian. Although I cannot pretend to keep abreast of his thinking, there is no man in the Church for whose mind I have a greater admiration or for whose integrity and single-minded devotion I have more respect.' Then he came to his own view: 'I have read *Honest to God* three times and it has taught me much. Although I might be described as a Liberal in my theological views I am basically orthodox; by which I mean that the traditional language of the Church presents few difficulties and I can recite the creeds with a clear and glad conscience . . .' He ended with another testimony to John: 'I am glad that I have in my diocese a suffragan bishop who has the intellect and competence to do what I cannot do.' It was an article which left John – and the diocese – and the Archbishop in little doubt where he stood.

Towards the end of April the Archbishop published a small booklet, *Image Old and New*, which although it again directly criticized some passages in *Honest to God*, showed a much greater understanding of John's approach. At the beginning of May the Archbishop informed the Bishop of Southwark that he would be making a statement on *Honest to God* in his presidential address to the Convocation of Canterbury. As no copy had been sent to him the Bishop of Southwark decided to absent himself. Instead, after seeking the advice of Canon Max Warren, he wrote to the Archbishop:

As the Bishop of Woolwich works in my diocese two points occur to me: If you state publicly that the doctrines of God and the deity of Christ in Robinson's book are incompatible with the doctrine of the Church, it is possible that pressure will be brought to bear upon me to take action against the Bishop. If this were to happen I should have to make up my mind about what action, if any, to take. I have and am consulting theologians but there is a division of opinion. I shall, of course, treat your verdict with the utmost respect but, until it has been carefully considered by our best theological minds, I cannot at this stage commit myself. It is my hope that a situation will not develop which might lead to estrangement between my Diocese and the Province with the possibility of the

Archbishop and the Diocesan Bishop on different sides, and perhaps in open conflict.

So far as my Diocese is concerned I am striving to bring the different parties together to talk over their viewpoints. I am refraining from saying anything that might be interpreted as an official pronouncement because it would hinder constructive discussion and encourage men to harden their attitudes.

Although bishops have been receiving many letters of protest from the critics, we must not be allowed to forget the people on the other side who have not written. My guess is there will be a reaction, perhaps a strong one, in favour of the Bishop of Woolwich. This could be disastrous as it might lead to the sort of situation that existed a hundred years ago at the time of *Essays and Reviews* when the book was condemned synodically in Convocation, when eleven thousand clergymen declared their hostility to the doctrines it expressed and when only three bishops were willing to take part in Frederick Temple's consecration. No doubt we shall be more circumspect today, but the cleavage might be as serious.

On 7 May in his presidential address the Archbishop said:

There is a saying of Mandell Creighton, Bishop of London, that the Church of England strives to combine the right of the individual to be free with the duty of the institution to be *something*. Those words put in epigrammatic form the role of at once encouraging freedom of enquiry and adhering to a definite faith revealed in Holy Scripture and summarised in the historic creeds. That double role is a difficult one. As long as I hold my present office I shall strive to help the Church to fulfil it in both of its aspects, for if heresy is a danger so too is an obscurantist spirit in respect of the study of truth.

The considerable liberty of thought which we enjoy as a Church does however carry with it certain obligations of consideration and restraint. Unless those obligations are respected, hurt of various kinds is liable to arise. There can be on the one hand the giving of hurt to students in their explorations of truth, or on the other hand the giving of hurt through inconsiderate utterances to the many struggling faithful members of the Church. In either or both of these ways there may be danger to the twofold role of the Church which I have tried to describe.

With great reluctance I refer to the matter of the Bishop of Woolwich. I would far rather not do so, but there is an obligation not to allow the position of our Church to be obscured, and to prevent the spread of serious misconceptions about the Faith to which we are pledged.

Let me first say that the questions discussed in the book *Honest to God* are real questions. How I wish that they had in this case been initiated in terms of 'thinking aloud' and of 'tentative inquiry' without the troubles which have arisen. So sure am I that the questions are real questions that I ventured ten days ago to publish a small booklet about them, partly to show that what I might have subsequently to say in Convocation implied no obscurantist spirit on my part, and partly because I wanted to give some help to people whose minds have been confused.

I was specially grieved at the method chosen by the Bishop for presenting his ideas to the public. We are asked to think that the enterprise was a matter of being 'tentative', 'thinking aloud', 'raising questions' and the like. But the initial method chosen was a newspaper article, crystal clear in its argument, and provocative in its shape and statement, to tell the public that the concept of a personal God as held both in popular Christianity and in orthodox doctrine is outmoded, and that atheists and agnostics are right to reject it. Of course the association of this thesis with a Bishop of the Church caused public sensation and did much damage. Many of us who read the article and its slogans might not have the opportunity or the necessary brains for reading the book referred to; and the message which the Bishop succeeded in disseminating in the country was the negative one which I have described. No other result could have been reasonably expected.

As to the book, I repeat that the questions discussed in it are real questions and the effort to open up new modes of contact between our Faith and a secular age is one with which I feel much sympathy. We state and commend our Faith only in so far as we go out and put ourselves with loving sympathy inside the doubts of the doubting, the questions of the questioners, and the loneliness of those who have lost their way. But again, the book appears to reject the concept of a personal God as expressed in the Bible and the Creed. The presence in the book of gentle remarks for the comfort of orthodox believers does not cancel this fact. In place of the doctrine of God which is to be rejected there emerges instead some doctrine about God and about the deity of Christ. But I doubt whether any argument could show that the doctrine which so far emerges is properly the same as the doctrine of the Church. The Bishop however assures us that he upholds the Biblical and Catholic Faith and that the thought of the book is tentative and exploratory. It is fair and right that I should say this as clearly as I have made my criticisms.

Forgive me for repeating some words which I wrote recently: *It is possible for Christians to bear shocks, and not to find them wholly destructive . . . Today it is for us to be ready to find God not within the cosiness of our own piety but within the agony of the world and the meeting of persons with persons every day. But wherever we find Him He is still the God who created us in His own image, and sent His Son to be our Saviour, and to bring us to the vision of God in heaven.*

Immediately after the Archbishop's address, and after consultation with the Bishop of Southwark and Canon Max Warren, John issued a statement:

> The Archbishop of Canterbury has spoken of my book with reluctance and charity. It is in the same spirit that I feel obliged to clarify my own position.
>
> I am bound to say that some of His Grace's statements appear to me to misrepresent what I believe. In particular I would draw attention to two points:
>
> 1. The intention of the book is a missionary one. Its whole argument depends on the fact that I am trying to help those who are on the fringe of the Faith or outside it. This concern determines almost every line of what I wrote. In the light of this event I regret the Archbishop's statement that 'the book appears to reject the conception of a personal God as expressed in the Bible and Creed'. I would insist that my arguments do not lead to this conclusion. On the contrary I affirm in my book as strongly as I can the utterly personal character of God as the source and ground and goal of the entire universe. I wholly accept the doctrine of God revealed in the New Testament and enshrined in the Creeds. My sole concern is to question whether the doctrine must necessarily be expressed in certain images and categories which might have the effect for many in our generation of making it unreal.
>
> 2. The Archbishop disputes 'whether any argument could show that the doctrine which so far emerges is properly the same as the doctrine of the Church'. His Grace refers to my doctrine of God and to the deity of Christ. I maintain that what I have said is both Biblical and in conformity with the Creeds. I have for instance, categorically affirmed that I stand with Athanasius against certain liberal humanist views. This, I say, can never add up to saying that Christ was of one substance with the Father, and on that line Athanasius was correct in seeing that the battle must be fought however much one may legitimately deplore the categories in which the ideas of orthodoxy had to be framed. To explore new ways in which the truths for which he stood may be communicated is not to quarrel with the truths themselves. I regret that the tentative character and obscurities have led to these misunderstandings, and I hope in due course to write more fully to say how the ideas that have been partially expressed in *Honest to God* are compatible with the doctrines of the Church of England. Meanwhile I reject emphatically any suggestion that what I have written is contrary to the Catholic

Faith. As a Bishop it is my duty to defend it. This I do. And it is my earnest wish to commend it to those who are as yet unable to accept the Living Christ as their Lord and Saviour.

On 21 May Michael Ramsey and John were both among the guests at Mervyn Stockwood's fiftieth birthday party. It was a marvellous opportunity to mend fences and both John and the Archbishop took it. Mervyn's champagne no doubt helped. The eighty-year-old Earl Attlee sitting in a corner said tersely, 'Never read the book.'

At the close of his thirteen years as Archbishop of Canterbury Michael Ramsey wrote with great humility and candour in *Canterbury Pilgrim* that: 'I found myself a learner amidst the changing and unpredictable scenes of the 1960's.' He confessed his 'initial error in reaction . . . I was soon to grasp how many were the contemporary gropings and quests which lay behind *Honest to God*'.

Part of John looked on helplessly at all that was happening, like someone who had dislodged an avalanche. He had observed with a kind of detached dismay, but little surprise, the comment of the *Church Times*: 'It is not every day that a bishop goes on public record as apparently denying almost every Christian doctrine of the Church in which he holds office.' (He was touched that some members of the *Church Times* staff should send him a letter dissociating themselves from this leader.) There were many responses – for and against – which were virtually predictable. John was most interested not simply in those which agreed with and supported him but in those which responded creatively. 'Have you seen what Herbert McCabe has written in *Blackfriars*?' he would ask; and 'You must get hold of *Encounter* – Alastair McIntyre has a fascinating piece in it.' There is little doubt that one of the reviews which pleased him most was the one that Canon Max Warren wrote for *The Bridge*, the magazine of the diocese of Southwark. There were few men more respected in the Church of England, by all shades of churchmanship, than Max. What he wrote in *The Bridge* appeared in most of the parish magazines of the diocese of Southwark:

Do you know somebody who thinks quite hard, finds life extremely difficult to understand, but who can make no sense whatever of the Christian religion? – the nice man next door who catches the same bus as you do each morning, the fellow at the office you sometimes have lunch with, that chap at the works, a pal you meet at the pub – and, of course, the feminine equivalent of all these?

With the best will in the world these folk just do not understand what the Christian means when he talks about God. Jesus is something of a mystery man, very wonderful, but he lived a long time ago. The Holy Spirit – that just does not register. The Bible – Sunday School stuff. Religion – all right for those who like it, but it doesn't seem to fit into Telstar, automation or even Emergency Ward 10, though perhaps . . . We all know people like this. And most of us feel a bit hopeless about doing anything about them from a Christian point of view, except being good neighbours, though that is an indispensable first step.

But the Bishop of Woolwich's new book will perhaps help some of us to meet some of these people. First, let it be said, this is an *honest* book. Dr Robinson, as we have learnt to expect, looks fearlessly at the real problems which the thoughtful man has about all religion, and about the Christian religion in particular. He also looks quite fearlessly at our Christian vocabulary, and he asks whether that vocabulary is good enough. It may be all right as a sort of religious shorthand for use among those who accept the Christian Faith. But can it be used to commend Jesus Christ to those who don't know our shorthand? That is an honest question. It calls for an honest answer by the reader. Dr Robinson burkes none of the difficulties.

Then, let it be said, this is a *gentle* book. That may seem a curious adjective to use about one of the hardest hitting books the reader is likely to have met. Yet Dr Robinson remains all the time very gentle, very sensitive not only to those whom he is trying to reach but also to those Christians who will find his approach very disconcerting and puzzling, and who will not be able to follow him. For all that it is very powerful writing this is not a dogmatic book. All through it the reader will recognize that Dr Robinson is asking himself questions. He is an explorer. Finally, let this be added, the book is fairly tough going. If you take it to bed with you it will either send you off to sleep in five minutes or keep you awake all night! It is that kind of book. But honest to goodness, it is worth reading.

But it was of course only a part of John that observed the avalanche. There was little time to stand and stare. In the first three months after the publication of *Honest to God* he received over a thousand letters, and the invitations to write and speak and broadcast and appear on television came in droves – and not simply on religious television. John was a welcome guest, for instance, on *That Was The Week That Was*, the Saturday night TV programme with an audience of twelve million, whose personalities, for example David Frost, and style of satire typified the Sixties.

On 22 October 1963 *The Honest to God Debate* was published. In the seven months since publication 350 thousand copies of *Honest to God* had been sold and seven translations were about to be published. 'No new book of serious theology has sold so quickly in the history of the world,' claimed David Edwards. The new volume contained fifty of the letters John had received and twenty-three reviews, a fascinating collection and meeting (or collision) of minds, for example C. S. Lewis, E. L. Mascall, Rudolf Bultmann. There were three fresh contributions to add a critique and assessment of what had been happening: from John Macquarrie (Professor of Systematic Theology, Union Theological Seminary, New York); David Jenkins (Fellow and Chaplain of the Queen's College, Oxford – now Bishop of Durham); and Daniel Jenkins (Chaplain of the University of Sussex). David Edwards wrote a preface and John wrote 'The Debate Continues', which he refused to call a 'sequel' to *Honest to God* or a reply to his critics: 'The issues raised by the debate, theoretical and practical, are too big to be taken up so soon or within the scope of an essay, and the atmosphere at some points is still too emotionally charged.' The last article in the book was by Ruth (reprinted from *Prism* and *The Sunday Times*): 'Honest to Children'.

John was undoubtedly right to say 'The Debate Continues', for certainly no theologian – or ecclesiastic – had succeeded in speaking conclusively either for what John had written or against it. Indeed it had become clear – not least to the Archbishop of Canterbury – that *Honest to God* was part of a larger scene. The Second Vatican Council, for instance, had opened in Rome in October 1962.

John had undoubtedly been hurt by some of the reactions to what he had written. R. C. Mortimer, Bishop of Exeter, for instance, said that there was 'nothing novel' about the ideas in *Honest to God*: 'It is however unusual for such opinions to be held by a bishop of the Church of England and unusual for a bishop to express himself quite so incoherently.' Later he admitted he had never read the book.

If the furore at the publication of *Honest to God*, the pain John had undoubtedly caused to some, and the pain that some reactions had caused him, gave rise to any regret in John that he had published it – and there is no shred of evidence that it did – the size of the sale of the book and the volume and nature of so many of the letters he received would surely soon have removed any such compunction.

Some years after *Honest to God* was published, Dr Robert Towler, then teaching the sociology of religion at the University of Leeds, happened to mention to John that the letters he had received, had he kept them, would have been an invaluable source for contemporary religious ideas. To Dr Towler's surprise John told him he had kept them, and, to his even greater surprise, offered to lend them to him. The results of Dr Towler's analysis of the four thousand letters are contained in *The Need for Certainty: A sociological study of conventional religion*. In fact the *Honest to God* letters, Dr Towler states, are:

> not about *Honest to God*. A small minority of the people who wrote to Dr Robinson had read the book, and almost all of the letters follow the same format: they make a reference to the book (or to a television appearance, or to a printed article referring to the book) in a short sentence or two, and then begin 'What I believe is . . .' The book's publication gave rise to public controversy about 'the truth of religion', and it was this controversy, not the book, which prompted people to write with their own opinions . . . The reason the letters came to be written, of course, was that there was a person to whom people could write. To some people he was a villain, to others a man of great courage, to others a person who was at least prepared to have an open mind, but anyone could write to 'The Bishop of Woolwich, Woolwich, London'. And very many did.

The sociologist Graham Howes rightly refers to the 'substantial intellectual legacy' which John has left us in the form of 'the credal responses *Honest to God* called forth from many non-theologians'.

It is no mean feat simply to acknowledge four thousand letters – or the vast majority of them. But John felt an obligation to answer, however briefly, those that were clearly from a mind and heart in pilgrimage – and particularly those that revealed some pain and distress; and Dr Towler concludes: 'One of the strongest impressions one gains from reading the letters written to Dr Robinson is that, no matter what form it takes, the quest for religious certainty is an agonizing affair. The most striking thing revealed by the letters is the amount of anguished pain experienced by religious people.'

There is no way in which a small selection from four thousand letters can be representative. Yet such a selection can at least serve to indicate something of what John had to contend with in his mail in some of the most crucial weeks of his life.

A rural dean wrote:

> I have read your book. There is only one course open to you, honest to God, and that is to resign your bishopric and get out of the Church of

England. So long as you remain, you are a stumbling block and an offence to all who have not your intellectual pride.

An archdeacon wrote:

I want you to know that I speak for many clergymen besides myself in and around – when I say with the utmost force at my command that I deplore the way in which you are damaging the Christian cause and particularly the Church in which you are serving as a bishop. I fully allow your right to your own opinions and to the expression of them, but I do not think you are justified in taking advantage of your position in the way you have. I could wish that you had been content to remain as a don at Cambridge, where I suppose you would have been in good company. At least there you would have been less of an embarrassment to those who have more first-hand experience of ordinary pastoral work in the Church at home and overseas.

A woman wrote from Canterbury:

I personally found the chapters on prayers and church-going in particular removed a vast load of guilt and misery. So many of one's repeated efforts merely ended in failure and a despairing effort to do better next time, and then more failure and guilt. Unlike the medievals we are now educated to think for ourselves, and cannot help thinking about, questioning, and reading about all aspects of our belief, and finding things which strike with an inner certainty of truth. It is just so marvellous to have all this coming from a bishop of the Church, and having one's thoughts and hopes confirmed, not rejected, from inside the Church. I am certain this must help a great many thinking people to remain in the Church, and to bring back others who have felt increasingly alienated from it.

A woman wrote from a vicarage:

There are many causes for this indebtedness to your book, the greatest being your reconciliation of the divine and the human in Christ. The orthodox teaching has always maddened me; so many other humans have sacrificed themselves for us, endured more sustained and prolonged torture, without the comfort of being the 'favourite son'. If, however, as I have understood from your book, Christ's divinity lies in his struggle, as a mortal, and his success in emptying himself of self, so that God might shine through, this truly is of God. Any of us knows the impossibility of the struggle; what you have helped me to remove is my constant annoyance that Christ always had an unfair advantage.

Perhaps one of the greatest blessings is that you – and the men who have inspired you – have made the Church seem alive again, when for years it has seemed so unbearably dead!

A male correspondent wrote:

I have been an actor for twelve years, and this is the first time I have seen another actor reading a religious book in a dressing room.

All the more fortunate that your book has been attacked and you yourself reproached by the hierarchy! The one way in which what you have had to say could have been killed would have been for the 'official Church' to have taken it to its already overcrowded bosom and pronounced it blessed. If that had happened all the people I know, who are religious but not ecclesiastically inclined, could only have turned yet again to the Church to find a theoretical welcome, but a fundamental rejection by defunct forms expressing dead thoughts.

A medical professor wrote:

I had become increasingly out of feeling with church activities; and indeed was only continuing to go to church on the grounds that one just cannot generate moral insights by oneself. But I won't go through the doubtless familiar reasons why this sort of thing happens – especially I think to doctors and biologists, who have their noses rubbed daily in certain problems – and who also (this isn't always realized) have (at least for physiology and pharmacology) a very real and genuine scientific fellowship by which to judge other fellowships. The point was that Holy Week impended and I was seriously envisaging not communicating – for the first time since confirmation. Why? – because I was feeling increasingly dishonest in attaching myself to a church of which I was so critical and which often made one angry. Since I don't think one can ever detach oneself from Christianity, once exposed, the prospect of keeping one's Bible-reading going in sanctimonious isolation was all that offered!

However, to find you voicing so many of my feelings, in the same mood, and from a position firmly within the Church, made me feel that I could and ought to tag along (I can't dignify it by any better name), because there was at last hope that there would be room for 'unreligious' people. Also one of your main themes, of God as ground substance, rang a terrific bell. 'Ground of being' has I suppose been a phrase in use for decades or centuries; but you unpacked its meanings and implications in a way which converted it from one of the phrases one used to resort to to translate a church archaism into something meaningful; out of this to an expression carrying, for me now at any rate, more meaning than the whole of Christology put together.

A young priest wrote:

> I had come to the same conclusions as you have described in *Honest to God* some time ago and I was beginning to feel that I couldn't stay within the Church any longer as I felt that I was the one out of step. Recently I have read Bonhoeffer and Tillich and realized that I wasn't alone by any manner of means, and now your book which draws the strands together and beds them in the New Testament has filled me with a joy that comes from being liberated from a sense of guilt about not being able to believe what I felt I ought to believe. Your book has given me the last bit of courage I needed to go looking for the truth with no reservations of any kind: to follow where love leads, to trust in life, to glory in the depth and mystery and not be afraid of what may be found in the depth or through the mystery.

Everything in John's life did not suddenly stop for *Honest to God.* On the contrary he was determined that no one should be able to say that it was to the detriment of his pastoral duties in the diocese. There was diocesan staff meeting as usual for him the day after publication day. The next day he gave his weekly lecture to the Southwark Ordination Course. The following day he conducted a confirmation at Felbridge, and on the Sunday he baptized, confirmed and celebrated the Holy Communion at St George's, Camberwell. Maundy Thursday, Good Friday, Easter Eve and Easter Day – in the third week after *Honest to God* was published – John spent at Roehampton, a vast parish containing the largest post-war housing estates to be built by the London County Council. John preached there – as he always did on the Cross and Resurrection – simply, positively and directly, yet taking difficulties seriously.

The pressures on him – and on all at 17 Manor Way – were of course huge and continuous. (He had visited Dr Cyriax again in January 1963, an osteopath in February, and a Harley Street doctor on the Friday before *Honest to God* was published. It was about this time that he was fitted with a support belt, and from then on he carried a cushion about with him which was always put on his chair when, for instance, he was confirming.) Marjorie Smith – his secretary from 1959 until 1966 – would arrive at Manor Way each weekday at 9.00 a.m. Before then John would aim to have completed a tape of letters, ready for her to start work while he opened the morning's post or began his interviewing. Sometimes he would do the tape last thing at night. 'You go and run the bath while I dictate a few letters for Marjorie,' he would say to Ruth (or at breakfast time: 'Call me when the tea is ready'). Most days during the morning he would be in the study interviewing, 'phoning or dealing with the post. He always packed interviews in too tightly, at about half hourly intervals, making no allowance for late-comers or for the fact that half an hour was rarely enough for him. So there was often one, if not two, waiting their turn – probably drinking coffee in the kitchen with Ruth – and maybe staying to lunch so that John could catch up with them. From lunch-time onwards, if John was interviewing, Ruth was on telephone duty – a constant interruption, and often taxing when it involved dealing with the media. Sometimes the children had to take messages, which they hated.

Honest to God – like the *Lady Chatterley* affair – was a mixed blessing for the children: sometimes exciting, sometimes embarrassing. Buffy writes of this time: 'We loved reading about Daddy in the newspapers, but after a while we stopped watching him on TV because the programmes were so boring.' One day John and Ruth took all the children to Guildford to see their father's book rolling off the presses. That was exciting. So too were the men from the media and the growing numbers of VIPs who came to see John and Ruth – such as Nubar Gulbenkian, who took the initiative in writing to John, Sir John Betjeman, David Frost, Donald Swann, and the Day-Lewis's. But for the children, entertaining such visitors could also be embarrassing. The pressures of the post and of engagements meant inevitably that when John was at home he was even more the prisoner of his study – not least to the children: 'We always had to knock, and often he didn't look up from what he was doing. Sometimes he would look over his glasses to see whether it was an important person or just us.'

There was one member of the family for whom *Honest to God* was not very exciting, John's mother, then eighty-three years of age. She wrote on 13 May 1963:

My dear John
I do so want to thank you for the gentle and patient way you bore with me yesterday. I can't bear to think I may have hurt you or seemed to misjudge you in anything I said – I know I express myself badly – please forgive me. The more one loves, the more sensitive one is to any suspicion of possible harm to what is precious.

I am so convinced of the great things you are bringing and are being called to bring to the Church. All this storm has been so bewildering. I have not been able to keep my feet or see things in perspective. But when

I get so close to you and to what you are doing as I did yesterday it brings back all my complete and utter trust in you. The mere thought of any loss of hold on this has been so unbearable. Indeed I do 'thank God and take courage'!

John did not lose any time in thinking out how to use *Honest to God* profitably, particularly in the diocese. Martin Preston, one of his former students in Cambridge, Chaplain of St Dunstan's College, Catford, read the *Observer* article with great enthusiasm and wrote immediately to thank John – who replied by return, promising to address a meeting of sixth formers after school hours. It was held exactly a week after *Honest to God* was published. The school library was crammed with over a hundred boys. Typically John agreed to fit in a second meeting, which was equally well attended. There were dozens of such events crammed into the diary, mostly of course for the parishes of John's area of the diocese.

He was particularly keen to do what he could for those who had written to him. With the help of Werner Pelz (author of *God is No More*) – with whom John had made a notable broadcast on *Honest to God*, together with Werner's wife Lotte, and Ruth – and with others helping such as Canon Harold Wilson, the Revd Lawrence Reading and the Revd Rupert Bliss, John and Ruth together held a series of conferences to follow up *Honest to God* at Wychcroft, Blechingley, the diocesan training centre of which Canon Douglas Rhymes was warden. These 'Hooks and Eyes' conferences, as John called them, were held several years running:

> Just before Easter 1964 I invited to a week-end at our diocesan training centre a group of some of the many people who had written to me over the past year. They represented a cross-section of those to whom the Church as it at present exists appears to have no hooks for their eyes. They were either 'insiders' hanging on because to come out would have seemed the greater betrayal, or 'outsiders' who would have liked to be in but felt that to do so would have meant denying too much in themselves which they knew to be true. Or they were Christians who had given up more than occasional church services because they knew their limitations and found that their faith, hope and charity were just not strong enough!

There were some people – like Sir Richard Acland (who founded the Common Wealth Party in 1943) – who pressed John to form some kind of association, even a movement, of those who were responding to his ideas and his leadership. John firmly rejected such a suggestion believing it would harden people into supporters and opponents, and deliberately used the facilities of the Church of England Board of Education when, for instance, setting up the 'Hooks and Eyes' conferences.

There was no end to *Honest to God* for John until his dying day. There were not only the four thousand letters researched by Dr Towler in 1973–5, but each year till the end there was another file full of *Honest to God* letters from around the globe. There was correspondence concerning scripts for TV programmes, and a steady stream of visitors who wanted to talk with the author. When John was dying many who had not got round to writing to him before wrote their thanks for what *Honest to God* had meant to them. The last letter to be placed in the *Honest to God* files was from a young priest, born – like so many of the latest correspondents – only shortly before *Honest to God* was published. It was sent to John's literary executor shortly after John's death as an attempt to find words to express what the book had only recently come to mean to the writer:

> During my first year at Oxford, I joined a well-known evangelical church. This gave me a great deal – a circle of friends, chance for service and giving to others, and a realisation of the need for conversion – which came when I was helping run a mission to others! It would be so easy to dismiss that now as merely succumbing to the emotional pressure that I knew was present, after a hectic, exhausting fortnight's work. But I still value that opportunity I took to express my commitment: that is, positively to assert my acceptance of the Christian tradition in which I had been brought up and which had surrounded me for all my 18 years. It was for me where I wanted to be.
>
> As my second year passed, I quickly found that particular church was not where I wanted to be, and their expression of the Christian faith was not where I was. I finished the year as a disenchanted, puzzled member of the church – reading in my final week a copy of *Honest to God* which was somehow on my bookshelf. One of my clearest memories of that week is a walk late one summer evening along the canal with my girl-friend. I was saddened that she could not grasp what a splendid, awe-inspiring book this was. Unsuccessfully I tried to explain how reading this was my second conversion, how I had arrived, and how I felt taken up by it.
>
> After two years of being told what to believe, to do, to feel – how to 'succeed' at the Christian 'game' – here was freedom. Here was

challenge and responsibility. I was inspired by John's passion that shone out so clearly. He was not only intellectually stimulating, he spoke to the depths. It was a book full of guts, courage and feeling. It moved me, not because of any need I was told to have, but because it seemed so right, so hopeful. Crude adolescent feelings? – but that is what he found and released. Re-reading the book now, I am still moved by his quotation from Kierkegaard: 'a deeper immersion in existence'. That's what John showed the way to, and showed it as one on the way himself.

This deeper immersion in existence was possible because of something else John conveyed. That is, that the darker side of humanity, of me, is acceptable. Doubt, fear, anger, pain are no longer obstacles to Christian living, but are just as precious as their counterparts.

I was always puzzled by the criticism that John had misunderstood symbols. He had, they said, replaced one metaphor with another, equally limited one. It was soon after reading *Honest to God* that I began again to be interested in poetry. I am sure there is a connection here, for John's method was to use metaphor, myth and story to hint at the divine, the inexpressible. I now find the most regular source of inspiration to be the poetry of T. S. Eliot. His way of approaching God ties in so well with John's confidence that at the end of our journey, the ground of all being is love.

It was a joy to find again the sentence which I suppose gave the book its title: 'All I can do is to try to be honest – honest to God and about God – and to follow the argument wherever it leads.' That is how I work out my ministry now day by day. Not asking whether God exists but what it/He is like. Accepting others as they follow the argument wherever it leads them and encouraging them in their way.

Too strong words? Not for conversion experience. In his own words, for me John's books have 'defined without confined' the way, the truth and the life.

John would have found that letter 'after his own heart' and sufficient reward for all the pains he had taken with *Honest to God*.

In 1963 a new phrase entered the English language. The Bishop of Southwark was able to write an article for the *Evening Standard* of 11 July 1963 knowing that all his readers would understand what he meant by 'South Bank Religion – What I'm Trying To Do'. The bishop related the term to three areas – doctrine, sexual ethics and pastoral methods. 'Doctrine' related primarily to John's writings. It is significant that 'sexual ethics' was not concerned with what John had written but with a series of sermons preached by Canon Douglas Rhymes in the cathedral at Southwark, afterwards developed into the book *No New Morality* (1964).

Despite the usual tendency of the media to fasten on morals, the chapter in *Honest to God* headed "The New Morality" (carefully put in quotation marks to show that the phrase was not John's but had been coined by the Holy Office) provoked virtually no controversy at all for three months. Then suddenly morals were at the eye of the storm – including what John had written.

As Bernard Levin wrote of John in his brilliant book, *The Pendulum Years: Britain and the Sixties*: 'He would have had to be very naive (in some ways, it is clear he is) not to realize that a remark like "Nothing can of itself always be labelled as *wrong*" would cause great scandal, especially since he promptly illustrated its meaning by examples in the field of extra-marital relations.'

John wrote that he tended to classify his engagements by 'whether they were contracted before or after the flood – the date of the flood, for archeological purposes, being March 19th 1963'. There was one 'antediluvian' commitment he particularly wished he could have got out of:

> for the atmosphere at the moment is still so heavily charged and so emotional – not least within the church – that almost anything one says is likely to add fuel to the flames . . . I would infinitely rather say nothing: indeed, it is only a strong sense that keeping promises is a rather important part of Christian ethics that has prevented me begging release.

The commitment, which he had entered into two years earlier, was the promise he had made to the Bishop of Liverpool, Clifford Martin, to deliver three lectures on Christian ethics at the end of October 1963 in Liverpool Cathedral.

John's three Liverpool lectures (first published as *Christian Morals Today*, and reprinted in *Christian Freedom in a Permissive Society*) widened and deepened what he had to say on ethics in *Honest to God*, and were models of careful thinking and writing:

> At the expense of being fundamental rather than quotable, I want to try to dig down a bit, to see if we cannot establish some mutual confidence and common ground . . . I am deeply concerned that at this juncture there shall be a real attempt at mutual understanding and communication. For I believe that the 'old' and the 'new' morality . . . correspond with two starting-points, two approaches to certain perennial polarities in Chris-

tian ethics . . . or really it is the same polarity under three aspects. The first is that between the elements of fixity and freedom, the second that between law and love, and the third that between authority and experience. The first of these is thrust upon our attention at once by the overall title chosen for these lectures 'Christian Morals *Today*'. In what sense are Christian morals today different from Christian morals yesterday? Is there not an abiding Christian ethic? Indeed, can you have a new morality any more than a new gospel? The tension here is between the constant and the variable, the absolute and the relative, the eternal and the changing. Now, neither side in the present controversy, I would submit, has any interest in denying either of these complementary elements . . . The 'new morality' [he protested] is not in the least interested in jettisoning law, or in weakening what in *Honest to God* I called 'the dykes of love in a loveless world'. But it also believes it has something to say which is not an incitement to immorality or to individualism, and for which it craves a quiet, unemotional and honest hearing.

John protested in vain. He was now to his enemies the high priest of the Permissive Society; and they were deaf to what society meant to him:

Permissiveness – what does it suggest both to those who like and to those who dislike it? Freedom from interference or control, doing your own thing, love, laxity, licence, promiscuity – and in terms of verbs, swinging, sliding, eroding, condoning.

Christian freedom, on the other hand, has its ambience, both in the New Testament and outside it, in a very different language world – that of freedom for self and others and God. Its concomitants are truth, grace, love, service, responsibility, wholeness, authenticity, authority (the freedom which Jesus had that comes from going direct to source), maturity, sonship, coming of age, self-possession.

On 2 January 1964 John – on holiday in Rome with Ruth, Stephen and Catherine – slipped away to meet Cardinal Bea, the gracious head of the Vatican Secretariat for Unity. The meeting had been arranged by Father Charles Walker, a friend of John and Ruth and former Chaplain of St Catherine's College, Cambridge, who was preparing for the Roman Catholic priesthood at the English College in Rome; and Father Alan Clark, formerly the Roman Catholic priest at Blackheath but by then Vice-Rector of the English College in Rome. (When Alan was the Roman Catholic Bishop of East Anglia he continued to be a good friend on John's return to Cambridge in 1969.) John's conversation with Cardinal Bea sowed the seed of the lectures he would be giving in the United States in May that year – the Purdy Lectures at Hartford Seminary, Connecticut and the Thorp Lectures at Cornell University (published in 1965 as *The New Reformation?*). John was not alone in asking that question. Roger Lloyd, the much respected Canon of Winchester, wrote: 'The prospect of a New Reformation is clearly in sight.' Professor Tom Torrance of Edinburgh uttered similar words: 'Without doubt we are in the midst of a vast new Reformation . . .' But John's mark of interrogation was important to him:

> I am not so sure [he wrote]. All this is a good deal too fast for me . . . the present ferment is far more likely to represent a 'theological fashion' than a turning point in Church history . . . On a world scale, such as we are forced to use today, the Old Reformation cannot but look a rather provincial quarrel within the confines of the Christian West. It is certain that any theological revolution that will match our hour cannot be a purely Western product . . . Christians can no longer indulge in domestic discussion as though the other world-religions scarcely existed . . . I welcome, rather than fear, the sympathy with which much that I said in *Honest to God* has been received by many within the Hindu and Buddhist traditions . . .

John pushed the question even further: 'A Reformation presupposes that the Church can be reformed . . . There is, however, much from within the organized Church, and still more for those observing it from without, to raise the question rather insistently: "Can it possibly be the carrier of the new life for the new age?"'

Having put the question – and reviewed the thought of some of the more radical 'Death of God' theologians of the time – John called a halt, and dissented from their conclusions: 'The hound of heaven still dogs us, the "beyond in our midst" still encounters us, when all the images, all the projections, even all words, for God have been broken.' He quoted approvingly the words of a student: 'We must try to be at one and the same time *for* the Church and *against* the Church. They alone can serve her faithfully whose consciences are continually exercised as to whether they ought not, for Christ's sake, to leave her.' John concludes: 'As one who knows in his bones that he could not put himself outside, I want to plead for those who feel they must.'

John was, in fact, at the sharp end of all three prongs of Mervyn's South Bank trident – doctrine, sexual ethics and pastoral method: and the publication of the Paul Report in January 1964 meant that John's leadership in the third was crucial. As chairman of the Keble Confer-

ence Group he had had much to do with the genesis of the Report –
which in theory was concerned only with the payment and deployment
of the clergy of the Church of England, but in practice concerned its
whole future. He had been wholly in favour of the merger of the Keble
Conference Group (which was more to do with organizational reform)
and Parish and People (which was more about Liturgical renewal) into
one new Parish and People movement with an 'open and militant
approach to reform and renewal'. The merger had been concluded in
October 1963, and in January 1964, with John's blessing, Eric James
agreed to leave St George's, Camberwell to be the full-time secretary
of the new movement, and 'stump the country' in the cause of renewal –
with a particular concern for the implementation of the Paul Report.
There was much enthusiasm and excitement and many high hopes at
the time. As John wrote later, it sometimes seemed a time when, to him
and to others, as for Wordsworth at the French Revolution:

> Bliss was it in that dawn to be alive
> But to be young was very heaven.

The response to the Report by the Church Assembly was clearly
crucial. The Archbishop of Canterbury's speech was in fact rather a
damp squib – Eric James called it in *Prism*, 'The speech that never was'.
The Assembly awaited the more eagerly what John had to say. The
Assembly's '*Hansard*' records:

> The Bishop of Woolwich said this was not only a masterly Report in itself
> but represented a moment of truth for the Church of England . . . his
> qualification would be that it was not radical enough . . . it did not seem
> to go nearly far enough in assimilating the whole basis of the pay and
> pensions of dignitaries to the rest of the clergy. He was doubtful about
> the whole assumption that hundreds more clergy were needed in the
> full-time employment of the Church . . . He doubted whether the
> Report – which had a section called 'The Laity to the help of the
> Ministry' – had yet grasped the real revolution required of them . . . This
> was a moment of great stirrings and expectancy all over the world and in
> all parts of Christendom. He was convinced that the theological re-
> formation had a priority over the political, and unless they pushed
> through with it, they would not meet 20th Century man at all. Neverthe-
> less, if they refused the political, the instrument they loved and served
> might be shattered in their hands . . . This Report was about the most
> radical reformation that there was a hope of getting through, and it was
> about the least radical required if there was such a hope.

At another session of the Assembly, debating the fees of the legal officers of the Church of England John requested a radical review not of the fees but of the whole work of the legal officers. He had come to believe the law ought not to be involved in many of the Church's operations.

John had one more major speech for the Assembly in 1964 – on the British nuclear deterrent. It was short but succinctly expressed the position he was to hold – and to witness to – for over twenty-five years. He said he did not believe that any simple solution, unilateralist or otherwise, was sufficient. He gave four reasons why the independent deterrent was something he believed Britain should be prepared to forgo:

    (i)   It was an appalling example to other nations who had no such deterrent.

    (ii) It represented a waste of precious resources

    (iii) It threw away the opportunity of creative leadership.

    (iv) It prevented the building up of the screen of conventional defence.

He concluded: 'At present, our stance is making us almost a positive menace to peace.'

It is difficult to exaggerate the ferment in the Church, the heady atmosphere when John went to the USA in May 1964 to deliver the Purdy and the Thorp Lectures. Later that year *Time*, in a notable piece of journalism on 'Christian Renewal', showed how widespread was the sense of an 'eve of Reformation' spirit running through the Church, demanding of it an openness to quite radical change. John went not only to Hartford and Cornell, but to the community at Kirkridge, Pennsylvania – the American equivalent of the Iona Community – over the Canadian border to Niagara and on to Washington, D.C., St Louis, Chicago, San Francisco and Los Angeles. Wherever he went he was now – as he had never been on his previous visits – the famous author and theologian, and on occasion was apt to receive something like secular 'star' treatment from the US media.

Ruth, Leslie Paul and Eric James were with John in St Louis for an important national conference on 'The Church and Urban Society', which was the culmination of a series of previous conferences. Five episcopal dioceses had been selected in a national urban programme to look carefully at the extent to which the Church was engaged in the vital issues of modern urban society and to diagnose what blocked the

Church's urban effectiveness. John's writings before *Honest to God* and his experience in urban south London, and Leslie Paul's preliminary work on his Report, had caused them to be invited as external consultants, to make unbiased and unfettered comments.

John was already exhausted when he arrived, and Ruth and Eric had the greatest difficulty in protecting him and keeping him free to do the work which had brought him to the conference. It was not only the press and the media which tried to engage him at all hours; many of the hundred or so members of the conference – lay people and experts in urban work as well as bishops, archdeacons, deans and other ecclesiastical 'brass' – wanted him to talk *Honest to God* till the small hours as well as, and even instead of, addressing the material produced by the conference. But John's notes reveal that he somehow managed to keep his head down. His comments on 'Eight "roadblocks" impeding the Mission of the Church in urban society' still ring true, nearly twenty-five years later. He noted, for instance, planning for new congregations, the preoccupation of the Episcopal Church with the newly developing white middle-class suburban areas rather than with the low-income non-white neighbourhoods.

It was again relief and refreshment for him to escape for a month from the pressures of life in England, but he could not pretend that he had been on holiday in the USA. He had been fulfilling some of the engagements, and taking some of the opportunities that were now showered upon him.

On the 4 August 1964 John sat down and wrote a very long letter to Mervyn. It was five years almost to the day since he had moved to Southwark. It was half way between his leaving Cambridge and his return. In spite of its length, the letter must be quoted almost in its entirety:

> Now that I have a little time to stand back from the rush of things at the beginning of a holiday at home, I should like to think aloud with you about the possibilities of my future which I have more than once raised with you.
>
> Let me say at once that these thoughts are not in the least induced by any sense of being browned off with the job or of wanting to pull out. On the contrary, I can't really imagine one that I should more enjoy being in, and I feel strongly the importance of all we are trying to do and the need for seeing it through. Indeed, like you, I feel we have only just finished the first stage. I do not at all want to move. The new factor however that

has come in is that, largely as a result of *Honest to God*, almost indefinite opportunities have been opened up across what Max Warren in his Toronto speech called 'The Religious Frontier' which perhaps I alone can seize. There is also I feel a sense of *kairos* about all this if what holes have been made are not to be allowed just to close up again. Naturally one finds it difficult oneself to believe that what one says or does is of very much importance, but I find it being constantly urged upon me by those whose judgment I respect that I should not allow what has been started simply to get buried under the demands of the local job. Perhaps as an illustration of the sort of thing I mean I could quote two letters, though they are embarrassingly fulsome. The first is from Alec Vidler to David Edwards: 'I have read *Christian Morals Today* and think it very good. I marvel that J.A.T.R. finds time for writing of this quality. All the same, if the C. of E. had any sense (which is probably either a meaningless statement or a contradiction in terms) it would get him at least six months quite free to think things through further.' The second is from Harold Wilson's assistant at the Church of England Board of Education, writing after the second of my 'Hooks and Eyes' week-ends with those on or beyond the fringe who have written to me: 'I have just spent three days with 70 of the younger clergy from the Chelmsford Diocese. The programme did not include it, but the debate went on all the time. It seems to me the need in that area is just as great as amongst the people you had at Wychcroft. My suggestion that you should have more time for this kind of thing wasn't a flippant one. It appears such a misuse of your very great gifts that you should be burdened – or over-burdened – with administrative tasks, when folk are crying out for the very things which you can give. *Honest to God* has shown the need and made it possible for the need to be met, and some acknowledgement by the Church in an imaginative way would meet with an immediate response.'

I am increasingly aware how impossible it is to do in effect two full time jobs at once, and I know how both are suffering. At the same time I don't in the least want to pull out of Southwark and, indeed, if what one writes and thinks is not to become airborne it is extremely important that it shall come out of a wrestling with the actual problems of the Church on the front. If I am not however to run into the ground I would like to consider very seriously two propositions on which I should like your mind. The one is short term, the other long term.

1   I feel that whatever else I do I must somehow try to get the sort of break to which Alec Vidler referred. By the summer of 1965 I shall have been here six years, which in a university job would entitle one to a year's sabbatical. I know of course that the Church has no such system, though the two sabbatical terms which I took during my period at Cambridge

were as I look back on it quite essential to one's continued creativity. I know that one cannot expect the Church to pay for this, and to provide for a substitute in this job is much more difficult than making arrangements for lecturing and teaching. Nevertheless, when I come later to ways and means I would seriously like to consider what possibilities might be open.

I feel I very badly need a spell in which I can take stock, think things through, and try and take further many of the things that have been left unclarified. I want if I *can* to try and revise and expand for publication during this holiday at home the lectures which I gave in the States, though even this involves reading a very large pile of books which I brought back with me from America, including the very substantial third volume of Tillich's *Systematic Theology*. But even if I could get this done, there is still very much on my mind the book which everyone is urging me to write on Christology. I said in *The Honest to God Debate* 'I am deliberately not touching in this essay on questions relating to the person and work of Christ, as I should like, when time allows, to follow these up in a separate book'. I originally wrote 'if time allows'. You said that was a silly thing to put and told me to alter it to 'when'! I was only trying to be realistic, as I know well that such a study if it is to be worth doing at all could not possibly be done off the cuff. This then is the most pressing priority – time simply to breathe and think.

2   What I would like to see explored as a matter of some urgency is whether there really might be a possibility of getting an extra suffraganship in this diocese, such as you indicated might be conceivable all round. I would urge that this is not argued on the grounds that we wish to divide the geographical areas of responsibility any further. I believe in fact that it would be a mistake to have a third Bishop, say, for the southern half of the diocese, as I think that a great advantage of our present division is that we both have a complete cross-section. Nor do I think that smaller geographical areas have much to be said for them unless we really are going the whole hog and having a lot more bishops – which at the moment is obviously not practical politics, even if it were desirable. I would urge, therefore, that the case should rest on the increasing need, as a result of initiatives and experiments undertaken in this diocese over recent years, to have a bishop whose frontier would not be geographical so much as missionary. There are so many initiatives we have set in motion, and certainly more that could and should be, which are not primarily based on the ministry of the geographical parish (though it would be disastrous if they got cut off from this) which will increasingly need *episcope* and coordination. Apart from the longer established work of the Canon Missioner and South London Industrial Mission, there is

all the new work connected with our priest-workmen, Southwark Ordination Course, lay training, religious sociology, clinical theology, press and publicity, etc. There is also a great deal which I think we *could* be doing along the line of exploratory ministries, rather than experimental (to use the distinction which I tried to elaborate in my American lectures), which start not by pushing out from established church bases but from the other side of the fence. (The difference is perhaps exemplified by that between our ordinary lay training courses which start from 'tame' laity provided by the parishes and the sort of thing I have tried to do in my 'Hooks and Eyes' week-ends). My experience indicates that it is very important that a *bishop* should be involved in this sort of work. It indicates to the world that the Church really takes it seriously and that such exploration across and beyond its frontiers is being done by someone who has (incredibly) the full authorisation of the institutional organisation behind him, and is not simply a scout or a free-lance. Such a bishop would continue to be an integral part of the diocesan episcopate and take his share in its work. I would not think at the beginning that it *ought* to be a full-time job which never left him a moment to think. Indeed, I would regard it as an essential part of trying to be a missionary bishop in twentieth century secular society that he should have time to give himself to the *theology* of this. If the Church does not think this is a justified use of its finances, then I would be perfectly prepared to consider being in part a bishop-workman, though of course if I had to earn my living (largely I imagine by lecturing and writing) I should have correspondingly less time to give to the direct work of the institutional church. There is also, of course, the very considerable amount of work (particularly if one is living in London) which takes one across the frontiers both of diocese and of denomination which it is important that we should all be more free to do than we are.

3   *Ways and Means*

Perhaps I could reflect on the longer term question first, since it may have bearing on the shorter term issues. Would you be prepared to back setting in motion a request for a third suffraganship on the sort of grounds which I have outlined? If necessary, as I have said, I could conceive this as a part-time job as far as the financial contribution of the Church was concerned. I think on balance I should prefer that it should not be so regarded, though I think that an episcopal equivalent to a priest-workman is a category which certainly should be explored. Moreover, the case could be argued, if necessary, as a deliberate experiment, not committing the Commissioners in the first instance beyond this term. For what it is worth, there seems a real parallel in the creation of the suffragan See of Maidstone which was thought up for

Leslie Owen during the war for a non-territorial (and indeed extra-diocesan) job and which was subsequently vacant until it was revived for a similar sort of purpose for Stanley Betts.[1] My own personal preference (since it would save so much coming and going and confusion) is that I should continue to be Bishop of Woolwich and that the territorial responsibility for the Eastern half of the diocese (for this turn anyhow) should be assigned to the new Bishop of Sutton (or whatever anyone liked to call him). Even if such a move were ecclesiastically and politically possible, I have no idea how long it would take. How long did it take Norwich to get his *two* new suffragans? My instinct tells me that it might take the best part of two years, but of course *if* there were the possibility of getting it a year from now then the question of a substitute for me during a sabbatical break would solve itself. Indeed, if there were a firm promise and a definite date ahead, I should be prepared to consider postponing thought of a sabbatical till that date. This would make things much easier.

On the other hand, unless there is a firm prospect I should like to explore how it might be possible to get a break beginning in September 1965. On the assumption that the Church, unlike the University, cannot pay me for this, I should have to support myself. On the assumption that I shall by then have been able to organise my royalties into *Christian Initiatives* (and this is proving more tiresome than I thought), I should of course be prepared to use some of them towards this. With my heavy family and schooling commitments at the moment, however, I could not contemplate existing with nothing else coming in. My mind has therefore been turning on the possibility of getting a fairly light-duty visiting professorship in America or even trying for a grant from something like the Institute of Advanced Studies at Princeton. *If* we went to America and uprooted the girls from school, it couldn't be for less than a year, though of course if it were possible financially to stay here, it would be better for the children and the timing would be more flexible. There would still remain the difficult problem of supplying a substitute for my work here, unless a third suffragan was in question. Theoretically I could do an exchange with an American Bishop (such as the Bishop of Western New York and Bradford are I gather doing next year). But this would simply be out of the frying pan into the fire, and what I saw of American suffragans does not incline me to take on their job. A possibility that has passed through my mind is whether there might be someone (e.g. like Leslie Brown of Uganda, who of course would be superb) who might be considering resigning to make way for an indigenous bishop and who would like a year to look around to find the right permanent job in this

[1] Bishop of Maidstone and Archbishop's representative with HM Forces 1957–66.

country . . . My salary would I presume be available to pay him, if I were given leave of absence without pay. All this, of course, raises great problems and you may not feel that it is a practical possibility. In which case, the only alternatives I should have would be to carry on in the unsatisfactory state I am in or to resign, and I am not keen to do the latter for your sake or for anyone else's.

In any case, I am anxious not simply to let time slip by and if any lines are to be put out I would rather begin doing them fairly soon. If there were no bites, then at any rate we should know where we are.

I am sorry this has gone on so long, but the issues are fairly complex and fundamental. The natural man in me says simply 'carry on and do nothing', but I am only too conscious of how much is going by default, in the diocese and elsewhere.

As John makes clear in his letter – and it underlines how serious the situation was for him – this was not the first time he had written like this to Mervyn. He had in fact written an equally long memorandum to him only five months before, covering much of the same ground. Such was John's creative ability, that in addition to all the problems – and possibilities – that arose for him from *Honest to God*, there were also very considerable pressures upon him – above and beyond those of a 'normal' episcopate – from his pioneering work on the shape of the ministry in the diocese.

Mervyn's reply to John's letter was brief but sympathetic. He offered to talk over the points raised, and told him that his earlier memorandum had caused him already to raise several of his questions with the Archbishop. But what was immediately clear was that Southwark would not be allowed extra episcopal help in a hurry. The question of increasing such help affected not only Southwark but all the dioceses in and around London. Indeed within months, in January 1965, the Archbishop of Canterbury was to set up a commission under the chairmanship of Sir John Arbuthnot, which would not report until September 1967, which would consider 'the organisation of the Church by dioceses in London and the South-East of England'. It was obviously impossible to make arrangements which would pre-empt the recommendations of the Arbuthnot Commission. In any event it was not at all easy to separate the problems and possibilities which related to the particular genius of John from the questions which would be there in the future for any Bishop of Woolwich and for the episcopate of Southwark in general.

Although John's March memorandum to Mervyn was a much less thought out affair than his August letter, it contains several passages which reveal rather more clearly than the letter the way John's mind was working:

> There is a part of me which views with horror the prospect of spending the rest of my life as the maintenance-man or manager of a religious club. The other half recognises that we have got to go from where we are to where we want to be by changes in the structure, and that there is no escaping taking responsibility for it . . .
>
> The demands of the organization are so consuming that it is all one can do not to get sucked down by them. *Someone* must break through, while working in harness with those whose main job is, inevitably, keeping the show going . . .
>
> I have found my position as a suffragan (or what I have made of it) in many ways ideal. One's standing as a bishop gives one immense opportunities and at the same time one is thankfully aware that one hasn't finally to carry the can, and that a great deal of the sheer routine administration of the diocese passes one by. I *wouldn't* say that I am bogged down in administration and committees. It has been a splendid platform, and being in London has meant that one has also been able to do a good deal at the centre without being too distracted from the Diocese . . .
>
> I am guiltily aware that I spend a very limited amount of my (seven day) week being Bishop of Woolwich. I don't think I have actually fallen down on the job – but one is constantly aware of the people one has seen practically nothing of during the past year. Whole hosts of things *never* quite get to the top of the priority list, and one simply deals with what hits one, concentrating on the problems and the trouble-spots . . .

The one practical outcome of John's memorandum and letter was that Mervyn readily agreed that John should have a period of sabbatical leave in 1966.

On 7 October 1965 the first edition of a new fortnightly journal, *New Christian*, was published. It replaced the monthly *Prism* and owed its existence to the creative imagination of Timothy Beaumont, who was then rich and generous enough to provide a massive subsidy to guarantee its losses throughout its five-year life. Half its readers – ten thousand at its height – were lay men and women; half were clergy. It was ecumenical and unashamedly radical, though half its readers were

Anglican. It owed its success not least to the gifts of its editor Trevor
Beeson (now Canon of Westminster and Rector of St Margaret's), who
until his appointment had spent fourteen years as parish priest of
several housing estates in the diocese of Durham. He had served no
Fleet Street apprenticeship, but had edited the journal *Parish and
People* and been close to the centre of the ecumenical movement for
'renewal'; and was thus well known both to Timothy Beaumont and to
John. (When John was Chaplain of Wells he had spent a fruitless
afternoon bowling at the immovable Trevor in a cricket match between
Wells and King's College, London, when Trevor was still a theological
student!) Timothy Beaumont had involved John in all the preliminary
planning for *New Christian.*

The phenomenal success of *Honest to God* undoubtedly contributed
something to *New Christian.* Most of its readers had rejoiced at *Honest
to God.* John contributed a major article to the first edition of *New
Christian* which, like several others, would be reprinted in *But That I
Can't Believe!* The mood of the new journal was expressed not least by
the fact that its editorial was entitled 'Honest Interpretation', and its
first two issues had articles by Daniel Callaghan, a young Roman
Catholic layman, on 'Honesty in the Church'. In the third issue John
reviewed a book on the Holocaust. In the fourth he wrote a major
article on 'Bearing the Reality of Christmas'. The following February
he wrote another such article on 'Ministry in the Melting', in which he
welcomed the decline in the number of ordinands and suggested a new
approach to the priesthood. It was very much the kind of writing *New
Christian* readers were hungry to receive. The article was itself a sign of
the times. It was provoked by a 30 per cent drop in a single year of
candidates recommended for training for ordination within the Church
of England. John began with one of his characteristic openings:
' "When are you going to send us another curate?" The answer, if the
Bishop is honest, is increasingly likely to be "Never" '. John's point was
that this did not drive him to pessimism:

> Let me put it this way . . . In the inner city areas at any rate (where the
> next ten years will see the real crunch), I trust we shall be relieved of
> mountains of masonry that at present divert almost all energy from
> mission to maintenance. And we shall have to operate with fewer
> full-time clergy grouped around fewer historic parish churches. But in
> between there will be an almost unlimited need for housing (including,
> where necessary, meeting rooms for house churches) for community

leaders, ordained and lay, from which Christians may exercise their ministry in and to the neighbourhood. The greatest help the diocese can give to a down-town area is likely to consist in the provision through its own housing association, of accommodation at a reasonable rent for priest-workers, teachers, doctors, social workers, etc. to live in the area they serve. Everything must be done to build up indigenous leadership, but where it is impracticable to say 'Look out from among you' the Church must be able to say 'I am among you as one – or as half-a-dozen – that minister'.

It was heady stuff but underestimated how long it would take to move the mountains of masonry – and not only the masonry.

John was a regular contributor to *New Christian* throughout its existence – not least through book reviews. It is worth noting that in the ten years he was Bishop of Woolwich he managed to read 353 books, two-thirds of which were theology.

The invitation to give the Raymond Fred West memorial lectures at Stanford University, California in May 1966 provided John with the stimulus to explore further the meaning of 'God'. Later he expanded the material into *Exploration into God*. He had been encouraged to press on from what he had written in *Honest to God* by some words the much respected philosopher F. C. Coplestone, SJ had written in *The Month* in an article he called 'Probe at Woolwich':

> My basic idea is this. By publishing *Honest to God* the bishop won for himself an extremely wide circle of readers. He succeeded in shocking or startling many people into thinking and talking about theological matters. If therefore he could write for his public, in similarly popular style, a book exhibiting more positively and fully the foundations of his Christian vision of reality, he might do a tremendous amount of good. Perhaps this is an impertinent suggestion to make. But it seems to me that the Bishop of Woolwich is faced with an opportunity which rarely comes to anyone in his position.

The lectures were of course prepared for university students, but they were not addressed primarily to those with a professional interest in theology. John deliberately tried to combine a 'lay' approach with an academic rigour:

> The theologising and the popularising [he wrote] have to be done at one and the same time . . . the digging has to be carried on so to speak on an open site, with the public looking on, and being welcomed to join in . . .

What I suspect we are going increasingly to see is the market place rather than the library, the secular city rather than the monastery, as the normal place where the *original* work of serious theology is done.

John had come to the conclusion that the real failure of communication with *Honest to God* was 'much more at the level of presupposition than of proposition'. And now he felt he must look carefully at the presuppositions.

In the prologue to *Exploration into God* John was unashamedly autobiographical:

All my deepest concerns both in thought and in action – and I cannot separate the theological, the pastoral and the political – find their centre in a single, continuing quest. This is to give expression, embodiment, to the overmastering, yet elusive, conviction of the 'Thou' at the heart of everything. It is a quest for the form of the personal as the ultimate reality in life, as the deepest truth about all one's relationships and commitments. How can one give shape to the conviction that the personal is the controlling category for the interpretation of everything, both conceptually and in action? That it is this is one of those basic acts of trust which it is impossible to say whether it comes from one's Christian commitment or whether Christianity authenticates itself because it provides its definition and vindication. At any rate it is, as near as I can determine it, my central concern, that which chiefly decides what rings a bell, what I respond to as meaningful, significant, stimulating . . .

And I think the phrase 'respond to' is the key. What I have in mind is that which makes one say, 'Yes, that's true, that's real – for me.' There are so many things one could have thought up or even expressed, but when one hears them or sees them one says 'Yes'. There is the sense that what is most deeply real is there before one: one is simply catching up on it, entering into it. Pascal's remark has always haunted me: 'Thou wouldst not be seeking me if thou hadst not found me' . . . life is response – and hence responsibility – to something that encounters one, as it seems, with the claim of a 'Thou'. This is the mystery that lies at its heart.

Exploration into God undoubtedly cleared up much that John had left unclear in *Honest to God*.

Buber was never able to satisfy me, any more than John Wren-Lewis subsequently, that he really did justice to the dimension of transcendence required to make meaningful talk of divine-human encounter as distinct from purely inter-personal relationships . . . the truth as the

Christian knows it, is always a relationship a person must be 'in' if he is to understand it aright, as a subject in response to a 'Thou'. It can never, without distortion, be stated objectively or propositionally ... I was concerned not to abolish transcendence (for without transcendence God becomes indistinguishable from the world, and so superfluous), but to find a way of *expressing* transcendence which would not tie God's reality to a supranaturalistic or mythological world-view which, if not actually falsifying, was largely meaningless for twentieth-century man.

John tended to read novels as a discipline! (He would sometimes set himself to read one in Lent.) He liked particularly those that illustrated and illuminated theology – not least his theology! In 1965 he came across *Incognito* by the ex-Communist Rumanian writer Petru Dumitriu, which, he wrote, 'stimulated me to pursue this particular line of exploration into God as much as any of the more purely theological influences to which I have found myself responding'. In *Exploration into God* John quoted extensively from *Incognito*:

This was it, the sense and meaning of the universe: it was love. This was where all the turns of my life had been leading me. And now everything was truly simple, revealed with a limpid clarity to my eyes as though in a flash of light *illuminating the world from end to end*, but after which the darkness could never return. Why had I needed to search so long? Why had I expected a teaching that would come from outside myself? Why had I expected the world to justify itself to me, and prove its meaning and purity? It was for me to justify the world by loving and forgiving it, to discover its meaning through love, to purify it through forgiveness ...

What name was I to use? 'God,' I murmured, 'God.' How else should I address Him? O Universe? O Heap? O Whole? As 'Father' or 'Mother'? I might as well call him 'Uncle'. As 'Lord'? I might as well say, 'Dear Sir' or 'Dear Comrade'. How could I say 'Lord' to the air I breathed and my own lungs which breathed the air? 'My child'? But he contained me, preceded me, created me. 'Thou' is His name, to which 'God' may be added. For 'I' and 'me' are no more than a pause between the immensity of the universe which is Him and the very depth of our self, which is also Him.

This understanding of the meaning at the heart of everything comes in the novel only after three-quarters of it has elapsed, and at the moment of most utter dehumanizing degradation and torture:

They went on beating me, but I learnt to pray while the screams issued mechanically from my ill-used body – wordless prayers to a universe that could be a person, a being, a multitude or something utterly strange, who could say? We say 'Thou' to it, as though to a man or animal, but this is because of our own imperfection: we may no less say 'Thou' to the forest or the sea. We say 'Thou' to the universe and hear its voiceless answer in our hearts as though it were a person and had heard us. But it is He who prays within us and answers the prayer which is His gift . . .

God is everything. He is also composed of volcanoes, cancerous growths and tapeworms . . .

If I love the world as it is, I am already changing it: a first fragment of the world has been changed, and that is my own heart. Through this first fragment the light of God, His goodness and His love penetrate into the midst of His anger and sorrow and darkness, dispelling them as the smile on a human face dispels the lowered brow and the frowning gaze . . . Nothing is outside God . . .

It was natural for John to follow his further exploration of the meaning of 'God' with a chapter on prayer – as he had done in *Honest to God*. At the head of the chapter he set a quotation from Dag Hammarskjöld's *Markings*:

> The longest journey
> Is the journey inwards

and began the chapter with a clear statement of how he saw the relation of prayer to theology: 'In the last analysis the way of exploration into God is the way of prayer. It is not an exercise in theology. And yet theology can have the effect of seriously distorting the map. And nowhere perhaps is the effect more powerful than in the area of prayer itself.'

As in *Honest to God* John was concerned to deliver clergy and laity from 'largely unadmitted guilt'. He used, not least, the experience of his 'Hooks and Eyes' groups to illustrate his conviction that 'the starting point . . . is the recognition, common to all, that prayer has to do with life at its most personal – and that means not simply with relationships between persons, but with response to all reality as "Thou"'. The chapter reveals John's familiarity with the mystics, ancient and modern – and not only of the Christian tradition.

John was himself undeniably a man of prayer, a holy man – by his own definition of prayer and the holy – which was clearly a deeply theological definition. No one who attended a service he conducted – particularly the Eucharist – could ever doubt that here was a devout believer. Much of the controversy surrounding him would undoubtedly have been silenced had those who found his writings unacceptable had opportunity to be present at worship he conducted.

There are certain prayers which John loved which those who heard him use would ever after hear him praying them. And it was often remarked that his usual somewhat grating voice was not at all grating but gentle when he said those particular prayers and when he celebrated the Eucharist. He would often say at the beginning, or before the beginning, of a service the prayer which the former Dean of York, Eric Milner-White, had composed: 'Look graciously upon us, O Holy Spirit; and give us for our hallowing, thoughts that pass into prayer, prayers that pass into love, and love that passes into life with thee for ever.' Each word as he said it was instinct with his sincerity, faith and devotion. And there was the prayer Ruth and John so often said together – from the Book of Common Prayer – the collect for the fourth Sunday after Trinity: 'O God the protector of all that trust in thee, without whom nothing is strong, nothing is holy: Increase and multiply upon us thy mercy; that, thou being our ruler and guide, we may so pass through things temporal, that we finally lose not the things eternal: Grant this, O heavenly Father, for Jesus Christ's sake our Lord.' It is significant that these prayers were 'traditional'. John treasured the book of *Prayers New and Old* written or selected by his father, which was published by the Student Christian Movement in 1932, four years after his death. John himself was always on the watch for 'prayers new and old' that particularly commended themselves to him. His own prayer book bulged with copies of prayers that had caught his imagination. He surveyed each prayer critically – with an eye to its language as much as to its theology. It was in 1963 that he first came across Michel Quoist's *Prayers of life* and was attracted to them not least because they started from life 'just as it comes'. 'Lord, why did you tell me to love?' was the first he dipped into, and he wrote: 'It remains unforgettable.' He was equally attracted to the *Litany from the Ghetto* by the Episcopal priest Robert Castle, which caused a furore when it was used in 1965 by the Chicago black minister Archie Hargreaves at the biennial convention of the United Church of Christ.

> The identification between God and the city [John wrote] is such that grammar is strained to breaking point in bringing together the 'Thou' addressed and the third person indicative of those who *are* the city:

> O God, who lives in tenements, who goes to segregrated
>   schools, who is beaten in precincts, who
>   is unemployed . . .
>   Help us to know you
> O God, who is cold in the slums of winter, whose playmates
>   are rats – four-legged ones who live with you and
>   two-legged ones who imprison you . . .
>   Help us to touch you

and so on, ever nearer the bone.

John commented: '*The Litany from the Ghetto*, with its identification of God with the scene rather than the spectator . . . has provoked the inevitable charge of pantheism. But it is not asserting a metaphysical identity; simply that at the given moment for the subject in prayer this is where, and who God is – and there is no turning aside, not even to Another.'

He queried what he called 'the "telstar" image of prayer, of redirecting messages off a celestial being'. He believed in 'the Quaker tradition of spirituality, which has its ambience much more *in* the Spirit and sees the Presence rather in terms of that which lights up every man from within, or, as Buber would put it, is "*between* man and man"'.

In *The New Reformation?* John had written of the vocation held out to the theologian:

> It is a call in the first place not to relevance in any slick sense but to exposure, to compassion, sensibility, awareness and integrity. It is the call to bear reality, more reality than it is easy or indeed possible for a human being to bear unaided. It is to be with God in his world. And in each epoch or culture the place of the theologian is to stand as near as he may to the 'creative centre' of God's world in his day.

Now, in *Exploration into God*, he affirmed that this is also the place of the man of prayer. It was undoubtedly so for him personally.

In the same year (1967) John's paperback *But That I Can't Believe!* was also published. It consisted mainly of pieces done for a mass-circulation readership and for that reason was easy to dismiss. But it is masterly journalism – profound theology written in the vulgar tongue. Some of its pages had appeared in the *Sunday Mirror, Tit-Bits, The Sun, Sunday Citizen* and *TV Times*; some had not been published before, only a few were for a predominantly Christian audience. (As John later revealed, Ruth had written some of the best items in the book!) He was of course at his best when writing of 'The Second Coming':

To skin your eyes watching the skies for the return of Christ is as misguided as to wait for the archaeologists to dig up evidence for the fall of Adam. For both are ways of trying to make vivid what Christians believe is true not just of one moment but of every moment.

Everywhere, at any moment, *Christ comes in.* That's what the doctrine of the Second Coming is concerned to assert. The trouble about the *phrase* 'the second coming' is that it suggests that Christ is only coming again once – and that till then he's well away. But you won't in fact find that phrase in the Bible. It speaks simply of 'the coming' of Christ, and the word it uses means 'presence' . . . It's that man again! There's simply no getting away from him. You won't meet him, literally, in the high street – or in the clouds. But his life, his standards, his love will find you in the end.

But it's not only in the end, so that we can put off reckoning with him, as we say, 'till kingdom come'. Even now, he insists on coming in.

Maybe it was in the man you travelled up with the other morning in the train, as you turned away and buried yourself in the paper. *Jesus* could have been meeting you in that man's loneliness.

Perhaps it was in the coloured couple asking for accommodation. Was there no room for *him* in your home? But it's not only in our personal choices that Jesus confronts us, but in everything that hits us out of the headlines. The New Testament writers couldn't describe even the most secular, political events without seeing Christ meeting and judging men in them.

In the late autumn of 1965 John was laid low again with back trouble for nearly two months. Much as he looked forward to his sabbatical in 1966 he was well aware that his back was likely to give more trouble. He was in any case unable to sit or stand for long. In January 1966 he and Ruth managed five memorable days in Sweden at the invitation of Margit Stahlin, their first woman priest. But in February the back trouble returned and John went away to a convalescent home. While he was away the Archbishop called at his home – which gave John the opportunity to unburden himself in a letter dated Ash Wednesday, 23 February 1966.

My dear Archbishop
It was so good of you to call at my house recently and I greatly appreciated it. I am away till the end of this week at a convalescent home really trying to get my back right. It is giving me a wonderful opportunity for writing and I am pressing on with my lectures for Stanford in May – under the title (borrowed from Christopher Fry) 'Exploration into God'. I have

been trying to hold together the 'secularizers' and the 'mystics', and in due time I shall greatly value your judgement on them.

Meanwhile, though the rest is doing me good, there is not much change in the back. It is clear that it is a fairly long-term process, and though this bout will doubtless mend itself in time I am strongly urged that I cannot hope to be clear of it unless I reduce the pressure somewhere.

As I try to assess it, I am sure that the real strain is having to balance endless openings which in themselves one feels are real priorities, against the job one was appointed to do, namely, to be the suffragan with responsibility for the eastern half of the Southwark diocese. In this vital job I know I am falling down badly. There are parishes and clergy I have not properly seen for three years, and a growing number of newly ordained men whom I really don't know. Increasingly one does not go out looking for things, but waits for them to hit one. And this is the abdication of pastoral leadership, and it is much on my conscience.

Of course, an obvious course would be to resign. I am not sure that this would do more than transfer the problem somewhere else, and I am deeply attached to my work in Southwark. It would also remove the platform which has come to give me most of my other opportunities, and I see nothing creative in simply being in the ecclesiastical wilderness.

As I try to wrestle with what I should be doing in the period ahead, there is nothing I would rather do than continue as Bishop of Woolwich. At the same time I cannot honestly discharge the remit originally given to me. What is increasingly engaging me within the diocese is the oversight and coordination of the whole work of exploration and experiment in the field of ministry and mission . . . There would seem to me to be blowing up the most urgent necessity to explore, and pioneer with, new forms of ministry, especially in the inner city areas. I believe the straws in the wind point to the near collapse of our traditional structures in considerable areas over the next ten years. Indeed, like the Free Churches, we are approaching, if we have not passed, the point of no return in many places already. I am sure that it will be spiritually disastrous if we simply soldier on till the shortage of manpower and money finally overtakes us. Some-where we should be planning and training for what might conceivably be put in the place of what is now going under.

It is in this field that I feel the challenge, and, if it were possible, what I should like to do would be to continue as Bishop of Woolwich with special responsibility to Mervyn for this work . . .

The rest of the letter is virtually what John had written to Mervyn in his long letter of August 1964. The answer to it, John knew, was bound to be much the same as it had been then, for the publication of the Arbuthnot Commission's Report was still a year and a half away.

On 9 March John flew to the USA – not this time to move from place to place. Wisely he had accepted the offer of a fortnight at Wabash College, Indiana where he could continue preparing the lectures for Stanford University. But from Wabash he made one sortie – to Chicago – to meet Martin Luther King. While there he paid his first visit to the Chicago Urban Training Centre. It soon became clear to him that such a centre was what was urgently needed by the Church in England – not least in Southwark; and on his return he soon set to work to establish a special relationship between the Diocese of Southwark and the Episcopal Diocese of Chicago which would enable there to be a continuing exchange between clergy and laity of the two dioceses – particularly from the inner-city areas – with clergy from Southwark thus being enabled to attend courses at the Urban Training Centre.

It was at the Chicago Urban Training Centre that John came across something which particularly gained his interest and enthusiasm (he wrote it up in *New Christian* and *But That I Can't Believe!*), the liturgy recently prepared for St Mark's-in-the-Bowery, in the notorious Lower East Side of New York. The Revd Michael Allen had gathered together a group of people from the parish, which numbered in its congregation many college and university students, to fashion a liturgy that was ecumenical and paid attention both to the historical 'shape of the liturgy' and to the contemporary community. The group worked at the liturgy over several months, eventually involving W. H. Auden, a member of the parish. After the summer of 1966 there was scarcely a committee in Southwark of which John was chairman or a group in which he was involved, which did not on occasions use the St Mark's-in-the-Bowery liturgy – these were the days when the Church of England's Liturgical Commission was working away at the draft of a new liturgy. The St Mark's liturgy became personally associated with John as much as some prayers had. He did not advocate its unaltered use; indeed he drew attention to it as an example of 'essentially local liturgy'. 'I doubt whether its confession transplants altogether easily from the world of the ghetto which shaped it,' he wrote. Nevertheless that confession certainly conveys the flavour of the liturgy as a whole:

PRESIDENT AND ASSEMBLY:
We are here because we are men – but we deny our humanity.
We are stubborn fools and liars to ourselves.

We do not love others. We war against life.
We hurt each other.
We are sorry for it, and know we are sick from it.
We seek new life.
PRESIDENT:
Giver of life: heal us and free us to be men.
PRESIDENT AND ASSEMBLY:
Holy Spirit, speak to us.
Help us to listen, for we are very deaf.
Come, fill this moment.

The little phrase 'for we are very deaf' was one of Auden's additions to the liturgy.

John was home from the USA for Holy Week and Easter, and on 30 April flew with Ruth to Stanford to deliver his lectures. When they were over, he and Ruth were able to see a good deal of Jim Pike, the controversial Bishop of California, and of Alan Watts and his wife. Alan, born in England and for a few years a priest of the Episcopal Church, and author of the much praised *Behold the Spirit: A Study in the Necessity of Mystical Religion*, since he moved to the USA in 1938 had become an interpreter of Zen Buddhism in particular and of Indian and Chinese philosophy in general. Alan was, as Monica Furlong has written, an incongruous figure: a 'combination of spiritual insight and naughtiness, of wisdom and childishness, of joyous high spirits and loneliness'. John and Ruth knew they had much to receive from Alan, and delighted in the bare but exotic eastern and Mexican Indian simplicity of the Watts' house-boat at Sausalito. On 8 May, after preaching at Grace Cathedral, San Francisco, John did a 'double act' with Jim Pike at the Esalen Institute on Big Sur. Ruth and John were lent a house for the next days amid the redwood canyons that look down sheer to the Pacific. The whole atmosphere of the Institute in its early days – under Mike Murphy, who had recently returned from India and was waiting to share the insights he had received – was a spiritual one: the exploring of the religious, philosophical and psychological frontiers – and of the arts – to emphasize and enlarge the potentialities of human existence. John was of course intrigued and curious and open to what Esalen might have to offer him – he was well aware that he was not without his own inhibitions, social and psychological. Yet it was then, as always, the exploration of ideas that John primarily warmed to. As later with yoga, he was eager to understand and share but remained essentially the observer. After Esalen John and Ruth were able to enjoy a memorable week together in the Yosemite National Park before flying home at the end of May.

One evening that June they spent a relaxed evening with Dr Billy Graham and his wife Ruth, after which Billy wrote:

> It was a great delight and pleasure to us to be with you the other evening. In some ways it will be the highlight of my trip to England. Isn't it strange what misconception we Christians have of each other, and how personal encounters often dissipate some of our prejudices and fears? You and your Ruth are two people with whom we would like to get better acquainted and become closer friends. I am sure there is much I can learn from you . . .
>
> With warmest Christian greetings, I am
> Cordially yours,
> Billy.

After a family holiday in Cornwall in August John was determined to settle down again to work in Southwark. At the start of his sabbatical his secretary Marjorie Smith had retired, and he had engaged a new secretary, Stella Haughton, to begin work in September 1966, with the prospect ahead of several years work in Southwark with John. Stella began work as planned in September, but it was not long before John's back trouble assumed dire proportions, and it was decided that only a spinal operation held any hope of solution. Armed with books, agendas, tape-recordings and numerous files – back trouble had never made him stop work but only change its location – he entered the Brook Hospital, Woolwich on 19 November. A small room had been set aside for him. Stella had quickly got used to the Robinson routine of one Grundig tape succeeding another, with forty letters and postcards to be typed each morning. Now there were daily visits to the hospital to deliver letters for signing and to collect the next tapes.

The neuro-surgeon removed two discs on 22 November, and outside engagements had to be cancelled until the end of the year.

Stella now opened the post, which was a revelation to her:

> Pages and pages of intimate spiritual outpourings, letters of abuse, of Christian repudiation, and, worst of all – three years after *Honest to God* – obscene, unsigned missives which made me blench and long to burn them. But they were all sorted into 'the sad, the bad and the mad', and as many answered as were helpful or feasible. Larger packages

were mainly manuscripts which aspiring writers sent for criticism and comment (usually without the return postage!).

The first manuscript of a book which Stella typed for John was *But That I Can't Believe!* She was to type the manuscripts of all the rest of his books. 'John was essentially practical and businesslike,' Stella wrote. 'Every minute of my time was utilised to the full, and always there was more left over for the next day. Yet never could I fault my employer for working less hard than I.'

In March 1967 he was still attending the Brook Hospital, and not doing any confirmations or other long services; but after Easter the diary returned to normal. In May that year John spent a very happy week in France with a group of clergy and laity from the diocese. The first days were spent at the seminary for worker-priests of the Mission de France attached to the Abbey at Pontigny, where John gave a lecture; and the last days with the community at Taizé. At Pontigny Cardinal Lienart gave John permission to celebrate Holy Communion in the chapel, for the worker-priests as well as for the Southwark group. At Taizé Father Roger asked John to address the crowded chapel before the evening office. John, open-necked and in shirt-sleeves, spoke of the seamless robe of Christ as the symbol of Christian unity. (At Taizé the Southwark clergy were delighted to hear an over-confident student pointing out John to a fellow student and saying: 'That is the Bishop of Woolwich, who wrote *Honest to God*. He also wrote a book about *Lady Chatterley's Lover* called *The Body*!') On the way back through Paris John met Roger Garaudy, the leading French Marxist philosopher, whose book *From Anathema to Dialogue*, published the previous year, had made a great impression on him. It was a meeting on which he wanted to build.)

John had attended the February 1967 session of the Church Assembly. His presence was greatly needed, for the complex Pastoral Measure – providing sweeping powers to reorganize the Church of England – suspending patronage and freehold; uniting parishes and creating team ministries – was in the last stages of consideration. John's seven years experience in Southwark as well as the clarity of his intellect enabled him to make an invaluable contribution to the debates on the Measure. He held within the grasp of his mind the powers of all the different bodies who were involved – Parliament, the Law, the Church Commissioners, the Town and Country Planning Act, the various diocesan advisory bodies, the parochial powers, and so on. Time and again he would make bold and imaginative suggestions which if enacted would give the Church greater freedom to deploy its buildings and its clergy with a greater flexibility. His suggestions were of course fiercely opposed by those who did not desire such flexibility. The Minutes of the Church Assembly for 14 February 1967 record a Pastoral Measure debate. The Bishop of Warrington, Laurie Brown, referred to 'this important new proposal since the Measure was last before the Assembly. It is right that I should acknowledge its authorship as that of Bishop John Robinson, the Bishop of Woolwich and Canon Eric James . . .' (Eric James would be the first to say that the proposal owed its origin to the Bishop of Woolwich):

> The intention is that in certain defined circumstances it should be possible within the terms of this Measure for a parish to continue in existence as a parish, even though the parish church has been declared redundant and disposed of, without being replaced by another consecrated building . . . It is accepted that in either case there must be some definable centre of worship in the area which is to enjoy the nature of a parish.

Ivor Bulmer-Thomas, director of 'Friends of Friendless Churches', protested: 'This motion proposes a revolution in the English parochial system.' It did not quite do that! However John's motion was passed.

He left no doubt where he stood when in July 1967 the Assembly decided that 'there are no conclusive theological reasons why women should not be ordained to the priesthood'. He recognized that the question of the attitude of the Roman Catholic Church might well be crucial and referred to an article he had received from a Roman Catholic priest in France, which underlined 'that there is no serious theological argument against it but only masculine inertia and self-sufficiency . . . ecumenically, so far from being an argument for doing nothing, it is an argument to do precisely the reverse'.

The same year a study group of Parish and People produced a *Prism* pamphlet, *Putting Together*, which attacked the theological base and the caution of the *Report on the Sharing of Churches* by different Christian bodies, which had been published in September 1966. John was at the centre of the group. As a result, after the debate in the Assembly of November 1967, the proposals of the September 1966 Report were virtually abandoned and replaced by the proposals of the Parish and People group.

Behind the scenes as much as in debate in the Church Assembly and in Convocation John the Reformer made his presence felt – whether it was concerning the reports on Crown Appointments, Government by Synod, Partners in Ministry, Diocesan Boundaries, the Pastoral Measure or the Sharing of Churches. He was, in 'the Church's Parliament', the recognized, respected and unchallenged episcopal leader of the forces for radical reform. The Bishop of Southwark did not attempt to make his mark in Convocation or the Church Assembly, leaving that field to John. In November 1968 there would be one more Assembly debate at which he would make an important contribution on Intercommunion Today. He spoke as a member of the committee that had produced the Report and said:

> Confronted by the challenge of the world, the difference between Christians with episcopal and non-episcopal ministries seems almost blasphemously irrelevant. The question has been put like this: 'On the march to Selma, would you or would you not have been prepared to share communion with or take communion from Martin Luther King?' . . . The impatience of so many today at fencing of altars springs, I believe, from a high doctrine of the kingdom, of the priority of involvement in the world . . .

John was in the USA briefly in April 1968 at St Mark's-in-the-Bowery, and at Princeton and Chicago. The *Theology Today* Colloquium on 'Next Steps for Church and Theology' at Princeton, at which he gave a lecture (published in *Christian Freedom in a Permissive Society*), was an opportunity for him to consult many of his fellow theologians. John was glad of every chance to meet, for instance, Charles Davis, Professor of Religious Studies at the University of Alberta, Edmonton (formerly Professor of Dogmatic Theology at Heythrop College and editor of the *Clergy Review*), who on leaving the Roman Catholic priesthood had written *A Question of Conscience*. He gave the lecture which preceded John's. James Pike (resigned Bishop of California) was also taking part. Pike's *A Time for Christian Candour* was in many ways a parallel to *Honest to God*. The Princeton Colloquium was a conference of theological 'stars': Thomas Altizer, Peter Berger, Robert McAfee Brown, Harvey Cox, Paul Lehmann, Martin Marty, Jurgen Moltmann, Schubert Ogden; to name but a few.

For almost the whole of August that year there was the Lambeth Conference. John gladly went down to Canterbury Cathedral for the opening service on 25 July. He was glad also to be in the sub-committee on 'The debate about God', in the section on 'Renewal in faith' – which had Howard Clark (Primate of All Canada, Archbishop and Metropolitan of Rupert's Land) as its chairman; Ian Ramsey (Bishop of Durham) as its vice-chairman; and John Howe (Bishop of St Andrews, Dunkeld and Dunblane, later Secretary General of the Anglican Consultative Council) as its secretary. John was inevitably in considerable demand at the conference, the first after *Honest to God*. He worked closely with Ian Ramsey and John Howe and was well satisfied with what the published Report of his section had to say.

It was as much in the Diocese as in the national councils of the Church that John was looked to for leadership in pastoral reform. The Report *Tomorrow's Parish* – the work of a sub-committee of the Pastoral Re-organization Committee appointed in March 1967 under John's chairmanship – anticipated several of the recommendations of *Faith in the City*, the Report of the Archbishop's Commission on Urban Priority Areas, nearly twenty years later. It was assisted not least by the pioneer work of the diocesan department of Religious Sociology John had caused to be set up under the Revd Leslie Harman. The diocese was forced to face both the historical and contemporary facts and figures, especially of the inner city areas. It was revealed that in Battersea, for instance, the churches of the Church of England in 1965 provided seating capacity for nearly eight thousand people, but less than a thousand made use of them – an average of fifty-nine per parish on a Sunday. Easter communicants in the area were about half the rate for the diocese as a whole, and that – twenty-four per thousand population – needed to be compared with 135 per thousand of Hereford diocese.

John was concerned that the facts and figures should not lead to pessimism but to positive action, to freedom from the burden of maintaining:

> impractically large and often almost empty buildings inherited from previous generations . . . The first need of church buildings is that they should be suitable for the essential functions of the Church . . . This can normally be met by very simple provision. This simplicity need not prevent part of the building from functioning as a place of quiet and retreat. We would indeed regard the creating of opportunities for sanctuary and silence as an essential consideration in the planning and use of church buildings. At the same time, we do not think the use of the Church's plant as a whole – especially large places of assembly

suitable for general community use – should necessarily be restricted to 'religious' functions.

The Report recommended that the diocese should 'aim to provide a suitable and effective Christian presence at three levels: (i) at the neighbourhood level; (ii) at the larger locality or natural grouping; (iii) at the level of the London Borough. Forms of ministry appropriate to these various levels within the pastoral structure must be worked out.'

John's realistic pastoral and intellectual leadership undoubtedly gave to many clergy – particularly in the inner city areas of the diocese, and especially, but not only, the younger clergy – hope, encouragement and a sense of partnership in ministry and mission. But it was not only in the realm of ideas that John was a pastor to his clergy. John Bowden, managing director and editor of SCM Press, tells of a curate in John's area who had contracted leukaemia and had only a few months to live.

> He spent some time with the community at St Julian's, but John was determined that he should have something positive to occupy his mind and enable him to make a contribution in the last months of his life. John hit on the idea of approaching us to see if we could find some copy-editing; which we did, and the curate spent some of his last weeks at SCM Press: a brief episode which none of us who were there will ever forget.

One of the most important parishes strategically in John's episcopal area was that of Woolwich itself – four miles from where he lived. In March 1960 the Bishop of Southwark had inducted Nicolas Stacey to the living as Rector of St Mary's, a grey eighteenth-century church with great square balconies, standing on an eminence overlooking the main road and the industrialized river Thames. Nicolas was a man of many and great gifts: when in 1968 he left Woolwich and the full-time ordained ministry he became successively Deputy Director of Oxfam, then Director of Social Services, first for the London Borough of Ealing and latterly for the County of Kent.

Much of what John's committee wrote about *Tomorrow's Parish* was exemplified in St Mary's, Woolwich. Nicolas found the church with an average Sunday attendance of fifty and left it with an attendance – doubled – of only a hundred. But in the meantime he had transformed the church, enclosing the galleries to create a social centre with a coffee bar and lunch counter, opened a discothèque in the crypt and housed the offices of the local Council of Social Service. He had created an ecumenical team ministry, founded a successful housing association, engaged a professional sociologist, become the first Borough Dean, watched over the birth of the new town of Thamesmead, and proved that the Church cared. Nicolas did not see much more of John than John saw of any other priest working in his part of the diocese, but 'it was great knowing he was around,' Nicolas wrote. 'One knew he would understand and support what we were trying to do. He had no illusions about the problems and intractability of the situation in our kind of parish.'

In December 1964 Nicolas had written an article for *The Observer* colour supplement, called 'A Mission's Failure'. It was a sensation – in the Church – and caused great dissension. The loudest protests came from the bishops of the Church of England. The Archbishop of York, Dr Donald Coggan, accused him of 'rocking the boat'. Nicolas needed no one to tell him what he had accomplished in a social service sense and that some people were deeply moved to see this coming out of a Christian context. His point was clear: that in terms of the Christian longing to bring people to the redemptive gospel and to the fellowship of the faithful he – and his team – had failed to make a significant impression on 90, perhaps even 98 per cent of the population of the parish. The way he had expressed himself in some paragraphs was open to criticism; and four – even eight – years is a short time in the life of a parish. But the heart of what Nicolas was saying could not be denied. In his autobiography *Who Cares* he wrote: 'Amongst the bishops, Robinson alone openly supported me.'

It was towards the end of 1968 that John began to take seriously the feelers which Trinity College, Cambridge was putting out as to whether he would be willing to succeed H. A. Williams as Dean of Chapel. Harry Williams had written to the Master of Trinity, Lord Butler, at the beginning of December and told him John 'might well wish to return for a time to academic work, and that the College would be lucky, to say the least' if they got him; but at first John was not short-listed, partly because he had reacted negatively to earlier feelers. On 3 December Harry, who was not a member of the committee recommending his successor, wrote: 'I am more sorry than I can say, as there is nobody I should like more to succeed me than yourself. It would be a great honour for the College, and you would build this place up theologically and religiously as nobody else could or would.' But Trinity's hesitancy was not final. 'R. A. B.' Butler overcame the initial opposition in his inimitable way, and John's name was brought forward again with three other candidates. On 1 January 1969 the Archbishop of Canterbury wrote to Dr Keith Moffatt, Fellow of Trinity (now Professor of Mathematical Physics, University of Cambridge):

> The Master has encouraged me to write to you about Dr John Robinson, the Bishop of Woolwich, in connection with the coming vacancy in the post of Dean of Chapel.
>
> I have no doubt that your Committee will feel that Dr Robinson is a somewhat controversial figure. Having seen a good deal of him and watched his development, I believe that he could do very well in the post of Dean of Chapel at Trinity if the opportunity came to him. He is an adventurous thinker and went through a phase of being somewhat confusing in his efforts to grapple with the difficulties of the people right outside the Christian fold. I believe that he has been increasingly finding a grasp of things which is far more positive than negative and that this would be very apparent in his influence on the young men. He has immense pastoral sense but at the same time he is eager for quietness, study and the chance for thought and scholarly writing. I believe that with the assistance of two younger Chaplains (which is, I believe, your arrangement) he would give real pastoral leadership and exert a strong Christian influence while conserving himself for study and writing of a scholarly kind.
>
> I hope that this letter may be of service to your Committee.
>
> Yours sincerely,
Michael Cantuar.

On 6 January Professor Dennis Nineham, Regius Professor of Divinity, Cambridge, wrote to Dr Moffat a letter which also undoubtedly had much influence upon the committee responsible for making a recommendation

> Thank you very much for your letter about possible new Deans; it so happens that I know reasonably well all four of the people you mention and I am perfectly willing in a confidential letter to say what I can about them.
>
> Of the four I should myself unhesitatingly put John Robinson first. He is a man of very considerable academic distinction indeed; I remember how the late John Baillie, a good and experienced judge, once said that John Robinson's PhD was the best he had ever been asked to examine. It

is worth adding that his recently granted DD here was given almost entirely on the basis of detailed works on technical New Testament scholarship which were, as usual, submitted for judgement by outside experts. The fame – or notoriety – brought upon him by *Honest to God* was, I know, a great surprise to him, and I don't think it should be held against him if a popular paperback intended simply to set people thinking has been found, on minute examination by experts in philosophical theology, to be in some ways muddled and unoriginal. As subsequent work has shown, John Robinson has given further thought to the questions, so far as he could in the midst of his work as a bishop, and he is now anxious to get a post which would enable him to follow up his popular books with further thinking and more scholarly publication on the same issues. It was with that in mind that he became a candidate for, and was appointed to, the Hulsean Lectureship. His work at Woolwich has shown that he has considerable capabilities as an organiser and administrator, and what is perhaps less well known is that he is also an extremely good and devoted pastor. To that the Bishop of Southwark and many of the clergy in the Southwark diocese would testify, and so would the large number of students whom he helped when he was Dean of Clare. It may also be worth saying that his imaginative re-ordering of the services in Clare chapel at a time before liturgical reform became so fashionable was a very thoughtful and moderate venture which had a good deal of influence.

While he is not perhaps as easy socially as some people, he has become much more so during his period at Woolwich and I have no doubt that the Fellows of Trinity would find him an amiable and co-operative colleague, willing to take his fair share of College duties, and at the same time a person they could not fail to respect for his integrity and intellectual abilities. He can of course be an outspoken critic of various customs and institutions at times, but I have never seen any evidence of his being a seeker of publicity for its own sake, or one who would be likely or willing to bring undesirable notoriety on any institution to which he belonged. On all grounds I should see him as a very worthy successor to Harry Williams.

Finally on 7 January 1969 the Bishop of Southwark wrote to Dr Moffat:

Thank you for your letter. Perhaps the most helpful course would be for me to make a number of points in separate paragraphs.

1   Dr Robinson told me many years ago that he thought his tenure of Office as Bishop of Woolwich should not exceed ten years. He completes the ten years in September 1969.

2   Dr Robinson has indicated on several occasions that he wants to

devote the next period in his life to academic studies. He wants time to think, read and write. I cannot speak too highly of his work as a pastoral bishop, and of his readiness to accept the burdens of administration and episcopal chores, but I realise that his present position gives him insufficient time to pursue his interests as a New Testament scholar.

3   Matters were brought to a head a few weeks ago when Dr Robinson suggested to me that he might have sabbatical leave for twelve months from 1969 (midsummer) to June 1970. I told him that while in ordinary circumstances I should readily agree, I could not do so on account of the impending retirement, on account of age, of my other suffragan, the Bishop of Kingston. It would cripple the Diocese if both suffragans were to be absent from their duties in 1970. If Dr Robinson stays he must remain at his post until the new Bishop of Kingston has established himself – circ. June 1971.

4   The upshot of this conversation was a discussion with the Archbishop of Canterbury. This discussion made clear that the Archbishop agreed with Robinson that he should return to a university. He appreciated Robinson's pastoral abilities, but he felt that he should spend less time on such routine matters as boards of finance, pastoral re-organisation, and the re-building of vicarages and more time on study, writing and teaching.

5   Although I am reluctant to accept the Archbishop's advice, I am sure I ought to do so. Robinson was my curate in Bristol, we saw much of one another when I was Vicar of Great St Mary's, he has been my fellow bishop for nearly ten years. It will not be easy for me to part with such a colleague. But, taking the larger view and setting aside personal considerations, I know I must encourage him to go. His present job does not give him sufficient opportunities to develop his scholarly abilities.

6   If Dr Robinson goes to Trinity, the college will have both a scholar and a pastor. Although he will rejoice in the freedom to read, teach and write, he will not neglect his responsibilities as Dean.

7   I know Dr Robinson is a controversial figure. And he is not afraid to make his views known if circumstances seem to demand it. But he much hopes that for the next years he may find himself in a position which does not lend itself to controversy and which will enable him to devote himself to his academic pursuits.

8   Efforts have been made to secure Robinson for university posts in America. In some ways these are attractive because there are less 'chores' than here. But I think that he agrees with me that he should, if possible, remain in this country. That is a reason why I hope he will be considered favourably by your committee. Moreover I doubt whether he would be happy in America for there would be little scope for his pastoral

interests as a priest. To appreciate Robinson one always has to remember that in addition to his scholarship he has a deep concern for persons.

I hope these observations may be of some help to the committee. Do not hesitate to write again if you have particular questions to ask.

Your sincerely,
Mervyn Stockwood.

On 22 January 1969 John Burnaby (who had been Harry Williams' predecessor as Dean of Chapel as well as Regius Professor of Divinity) wrote to John: 'I should like you to know how warmly I should welcome your return to Cambridge and to Trinity, and how sincerely I hope that you may have a proposal from the College you would be able to accept.' Within hours the proposal came.

John was able to accept immediately. He wrote in reply to the many letters of congratulation he received:

What tipped the balance in my deciding to accept was that two Cambridge appointments simultaneously came my way which were clearly going to require a lot of preparation. The first was the Hulsean Lectureship for 1969–70. I had put in for this to bring to a head the intention I have had for the past five years of doing something further on Christology. The other is a course of four University sermons in the Spring of 1971 which are also intended for publication. (This is a new way of trying to make something of the University sermon and the Archbishop of Canterbury is giving the first series in 1970.)

It was these invitations that made me take seriously the feelers from Trinity. But I had for some time been aware that now that my disc (after an operation which had been about 80% successful) was no longer going to lay me flat(!) I must find some other opportunity for deeper reflection – which did not at the same time remove the stimulus of practical engagement which I need if I am to produce anything . . . The base at Trinity will provide great opportunities. And if I am ever going to do any academic work again, it is clear that it must be at this stage before too many more brain-cells rot!

Mervyn wrote on 24 January:

My dear John
As I told you on the telephone I have made my own grave! I hate the idea of losing you, but I am cheered by the conviction that the decision is right. You have so much to contribute to the life of the Church and I know that, at this juncture, it can best be done in Cambridge rather than

in Woolwich. You must be free to grapple with the deep theological problems on which everything in the last resort, depends.

You have always been such a wonderful friend and colleague and my life in Southwark would have been intolerable without you . . .

I cannot say more now. But I felt I must let you know as you prepare to leave how deeply grateful I am for all you have meant to the diocese and to me.

> My prayers for your future
> and my love as always.
> Mervyn.

The Archbishop of Canterbury wrote on 28 January:

My dear John

I am very happy and thankful that the Trinity post has fallen to you, and you have all my good wishes for your tasks and opportunities there. At the same time I feel full of thankfulness for your 'Woolwich' time – in what you have given to so many, both clergy and others in your shepherding of them so lovingly, in what you have given to us in the central discussions of our church, and in your pioneering in the theological tasks before us.

I reproach myself with having been rather 'slow' in understanding, but I have found myself increasingly learning from you and increasingly being grateful.

I enclose my latest little – very little book – as a tiny mark of love and thankfulness.

My wife wants to join me in very best wishes to you both.

> Yours affectionately
> Michael Cantuar.

Harry Williams wrote on 31 January: 'I have found that the opposition which arose when the suggestion was first made has completely disappeared, and all the fellows concerned are extremely enthusiastic at the prospect of your arrival and realise how lucky we are to get you.'

The Bishop of Southwark – understandably – lost no time in approaching a successor to John. On the Sunday evening of 26 January John, Mervyn and David Sheppard (then Warden and Chaplain of the Mayflower Family Centre in Canning Town; Bishop of Woolwich 1969–75; and now Bishop of Liverpool) met together for a first exploration of possibilities.

There were several more months in which John and Ruth could say their farewells to Southwark, and time for John to pay one more visit to the USA. He had committed himself to a day with the clergy of the diocese of Chicago on 17 June, as part of the Chicago-Southwark exchange, and to lecturing at the Chicago Summer Biblical Institute with Father Gregory Baum and Rosemary Reuther. Hugh Hefner (whom John had first met in 1966 writing an article on 'The Responsibility of Freedom' for *Playboy*) endeavoured to bring creative personalities together as his house-guests and wanted John to meet Jesse Jackson (later the black USA presidential candidate). The morning after their meeting Jesse took John to Operation Breadbasket, based on Jesse's black Baptist Church on the South Side of Chicago. In the 'operation' food and other assistance was given to poor black families and there was a never-to-be-forgotten service with preaching by Jesse, which gave those who took part an undeniable sense that though they were poor they were 'somebody'.

John then flew West to conduct two seminars at Esalen Institute, on 'Theological Reflection on the Human Potential' and 'The Human Potential: Does Christ get in the way?' Esalen seemed to be moving more in the direction of the psycho-physical. There was always a sense in which John seemed invulnerable at the emotional, as distinct from the feeling level – he was not a man *without* feelings but they were rarely expressed strongly on the surface. Because he was the least neurotic of men he was able to respond quite naturally – and ingenuously – to therapies aimed at the expansion of 'body consciousness', and could quite happily take part in them. In San Francisco he was glad to see something of Kilmer Myers (Jim Pike's successor as Bishop of California), and to see something more of Alan Watts, before ending his last visit to the USA as Bishop of Woolwich.

The decade at Southwark had, of course, seen great changes in the family and the children. Stephen had just had his twenty-first birthday in February 1969. He had left Marlborough with prizes in Classics and Chinese. In the summer of 1969 he finished his second year at Clare, Cambridge with a 'First' in Part 1 Classics, and was switching to Mathematics. He was too like his father to find relationships with him easy. He had once asked John: 'What do you do with feelings you don't know what to do with?' 'I don't have them,' John had replied. By the time John and Ruth decided to return to Cambridge Stephen had virtually flown the nest.

So too – but to a lesser extent – had Catherine. She was about to begin her final year reading English at Bristol. She, like Stephen, had known from an early age that she had to be as grown up as possible if she was to live up to her father's vision of her and for her. When she was only thirteen he had bought her a sophisticated-looking eiderdown – maroon with thin gold stripes – which, he said, 'you'll have for your room when you go to University.' Sometimes she felt proud of what was expected of her; sometimes it was a pressure and an anxiety; sometimes it was just part of the home life she shared. At the supper table she often had to listen to and even take part in intense discussions about the central issues of life: morality, freedom, theology, politics, relationships with each other and with God; with visitors from all over the world. Catherine had few school friends: 'at school a barrier existed because I was a bishop's daughter and often conversation fizzled out – about boy-friends and parties – when I was in the room'. One day she ventured to describe to her father the anxiety of trying to be grown up. Without the slightest self-consciousness he said: 'I have always thought of childhood as a necessary evil one has to go through before one really starts living.' It was of course a sad remark – sad that anyone should miss so much of life and of nature: but sad too that the person who made it seemed not to perceive its sadness.

Believing what he did about childhood, John needed no great pressure to escape to his study, but of course that pressure was exactly what he had, in abundance. All the children remember creeping quietly past the study door so as not to disturb their father, and hearing the constant drone of his voice as he dictated letters or talked on the telephone. ('I'm just finishing the last sentence' was one of the family jokes.) None of them would have thought of going into the study if they were upset or miserable. To Catherine 'one of the unwritten rules was that you don't get upset; or if you do, you find the quickest, most logical way of altering circumstances so that there's nothing to be upset about'. She would say she inherited from her father an inability to express anger. 'I learnt how to side-step feelings so that they glanced off me, barely acknowledged.'

Not only John's timetable but the very nature of his work created great difficulties in terms of family life. On Sundays the Robinsons had begun at Southwark by trying to go together wherever John went. But confirmation at Parish Communion was beginning to be the norm, and weekly confirmations at a different church was no family fare for four children. So the children and Ruth went to church locally. To begin with they had to go with Ruth whether they wanted to or not, as she could not leave them on their own; but in later years they made their own decisions, and if Ruth wanted to go with John she did. John tried to keep Saturday as his day off, when he could put diocesan affairs on one side; but that was not always possible. And a day off from diocesan affairs was not necessarily a day off from his own writing and reading, indeed he saw it as an opportunity for that. It was this which made John and Ruth strive to make something special of Saturday evenings. They had a family supper which they tried to turn into a sort of *agape*, wanting to share with the children the fact that communion in church involved relationships outside. They would open a bottle of wine and after a short grace share bread together. The children – most of them, most of the time – went along with it, probably for their parents' sake – though for Catherine it really was both the beginning of what took place the next day in church and a time of closeness with her father. All the children were glad to have their father's whole-hearted and relatively relaxed attention once in the week.

The decade at Manor Way was of course that of the unsettling Sixties. Most parents of teenagers – and most teenagers – had their difficulties. To read *Seventeen Come Sunday*, written in the first instance for Catherine by her mother (and 'Honest to the Children', in *The Honest to God Debate*, also written by Ruth) is to be made aware that the Robinson children had a mother who certainly did not think of childhood as 'a necessary evil'.

Buffy Robinson was seventeen and still at home when the news came of the move back to Cambridge. And Buffy was different. No one could call her unfeeling or imagine her concealing her feelings. Her description of the Robinson's Saturday *agape* is very much her account!

> Mummy and Daddy had some crazy idea that the family should all be together for a special family supper each Saturday night. Even if we had been invited to a friend's house we were not allowed to miss, neither could we have a friend round to the meal. I hated them all – anyway at this time! – and we had enormous rows over this Saturday supper. We had to have prayers and candles, and this is what triggered the violent rebellion I had against church and ceremony in general around this time. I reckoned the time had come to *do* something. One Sunday I refused to get out of bed. I knew they couldn't make me get up and go to church, and I absolutely wouldn't budge. After several weeks of this outright rebellion Mummy gave in and said that she would have to stay at home with me. Soon after that the others stayed at home too without any fuss; and from then on Daddy went to church by himself.

When John and Ruth – and Judith – moved to Cambridge Buffy's rebellion would take the form of leaving home and getting a job. She could have gone to school in Cambridge and done her A levels in a year, but she was convinced she was an academic failure. In time she would prove herself to be an artist in batik of very considerable distinction; but that was as yet 'the distant scene'.

Judith was fifteen with her O levels a year ahead, and therefore would become virtually an only child in the flat in Cambridge. Either because she was too young to be affected or was by nature more placid, events at Southwark which left a mark on the other children washed over her. She would maintain that she had a perfectly normal childhood; but she would acknowledge that seeking – and enjoying – father's approval was as important to her as it was to the others, and that she held him 'in awe'. She knew well, for instance, that when she got home from the Blackheath library he would ask what books she had chosen, and that it was important for her to avoid Enid Blyton and other 'mindless drivel', much as she wanted to read it; otherwise there would be the slightly raised eyebrow, a gentle scoff, or worse – much worse – the Robinson laugh. All the children disliked the laugh that could greet their solecisms, which although they would be told by their father time and again, he was 'not laughing at but laughing with', did not feel like that at the receiving end.

Judith remembers a game of bridge in which her father attempted to teach her to play. It ended with a sharp intake of breath and an 'Oh, Judith!' uttered with infinite dismay. That did it – for life!

There was another person who bore the marks of the Southwark years, whose importance in John's life can hardly be exaggerated. On 29 December 1969 John's mother was to celebrate her ninetieth birthday. Few sons with such heavy responsibilities as John can have been more diligent in the care of their mother than he was. Mercifully Blackheath and Canterbury were within easy access of one another. To read John's mother's letters to her son leaves no doubt what he meant to her:

My dear John
I do just want to send a message of thanks and say what a help and cheer our little talk on Mon: morning has been to me. I have felt more and more as time goes on what a wonderful sense of security it brings me that I have you to turn to. It is always this thought that comes to me when things seem to get beyond me: 'There is always John'! And you have never

failed me! Your Father's wise judgment and deep understanding and his *wider* view than that of anyone I have known, have given me such guidance and inspiration, and I feel as though he were living again in you, and you were carrying forward the great things he so reverenced – also the helps and support he gave, and still gives, to me.

Thank you for all you said and put so clearly the other day. You did indeed put things in their right perspective for me and I shall not forget it – neither your counsel to be 'honest with yourself', which I shall try hard to follow. It is everything to know that I have your prayers and to feel as I do the same trust in your judgment and wise understanding as I did in your Father's. I do see so much of him both in you and Edward.

It is good to be reminded to look again to the Prayer Book for a right view of things. Ps. 31:9 always delights me as summing up so beautifully what we have to give thanks for in our 'C. of E.', and the vision your Father gave us of it: 'Thou hast set my feet in a large room.'

Always your grateful and
loving Mother.

Within a few weeks of her ninetieth birthday John's mother would write:

My dear John
Just a little personal message for you I so want to send. That very wonderful letter you showed me telling what *Honest to God* had meant to that reader seemed to come to me that it was for me to read the book again – not having I think done so since that first overwhelming storm broke out and raged so devastatingly. Such terrible things said and written from all sides – quite impossible to know what to think or hold on to – except what I knew of *you*. And this has been everything to me in the years since and though indeed often things haven't been easy and I have often felt very insecure. Since getting home I have read all through the book again and find *all* was there all the time! – and *more*, in the light of what has been given me since. You have again brought me *back* and *on* to the right lines. All this has been rather difficult going for my 'Early Vic:' brain! – and that now increasingly dim! I just want to send this message of my very loving thanks . . .

Mother.

There was something of Monica's prayer for St Augustine in the love of his mother for John, set always within the context of her disciplined and daily prayer for him. Ruth knew she had a mother-in-law (almost an extra mother) and the children knew that they had a grandmother, of quite outstanding quality – not least through her regular visits to Blackheath and theirs to Canterbury.

It was after John and Ruth and the family moved to Cambridge on 8 September that they returned to Southwark for John's last day as Bishop of Woolwich: 28 September 1969, the eve of Michaelmas. In the morning he ordained new deacons and priests in Woolwich Parish Church. In the evening there was an unforgettable farewell party at the Church of the Ascension, Blackheath – where the previous November John had instituted Paul Oestreicher (now Canon Residentiary and Director of the International Ministry of Coventry Cathedral) to a notable ministry that was local, national and often international.

In 1962 Cecil Day-Lewis, Poet Laureate, had published *Requiem for the Living*, written for music but, in the words of the poet, 'waiting a composer'. John had persuaded Donald Swann to take up the challenge, and the *Requiem* was performed for the first time at the farewell celebration. In words and music it was a worthy celebration – with Donald Swann playing the piano and Jill Balcon – Day-Lewis's wife – as the speaker. Sydney Carter also recited some of his own poetry. Edward Petherbridge of the National Theatre read 'Farewell' from *The Prophet* by Kahlil Gibran (which John had just come across in San Francisco):

> Farewell to you and the youth I have spent with you,
> It was but yesterday we met in a dream.
> You have sung to me in my aloneness, and I of your longings have
>   built a tower in the sky.
> But now our sleep has fled and our dream is over, and it
>   is no longer dawn.
> The noon tide is upon us and our half waking has turned to fuller
>   day, and we must part.
> If in the twilight of memory we should meet once more, we
>   shall speak again together, and you shall sing to me a deeper song.
> And if our hands should meet in another dream we shall build
>   another tower in the sky.

At the end of John's ten years as Bishop of Woolwich the question remained in some people's minds: 'Should he *ever* have been a bishop?' That question went on being asked, particularly in academic circles. One thing is certain: it was rarely asked in Southwark. The answer was obvious. Some people – again outside Southwark – assumed he was able to be a bishop only to like-minded radicals. Again in Southwark there was, and is, no doubt what the opinion of the clergy and laity alike would be – with very few exceptions. Yet since John was shy and reserved, and because ideas meant so much to him, it is important to establish beyond all doubt what it meant to men and women in Southwark to have him as their bishop. Again the representative few must stand for the many.

Michael Mayne was Domestic Chaplain to the Bishop of Southwark 1959–65; afterwards Vicar of Great St Mary's, Cambridge; and is now Dean of Westminster:

My first memory of John is from the early 1950s, when I was an undergraduate and used to attend his lectures on New Testament Ethics. I found them stimulating and thought-provoking. I once went to his rooms at Clare to borrow a book. I found him kind but strangely awkward and ill at ease.

I met him again in 1959, when Mervyn invited him to Southwark. It was just before John's Consecration. Ruth was desperately ill. With Mervyn I visited Ruth in the Atkinson Morley Hospital in Wimbledon, and began to see and admire the integrity and courage of both Ruth and John, and understand the wisdom of Mervyn's battle to get John as his Suffragan.

I saw a good deal of John over the years 1959–65, and came to understand his immense contribution to a diocese which became a byword for new and radical thinking and excited and appalled the Church of England in equal measure.

As his clergy came to know John they discovered a scholar whose awkward shyness hid a man of immense natural kindness and pastoral ability. Those who went to him for advice or counsel, or who needed help, found in him someone who had great gifts of listening and caring – and total integrity. I often saw him when he was tired and overworked, but I never knew him to act 'out of character'. He was I think incapable of a betrayal of trust. You knew instinctively that whatever you told him was safe.

There were innumerable acts of imaginative kindness to which his clergy could bear witness. One personal example: when we got married and moved to a parish, he must have known we had very little money, and his wedding present was a fortnight's honeymoon in a villa on an Italian island – something which otherwise would have been quite beyond us.

Despite John's pastoral gifts, and despite the fact that at the time he wrote: 'I cannot imagine a job that I should more enjoy being in', he knew by 1964 that the administrative demands of his office and his gifts as a writer and scholar were tearing him in half. The response to the publication of *Honest to God* had shown him to be capable of touching a nerve right across 'the religious frontier'. He alone could seize and build on this response and he longed to do what he could do best – *write*. At the same time I believe he saw very clearly that what he was struggling to verbalise on behalf of so many had to be incarnated and come out of the 'nitty-gritty' of the problems of the Church in South London. In the end perhaps his decision to return to Cambridge was inevitable, but I think he returned there a very different man.

So far as Southwark is concerned, my estimate is that its greatest contribution to him was the stimulation it gave him to write *Honest to God*, and his greatest contribution to the Diocese (and perhaps to the Church of England) was the imaginative and prophetic Southwark Ordination Course, of which (with Mervyn's encouragement) he was the architect.

Frank Colquhoun gave up being Vicar of Wallington in Southwark to become Canon Residentiary of Southwark Cathedral and Vice-Principal, later Principal, of the Southwark Ordination Course which he served from 1961 to 1973. He was Canon Residentiary of Norwich Cathedral 1973–8:

The better I got to know John the more I came to respect him. I confess I did not always share his theological views, and I don't think he expected me to. But that made no difference to our friendship. Increasingly I felt a real kinship with him in the things of God. Like most Christian scholars I have known, he was a very humble, self-effacing man – and utterly sincere. Of course he made his mistakes (as I thought), but never for a moment did I doubt his complete integrity.

When the storm of controversy broke out on the publication of *Honest to God* – a book which admittedly left me rather cold! – my fellow Evangelicals sometimes asked me how I managed to work alongside a man of such unorthodox and 'unsound' views. My answer was two-fold. First, that the man himself was bigger than his religious opinions, and that though his head might sometimes be in the clouds, his heart was certainly in the right place. Secondly, that whatever differences there might have been between us, we had one thing in common: a profound love and reverence for the scriptures.

To me, this was the most significant feature of his life and ministry. Like Martin Luther, his conscience was captive to the Word of God.

He was a most attractive character. I shall always remember him with affection; not as a controversial figure, but as he was – a man of devout faith, a dedicated servant of Christ.

Christopher Byers has served all his ministry in Southwark. Ordained to a curacy in Bermondsey in 1960, he was Rector of Mottingham 1966–86 and is now Team Rector of Thamesmead:

> I remember people warning me that my new bishop would be a dry and aloof academic from Cambridge from whom I would not receive much support or sympathy. Nothing could have been further from the truth. From the very first meeting I knew instinctively that in him I had a friend and pastor. He was the one man who through the years was truly my bishop.
>
> I remember him asking to see me to find out how I was surviving amid the factories, flats and youth clubs that abounded in the Bermondsey of those days. He conducted the conversation while lying flat on his back with a slipped disc. He mentioned in passing that this period of physical inactivity had given him the chance to finish a book. Later I remember reading the galley-proof of *Honest to God* while sitting in the churchyard of Bermondsey Church, unsuspecting of what was to follow. All of us who knew and worked with John were aware of the 'before' and the 'after' surrounding the publication, and the cost to him.
>
> I recall one cold Sunday morning after Christmas when the church heating had broken down and I was preaching to a congregation huddled in the church hall. Quite unannounced, John was sitting there three rows back. To some young clergy that could have been an unnerving sight, but to us on that morning it meant only support and encouragement.
>
> I always knew I could be myself with him and I felt he knew what I was about and where I stood theologically. Through the years he would often ask: 'Where are you now and what is motivating your work and your study?' He knew how important it was for his clergy to believe in what they were doing and saying week by week. He taught me what it means to be radical: that it has something to do with being sure of where faith is rooted and grounded within experience, so that you are free to question everything and not to fear truth or reality.

Gordon Davies was Canon Residentiary of Southwark Cathedral and Diocesan Missioner 1955–72; and Archdeacon of Lewisham until 1985:

> John and Mervyn were a duo of the same creative mould, and under their combined leadership the Diocese experienced one of the most construc-tive periods of its life. They were turbulent days, and I received many letters expressing great unease from those who were unsettled by what was being written and done. But I knew from personal contact with John that he had the heart of the Gospel in him and the disturbance for me was

a challenge to be faced, not a reason for going elsewhere. What John did was to nudge me carefully but clearly into the acceptance of new ways of working, and several areas of diocesan life which were earlier part of my brief as Missioner were put by John under new management.

For instance: I introduced into the diocese seminars on Clinical Theology and Pastoral Counselling; working in close liaison with Frank Lake, the work developed. It was John, however, who perceived that this piece of work was too important to be left solely to me with my other commitments. He took the initiative of appointing a specialist to be full-time in promoting this field of ministry. I started courses for churchwardens and PCC members and was in on lay training generally. John saw the need for greater specialisation. Today, both departments are flourishing; and this must redound to John's credit, as they are the result of his drive and imagination.

I number myself among those who feel greatly indebted to him. His life and work were inspirational to the very end.

Peter Naylor was ordained to a curacy at St Michael's, Beddington, Surrey in 1961; and was Vicar of St Anne's, Lambeth 1964–77; he is now Vicar of St Paul's, Nork, Banstead, Surrey:

Of our five children, Ruth was the frailest. She was critically ill during my time at Beddington and had to be a patient in Queen Mary's Hospital, Carshalton. One evening I was chastised by the Ward Sister. I had not told her that a Bishop would be visiting her ward! I professed ignorance, only to learn that John had paid a visit earlier that day, asked to see Ruth Naylor, and prayed by her cot.

The week before I was instituted as Vicar of St Anne's, South Lambeth, I discovered on my prayer desk a paper on which was written: 'Prayers were said here today for you, Patricia and the children, and for your work in South Lambeth. John.'

The note had been deliberately obscured beneath the kind of books and papers usually found on such a desk.

Martin Coombs was ordained in 1961 to a curacy at St John-the-Divine, Kennington; after being Chaplain of Emmanuel College, Cambridge he was Domestic Chaplain to the Bishop of Southwark 1968–70; he is now Vicar of Pershore and an Honorary Canon of Worcester Cathedral:

Early in 1963, word was getting round the Diocese that John had written a book which was going to cause a great public stir. In March, someone lent me a review copy. I went to bed early one night and could not put it down before I had finished it. This book was certainly going to keep lots more people awake!

Two weeks after the publication of *Honest to God* I went to a Confirmation taken by John at St George's, Camberwell, with four candidates from our church. Someone said to me later, 'If you want to understand John, you have to see him in cope and mitre taking a Confirmation'; and it was sobering to see the man who had questioned traditional orthodoxies acting in a traditional orthodox manner! The sermon made an impression on me, as it was on a theme not often heard at my own church, or anywhere else at that time, I imagine: the new humanity brought about by Jesus. I remember seeing Ruth for the first time at that service, kneeling at the altar rails for Communion with two of her daughters leaning on her on either side. Afterwards I introduced one of our candidates to John. He was a West Indian called George Walters, who could look at someone's feet and make him a pair of shoes that perfectly fitted – as he had done for me and which I was wearing. I pointed them out to John and he congratulated George warmly on his shoe-making. How good it was to have such a humane person for one's Bishop! George was equally pleased and said he would make him a pair, but John modestly discouraged him and he never did.

Later, I returned to my own parish to meet one of the Sisters who lived in a house near the Church. 'What a wonderful sermon!' I said enthusiastically. 'Yes,' she replied, her eyes flashing angrily, 'but did you notice he did not mention God once?' I had *not* actually noticed this, as the whole sermon had seemed to me in one way to be about God. Many Anglo-Catholics as well as others were very furious with him at this time!

For my third-year project in the ministry I chose the subject of 'Existentialism'. Canon Stanley Evans gave me John as my tutor. From the autumn of 1963 I used to go down to Blackheath with another curate who had chosen the same subject. John's study was filled with responses to *Honest to God*. I remember on one occasion seeing a pile of letters several feet high!

My project was slimmed down to one of the novels of Iris Murdoch, whose work I was then reading with enthusiasm. John showed great interest in my essay, and I used to go and talk to him about her work. But as he himself said, he knew very little about her and was not able to discuss her works with me very closely. This rather confirmed my view that he was not a very literary person. John was however a great help to me by listening to my ramblings, and getting Ruth to as well (he said she knew far more about novels than he did, which was true).

For my project, John arranged for me to meet Iris Murdoch, and sent her a letter asking her to contact me, which she did. When I met her, we spent some time discussing *Honest to God* as well as her novels.

In 1968 I returned to South London to be Mervyn Stockwood's chaplain. John used to come to staff meetings and sit chewing the end of his spectacles in a ruminative way, and burst into occasional chuckles. By this time he had a firm grasp of all the parishes and their problems in the Southwark Diocese, and I was always surprised, in the light of *Honest to God* and his reputation, how bound up he was with the intricacies of church and parish life. In the large pile of papers he used to have on his lap, he always managed to produce the right one at the right moment. Mervyn was very fond of John, but in some ways he still treated him as his curate; but John was always delightfully good humoured, and lightened the mood of many a staff meeting.

John Chater was an undergraduate at Queens' College, Cambridge when John was Dean of Clare. He was Vicar of St Anne's, Bermondsey 1960–4. He is now Dean of Battle.

In 1960 I joined a group ministry in Bermondsey. It was late August, and Elizabeth and I have a vivid memory of John and Ruth arriving on our door-step unexpectedly, to see how we were settling in. They had come with fruit and vegetables from their Blackheath garden when they were setting off on their summer holiday. It was typical of the care and interest we were given during our four years in South London.

Whatever the shortcomings of 'South Bank religion' in the 1960s, there was a burning concern to communicate the Christian faith, somehow or other, to ordinary, non-church people. I always felt that the mainspring of John's theology was a personal commitment to mission. He wanted more people to come to faith in God in Christ.

I remember reading *Honest to God* in 1963 and being irritated by Chapter 2: 'The End of Theism'. To my somewhat simplistic, biblical, Evangelical faith, it seemed not only that 'our image of God must go', but that God himself had gone. Unsuspected by me, Chapter 2 had planted a time-bomb deep in my subconscious.

Seven years later, after five years as University Chaplain at York, I read David Edwards' *Religion and Change*. It crystallized for me many of the theological issues which had been part of the ferment of the 1960s. Almost overnight I found myself in the maelstrom of a crisis of faith. By then I was the incumbent of a Bristol housing estate – which had enough problems of its own without having to cope with a vicar who had lost his faith. In the midst of my struggle I sought John's help in Cambridge. I remember he claimed to be 'bilingual'. He could, he said, still use traditional categories of theology or the new 'models'. I was at the stage

Evening Standard

WEST END FINAL

42.416 THURSDAY, OCTOBER 27, 1960 ●●2½d.

'This book is not depraving'

CHRISTIANS SHOULD READ LADY C–Bishop

'Essentially something sacred'

Evening Standard Reporter

The Bishop of Woolwich, the Right Rev. John Robinson, 41-year-old father of a son and three daughters, stepped into the witness-box at the Old Bailey this afternoon and spoke in defence of Lady Chatterley.

Wearing a grey suit with his pectoral cross hanging round his neck against the purple cloth of his office, he said that D. H. Lawrence's book was "neither in intention nor effect depraving".

He said it was clear that Lawrence, who wrote Lady Chatterley's Lover more than 30 years ago, was trying to

Bank rate cut

Evening Standard Reporter

Bank rate—key to all interest rates—is DOWN. The Bank of England today announced a ½ per cent cut to 5½ per cent. Special deposits stay unchanged.

This is the first reduction in Bank rate since November, 1958, and the first greenlight move since the credit squeeze began last April.

It does not come as a surprise to the City. Indica-

It's an odd thing, but now one *knows* that it's profoundly moral and packed with spiritual significance a lot of the old world charm seems to have gone.'

Jury reach historic decision after 3 hours

THE INNOCENCE OF LADY CHATTERLEY

She's cleared after 6-day trial

APPLAUSE AT OLD BAILEY

Lady Chatterley obscene. S Bailey decided being out for

There was from the back of the jury anno cried loudly:

'NOW WE CAN GO AHEAD' SAYS PENGUIN CHIEF

Evening Standard Reporter

Sir Allen Lane, head of Penguin Books, ran from the Old Bailey this afternoon

12s. 6d.

Easter egg for

NEWS of the WORLD

AND EMPIRE NEWS

LATE LONDON EDITION

SUNDAY, NOVEMBER 6, 1960

No. 6.104 PRICE 4d.

EKCO HIGH-FIDELITY picture TV

LADY C CAUSES UPROAR IN CHURCH

Exclusive The Shah takes his wife home

From Our Own Correspondent

TEHERAN, Saturday.

Primate calls Bishop 'stumbling block'

REMARKS BY THE ARCHBISHOP OF CANTERBURY YESTERDAY ABOUT THE "LADY CHATTERLEY'S" ...FIED AN UPROAR AT THE OLD BAILEY HAVE PUBLICLY REBUKED ONE OF HIS BISHOPS WHO ...IDENCE.

His Grace does not approve

Headlines greeted the trial of D. H. Lawrence's *Lady Chatterley's Lover*. Cartoonists Osbert Lancaster and Trog added their comments.

John in the garden of 17 Manor Way,
Blackheath, at the time of *Honest to God*

The Bishop of Woolwich continues his day
to day ministry

The first edition of *Honest to God*, the
book that became a world-wide best seller

when the old had gone dead on me and the new meant nothing real. I still have the copy of *Exploration into God* which he wrote in and gave me at the time.

For me it had to become a true exploration. My wife and I with our four young children set off together into the unknown. I resigned my benefice with no job in sight. We were able to buy a small house, and, soon after, I landed an administrative job in the University of Bristol. For the next seven years I read no theology; spiritually I lay fallow. And when I came to myself, I had discovered a new wholeness and was able to re-enter a full-time parochial ministry with a new sense of freedom, personal and theological.

I last saw John at a clergy study day in Wells in the spring of 1983. I shall always be thankful to have known him as my bishop, teacher and friend.

Francis Longworth-Dames served in Southwark for nearly forty years. He was Vicar and Rural Dean of Lewisham and is an Honorary Canon:

I have always admired John, and supported him when the wave of bitter criticism came after *Honest to God.*

I was glad when we had him for Confirmations. He was so calm, no fuss at all, so that the slightly overwrought vicar, anxious over many things, was reassured, and knew that everything would be all right. The act of Confirmation, and indeed anything else which he did in the service, was never hurried.

On each occasion that I 'phoned, or went to him for advice, he gave me what I needed. I remember noticing that he allowed me to 'hear' his thinking as he considered this or that possible course of action; he didn't protect himself by laying down the law or by referring to higher authority.

I could be completely open with him. For instance, when I was considering I should move on from Lewisham, I was able to bring out all my mixture of motives. I was grateful for his advice then, including his remark that even if I had made a mistaken decision that wasn't the end! – implying that God would still be there helping and using me!

I remember at one of the meetings for Rural Deans in Bishop's House, when I was at Lewisham, John brought up the relationship between vicars and their curates, saying that this was often far from good – vicars often not discussing matters with them and giving them the opportunity to give their views etc. Some of the RDs thought this was nonsense, and that the curates were quite happy without all that – but, of course, John was absolutely right.

I think it was the depth of his faith which struck me most. That must have been one of the reasons why I was not knocked off balance by the

Honest to God crisis. I trusted him; I trusted his faith; and his preaching never failed to stir me.

Gerald Hudson first met John when they were theological students together at Cambridge. He ended his ministry in Southwark with nine years as Principal of the Southwark Ordination Course before spending four years as Rector of St Mary-le-Bow, Cheapside, in the City of London. He is an Honorary Canon of Southwark.

I first met John in 1942, at Westcott House, Cambridge. He was shy and a bit withdrawn, though respected for his scholarship. He seemed set for an academic life.

I had already been Vicar of St Laurence, Catford for eight years when John and Ruth came to Woolwich and had altogether spent sixteen years in the Diocese. I was amazed how greatly he had changed. Ruth had been very good for him. She had taught him not to take himself too seriously and he had acquired a good deal more confidence and ease in his relationship with others. Only the high-pitched nervous laugh remained.

One of the first episcopal occasions he had to negotiate was the institution of a curate of mine to the new church at Abbey Wood. John never quite managed to invest his episcopal occasions with the appropriate solemnity. He would set off in cope and mitre and walk in procession as though he were going for a tramp in the Lake District. He was happiest with informality, and there could not have been a greater contrast between him and Mervyn. John was, incidentally, enormously loyal to Mervyn, for whom he had the greatest regard. Sometimes it is assumed that their relationship was based on a shared radicalism both in politics and religion. Nothing could be more misleading. It was a relationship in which two greatly different men respected each other's gifts.

John and Ruth were generous in their hospitality at Blackheath, and their home became a real centre for those who had begun to see the extent of changes which were needed if the Church in South London was to be freed from the burden of the past and structured for mission.

In 1960 I went to Roehampton – mainly, I believe, because of John's advocacy. He had checked very carefully with my wife – something he frequently did, I gather, when a man was being moved to take on a major piece of new work. Certainly my wife appreciated this sensitivity – how the move would affect her; how it would affect the children's schooling; and so on.

I saw *Honest to God* in proof, and realised how helpful it could be to such people as my group of students from the Froebel Institute in the parish, all of whom were properly agnostic about what they assumed was on offer in Christian believing. They all found his book of immense value, and he agreed to come and meet them. He came to the College in June, and I chaired a meeting for him in the hall with the entire college, staff and students present.

He had spent Holy Week with us that year, preaching on Thursday, Good Friday and Easter Day. Those who thought him over cerebral, an intellectual out of touch with the common herd, can never have heard him preach, especially when he preached the Cross and Resurrection.

He was not a natural preacher nor a natural TV speaker. Many of the interviews he gave at this time gave the impression of abruptness or impatience. He found it far easier to wield a pen.

In 1971 it was John, as Chairman of the Council, who invited me to become Principal of the Southwark Ordination Course and so gave me some of the happiest years of my ministry.

Douglas Rhymes was Vicar of All Saints, Eltham 1954–62; Canon Residentiary and Librarian of Southwark Cathedral and Director of Lay Training in the diocese 1962–9; Vicar of Camberwell 1968–76 and Rector of Woldingham 1976–84:

In the early years of my ministry, my own temperament and the consciousness of what it is like to belong to a minority had led me to question the rigidity of much that the Church preached and practised. On the other hand, my Anglo-Catholic background led me to believe very strongly in the authority of the Church and the importance of belief in the dogmas and sacraments of the Church.

When I read the writings of John Robinson I found that not only did he stimulate openness of thinking in almost every sphere of life, but by his own honesty in searching for a spirituality to meet the life of the present day he encouraged others like myself to contribute their own part to the revolution in Christian thinking which began in the 1960s. I would never have written *No New Morality* or *Prayer in the Secular City* without the inspiration of *Honest to God*.

John set up groups of clergy and lay people who met regularly to ask questions and to think through problems; and in all those groups there was a complete freedom to be as open and as questioning of received traditions and thought as you wished. But each of us had to do our own thorough thinking, and read papers at the meetings, and subject ourselves to the merciless criticism of others if our thinking had been careless and research inadequate. It was because of the high standard expected of us in these groups that I have written out in full every sermon I have since preached and every lecture I have given.

But it was not only in theological matters that John took risks. When he asked me to be Director of Lay Training he was well aware of a trait in my own temperament which had caused disaster in the past and might well cause scandal in the future; but he took the risk which few dignitaries of the Church would have taken. I knew nothing of Lay Training as such, but he trusted me to come to that work without set answers, and, with the help of Cecilia Goodenough, who was associated with the work from the beginning, to learn from the laity what training they themselves felt they needed. It proved to be not simply training to be faithful members of the parish Church but to meet responsibly as Christians the complexities of the secular world.

There is no one who has given me so much or to whom I owe so much in my life as a priest.

Stella Haughton was John's secretary from September 1966:

My lasting impression of those days was inextricably bound up with the Robinson family, from whom I received nothing but warm affection. I could not but feel for them in their isolation, with the Bishop always out, or, even when present, fully preoccupied with church concerns. After a time I began to see his judgment of people was often unrealistic, and he would return from a meeting quite euphoric over what had taken place or what appointment had been filled, which everyone else knew was nothing but disastrous! How much of this was his innate kindliness or ingenuousness I never really knew, for people always showed their nicest side to him, and an aura of sweetness and light seemed to illuminate every vicarage.

I had been working for him for two years when he one day said, 'Let's dispense with the "Bishop" shall we?' This gives a good insight into our relationship. I always felt in awe of him, of his intellectual brilliance, his vast travel experience, his unflagging energy and his eclectic upbringing. This inhibited conversation on mundane and domestic matters – which would quickly bore him and he would mentally switch off. I suppose this made it difficult for me to call him 'John', and latterly I slipped into the 'J.R.', which he came to recognize, although I doubt if he ever watched *Dallas*!

He was always affectionate in a remote way, always willing to help if specifically asked, and quite unshockable. He could be alarmingly tactless by his sheer openness. Always he was quite unmoved by praise or blame, and he certainly came in for plenty from national and religious press coverage.

He did not find small-talk easy, and this communicated itself to others, so that free-and-easy companionship was difficult for him. Yet nobody could have had more friends in the wider sense of the word, nor helped more people on their way.

David Faull has been Registrar of the Diocese of Southwark and Bishops' Legal Secretary since 1963:

John Robinson said at the end of his time in Southwark that he had never been more than an enabler. This was, of course, typical of his modesty. But he was an enabler. He encouraged many of us to find new ways of communicating the gospel in the second half of the 20th century.

For many people John was a dreamer, a thinker; but to those of us who worked with him he was not only a theologian but a hard working every-day Bishop who put into practice his theological beliefs for making the Church a living reality. It was this which I found refreshing and inspiring. Pastoral re-organisation was a passion with him but it was only incidental. He gathered together and encouraged those who were concerned with re-organisation, but it was never dull. One always felt one was on a great adventure where the ultimate purpose was to reach out to people to communicate the gospel which was so important to him.

What I think was never fully appreciated was that the dynamism and the thrust of Mervyn Stockwood's first 10 years in Southwark was as much due to his choice of John Robinson as Bishop of Woolwich as to his own radicalism. And John clothed that radicalism in a theology. He spent many hours bringing practical sense into the Pastoral Measure 1968. Without this much of what can now be done under the Measure and its subsequent amending Measure could not have been done. And he did it in the face of much opposition and with little political understanding, for he was not a politician. It was he who led the opposition to the Report of Bishop of Leicester, Ronald Williams, on the Sharing of Churches with other denominations, and who drove through the Sharing of Churches legislation. It was not a pleasure to him and he was impatient. But he understood that in order to release the Church for growth he had to be prepared to wrestle with legislation to achieve it. For he understood that theology had to have a practical out-working. Likewise he threw himself into property development – not because it interested him in itself, but because it released resources for the Kingdom – and he would bring that sort of insight into a development discussion. 'South Bank religion', so-called, was theologically conceived and practically born. In fact it was a principal demonstration of his belief in and understanding of the incarnation.

As far as he was concerned, he preached the truth as he saw it, and he could not understand that the Church of England did not like it. He listened to and respected the humblest of people and he assumed that all people behaved in the same way.

John challenged the language of traditional thought but always, whilst he was in Southwark, his aim was to enable people to believe and to encounter Jesus Christ in their work and in their worship.

Above all to me he was the most humble and gracious of men. He was desperately shy, he was impatient of bureaucracy, and that gave a first impression of indifference and almost arrogance. But all I know is that I was an ordinary solicitor with no academic pretensions and he treated me as he would have treated any of his great contemporaries, and that I know was the experience of many. Commitment was all that he asked.

There must be one last – and lengthy – letter on John in Southwark: Una Kroll, wife of an Anglo-Catholic priest, mother of four, a family doctor practising on a large housing estate in Southwark when she first met John; their friendship had a particular importance to both of them – but not only to them.

I first met John in 1967 when I was trying to become a theological student with the Southwark Ordination Course. It was a course for men, some of whom felt called to combine priesthood with their secular calling or profession. I felt called to the same kind of ministry, but as a woman my tentative voicings of that vocation had been greeted with laughter and scorn. Rejection had worn me down, and the appointment to see John Robinson at his home was God's last chance as well as my own, at least in my mind it was. I had begun to see myself as a deluded 'silly' middle aged woman, 'puffed up' with unrealistic expectations. I had carried out every suggestion made to me by Bishop Mervyn Stockwood in his reply to my letter of enquiry which I had written after seeing a report about the Southwark Ordination Course in the *Evening Standard*. All doors seemed shut. It is important to understand that at that time of my life I had never met any bishop at a personal level. I had seen them, of course, knelt for their blessing, remained in the background at clerical gatherings where a bishop had been the principal guest, but I had never talked to a bishop about anything that mattered to me. At the time of my meeting with John I was a 'dyed in the wool' Anglo-Catholic, with all the traditional beliefs held by committed sacramentalists and with some of their prejudices against anyone who 'rocked the boat', as the Bishop of Woolwich had done in his highly controversial writings. I can, therefore, remember going to that meeting with very mixed feelings, among which fear and suspicion vied for equality and hope glimmered faintly in the background. I took my husband along with me as protection, and to do the talking for me if I ran out of words to say. I neither knew what to call a bishop when one met one face to face, nor exactly what to do, since my recollection of encounters in church suggested that one should genuflect. I was not prepared to see such a person answer the door himself. Of course, he did, and both his greeting and his stretched out hand of welcome made it impossible to do anything but behave normally to him as one would to any other person one met for the first time.

As we began, so we continued. Tucked into a deep chintz-covered armchair, given a cup of tea, surrounded by shelves of books, I began to talk to this unusual man who was prepared to listen without interruption, who did not immediately laugh at my gaucheness, nor deride my vocation, nor question my sincerity. I totally forgot he was a bishop, felt safe with him as a priest, and gained enough confidence to do most of the talking without needing the 'back up' which I usually did from my priest-husband. The only sign he gave of authority was towards the end of the hour long conversation (a longer time, incidentally, than anyone else had deigned to give me), when he said to me that he would recommend me to the Principal of the Course and that if he agreed I should be able to start training alongside the men. 'I don't see why not,' he said. 'Of course, you know you won't be ordained to the priesthood, but I can't see why you can't be trained with them.'

So began an experiment which was to pioneer a new kind of training for *women and men*. I was the first woman to do the Southwark Course in exactly the same way and under the same kind of strains as my brother students. I survived the three and a half year experiment of co-educational training that is now the norm throughout the Church and helped to prove the value of training ordinands with people who would serve the Church in ways other than the ordained priesthood.

During the years of my studentship I saw little of John. He never protected me from any hardships or struggles or showed the least bit of favour or friendship towards me. Just once, he admonished me to remember that Baptism was more important than Ordination, and that at a time when I was plainly sinking under the pain and bewilderment of struggling with a vocation which could not be fulfilled in the most obvious way of becoming a priest. When my period of training was coming to an end I found myself with nowhere to go. My own sponsoring Diocese could find nowhere suitable for me to be licensed. A move across dioceses to Southwark had proved itself difficult from my family's point of view and I had had to change jobs and return to general practice in a new area quite unknown to me. I could not have been made a deaconess without a parish to go to as a licensed worker. It was then that John stepped in again. He matched me with a parish priest in Morden called Donald Reeves (now Vicar of St James's, Piccadilly) who was a creative genius as well as being young and eccentric enough to accept a wounded feminist on his staff. Probably no one else could have offered me such a generous home, where I could learn and make mistakes, as Donald did for the first ten years of my active ministry. John's pastoral skill lay in his being able to discern the fact that Donald and I would increase each other's creativity rather than destroy one another. He threw us together and left us alone to work it out. I had nowhere else to go, but Donald could easily have said 'no'. I shall never cease to be thankful to both men who accepted me as I was, and who set me free to grow in all kinds of ways.

I was one of the first women to become a non-stipendiary deaconess-worker without first serving an apprenticeship as a licensed parish worker.

John assisted at my painful birth into the deaconess order. I can remember still the relief of his humorous and whimsical hands as they touched me as he and Dr Stockwood passed from the last of the men who had been made deacons and arrived at the end of the row to discover a woman lurking in wait. I do not suppose that either of us knew quite what we were doing that cold St Thomas's Day in 1970, but I was soon to discover that my commissioning as a deaconess worker was to lead directly to a committed pastorate among women who were struggling against the discriminatory laws and prejudices which were operative in English society at that time.

But John himself shall have the last word on his time in Southwark. He wrote in an article for the *Christian Century* series 'How My Mind Has Changed' which was published in the issue of 12 November 1969 and reprinted in *Christian Freedom in a Permissive Society*:

I am seldom happy except on a frontier; and I have a sense of constantly pushing out, or rather being pushed – drawn from ahead, yet held from behind, by a power that will not let me go. The centre remains the same but the edges and the ends are opening and expanding. This gives one the courage to go on not knowing where one is going, and to find doubt extending rather than bewildering. This, as Tillich insisted, is an essential meaning today of justification by faith – to know oneself accepted *simul justus et dubitator*. And my deepest wish for the church is that it should be an *affirming structure* of that trust. That the Church of England has been that for me over the past decade I can only gratefully acknowledge. I do not think I should have been so free in any other organisation, ecclesiastical or secular. That is why, despite all its failings, I believe in it and refuse to leave it, for my own sake as well as others'.

7

The Trinity Years

Founded by Henry VIII in 1546, Trinity is the largest college in Cambridge. When John became Dean of Chapel in 1969 the College comprised well over a hundred Fellows – an academic élite spanning the sciences and the humanities – and over eight hundred junior members, at that time all of them male. Half the Fellows formed the College teaching staff; others were professors in the University. Some were living in retirement; more than a dozen were young Research Fellows, elected for a limited period. Several of the Fellows were tutors concerned with the general welfare of the students. The unmarried Fellows lived in College; but all members of the College were encouraged to take meals in Hall as often as they could.

Not least because the College was so large, the role of the Dean of Chapel – defined by no precise job specification – was not without its importance. He was expected to mix freely and widely within the College, as were the two College Chaplains. Although the Dean was responsible to the College Council for the Chapel services – and would also be Director of Studies in Theology – his was clearly more than an ecclesiastical office.

It is in fact laid down in the Statutes of Trinity College that the Council shall each year

> elect from amongst the Fellows of the College a Dean of Chapel, who shall provide for the celebration of Divine Service in the College Chapel according to such rules and regulations as may from time to time be made by the Council, shall see that all persons conduct themselves decently therein, and shall perform such other duties as the Council may from time to time assign to him.

When Harry Williams resigned from being Dean of Chapel there was thought to be no Fellow of the College who could appropriately fill the office, and for the first time in its history, Trinity decided to look for a

Dean of Chapel from outside the College. The intention was to seek someone who could be elected to a Fellowship and then be elected Dean of Chapel. The appointment was considered so important that the Master of Trinity, Lord Butler of Saffron Walden, chaired the committee himself. It was clear that Lord Butler – no stranger to the power of appointment – was seeking on behalf of the College a man of stature, perhaps a future Regius Professor or diocesan bishop; a man certainly of whom the College could be proud in years to come.

It might be imagined that John's return to Trinity was a homecoming. He had been a research student at Trinity. He was a Doctor of Divinity (and a Doctor of Philosophy) of the University of Cambridge and had already been Dean of Chapel of Clare College. Yet perhaps it should be underlined that where Deans of Chapel of Trinity were concerned, John was the 'man who came in from the cold', the first Dean of Chapel to be appointed from outside the existing galaxy of Fellows. For John's return to Cambridge was not altogether easy. One of the two Chaplains of Trinity at the time, John Latham (now returned to his homeland New Zealand), who as curate of St George's, Camberwell had known John in Southwark, thought John 'lacked confidence when he started at Trinity'. Faced with John's assignment, only a man of consummate arrogance would have been totally confident. In his more than ten years at Trinity as Dean of Chapel and Tutor, Harry Williams had won a particular place in the confidence and affections of the Master of Trinity, Lady Butler, the Fellows and many of the undergraduates. G. M. Trevelyan, a former Master of Trinity, had once said to one of the Chaplains in his time: 'I may be anti-clerical, but I'm not anti-cleric.' The Fellows of Trinity were on the whole *for* their clerics; but the position of Dean of Chapel, as Harry Williams had left it, was not one that could simply be transferred and handed on. Indeed the kind of acclaim – even popularity – which John had achieved in Southwark, and not only in Southwark, counted for little in Trinity. The Fellows – most of them courteous and sensible, their courtesy characterized by the agnostic former Master of Trinity, Lord Adrian – were suspicious of the media and of the whole 'bubble reputation'. As John Latham remarked: 'Academics are not slow to believe that other academics "understanded of the people" must be lesser academics.' The Fellows of Trinity – and not only of Trinity – were, in short, wary of 'Honest to God' Robinson.

There is sometimes an 'effortless superiority' about Trinity. (Nobel

Prizewinners there are almost two a penny.) 'This is the only institution that matters', Trinity seems to say. John had therefore first to knuckle down to being again, and being seen to be, a 'Trinity man'. (Trinity men were sometimes known to observe that 'God himself is a Trinity Man'!) The task was not all that easy, and there were at least some good and sufficient reasons for believing it should not be for a bishop in the Church of God. The High Tables of Oxford and Cambridge colleges are undeniably comfortable, even somewhat cosseted, societies. But it was not the luxury that John found difficult. What clearly he soon missed – though in Southwark it had sometimes seemed oppressive – was being 'at the centre'. Not until he left South London did he realize, for instance, how much he had grown used to being consulted by the media.

This could, of course, be naked 'pride of man and earthly glory'. No doubt there was an element of this in John, but those who knew him best knew him to possess a profound humility. Yet with no prospect of becoming a diocesan bishop – itself a comment on the appointments system of the Established Church – and yielding to pressure and returning to Cambridge it is surely not surprising that John should have had what John Donne called 'some reclinations, some retrospects . . . a little of Lot's wife' in him, which made him look back to when some of his gifts were used which would rarely be used in Cambridge. For Cambridge was – for better, for worse – in *some* respects a backwater for John. The surprise in the circumstances, is that *no one* ever heard an embittered word escape his lips.

Ben de la Mare (now Vicar of St Oswald's, Durham), the other Chaplain when John arrived, would say that John immediately made his mark in Trinity, and not least by the way he treated the Chaplains.

There were now more regular staff meetings. John had a true humility. He made it clear from the start that he wanted to learn from us and that the pastoral care of the undergraduates and the care of the worship were mainly ours. He was loyal to the Chaplains and made us feel we were colleagues. Those who thought that John would have little time for the Evangelicals – the Fundamentalists – were quickly proved wrong. He took trouble over the members of the CICCU – the Cambridge Inter-Collegiate Christian Union – and they knew it. Paradoxically, John was more of a churchman than Harry Williams – though Harry had gone to be a monk at Mirfield – consequently John had more difficulty in relating to the secular institution that Trinity was and is. John wouldn't and couldn't play 'Trinity's games'.

There were other aspects of John which also made an immediate impact. His shyness and reserve and lack of small-talk of course contrasted with Harry's warmth and ebullience. Then there was John's voice. Perhaps the Fellows of Trinity should have been less irritated by that than they were; but big men can be surprisingly small men from time to time; and in the confined space of a Cambridge Combination Room one voice which can be heard above all the others – and an ugly and abrasive voice at that – can be very irritating and can easily personify the opinions – and indeed the person – you find irritating. John was virtually tone-deaf. Certainly he was deaf to the effect his voice had on others. (Music was *almost* a closed book to him.) Sir Desmond Pond, formerly Professor of Psychiatry at the London Hospital Medical College – who had known John as an undergraduate at Cambridge (he was President of the SCM two years before John was President) and had seen something of him and Ruth at Bristol, Wells and Woolwich – offered the suggestion that John's voice was 'another defence against too close a personal involvement'.

The departure from Southwark was undoubtedly a bereavement for John and indeed another watershed in the life of the Robinsons. There would never again be for all of them just one place that was home – as 17 Manor Way had been.

As early as 1964 John had written:

> One of the things I am feeling I should do with my royalties . . . is to provide a house for Ruth by means of an irrevocable trust-deed. I believe it is irresponsible to give it all away and then to leave her to other people's charity, if she were widowed. I don't mind which house I sink it in as long as it provides her with the capital, if necessary – and I would rather put it into a house I could use for my work than invest it or buy a country cottage.

The fruit of such thoughts would now greatly affect John's life at Trinity. In the spring of 1968, the week before Holy Week, John and Ruth had been exploring together the countryside within reach of Blackheath, and had chosen for one day the ridge of the North Downs above Reigate. On their way home they had spotted the 'For Sale' notice on Fort Lodge, on the bridle-path running along the ridge. John had immediately seen the possibilities of having a house in the southern part of the Diocese, only three-quarters of an hour's drive from home. While they were still in Southwark they could escape on a Friday evening, have an entirely private day off on Saturday; and John would still be within easy reach of his Sunday engagements – more easy reach of some of them. A few days later John and Ruth had gone to the auction, and when the hammer came down Fort Lodge was theirs.

It was a delightful home. Ruth adored the garden, which she set about transforming. After the years of *Lady Chatterley* and *Honest to God*, Fort Lodge, she felt, allowed her to be a private person. The house opened immediately on to the Downs. It was ideal for walks – for both John and Ruth, and for 'pastoral' walks and talks, in every sense of the word. The only disappointment was that, understandably, Buffy and Judith were not really happy away from their friends at Blackheath, and never developed any great affection for Fort Lodge. The decision to move to Cambridge clearly made Reigate not simply a bolt-hole but, during vacations, a necessary base for John's work, not least as an Assistant Bishop of Southwark – to which Mervyn had immediately appointed him. It was indeed the Robinsons' home to replace Manor Way; and plans were made to add a study to the house to make it a base for John to work in as well as rest, which, when it was completed, would be one of the places where he most enjoyed working.

Although in his farewell letter to the Diocese John had referred to 'the grass-widowhood of a don's wife', he had also said that Ruth would be 'much relieved by her not being house-bound (as she was last time) by four small children – and by the chinks of enlightenment that have penetrated these male preserves in the decade since we left!' Ruth in fact had looked forward to returning to Cambridge: to the intellectual stimulus – and music and bookshops – and to Pinehurst, the flat in Marlborough Court in Grange Road, of which they had taken a lease for John, herself and Judith. John was often to refer to 'the base at Cambridge' and to 'the base at Reigate'; but in reality he had two bases at Cambridge. In addition to Marlborough Court, he had the Dean of Chapel's rooms in Great Court, Trinity – with the possibility, and often the obligation, of lunching and of dining in Hall. For him there was again, as there had been at Clare, virtually a second 'domestic' Cambridge set-up.

Although at first Ruth enjoyed the Cambridge amenities, and getting to know places like the Pepys Library, which there had never been time for in the 1950s, she was unable to take on commitments or any sort of job. The garden at Reigate called – chaos would come again if it was left; and most of their possessions were now in fact at Fort Lodge.

There were of course some things for Ruth to join in at Trinity – though she felt diffident at hanging around too much – but most other wives had their households or their own professions. Ruth, having suddenly ceased to have a role as the wife of the Bishop of Woolwich, very soon began to feel that while John was busy finding his way into his new job as Dean of Chapel and getting on with the preparation of his lectures, she was simply filling in time until he had space for her when he left Trinity at the end of the day: she was fast becoming nobody. When John had referred to 'the grass-widowhood of a don's wife', consciously or unconsciously he may well have recognized – and not without some apprehension – that this was one of the least satisfactory aspects of his new appointment.

John had to get on with his work, for there were only eight months between his move to Cambridge and his Hulsean Lectures – which were supposed to be 'the big book on Christology he had in him'; and in those months there would also be for him many hours of supervising students reading theology. Nevertheless, as though clearing the decks, he put together his collection of essays, *Christian Freedom in a Permissive Society*, which garnered some of the things he had written as articles, lectures and sermons during the Sixties. The subjects were of course quintessential 'Sixties subjects': Abortion; Obscenity and Maturity; Mystique and Politique; The Ecumenical Consequences of *Humanae Vitae*; Let the Liturgy be Free, and so on. But it would be wrong to dismiss such a 'Farewell to the Sixties' – to quote the title of an article included in the book – which John had written for *The Observer* for the last Sunday of September 1969. On the contrary, twenty years after most of the contents of the book were written, it is clear that the subjects have refused to be dismissed and that John's arguments are as cogent now as they were then:

> The pervasive influence of Christianity is not promised to the strength of a self-contained ecclesiastical organisation, but to leaven and salt mixed and dissolved in the lump of the world's life. Movements and groupings there must be, clusters of action and sanctity and thinking, and these must be structured if they are to penetrate effectively. But basically the attractive power of love and hope, integrity and justice – and these are the signs of the Kingdom at work – do not depend on institutional orthodoxies and establishments. Ours is an age in which these things have ceased to carry their own authentication.

It was as John penned these last words of the book that he heard the news of the tragic death of Bishop James Pike – who had 'caused' John's essay in *Theological Freedom and Social Responsibility* to be written. Bishop Pike and his wife had wanted to visit Qumran in the deserts of Judah, where the Dead Sea Scrolls had been found. They had taken a wrong turning and their car had broken down in the desert. They had walked together till Bishop Pike was exhausted and could not go on. His wife had then walked on to get help – for ten gruelling hours. The body of Bishop Pike was found six days later. John dedicated *Christian Freedom in a Permissive Society* to him: 'seeker and contender for freedom and truth'.

At the end of his first term John immediately disappeared to Reigate – as would be his invariable practice in the next years – except when, like Elijah, he was 'in a journey'. He got away primarily to work at his lectures. Supervisions, visitors from the four corners of the globe, and his obligations as Dean, made that virtually impossible in term time.

As a bachelor Harry Williams had been 'around' most of the vacations. The College undoubtedly disliked John's disappearances – though his presence for some part of the vacations had not been specified when he was appointed. John simply could not see how he could produce the 'big books' Trinity expected of him if he stayed in his rooms.

On 16 May 1970, in Westminster Abbey, there was 'a Service of Presentation of the Old Testament and Apocrypha in the New English Bible and of Thanksgiving for the completed translation'. John was in the Procession of the Translators as a New Testament Translator. He was proud of his involvement in this great work; because it was so manifestly that. The translators agreed that they would accept corporate responsibility for the work and that no individual attribution should ever be made. But those who heard John read passages from the New English Bible version of the Revelation of John felt – rightly or wrongly – that they had good reason to believe he had had a particular involvement in the translation of that particular book:

I, John, your brother, who share with you in the suffering and the sovereignty and the endurance which is ours in Jesus – I was on the island called Patmos because I had preached God's word and borne my testimony to Jesus. It was on the Lord's day, and I was caught up by the Spirit; and behind me I heard a loud voice, like the sound of a trumpet, which said to me, 'Write . . .'.

John was proud to be involved also for a very characteristic reason: 'The effect of this and other versions has been to loosen a stranglehold of 350 years. For until very recently, "the Bible" for the Englishman meant one thing, significantly called "the Authorized Version" – though in fact it has never been authorized.' John loved the Authorized Version as English literature, but he was one of those who believed the Bible was never meant to be read primarily as literature.

John's book, *The Human Face of God*, began as the Hulsean Lectures, delivered to packed houses in the Divinity Schools in Cambridge in April 1970, to which John added material from the Nelson Lectures he gave at Lancaster University in February 1971 and the Owen Evans Memorial Lectures he delivered at Aberystwyth in April that year. He had of course been mulling over his subject for many years. Although he had written a chapter on 'The Man for Others', in *Honest to God*, in *The Honest to God Debate* he wrote: 'I am deliberately not touching in this essay on questions relating to the person and work of Christ, as I should like, when time allows, to follow these up in a separate book.' But in 1970 and 1971, he was aware that

> the state of the Christological question is fluid . . . I was aware of the difference of mood, for instance, at Cambridge and at Lancaster. In the former, at any rate in the Divinity Schools, the questions were still fundamentally Christian questions, and the answers were tested by those presuppositions. In Lancaster one had the healthy experience of 'playing away'. One sensed that what one was saying should somehow be starting from somewhere else.

By the time he came to write up the lectures into a book 'the scene had already changed quite markedly since I first delivered the lectures' (*Godspell* and *Jesus Christ Superstar* were both first produced in 1971). John had one central conviction: 'the Christ has once again to become the contemporary of each succeeding generation. And for the "Christ today" the "Christ yesterday" cannot be written off.' He was aware that

> there will be incredulity that serious men can still spend their time grubbing around the old holes. The question is not so much, *How* do we speak today of 'the humanity and divinity of Christ', or his historicity, his sinlessness, his uniqueness, his finality, or his 'full, perfect and sufficient sacrifice, oblation and satisfaction for the sins of the whole world', as *Why*? Who would think to begin there with the world perhaps a generation from disaster? Genocide rather than parthenogenesis,

Auschwitz rather than the empty tomb, look more relevant foci of enquiry for those who would really know 'What is in man'.

The simplicity of John's chapter headings – which represented different lectures: 'Our Man'; 'A Man'; 'The Man'; 'Man of God'; 'God's Man'; 'God for Us'; 'Man for All' – gave clarity to the whole complex subject. John also achieved his aim of making the book – give or take a few technical passages – one for the general reader not simply for the specialist.

John probably realized *The Human Face of God* was not the *great* book on Christology he had hoped it might be possible for him to write, but it is undoubtedly a very considerable book. He wrote in the preface: 'I am not so sure now that in any traditional sense Christology will be the next focus of theological debate. We appear to be in a particularly volatile situation, and this book could already be too late for some and too soon for others.' He had come to realize that *anything* written on the subject would be more provisional than definitive. Yet the book is surely one of the weightier books on Christology of this century:

'Who is Christ for us today?' I have suggested elsewhere that the gospel passages with peculiarly compelling power for our generation are those, like the Sheep and the Goats, the walk to Emmaus or the final appearance of Jesus by the lakeside, which 'tell of one who comes unknown and uninvited into the human situation, disclosing himself as the gracious neighbour before he can be recognized as Master and Lord'. In this, as in other respects, our thinking today has, I am convinced, to begin 'from below' and move from immanence to transcendence, from relationships to revelation, from the Son of Man to the Son of God, rather than the other way round. Hence the categories in which people have recently attempted to convey the meaning of Christ have been those such as the servant-Lord, the way, the man for others, the victim, the outsider, the representative, the incognito, even the clown or harlequin, whose pathos and weakness and irony, as well as whose gaity and freedom, 'all begin to make a strange kind of sense again'. Yet *in* all these he is to be seen as the embodiment of 'the beyond' – in the midst. Indeed, we should not forget that Bonhoeffer's now famous phrase 'the man for others' is in answer to the question 'Who is *God*?' For unless the dimension of the transcendent, the unconditional, is visible, however 'brokenly' (and this seems almost a *sine qua non* for our generation), there is no Christ at all. Perhaps for this reason the profoundest Christological statements today are likely to be discerned hidden in fiction or art, in psychology or drama – the equivalents in our age of apocalyptic. Our 'worldly' language may be that of poetry, or politics, or personal relationships. Yet, whether specific 'God'-talk is a help or a hindrance, it is 'transcendence *within* immanence' that we have somehow to articulate and express.

John had a real *affection* for certain of his fellow theologians – this is obviously true of his relationship to Dietrich Bonhoeffer. *The Human Face of God* probably depended more on his relationship with the American New Testament theologian John Knox than with any other theologian. They had become friends when Knox spent the year 1952/3 in Cambridge, when John was at Clare. From that time onwards John hardly ever went to the USA without visiting John Knox – first when he was Baldwin Professor of Sacred Literature at the Union Theological Seminary, New York, then when he was Professor of New Testament at the Episcopal Theological Seminary of the Southwest, Austin, Texas; and finally in retirement at Medford, New Jersey. When John was giving his Hulsean Lectures John Knox was in his early seventies. He was to write – in his mid-eighties:

> I was drawn to him, do I dare say, we were drawn to each other? in the mysterious way of all natural affinities. His capacity for friendship was indeed extraordinary. I can claim only a 'capacity' for accepting with my whole heart his proffer of it. Why he cared for me, as he evidently did, I do not know. But the fact that he did means more to me than I can say. Our minds were congenial, I think I may truly say, in a special way, especially as regards our theological thinking and interests ... I have been greatly moved by his willingness, in view of his busy schedules, during his American stays, to come to us in this rather out of the way place in New Jersey, not infrequently at the cost of considerable inconvenience and no doubt expense. I think I knew him well, and he was one of my dearest friends.

In 1967 John Knox had produced *The Humanity and Divinity of Christ*. In *The Human Face of God* John calls it 'one of the best recent books on Christology'.

Eight months after John had delivered his Hulsean Lectures he gave the course of four University Sermons at Great St Mary's, Cambridge, the University Church, which was crowded on each occasion. These sermons, expanded with extra material, he delivered as the Carnahan Lectures at the Union Theological Seminary, Buenos Aires in July 1971. They were published at the beginning of 1972 as *The Difference in*

Being a Christian Today. It was the third book he had published in less than three years. Trinity had good reason to be pleased with this aspect of their new Dean's work.

There were three stimuli behind his University Sermons. First the 1970 Reith Lectures of Donald Schon, the American business psychologist, on 'Change and Industrial Society', published as *'Beyond the Stable State*. John – carefully qualifying Schon's metaphor – called his introductory chapter 'The End of the Stable State'. Secondly John had come across W. H. Auden's Christmas 'oratorio', *For the Time Being*, and had been much moved by the explanation Auden put into the mouths of the wise men as to what led them to Bethlehem.

> The first says:
>> To discover how to be truthful now
>> Is the reason I follow this star.
>
> The second:
>> To discover how to be living now
>> Is the reason I follow this star.
>
> The third:
>> To discover how to be loving now
>> Is the reason I follow this star
>
> Then, to sum up, all say:
>> To discover how to be human now
>> Is the reason we follow this star.

'How to be human now.' John writes: 'That is the greatest single search that unites our distracted world. If the Christian message is to have any relevance, it will be because it comes to men as an answer to that question. This is an indispensable mark of distinctively Christian existence today.'

The end of the Auden oratorio also seemed exactly to sum up for John what he wanted to say.

> He is the Way.
> Follow Him through the Land of Unlikeness;
> You will see rare beasts, and have unique adventures.
> He is the Truth.
> Seek Him in the Kingdom of Anxiety;
> You will come to a great city that has expected your return for years.
> He is the Life.
> Love Him in the World of the Flesh;
> And at your marriage all its occasions shall dance.

The third stimulus was the fact that exactly a century before, in his Hulsean Lectures for 1871, 'another Cambridge man . . . the gentle and scholarly Dr Hort, Fellow of Trinity, who with Westcott and Lightfoot, steered the Church of England through the storms of biblical criticism in the 19th century', had used the same three heads 'The Way, the Truth, the Life'. As F. J. A. Hort had put it (and as John quoted him): 'The Way lies most on the surface as presented to our faculties; further down lies the Truth, and beneath the Truth the Life.'

John had accepted the invitation to give the Carnahan Lectures 'because it provided an opportunity to become exposed to the problems and questions of the South American scene which I knew I could not duck . . . I made it a condition that Ruth must come too, as her Spanish would provide us with openings and opportunities which would otherwise be closed.'

They flew first to Rio de Janeiro on 27 June 1971, and were met at the airport by the Episcopal Bishop, Ned Sherrill (son of a former Presiding Bishop of the United States); the Chaplain of the English Church, Eric Wilcockson; a Roman Catholic priest and a Protestant pastor. 'This was typical of the new ecumenism which is being fostered,' John wrote, 'though it is as yet a tender plant.' John had plenty of evidence in Rio de Janeiro of the police state – and also saw something of the *favelas* – the local name for the appalling shanty towns. 'It is so well armed,' wrote John. 'For the first time it is providing economic stability and rapid growth. But the cost of this in human terms is appalling.'

It was the same in São Paulo – an exploding city of approaching ten million people. John lectured at the Episcopal Seminary, run on an evening class basis. A paragraph he had added to his lectures to respond to the South America scene, had to be excised: a reference to Ruben Alves's book *A Theology of Human Hope*. (Ruben Alves lived in São Paulo.) John and Ruth saw something of the work of 'conscientisation' of a young Brazilian priest in a very poor area on the outskirts of São Paulo 'with real danger to their personal liberty'. He also met there a young Roman Catholic priest who described how one of his congregation had been arrested and tortured by the police. Early on Sunday morning they went to the prison where some Dominican priests were incarcerated. They were not allowed to visit them but they did get a message through to them.

The next stop was Buenos Aires and Argentina. They stayed at the

Union Theological Seminary, where John was to give the Carnahan Lectures, as guests of John Litwiller and his wife. (He had recently taken over as rector from José Miguez Bonino.) The ecumenical seminary was largely supported by Methodist funds. John also visited the Roman Catholic seminary. He described Buenos Aires in his journal as 'a run-down version of Barcelona'!

An earthquake had occurred in Valparaiso, the night before John and Ruth arrived in Chile. The airport clock in Santiago – where John was to lecture at the Catholic University – was stopped at the hour it happened. It was in fact only when he got to Chile, then under President Allende, that John 'felt able to talk freely about politics for the first time'. After the lecture the Anglican chaplain, Graham Jack, got together 'a considerable cross-section of people – including the Lutheran and Methodist bishops, a French Dominican from the Vatican Secretariat for Ecumenism, a Maryknoll Father and various sisters and laymen, Roman Catholic and otherwise.'

When they went on to Peru, John and Ruth were 'more than usually' limited by being confined to English-speaking contacts. But John added: 'incidentally, we were much impressed by the friendliness and hospitality of the British Embassies, almost wherever we went, having never expected to be fêted at this level!' The Anglican chaplain, John Baillie, enabled them to meet the Cardinal Archbishop of Lima. 'I got the impression that Roman Catholic priests and sociologists were among those making the most constructive contribution to re-thinking the structures of society,' John wrote. But he was baffled by the social problems – the *barriados* (the Peruvian equivalent of the *favelas*.) He wrote despairingly in his journal: 'How in the long run one tackles the immense back-log of social problems of the country, and above all enables the Indians to get out of their desperate poverty, without destroying their culture, I don't know.'

At the end of their visit to Peru John and Ruth became unashamed tourists, 'doing the rounds of the Lima museums, with their fantastic collection of Inca and pre-Inca pottery and textiles'. For John 'the high spot of our trip, literally and metaphorically, was the two-day trip which we took to the Inca cities of Cuzco, the Inca capital, more than 10,000 feet up on a plateau, surrounded by mountains, and Machu Picchu, the lost Inca city, rediscovered under the undergrowth in 1911'.

Ruth's Spanish came in useful (and the realization by the crew that they had 'Obispo and Señora Robinson' flying with them) when the plane was delayed on its return and the connection in Lima looked impossibly tight. Following her negotiations in the cockpit they were ushered off the plane, and baggage, passports and so on, all dealt with, and within five minutes of landing were seated in the Argentine Airways plane to Mexico City. John's characteristic comment was: 'It just shows what really can be done, and the hours of unnecessary time one normally spends in airports'!

John next lectured at Cuernavaca, an hour and more outside Mexico City, at CIDOC (Central Inter-Cultural Documentation), which centred round the charismatic figure of Ivan Illich – who had come to Mexico City from Europe via Latin America and Puerto Rico. To John CIDOC was 'partly a language school for American Christians going to work in Latin America, and partly a centre for social research of various kinds'. In the brief time John had with Ivan Illich – 'a monsignor at 29, now sitting very loose to the Roman Catholic Church' – John established 'a firm affinity of spirit'.

John and Ruth were driven back into Mexico City with the former Provincial of the Dominicans in Mexico now working with university students. John learnt much from him – not least that 'it is illegal to appear here in a dog-collar – a fact I did not realise when I arrived at the airport in my purple stock, in the hope of being recognized by anyone meeting us!' They stayed in Mexico City with Robert Jones of the American chaplaincy and his wife. His host for his lectures was the Mexican bishop of the Episcopal Church. It was time for more sight-seeing, and Ruth came away from the bazaar in the old Spanish part of the city with a splendid opal ring set in silver, for which she paid two-thirds of a pound! They found the museum of archaeology and anthropology enthralling, not only for its Aztec and other treasures but for the beauty of its order and display. On their last day they were taken out to the ruins of Tenochtitlan, where the pyramid temples and other buildings survive from well before Aztec times. On their last night they dined with the British Ambassador.

Finally Ruth and John flew to Puerto Rico. 'Few people in Britain realise the extent to which Puerto Rico is simply part of the United States,' wrote John. They stayed in San Juan with the Episcopal Bishop Francisco Reus-Froylan and his wife. John gave lectures in the Ateneo, a centre for preserving Spanish tradition and culture, in a new lecture hall of the University of Puerto Rico, and in the Episcopal and Evangelical seminaries. John was glad that he and Ruth were invited out of the city to see the work of a Dutch Dominican and a group of girl graduates from the University who had set up an informal religious order to live among squatters on the fringes and to help in the battle for their rights.

The Colombian airline plane that began their flight home started two and a half hours earlier than on their tickets. John was astounded. Seasoned traveller that he was, he never began to accept other people's habits where time – and not only time – was concerned. Yet when they arrived home, after precisely four weeks away, he was aware how essential it was to have been where he and Ruth had been if he was to 'do theology' as it needed to be done. Giving his lectures was of course important to him; but so too was his receiving – listening and observing: being 'exposed to the problems and questions of the South American scene'.

When John returned from 'earth's wide bounds' to the confines of Cambridge, some of his daily duties at Trinity must have seemed to contrast strangely with his experience in South America. There was, for instance, one major responsibility of the Dean of Chapel which embodied some of the characteristic complexities and ambiguities of the Church of England by law established. The Dean of Chapel of Trinity is the secretary of the College Livings Committee – though he is more than merely its secretary. The College is patron of about thirty Church of England benefices, chiefly in the North of England and the Midlands – including the living of Great St Mary's, Cambridge, four of whose successive incumbents in the last quarter of a century have become diocesan bishops, and the fifth, Dean of Westminster.

Trinity's attitude to its College Livings is simple. They are part of its history and heritage. Some of them have been in its gift since the fifteenth century. It is for the College to preserve and care for its heritage – though it ought to be added that half a century ago the College disposed of some forty of its Livings, feeling it simply could not do justice to them all. The College is conscious of the great benefit it has received from the lands associated with its Livings, and feels an obligation to give back something of what it has received – by paying part of the stipend of the priest or something towards the upkeep of the church or the vicarage. The College also tries to care for its members, and is particularly pleased if, to their mutual benefit, it can match a Trinity Living with a Trinity man in priest's orders. It is not possible to write to every one of the many Trinity men in holy orders each time a vacancy in a College Living occurs. So that if the Dean is to advise whether a particular Trinity man should be considered for a vacant Living it is for the Dean to know all he can about those on the register of ordained members of the College. But it is not only the man who might be appointed whom the Dean needs to know but also the place to which he might be appointed. It is the Dean's job therefore also to get to know the College Livings.

John assumed the duties of the secretary to the College Livings Committee willingly but warily.

The Keble Conference Group of which he had been chairman, the Paul Report and the Morley Report on the deployment of the clergy, which he had supported in the Church Assembly and in the Convocation of Canterbury, were in favour of the abolition of private ecclesiastical patronage. They were also against maintaining in isolation, with a freehold, every individual benefice. John well knew as an urban bishop that this way most of the clergy had been deployed in the more rural areas while most of the people were in the towns. John had also given strong support to the formation of teams and groups of clergy and parishes to end their isolation. With ten years of experience as a bishop he was also well aware how crucial it was to get the best man for the job when filling a vacant living – not simply a man from a particular college. As a bishop he had in fact taken a pragmatic attitude to private patrons. If the candidate of the patron was 'a good man' – 'all other things being equal' (a favourite phrase of John's!) – he would give him his support. He was aware nevertheless that a diocese usually had a larger pool of men to draw from than a private patron, and had greater opportunity than a private patron to see a parish in the context of a strategy for an area as a whole.

These were two positions sincerely and responsibly held and not necessarily in opposition. Neither John nor the College intended to act in any uncompromising way.

John however undoubtedly evoked suspicion by rarely calling a meeting of the College Livings Committee – a suspicion of 'John the radical' which needed little to foster it. There was also the quite different suspicion of his personal judgment of people in that 'all his geese were swans'. When John came to put into practice what he believed, suspicion therefore surrounded what he did – or failed to do.

John, too, had his suspicions – that Trinity was merely 'conservative' and failed to give due recognition to the changes which had been occurring within the Church of England and which were bound to affect the task of the secretary of the Livings Committee, whoever it might be. The severe and continuing decline in the number of clergy ordained in the Church of England – for example, from 598 in 1960 to 340 in 1972 – meant that many of the smaller livings *had* to be combined. And the local laity now *insisted* on a greater say in appointments. In fact in John's time only one Living disappeared altogether from the Trinity list, Wymeswold in Leicestershire (where Dean Alford had written 'Come, ye thankful people, come'); though several Livings were joined or grouped or teamed with others so that the terms of Trinity's patronage changed. Moreover it is difficult to find an incumbent of a Trinity Living who does not think John did a good job as secretary of the College Livings Committee.

John did not struggle over much to get to know all the Trinity men in priest's orders but he did all he could to get the best man for a vacant Living, whatever his college. He consulted the diocese – as well as the parish – at crucial times. He visited personally – and enjoyed visiting – the College Livings. Canon John Hodgkinson, Vicar of Kendal, has written:

> Most years, John would make a tour of the Trinity Livings, and I used to look forward to his informal and friendly visits. It was good to have someone from outside the diocese who showed concern.
>
> Shortly before he moved to Yorkshire, John and I spent a very long lunch at 'The Brewery Arts Centre' in Kendal. Diners came and went unnoticed as we wrestled with the theological issues of the day. A recent convert to Don Cupitt's position, I valued the opportunity to test my views with someone of John's calibre. I found that the author of *Honest to God* was now the champion of orthodoxy – although he could have been stringing me along.
>
> The Restaurant was almost empty by the time we had reached 'Eternal Life'. I put forward an analogy to the drops of water in a river that finally reach the end of their journey and are united with the ocean. John paused for a moment and then shook his head: 'That won't do for me, I hope for a more personal life after death.'
>
> Trinity incumbents were always welcome to visit and dine at Trinity; so all in all, John made Trinity's Patronage a relationship full of meaning.

One of the first appointments John had to recommend to the College was in 1970, when the Vicar of Great St Mary's, Cambridge, Hugh Montefiore, was made Suffragan Bishop of Kingston. John first spent much time trying to persuade a Trinity man – in fact, a former Chaplain of Trinity – to succeed him; and only when he refused did John recommend an Oriel College, Oxford man, Stanley Booth-Clibborn (now Bishop of Manchester) to the College.

It was with John's assistance as Dean of Chapel that the College Council and the Diocese of Southwark negotiated a system of joint patronage for the living of St George's, Camberwell, the parish in South London in which the College Mission had been established nearly a century before – but the patronage had hitherto belonged solely to the Diocese. John gladly played his part on the Camberwell committee, which was always chaired by the Master of Trinity, not least because he had seen much of St George's when he was Bishop of Woolwich. He did all he could to bring to a successful conclusion the plans for a new Trinity Centre in the parish – opened in 1982 – and to bring Trinity and Camberwell closer together. (Peter Adams, Vicar of St George's and Warden of the College Mission 1975–83, had worked closely with John as Chaplain of Trinity from 1970 to 1975.)

There was one ecclesiastical subject a Dean of Chapel could not avoid in the Seventies: liturgical revision; for in 1955 the Church of England had set up its own Liturgical Commission, and ten years later had authorized new services for experimental use. Since then the commission had prepared revised services in three distinct 'series'. The Worship and Doctrine Measure of 1975 would in due course lead to the Alternative Service Book of 1980.

John personally could not avoid this subject, for he had already made public his own views in *Liturgy Coming to Life*. He had also gained considerable experience as Dean of Clare in how to handle a Cambridge college where this subject was concerned. He had learnt that patience is not only required but rewarded, and that he could probably achieve what he wanted if the chapel-going Fellows and junior members of College were treated responsibly: if a fairly representative liturgy group were set up, and drafts of services carefully considered, and alternatives voted upon. There would of course be proposals and counter-proposals – and storms in Cambridge tea-cups! – and young undergraduates would sometimes prove more recalcitrant than aged Fellows: but if there was sufficient consultation – and if the Chaplains did much of the ground-work – all would be well. One of the earliest productions of the liturgy group John set up – 'an unrepresentative group only to the extent that it has brought together over the past year those who are particularly concerned to explore what liturgy should be doing and meaning today, especially in our own situation' – was a paper that is a model in mood and content of how such discussions should be carried on – not only in Cambridge:

> Worship is an expression of what we believe and we want to put it into our own language, not one that is far away from us. If we cannot put it into the same sort of language as that in which we live the rest of our lives, it compartmentalizes religion. We want in worship to be taken out of ourselves, but not into another culture. We need to be able to express the mystery and the transcendent *in* modern language: the world which the worship transcends must be that of the twentieth century not the sixteenth. We also want to worship in the same sort of language in which we *think* about God – otherwise the relationship between the two is broken. There should be no dichotomy or alternative between thinking and worship: 'I will pray, but with the understanding also.' And, as St Paul also recognized, it is not only a question of what *we* like: the impact upon and relevance to the outsider and the enquirer is important, even at the Eucharist. Many come in today through the parish communion and they do not come in with the old church background: indeed they may be refreshed to find its absence.
>
> The arguments advanced in favour of the old were understood and appreciated, but just did not seem relevant to the majority. It needs to be recognized how much a person gets out of the old language *because* it is old and familiar. For others, to whom it is not familiar, the new works just as well – though they too would urge that you get much more out of it as you become used to it. Taste in these matters appears very arbitrary and it takes time for someone brought up on the rhythms and periods of the old to appreciate the equally valid rhythms of the new, which are more like those of modern poetry.
>
> It was fully recognized that there is no clear-cut issue here. There are pastoral concerns to be respected, on both sides. The last thing anyone wanted was a liturgy that was *merely* contemporary, that did not carry the overtones of the ages. But the overtones are supplied by much more than the language – by the whole presentation of the service, the music, the building. To use words just because they are beautiful may miss the point: it may be better to use the words that clarify rather than lull and to allow other aspects of the worship – including silence – to give them their resonance . . .

'The whole presentation of the service, the music, the building' provided the Dean of Chapel with a continuing agenda, in addition to the question of forms of service.

'Only the walls and roof of the Chapel are of Tudor origin,' wrote G. M. Trevelyan, in *Trinity College: An Historical Sketch.* 'For the fine woodwork of the organ-screen, stalls, panels and the baldachino over the altar, we are indebted to Bentley and to his friends and enemies the Fellows in the reigns of Anne and the first two Georges. The elaborate scheme of mural decoration above, and the coloured glass windows are patently Victorian.'

In fact the nineteenth-century paintings on the walls and ceiling had been painted over when the Chapel was redecorated nearly ten years before John's appointment; but there was still much to be discussed – not least with the College Council – and handled carefully by the Dean, before the Chapel would shine as it shines now.

In 1976 John dedicated the renovated and restored organ. The old one had been dismantled, and a new one, incorporating parts of the original 'Father Smith' organ, had been built by Metzler of Zurich inside the original organ case. In 1978 the admission of women undergraduates to the College meant – to John's great delight – that the Chapel Choir could be composed of both men and women, which would so raise the standard of the Choir that evensong and the Epiphany carol service would be broadcast by the BBC. John, although he himself lacked any great musical appreciation, was well aware that for some, music was – as for George Herbert (Trinity College 1610–27) – 'the way to heaven's doore'.

John was willing to expend much time and many letters, and consult artist upon artist, in order to get the Chapel lit effectively and beautifully, and to get the right painting – or carving – for the huge baldachino that dominates the east end of the Chapel. That John cared for the Chapel at Trinity there can be no doubt. Eventually however the altar-piece of 'St Michael and the Dragon', painted for it in the late eighteenth century by Benjamin West, and banished to the Library staircase in the 1870s, was returned to its original place.

The final printed 'Order for Holy Communion' – containing carefully selected prayers and meditations, to which John had made a considerable contribution – is, as he had made sure it was at Clare, a thing of beauty. That John cared for the worship *within* the Chapel at Trinity there can also be no doubt.

But at Trinity John was judged primarily by what he was and did *outside* the Chapel – and his own theology approved of that. Some of those who were with John at Trinity are best able to voice that judgment. He took particular care (with others) in choosing the College Chaplains.

Philip Buckler, Chaplain of Trinity 1975–81, (now Minor Canon and Sacrist of St Paul's Cathedral) has written:

In October 1973 I received a letter from John Robinson asking whether I would be interested in a Chaplaincy at Trinity. We met in Cambridge towards the end of that year. I was struck immediately by that strange mixture of warmth and awkwardness that always surrounded him. He took me for a walk to the University Library, conversing all the way with an engaging intimacy about his latest interests and enthusiasms, and about particular people who he believed had something to say. He spoke loudly, unconcerned about others who might listen, and continued at the same volume even within the quiet atmosphere of the Library. Our walk continued through the grounds of Clare, and out on to the Backs behind King's College Chapel. As we sat in the watery winter sun, it was clear how much delight he took in the natural world about him.

Following that meeting I received another letter, characteristic of many that he would write in subsequent years. It was full of the most generous warmth and friendship. It is perhaps significant that it was primarily in his preaching or writing, and especially in his letters, that he was best able to expose the depth of his feelings.

John was not an easy friend – yet he was much loved. He could be demanding of those around him. For there were times of loneliness when he needed companionship and affection. These resulted from his style of life – living during term time in College, concentrating on his work, and returning home to Reigate, or later Arncliffe, in the vacations. Only occasionally would Ruth come to the College – though she was always welcomed by John's friends, who had often been welcomed by them both in visits to their home during the vacations. Their pattern of life meant that John came to rely heavily upon his Cambridge friends for company in moments of relaxation during term. There would be walks around the Cambridgeshire countryside, visits to the cinema, journeys to watch cricket – occasions when he relished company and displayed the vulnerability almost of a child. The people with whom he chose to spend such time would be drawn from among his pupils, a few undergraduates he had come to know in College, the College Chaplains and one or two others.

There was the annual visit to Lords for the Test Match. John claimed that he liked to appoint chaplains who were members of the MCC to ensure that he could always get tickets for the cricket! Invariably the day John chose would be the day it rained. One year, rain delayed the start of play till mid-afternoon. The umpires came out at last, only to return to the Pavilion immediately. The crowds started shouting and booing; and there was John standing on his seat, yelling in anger at what he considered bad sportsmanship. The umpires were vindicated five minutes later when the rain began again and settled in for the rest of the day. We retired again to the bar, John talking about a book he had just received – *The Myth of God Incarnate* – before we all set off home again, starved of sport.

At the end of my first term, John wrote me a letter in which he said 'I remember Thirks, the old Master of Clare, saying to me at the end of my first term "I am so glad you came". Knowing what encouragement it gave me I pass on the same message. I am indeed glad, as we all are, that you came.' Such words certainly offered encouragement, and displayed another side of John which some might not immediately recognise – his sensitivity. For to call John a sensitive person would demand substantial qualification. He could also be one of the most insensitive people imaginable. His glaring insensitivity none of John's friends could deny. For whatever reason, there were jarring moments of speech or action which sadly obscured for many the gifts he had to offer. Few of John's friends cannot recall times when through carelessness John managed to hurt them quite deeply. Had he realised, he would probably have been distraught; but it was often this lack of realisation or consideration in apparently small matters that usually created the situations. For one so clearly sensitive to the world at certain levels, so brilliant a communicator in words, both spoken and written, it was a surprising fault. Yet it could not be overlooked, and the tragedy is that it caused so much damage at Trinity. Yet there was sensitivity there, and many could point to moments when his words or actions displayed a deeper awareness and concern than they might have expected. He was a wise and loving father-in-God to Linda and myself as we talked over the possibility of marriage (especially as this was not considered appropriate by many for a Chaplain to the College in those days). It was John who took great delight in conducting the service on our wedding day – though he needed to be prompted on a number of occasions! John also made the effort to hurry to see Linda in hospital one day after she had suffered a miscarriage. In the rather awkward setting of a hospital ward he expressed loud surprise at the situation, saying 'I can't understand it. Ruth never had any problems with children.' Such statements will be recognised by many who recall cringing at John's ability to say the wrong thing. He could be the master of the inept comment or the disastrous timing.

It was often this careless insensitivity that people remembered, rather than those other moments of deep perception and concern for a wide variety of persons who were around him or might seek him out. The fault lay, probably, in a kind of carelessness. A lack of care or concentration in the ordinary everyday things is the charge which could be levelled against John. In his defence it might be argued that he was busily concerned with what he considered matters of importance, and had little time for all the niceties of social convention. Yet he clearly was perceptive about such aspects of social behaviour, for it was often at these points that his preaching would begin; and his sensitivity to the world and its concerns was what made him unquestionably a fine preacher and teacher of the faith.

It was in the short sermons at the College Eucharist on a Sunday morning that John most revealed his remarkable skills as a teacher. One of his favourite expressions was 'grist to the mill', and his pithy imaginative illustrations would provide just that for those who were thinking out their faith. Although John would only have opportunity to get to know a small number of the College's undergraduates, those who were of that number were richly rewarded. But nearly all of the students who came across him, even at a distant level, held him in respect. His ministry in the Chapel, or his hospitality to interesting visitors he would introduce at his Dean's Evenings, were appreciated by all sorts. After Sunday morning Chapel, breakfast would be served in the rooms of the Chaplains and the Dean. Those whom John invited to join him knew they were likely to be in for a time of listening, as he would hold court upon his latest enthusiasm, or else converse at length with a particular guest who might be visiting. Nevertheless they realised they were privileged – if not always comfortable.

In a sermon preached in October 1980 John said:

> The more I go on, the more rooted I feel I want to be at the centre – biblically and doctrinally – and the more radical at the edges. It is my deep roots that over the years have driven me to radical stances both in doctrine and ethics.

This rootedness, both in the Christian Gospel and in the Anglican tradition, was kept alive and fresh by his own personal devotions. For the leader of so much new liturgical experiment was also the person who would each morning be in the little 'upper room' that we used as a Chapel, to join in the saying of Mattins and to share in twenty minutes corporate silence. But although silence clearly meant a great deal to John, he could hardly be described as a person of stillness. He would fidget unmercifully. On Saturday evenings, late at night in the candle-lit College Chapel, Compline would be sung by the choir. It was always a surprise to John that students would turn out for such a traditional act of worship at such an unusual hour in student life. Nevertheless he clearly enjoyed it himself and would sit there, as moved as the rest, by the singing and the setting. But he would fidget with the candle fitments loudly – to the irritation of those around him.

Acknowledging the necessity of institutions, John was fiercely critical when their trappings obscured their very purposes. It was partly this, coupled with his carelessness with matters not engaging his immediate attention, that led him to be so unpopular a figure amongst his colleagues. Undoubtedly he failed to appreciate much of the life of the College, and never became the College man Trinity wanted. He may well have been irritated by many of the sillinesses that occur in a close community such as a High Table, but in choosing to ignore them completely he cut himself off from those to whom he was supposed to be not only colleague but pastor. There were, of course, some who found in him the most rewarding of personal guides, but they were the exceptions. The Fellows prided themselves upon a style of life and tradition that contained its own unwritten rules of communal living and concern. With these John proved careless in his disregard. This was aggravated by his angular and loud or brash manner.

His colleagues would often only hear of the more popular items that engaged his interest, rather than the serious study that occupied the majority of his time. The people he attracted and welcomed as his guests were occasionally to prove a liability in such an environment. It is easy to see the shortcomings of a close community such as Trinity at this level, but it was never itself closed to new people or ideas. John was at fault, perhaps, in not being prepared to take its conventions seriously. This was all the more sad as he could have been so very much at the heart of the College as its Dean of Chapel. Many looked for one who would be committed to the College, critical certainly – even awkward – but at least committed. This they felt was lacking in John. It was symbolised in his hurrying away from College at the first possible opportunity, only just fulfilling the requirements of residence. All would acknowledge that a College system of this sort should offer ample facilities to support the research of its members; it was hoped that many would contribute something in return. It was expected that a Dean of Chapel would be one whose contribution to the College would be substantial. Yet many saw John only taking the benefits without apparently offering much in return. That was undoubtedly a false impression, but easily gained in comparison with his predecessors such as Harry Williams and John Burnaby, both of whom were still in touch with the College and many of its Fellows. These difficulties were clearly not helped by the fact that the Divinity Faculty did not – perhaps could not – offer John the recognition he deserved. Consequently he was financially supported by the College, and many felt as a result they deserved more from him.

With Ruth and Father Johannes Rakale in Soweto, Johannesburg

With the Reverend Professor C.H. Dodd in the procession of the translators
of the New English Bible, Westminster Abbey, 16 May 1970

The Dean of Trinity at the wedding of a Chaplain of Trinity

John and Ruth in the Botanical Garden Cambridge, during his last illness

Of the hostility towards him he was probably more aware than at times his behaviour suggested. Yet I doubt he understood how widespread it had become.

He had forged the situation where his presence was not always welcome, yet his absence was most often resented. It usually fell to the Chaplains to act as intermediaries, interpreting the Dean to the College, and the College to the Dean.

Many of us owe a great deal to John. I have already mentioned his concern and support for Linda and myself. It was he who later also prepared Linda for Baptism and Confirmation. Each week she would go to see John for preparation. He would have ready a pot of his latest tea – perhaps peppermint or jasmine – and would talk about his latest ideas or enthusiasms, or tell of the exciting people who had attracted his attention that week. It was hardly preparation for Confirmation, and often proved for her more frustrating than helpful. One evening she returned to my rooms exploding with irritation, determined never to go again, only to discover Eric James – who had been with John prior to her visit – saying how much John looked forward to these occasions and what it meant to him. It proved a happy day when John himself confirmed Linda in the College Chapel, along with other members of the College, at the annual College Confirmation.

The Revd Dr John Polkinghorne, FRS, a Fellow of Trinity since 1954 and Professor of Mathematical Physics, Cambridge 1968–79, now Dean of Trinity Hall, Cambridge, writes:

More than anyone else I have ever known, John Robinson was an unresolved mixture of differing attitudes. Endowed with the learning of the scholar, he possessed also the instinct of the journalist for an issue which would catch the public imagination. He dearly loved to set the cat among the pigeons. His fascination with the Shroud of Turin displayed all these characteristics to the full. He came of a clerical line; 'My uncle Armitage' was often mentioned. Added to this weight of tradition was, however, what seemed at times an instant alignment with the changing attitudes of society. Mention a topic such as the lowering of the age of consent and John appeared to move into a kind of radical overdrive which produced a reaction less considered than the complexities of the situation required.

A man of warm friendship and great kindness, John could also be tactless in the extreme and remain quite unconscious of the effect his words produced. At the private lunch when he was being interviewed as prospective Dean of Chapel he said with his characteristic sharp laugh: 'I'm rather good at closing down churches.' It created an impression of harshness which was an unfortunate and inaccurate comment on his time as Bishop of Woolwich. Once when we were chatting over lunch at the High Table, John said to me (apropos of what I cannot now remember), 'a Protestant rationalist like you would not understand that'. I burnt with indignation at this (I believe) totally unfair characterisation, but John seemed quite unaware he might have given offence. Through *Honest to God* John became a media figure in a way that is given to few bishops and hardly any scholars. It must have been a heady experience. He clearly enjoyed it with a naive enthusiasm. Once, when we were talking in the Parlour, he pulled out a wodge of press cuttings about himself in some controversy which was then attracting attention, and invited me to read them. It was a self-regarding act redeemed by the simplicity with which he did it. Scholars as a whole tend to regard such public fame achieved by one of their number with suspicion and not a little covert envy.

In the general life of the High Table in Trinity the odder, less-endearing, sides of John were sometimes more visible than those which caused some of us greatly to value his friendship. Most Fellows would read in the paper of some half-considered comment John had made on a moral or political issue. Very few had read *The Human Face of God*, the only serious contribution to Christology by an English theologian in recent years. This slant, combined with the robust anti-clericalism of some Fellows, meant that John had some hostility towards him during most of his time at Trinity. It was not widespread but it was unfortunate, and reduced his influence in the College as a whole. It was not clear how aware John was of this, but to the extent that he was aware he took it with good nature. It was wholly dispelled by the dignity and courage with which he lived his life following the diagnosis of terminal cancer. Some of those who had been most in opposition were generous in seeking to help him by arrangements to minimise the problems presented by his illness.

No one can rightly assess John's time in Trinity who did not share in the worship of Chapel and the activities associated with it. He was an excellent preacher who always drew a good congregation to hear him, including many from outside the College. His fertile mind was manifestly engaged in the search for truth. Although in *Honest to God* John had spoken of the difficulty he found about prayer, there was, during his time as Dean, a reverent and prayerful atmosphere in the worship of Chapel which remains a subject for gratitude for those of us who shared in it.

It was a great pleasure to me, and I think to John, that, by kind permission of the Bishop of Ely, he ordained me priest in Trinity Chapel on Trinity Sunday 1982. As it turned out, I was the last priest he was to ordain.

David Reindorp, who had spent several years as a social worker and went up to Trinity as a mature student aged twenty-seven in 1979, and is a Team Vicar in Hitchin, writes:

When I went to Westcott House in 1978 to be interviewed – for ordination in due course – somewhat to my surprise Westcott had organised an interview with John Robinson with a view to my reading Theology at Trinity. It was a classic encounter. Suzy, my wife, was with me, and John was knee-deep in galley proofs. Suzy's experience in publishing enabled her to help him with those; then he stumbled upon his address book, and asked us if we knew where so and so now lived: and away we went on that. We touched briefly on theology, and then our time was gone. He airily said, 'See you next year,' and that was that!

In 1979 I came up to Trinity. J.A.T.R. was most welcoming. He had a concept of life outside the University, of the trauma of giving it up and what having a wife and child meant – not all that common in Trinity!

J.A.T.R. was something of an ageing lion when I first met him. We all knew of *Honest to God*; the Shroud saga was a recent event. But, as one fellow undergraduate very gently pointed out to John, he was only two in the year of *Honest to God* – 1963.

John's position at Trinity was not easy. Harry Williams had been much loved, had relished High Table and was essentially clubbable. He was a hard act to follow. John was too serious a man for that; he would have been forgiven for that, but for his own ego. Trinity is no stranger to distinguished men, indeed, takes rightful pride in that; but it is of a subtle kind. The last *Annual Record* put under 'Other Appointments' Rajiv Gandhi – Prime Minister of India; Douglas Hurd, Secretary of State for Northern Ireland. As the Diarist of *The Times* asked: 'What do you have to do to make the main list?' That is the kind of distinction Trinity likes – there, but understated. But there was nothing understated about John; he relished the limelight and gloried in media exposure. Nothing pleased him more than to lecture to a crowded Dining Hall on the Turin Shroud.

His fellow dons found such blatant playing to the gallery unattractive and opportunist, and were sometimes just jealous. But it also made those who were serious about academic work look upon his serious work in the same light. No man could have meant to be kinder – but sometimes John was totally lacking in awareness. When we were having an End of Year dinner for all Trinity theologians, somewhat at the last minute we invited Dr Eamon Duffy – Fellow, Tutor and Director of Studies in History and Theology at Magdalene College – to join us. J.A.T.R., in welcoming him, said, 'Eamon, thank you for coming; we were really scraping the barrel when we asked *you*.' What he meant was entirely different. The *frisson* caused by this remark was dissipated by Ruth saying how ghastly it sounded; and we were all able to laugh it off.

On another occasion, we were discussing in the Faculty a book written by a highly regarded pupil of Owen Chadwick's. J.A.T.R. suddenly said it was a much better book than he thought it was going to be! His meaning was entirely different – but the damage was done. John was like a porcupine with its bristles up, walking backwards into people, totally oblivious of the offence caused. Never did John mean to give offence, but he had a childlike naivety with regard to social niceties that often presented him in a totally undeserved unflattering light. Not for nothing did Ruth describe him as 'my lovely impossible man'.

Why then did I love John?

He was not a good teacher in the supervision sense of that word. A great teacher and an original mind are not necessarily the same gift. But you knew that John was a great man. His words were from the horse's mouth; he was a leader in his field, and if you wanted his teaching, there it was in his books – and what an output! Why I loved him as a teacher was his endless ability to ask questions. 'What think ye of this?' was his by-word. He taught you always to ask questions, never to accept orthodoxy – all must be tested and tried. In this sense *Redating* was quintessential J.A.T.R. Intellectual timidity was not in his nature.

I loved him for his moral courage. If he felt something was right he would go for it. I so well remember sitting in the bath one Sunday morning and hearing him on the radio denounce the Falklands war. I thought, 'Oh, crumbs! this will mean trouble!' For J.A.T.R. that kind of thought wouldn't enter his head. The successive Lambeth Conferences had condemned war as a means of settling disputes, and for John that was what it meant.

I loved him for his boyish enthusiasm – vegetarianism, nuclear war etc. – and his intellectual vigour. You name it! He never tired of exploring new avenues. It did not make his life easy, for his fellow academics suspected him of 'bandwagonism', and it was often dismissed as John's latest scheme. This restlessness spilled over into his professionalism. He should have been a round peg in a round hole as Dean of Trinity. He had income; time for teaching; time for travelling. But he was always searching for a new interest, and – in later years – for the possibility of a new job; with the result that Trinity felt his heart was not in the College and that he could not wait to escape from it.

I loved him for his awkwardness. Great men often have great weaknesses. Because they loom large in public life, their strengths and weaknesses, likewise, loom large. John's childish awkwardness resulted in terrible *faux pas* that obscured much of his pastoral work in the

College. Undergraduates would mime his accent. But you mostly mimic those who are worth mimicking.

But he *did* care and *did* love. His friendship to me, and care of Suzy, when I had my breakdown and was in hospital, showed J.A.T.R.'s pastoral strength.

I loved him because he was so vulnerable. College life is not easy for wives. The Master's wife has an essential role – unlike the Dean's. John and Ruth resolved the essential bachelor existence of the Dean of Chapel's role with J.A.T.R. being on his own during term time and going home for vacations. Although totally understandable, it meant that in term time J.A.T.R. missed Ruth's eirenic qualities and those qualities of hers that softened him. His absence in vacations contributed likewise to a feeling amongst dons that he was never there.

I loved him also for another aspect of his character. He was a complete *child* of the Church of England, born into the Canterbury precincts. That childlike quality never left him and did much to explain his naivety. But his being centred in the Church of England and being so totally part of it meant that at times he played the role of *enfant terrible*. And, like any favoured child within a family, he felt secure to do just that, knowing no harm would come to his family. He never feared to rock the boat for he knew the boat was safe.

I loved him also for the manner of his dying, and will always be thankful for popping into his rooms just as he was leaving Trinity for the last time, and being able to pack him into his car, and bid him farewell. He faced death with his customary intelligence and drive, exploring all avenues. His dying gave Trinity the opportunity to show him some of the love that he had failed to evoke earlier. As his dying brought out his own best qualities, so Trinity rose to the occasion.

Dr Sarah Coakley, who with her husband Dr Chip Coakley shares the Lectureship in Religious Studies at Lancaster University, has written:

My first chance encounter with John, under slightly bizarre circum-stances, was memorable for several features in him which, as I much later discovered, were wholly characteristic. It had been the custom at the Blackheath High School for Girls, for some obscure reason, to invite a clerical father of one of the girls to give a short sermon at 'prayers' (assembly) on Ascension Day. Accordingly I remember craning my neck up from my cross-legged position at the front amongst the youngest senior girls (I was ten) to hear this youthful-looking bishop with a red boyish face and a curiously compelling grating voice expound the Acts account of the Ascension. It was my first experience of demythologiz-ation, and I was both excited and shocked. It was doubtless not a coincidence that thereafter the school's Ascension Day observance lapsed (in any case it was, I think, the next year that the *Honest to God* furore broke). Bishop John Taylor – of Winchester – wrote to me after John died that he thought John's essential spiritual attractiveness lay in his evoking a powerful combination of little boy and wise old man archetypes; that was certainly true of this first occasion of my coming across him (it is significant that I remember it so vividly), as was the much more obvious, and somewhat naive, capacity to rock the boat.

Much later, when I came to be taught by John at Cambridge (I had met him briefly at a party the year before going up, and was both surprised and flattered when he extended an invitation via my Director of Studies to take me on for New Testament), I found the supervisions at first absolutely nerve-wracking. In my first year I was coming to New Testament study completely cold, and had almost no equipment yet for distinguishing good from bad secondary literature. John, it must be said, was virtually no help here: he made no concessions to the weaker brethren, and always looked faintly irritated if one asked for bibliographical suggestions (the answer in any case would almost invariably be one of his own books or articles, or failing that, something that in some other way he had had a hand in). My first essay for him was in fact the only one for which he even supplied a title (the dating of Acts, I remember), and for this he threw off the suggestion that I look at John O'Neill's book on Acts, which, it turned out, was based on a thesis supervised by John himself. Thereafter, he simply left me to choose my own titles and concoct my own reading lists; the effect, educationally, was excellent, as far as training in initiative was concerned, although I probably emerged with a rather idiosyncratic package of learning, rooted primarily in John's own work. A supervision with John was, however, always an occasion, whether of a positive or humiliating nature. I never learned to relax in his company as an undergraduate, and found his particular form of gaucheness unerringly *uncomfortable*: the booming voice and rather penetrating gaze were fairly fearful opponents in themselves, the more so if one was taking a line opposed to his (which I increasingly did, sometimes just for the sake of it). Also he could be critical in an off-hand and pretty devastating way; but he never talked down; in fact, much more than with other teachers, one felt oneself to be engaged as an equal. Thus he often lent out unpublished material of his own, asking for comment at the next supervision, and he positively welcomed any new bibliographical leads that one could come up with for him. Thus he used his students more as sounding boards and sources of information than as charges to whom certain responsibilities were due from his side.

As a teacher, then, John could be quite disastrous if one was looking for a safe passage through the Tripos, but enormously challenging if one was willing to play the game according to his rules. Even if many sessions revolved wholly round his own recent theories, he could also be surprisingly, even touchingly, interested in one's own intellectual concerns and development. I recall, after a frustrating term on historical problems in the Gospels, voicing a complaint that my disagreements with John were probably more a product of underlying philosophical and christological issues than of the minutiae of gospel criticism. John's immediate response was that I should go away and write an extra essay expounding these problems, and I think he was genuinely concerned that I get them straight in my own mind. (Ultimately in fact this resulted in my doctoral thesis on Ernst Troeltsch and his christology.) Once again, this illustrated both John's blithe disregard for the constraints of the syllabus, and also his willingness to listen seriously to a student's particular 'line', his concern for the individual's integrity and growth. This was the sort of touch that belied the (superficial) impression that his teaching was little more than egotistical booming, as some snidely complained.

Overall, I found John much better on Paul than the gospels. Indeed reading *The Body* (in my view possibly even his best book) and exploring the central themes of Romans under his guidance, were a real spiritual and intellectual tonic. On the gospels I felt his concern to show that a lot more material than was generally allowed was 'early' and 'authentic' arose from presupposed christological needs and led to a lot of special pleading. (Chip, incidentally, would not agree with me.) And perhaps I do an injustice to John here, because there are strands in *The Human Face of God*, and elsewhere, which show that he was not wholly hide-bound by the historical Jesus. None the less this was his basic starting-point where christology was concerned, and I don't think he really ever understood the objections to it. Others, of course, found it enormously refreshing, typically, Catholics rediscovering the human Jesus after Vatican II. John once asked me who Ruth Burrows was, who had been writing enthusiastically to him from Quiddenham about *The Human Face of God*. It was significant that John had no idea that she was probably the country's leading expert on the distinguishing marks of 'union' in St John of the Cross. I never discussed prayer with John, and although I'm sure he was a faithful pray-er, I don't believe there was any contemplative streak in him.

Although John was essentially British in his christological method, in another way he was quite Germanic, in the sense of *systematic* in his thinking – more so, probably, than other theologians at Cambridge alongside him. Perhaps this is another way of talking about his intellectual integrity. He wasn't at all ponderous or self-conscious about it, but whether discoursing on a minor pericope in the gospels, or the state of the Labour Party, or the Falklands war, or the age of consent, the outcome was slotted into the complete Robinsonian framework. Perhaps this was partly why he was an offence to some members of the Cambridge Faculty: he was concerned with the big picture, and with the application of biblical theology to contemporary issues, and with the making of it known to one and all. He could never have been contented merely with dense articles written for the scholarly élite, although he certainly desired to be taken seriously at that level too. The fact that he often wasn't must have been deeply painful to him. It must be said, however, that I never heard him utter anything disparaging or bitter about his Cambridge theological colleagues, despite their discernible hostility, with one sole exception that surely proves the rule! But, as with so many sides to his character, John's charity towards others seemed not something actively sought or achieved as a virtue, but simply John being himself. He was charmingly 'without guile', and perhaps it was partly *because* he was naturally so remote from the plotting and scheming that characterizes much of academic life that he was disliked by so many within it. (That was not the only reason of course. His notorious tactlessness was another; again, just John being himself.)

Intellectually, I owe John an enormous amount. Looking back I see that he was the dominant influence during my undergraduate days, and that by putting me agonizingly on the spot, he, more than any other of my teachers, made me think for myself. (After ten years of my own university teaching I now know how strangely difficult it is to nurture that capacity.) At the more personal level, I owe John of course even more: it was he who introduced me to Chip, fostered the match (he was half-way through proposing on the reticent Chip's behalf when Ruth mercifully interrupted with an expostulation from her cooking over the Aga), and eventually married us. He remained our most important mentor, and was an especially good friend when we were first setting up house in Cambridge.

John was always a bit larger than life. But had I been asked before his final illness whether he was a great man I might have hesitated, wondering if his work would stand the test of time. Having witnessed the manner of his dying, I have no hesitation at all. I vividly recall going to see him in Addenbrooke's the week-end after his terminal cancer had been diagnosed. It was the same John, but he was already changed, his actual physical vision sharpened, for he looked at me as if he was seeing me for the first time. In a way that I find impossible to delineate, let alone relate concretely or clearly to the 'historical Jesus', I would like to say with conviction that I saw Christ in him there.

Dr Jim Garrison, author of *From Hiroshima to Harrisburg: The Unholy Alliance* and *The Darkness of God: Theology after Hiroshima* has written:

I first came across John Robinson's name while studying at Harvard Divinity School. I was considering applying to a doctoral programme at a British University. Also studying at HDS was an English woman, Sarah Coakley. In the course of several conversations, John's name came up as someone she had studied under, admired, and who would probably be sympathetic to someone like myself who wanted to write a thesis on a socially relevant subject. She recommended I read *The Human Face of God*, as I was particularly interested in different perceptions of Christology.

I read the book with fascination. It was the first Christological work that filled the humanity of Christ with divinity rather than the other way around, and in so doing made the person of Jesus accessible to me in a way no other theologian had done. I was particularly struck with Robinson's query as to whether Jesus ever had an erection. I thought to myself: 'I'd like to study under that man.'

So I applied to Cambridge, and was accepted at Emmanuel College for the Fall of 1975. By this time, I had become increasingly concerned with the nuclear issue as well as with the feminist critique of theology. It seemed to me that these two issues – the development of a technology that could destroy the world and the equalization of the sexes – were perhaps the most compelling issues of the 20th Century.

I can clearly remember my first meeting with the Bishop, in his rooms on the Great Court of Trinity. I was quite nervous, knowing of his fame and reputation; knowing, too, that Trinity had rejected my application for admission. In fact his first words were to recall that Trinity had rejected me and to register surprise that Emmanuel had not! I felt myself perspiring, and said quickly that I had come specifically because I wanted to study under him. He asked why. I told him my impressions of *The Human Face of God* and how struck I was about his query about erections. He looked at me with incredulity. I rambled on, saying something about the courage it took to ask questions like that. I had clearly made him even more nervous than I was.

He then asked me what I wished to study. I said I wasn't sure, but the interconnection between the advent of nuclear weapons and the liberation of women was a topic which I was seriously considering. His little eyes got big: he leaned over his desk at me and said: 'Mr Garrison, I don't think you belong here, and I certainly don't think I would be a suitable supervisor. As for studying the liberation of women, that's completely out of the question. The Divinity Faculty is not equipped to handle it.'

I felt completely devastated and suggested that I think things over and get back to him. He reluctantly agreed. Over the next months I read extensively, mostly Teilhard de Chardin, Bultmann and Bonhoeffer, trying to come up with something else to study. Finally, in March 1976, I was offered a job working on nuclear policy at the Office of Social Ministries of the Jesuit National Conference in Washington, DC. Feeling isolated and unwanted at Cambridge, I took a year's leave of absence to work for the Jesuits. When I informed Robinson I was taking a leave, he was enthusiastic! Cambridge was a very narrow hoop, he said; I would probably be happier elsewhere.

During the remainder of 1976, I worked with the Washington Inter-religious Staff Council in the area of policy development with regards to nuclear technology. I read Pedro Arrupe's *A Planet to Heal*, which spoke of the importance of Hiroshima and the challenge it posed to Christian theology and faith. I realized that this issue was the only one I could explore with any sense of integrity. I also felt personally challenged by Robinson's coolness, and became determined not only to return to Cambridge but to insist that he be my supervisor.

When I returned in January 1977, I tried a new tack. I proposed that I take up the question of the relationship between the visions of apocalyptic destruction and renewal articulated by the Jewish prophets in the centuries just before Christ and the technology which could now actually destroy the world. Bonhoeffer had said that a secularized world had pushed God beyond present existence. We no longer had need of recourse to God for our everyday lives. Nuclear weapons, I argued, were pushing God even beyond the possible *end* of existence, and were, therefore, a direct challenge to the Judao-Christian prophecies which said only a wrathful God would end the world.

This was the first time the Bishop had looked interested. I asked his permission to try a draft. He reiterated his distaste for 'woolly thinking', reminded me that Cambridge PhDs were supposed to be very technical treatises about very narrow subjects, and then said apocalyptic was completely out of his field, to say nothing of nuclear weapons. Couldn't I find another supervisor? I almost begged him to be patient and let me have a go. With reluctance he agreed.

I don't think I have ever worked so hard in my life. For the next six months the University Library was my home. I was too frightened of Robinson to see him, although I remember bumping into him one day at the Divinity School and saying work was in progress. I gave him my essay, some 40,000 words, in June. He read it in a few days – he was always very quick to do things – and told me he was impressed. I was so relieved I almost cried. What I remember most clearly about this conversation was the way he sucked his teeth and pointed out all my split infinitives.

I decided to take another leave of absence at this point to return to Harvard to study with Paul Hansen, a specialist in apocalyptic, whose book had had a major impact not only on my understanding of prophecy but on how the Biblical tradition evolved. I was also interested in studying with Harvey Cox. I think John was slightly disappointed I was taking leave at this time, but gave me his permission, saying it was clear to him I was on to *something* original – an essential requirement for a Cambridge PhD – even if he still wasn't sure what that something was.

The year at Harvard was of major importance, as I was not only grounded more deeply in the complexities of apocalyptic but introduced to the Process Theology of Whitehead and Hartshorne and the Depth Psychology of Carl Jung. Hartshorne and Jung amplified my understanding of 'panentheism' – which I had learned from Robinson and Norman Pittenger – and provided a method of linking the ancient apocalyptic visions of the end with the 20th Century capacity to achieve it. I also continued my involvement in the politics of nuclear protest, which only deepened my conviction that nuclear weapons were the most critical theological issue of our time.

I returned to Robinson in the Fall of 1978, full of enthusiasm and with an entirely new draft. My thesis was that Hiroshima was to Christianity what Jesus was to ancient Judaism – it was filling the old wineskins with new wine. It was radicalizing our category of apocalyptic by giving humans the power to enact what the religious community formerly believed only God could do. In the process, it was forcing us to take more seriously that humans and God create history together. If apocalyptic was characterized by an outpouring of human sin and divine wrath, we had to explore our own psychic depths to discover these qualities now – something the Depth Psychology of Jung could help us to do. In the process, this opened up new insights into the reality of evil, the darkness of God, and the capacity of God and humanity alike to engage in darkness as well as light – to bring about a creative integration of both that was ultimately saving. The polarity of the crucifixion and resurrection and the sacrament of Baptism, which Robinson himself had written of in his *Twelve New Testament Studies*, offered the central symbol with which to understand the potential power of Hiroshima for human history and consciousness.

At this point, Robinson began to get positively excited. Thus began the friendship between us and some of the most interesting theological discussions I was to have with him. We learned together, and he told me he was preaching about the subject. By coincidence, 1979 marked the year in which public attention was dramatically focused on the nuclear issue by the decision of the NATO Council to deploy the Cruise and

Pershing II missiles. As usual, John was courageous in his stand on the greatest social issue of the day. I was of course delighted, and eagerly accepted his invitations to join him for dinner or address the evening series of discussions, held in his rooms.

It was John who got my first book published by SCM in 1979, *From Hiroshima to Harrisburg*; it dealt with the interconnection of nuclear power and nuclear weapons – a point which took me a long time to convince him about, but which he finally came to agree – that atoms for peace and atoms for war were but two sides of the same coin, and therefore both had to be opposed. It was John, too, who encouraged me to publish my thesis, and who even came up with its title: *The Darkness of God: Theology after Hiroshima*. It was during this time he was writing *The Roots of a Radical* and *Truth is Two-Eyed*.

The last time I had dined with John, he complained of stomach upset but thought it was probably the rich food at Trinity's High Table. We laughed about the battle of the waistline all of us inevitably fight. The next day Ruth took him to the doctors where tests confirmed his cancer. But even facing death he continued to speak out on peace, telling me several times it was the most important issue with which he had dealt.

Dr Paul Hammond, Lecturer in English at Leeds University, has written:

I first met John in the autumn of 1972, when I came up to Trinity as an undergraduate. I had heard of him, but had not read any of his work. Excited by the possibility of getting to know a notorious bishop, I bought a couple of his books and asked him to sign them. The result was an invitation to lunch, and the beginning of a friendship with one who has shaped my thinking more than anyone else.

I stayed at Trinity for six years, as an undergraduate and research student, until I left in 1978 to take up a university lectureship at Leeds. In the same year Trinity elected me to a research fellowship which enabled me to return to Cambridge for 1980–82. So for eight of the last eleven years of his life I saw John regularly while we were both living in Trinity.

That lunch in October 1972 was the first of many which I had with him; simple affairs of soup, bread and cheese and fruit, they always had a domestic air. That was characteristic of his room – in spite of the hundreds of books, the atmosphere was less donnish and more domestic than in the rooms of many Fellows.

I think that when I was an undergraduate there were always a few (two or three, perhaps, in any year) who were devoted to him; the others tended to find him intimidating. This was not a donnish hauteur, but something much more deep-rooted, a shyness which became manifest in talking *at* people rather than *to* them. Shy, and perhaps a bit lonely even, in those days; he was always the last to leave. It was typical of him that at the end of an evening when I had celebrated my 21st birthday with a dinner for some friends, he should get up to leave, and then spend an hour standing on the hearth-rug talking at us. (It was also typical that his present was a copy of *The Human Face of God*!) During my first two years at Trinity his undergraduate friends formed a 'Liturgy Group'. We met fortnightly in John's rooms, over lunch, to write liturgies for group use. We took it in turns to make a draft which we then worked on together, though each one retained its individuality (some were very peculiar). When each reached its final form we would use it, as a group, for a eucharist; two were duplicated for use at weekday services in chapel. In the meetings we learnt a lot of theology informally from John, and our liturgical experiment became a way of thinking about what sort of religious language was possible for us and for our circumstances.

This was obviously an offshoot of John's interest in liturgy which had blossomed at Clare, but it was perhaps significant that we were a small group, confessedly on the 'fringes', both ecclesiastically and theologically: it wasn't really a 'house church' of the kind that seems to have flourished at Clare. Only once did John really produce a liturgy for the whole College, and that was in 1977, when we made our own communion manual, based upon Series 2. Although a lot of the detailed drafting was done by Philip Buckler and myself, the manual was debated and revised at a series of open meetings held in John's rooms. He chaired them with great sensitivity and skill. It was an example of his insistence that the College Communion should be open to all – not just technically open, but conducted in such a way that no one party felt alienated. Naturally, many of the CICCU went off elsewhere, but there were always some evangelicals who came regularly to the College Communion and to Chapel meetings; they respected his sincerity (and his biblical scholarship) even though they disapproved of his theology; and he always kept dialogue going. Indeed, I can recall quite a lot of evangelicals (both undergraduates, and research or mature students from the American bible belt) with whom he was on very good terms, and took special pleasure in being so. It is a sign of change, both in John and in the student body, that whereas there were full-scale debates in College in the mid-1970s over Series 2 and 3 and the manual, the production of a new manual for the ASB rite in 1982 was done almost entirely by John, the Chaplains and myself.

The 'Liturgy Group' was one example of the 'fringe' groups which came and went under John's leadership. Later there was a group which met weekly to discuss *Can We Trust the New Testament?* chapter by chapter, before it was published. Some of our comments affected the final book, though I don't remember any details. Later still, in 1981–2, there was a group called 'fringe theology', made up largely of dons and research students. This was more of a Cambridge than a Trinity group.

This leads to the main point which has to be made about John and Trinity: it was not a happy or creative relationship. There is plenty which appears to contradict that assertion, such as the many friendships and books which stem from these years. But although Trinity gave him a job, and was generous in giving him time off from it, it was not a community in which he felt happy – or one which felt happy with him. He never found Trinity really congenial, and his relationship with the College got worse in the last few years.

I can't help thinking that he was losing his touch during his period at Trinity. In the early 1970s the sermons which he was preaching in Chapel were clear, strong and stimulating, but many of them were restatements of his earlier work. Looking at my file of his sermons, I find a series called 'A Statement of Christian faith', from 1974, and a set on the Eucharist which may be a year or so later. Good pieces, but not significantly different from *Liturgy Coming to Life* or *Exploration into God*. When his books were re-issued, he often said that he found little that he wanted to change. His theology wasn't on the move in these years – indeed, was he ever, strictly speaking, a theological thinker? His theology was characteristically a bundle of quotations. I don't mean that disparagingly at all, but he did not seem to have enough of an original philosophical streak to make him a creative theologian. He was much more of an apologist, an interpreter of the church to the world and vice versa, insisting that you started your theology from where you really were, not from where others thought you should be. And so I think that in these last years his theology suffered from his not being really sure where society started from, where the points of pressure were; when he was at Woolwich he seemed to see this more clearly. At Trinity, instead of asking where society started from, he seems to have asked instead where *he* started from, and the last years were marked by a new kind of radicalism – an even stronger sense of his family and the scholarly achievements of his forebears, an interest which coincided with his new radicalism in biblical scholarship. It was surely significant that this radicalism into which he put so much of his truly creative self in the last years has been and will be seen by many as a neo-conservatism. He was, after all, a conservative of the best kind.

John as a prophet seemed increasingly unsure of the people he was addressing. In the late 1970s we expected John to take up a new cause each term – women priests, followed by nuclear power, followed by nuclear disarmament. All were real issues, but John never quite became the voice that people listened to on those issues. Over the Falklands, he felt passionately that the Church should be heard, but was not really quite sure what the church should be saying. This partly reflects on John and the difficulty of being a prophet from a platform like Trinity; but it may also be put down to the late 1970s and early 1980s being a period of transition. The state of our society is clearer now than it was two or three years ago, so that people recognise the urgency in what David Jenkins or Bruce Kent are saying; perhaps the late 1970s were just a comfortable muddle.

But this intermittent connection with the needs of society coincided for John with an intermittent grasp of College life. He refused to be a tutor, or to serve on the College Council; worse, he broadcast that refusal. He studiously avoided College administration and politics. As a result he often made political errors when dealing with (say) Masters and Bursars. This, combined with the small numbers of students reading theology, made it almost certain that when he left he would not be replaced: the College would employ no more theologians, and would make the senior Chaplain Dean. As it happened, the dignity and scrupulousness with which he behaved towards the College in his last months, together with a College Council which happened to be comparatively sympathetic to Chapel matters, meant that there was (so far as I am aware) no serious pressure in this direction. But things could easily have been different. John never really settled into Trinity as a community. He kept very strict terms, and during term would almost never dine at 8 p.m. except on Sundays; during the week he would dine out, or with undergraduates, or at the 7 p.m. informal sitting. Lunch he would often take in his rooms, usually with students or visitors. When he did dine, it was often with guests, which increased his unpopularity. One night I saw the Fellows' attitude vividly demonstrated at dinner: at the top table sat the senior Fellows, John and John's guest; at the second table sat some two dozen other Fellows. It is hardly usual for Fellows to be awkward or dull, but John annoyed by the frequency with which he talked about himself (his books, TV appearances, trips abroad). He was spoken of (always as 'The Bishop') in a tone which I heard used of no one else: exasperation and mockery, with a tinge of respect. Trinity's tolerance is legendary (it has to be!) but even so John just wasn't 'one of us'. Partly this stemmed from pique at his constituency being so much wider than academe, while he was at the same time a scholar of unimpeachable credentials. But John contributed to this himself by his conversation, and by never giving the impression that he was dining out of an interest in the company of the other Fellows. Many never forgave him for not being Harry Williams.

John's own awkwardness socially contributed to this problem. You could never predict whether his extraordinary sensitivity or his equally amazing lack of it would come out on any particular occasion. Either was possible, quite regardless of the company. When, as a research student, I proudly told him that I had been appointed to a university lectureship at Leeds, he just said, 'Oh, is that a good thing?' On another occasion, on one of our walks, I discussed with him whether I should apply for a particular job in Cambridge; he listened attentively, and gave good advice; we agreed that it would stay strictly confidential, Cambridge gossip being what it is. A few days later at dinner on High Table he called out to me from three places down the table to ask what I'd decided to do about applying for that job. But enough of the gauche side, which seemed to be produced by a deep shyness (he was surely incapable of malice, though some people got the anecdotes they deserved). His sensitivity was even more remarkable; he had a great gift for pastoral care which rarely looked like pastoral care, and he was very accomplished at making it look like straightforward friendship, thus avoiding that terrible impression of calculated sympathy which many clerics cannot avoid. As well as seeing when students needed special care, he had an eye for the needs of College servants, and was also very generous of his time and friendship with some of the odd hangers-on who drift around Cambridge.

Odd though this combination of the gauche and the delicate was, it was the combination itself which was one of the lovable things about him, for it was an example of his total honesty. He had real integrity; *Honest to God* was a very true description of him (all the more so for being a title forced on him). 'Honesty' and 'integrity' sound a bit unexciting, so I'd better add that one of his captivating qualities was his energy, that truly radical cast of mind which kept him on the move.

I can't bring myself to say anything of the last months; it would be superfluous anyway. But opening *Truth is Two-Eyed* again recently, it did strike me that the beginning of the first chapter spoke more truly than John realised. He talks there about the Hindu stages of life, remarking that he himself is now at the penultimate stage of withdrawal into the forest after the earlier stages of shouldering the burdens of office. The final stage is of withdrawal of attachment to the world. Now, I wonder in retrospect whether his last five or six years, which he saw sometimes as being irritatingly detached from the chores of office, were part of that penultimate stage which was arriving prematurely: a deliberate return to the roots, in his biblical scholarship, recovery of his ancestors' achievements, his unexpected call to India, his sermons on Julian of Norwich and Richard Jefferies, and perhaps, too, his new appearance at daily Mattins and Evensong for meditation. Perhaps in all this one might see signs of that drawing away from worldly routine towards the Ground of our being which characterises the last two stages of the Hindu life; a kind of preparation, perhaps, for that final prising away of the soul from the body about which de Chardin wrote in that profoundly moving passage which we heard at John's memorial service.

Some of those who knew John best have given their account of him at Trinity. It is against that back-cloth that specific events in John's life can best be seen. But it is well to remember how different that back-cloth was from the South London with which John had become so familiar. Bob Reiss, Chaplain of Trinity 1973–8 (now Team Rector of Grantham), has written:

> By the time I arrived back in Trinity as Chaplain the intellectual tide in the college was turning. Such left-wing radicalism as was present in Trinity in the 1960s was in sharp decline and many of the most able and articulate amongst the undergraduates were both temperamentally and politically conservative. For them John was a slightly out-of-date figure and one out of touch with the undergraduate mood. A few undergraduates had the perception and sensitivity to see what he was getting at, but many more, I fear, simply dismissed him.

Not long after John went to Trinity, there was the Rudi Dutschke affair. Rudi had been the German student activist of the 1960s. Despite his reputation he was a loving non-violent person and a restraining influence on many a student hot-head. In 1968 he was the victim of a bomb-attack (in church) which all but killed him and for a long time stopped him either reading or writing. His pastor and professor of Theology in Berlin, Helmut Gollwitzer, had written to Paul Oestreicher for help. Paul had conferred with John – when John was still in South London. The Dutschkes had first stayed with the Oestreichers. With great courage Rudi gradually fought his way back to health. John got to work to obtain a postgraduate doctoral research job for him in Cambridge – and had been successful. Rudi was placed under Home Office orders not to take part in politics. He stuck to that, but others came to see him and consult him. Their visits were monitored by MI5. A witch-hunt started for deporting him as a danger to peace. There was massive protest at this from the University; everyone was united, from the Vice-Chancellor to the students. John was in the forefront of the public liberal lobby which fought the expulsion order and attended the debate on Rudi in the House of Commons. The government won the vote and deported Dutschke to Denmark, which readily received him. Rudi continued his research at the University of Aarhus – where John later visited him, before Rudi's tragically early death.

In April 1972 John and Ruth celebrated their silver wedding. In May Elizabeth (Buffy) married Simon Rickard at a Reigate Register Office. John's obvious love and respect for Simon meant a lot to Buffy, for 'he didn't fit Daddy's normal requirements as someone to be given consideration – he didn't have a degree and worked as a graphic designer and typographer'.

In December 1972 John took part in a public discussion at the Royal Society of Medicine with Lord Justice Edmund-Davies and Dr Colin Murray Parkes, on 'The Patient's Right to Know the Truth'. In view of what was later to befall John it is significant that he spoke of two experiences – of a man who had died of cancer who had been urged not to tell his wife he had only a few months to live; and of another man who had an inoperable growth, of which John knew but the man himself had not been told. John said:

> What I would look for more than anything else in my doctor would be a preparedness to be absolutely honest and truthful with me. As soon as I got the impression that he was being evasive or equivocating or withholding something, even if it is, as he thought, for my good, my suspicions would be aroused and I suspect that in that situation a healing situation would become progressively more difficult. A priest who has been trained for this situation knows, perhaps more than a doctor, that *how* one tells a patient the truth about himself makes tremendous demands upon both. It is a great burden that is laid upon us but one which I feel we must nevertheless accept.

In September 1973 Judith went off to Birmingham University and John and Ruth moved from Marlborough Court to a small bed-sitter in King Street, Cambridge. But soon Ruth began to feel that if she spent term-time in Reigate as well as vacations life would be less complicated for John, and that she would have the space she now felt she needed to develop her own inner resources. John could come home to Reigate for a couple of nights in mid-term and she could always spend a night or two in John's rooms at Trinity. This arrangement suited them well. John 'phoned Ruth every evening. Whatever the world outside surmised and said, they never thought of themselves as anything but a happily married couple: never questioned the mutual love which was theirs. Indeed Ruth believes their way of life made opportunities for their relationship to be deepened. She particularly remembers one mid-term driving John to Redhill station after he had had a couple of days at home. He had come for a complete break from the job, so they had walked and gardened, read and played chess. As he got out of the car at the station he said, 'Thank you for a lovely weekend.' Ruth remembers not only the words but the feeling behind them – and how moved she was that John should say what he had said after thirty years of marriage. 'Such words did not come easily to his lips.'

In March 1973 John had paid his first visit to the USA since he had left Southwark. He visited John Knox, as usual, and Paul Van Buren, William Johnston, John Wren-Lewis and many other friends. He was as indefatigable as ever in his journeying, taking in Princeton; Kirkridge; Richmond, Virginia; Washington, D.C.; Ohio; Chicago; Los Angeles and San Francisco. The preliminary work he had been doing on *Redating the New Testament* provided the material for his lectures.

John had for many years, and for diverse reasons, wanted to visit South Africa – not least because of family connections. His uncle Edward, for instance, had been a headmaster in Namaqualand. Edward's interview with President Kruger in 1899 – in the presence of 'the State attorney' J. C. Smuts, who had been with Edward at Christ's College, Cambridge – is described in Forbes Robinson's *Letters to His Friends*. John had also read his uncle Forbes' vivid account of his own visit to South Africa just as the Anglo-Boer war was beginning. Edward's son Arthur was born in South Africa and had lived most of his life there, but had stayed with John's family in Canterbury when they were both schoolboys. They met again at Blackheath in 1960, just after the Sharpeville shootings. Arthur had been a political prisoner in Port Elizabeth for several months and had come to England as an exile. He was struck by the way John 'listened in sympathy and concentrated deeply on the picture as it unfolded. I described the agony of the way in which thousands existed.' At this time John spoke at the Sharpeville rally in Trafalgar Square and took part in the vigil of protest.

John and Ruth were invited to spend five weeks in South Africa in February and March 1975. John was the guest of the Theology Department of the University of South Africa. He lectured in centres all over the country and visited 'the heart of cities and depths of the bushveld, the richest White suburbs and the most desperate Black locations' in Pretoria, Johannesburg, Cape Town, East London, Durban and Pietermaritzburg. He 'listened to just about every voice in the spectrum: English and Afrikaans, Black and White, Coloured and Indian, liberal and conservative, urban and rural, young and old' including Dr Beyers Naudé of the Christian Institute, the editor of the *Rand Daily Mail*, Alan Paton, and Helen Joseph under house arrest. To their amazement John and Ruth discovered that the house in Natal where, by the merest chance, they were staying had previously been the hospital run and lived in by John's uncle Frederick, the missionary doctor. Before leaving South Africa, John was invited to give a public lecture on how his image of South Africa had changed during his stay. It filled almost a page in the *Pretoria News* of 31 March 1975. He had some strong and courageous things to say:

> To come to a country where detention without trial is a normal part of the State's working and where freedom can be removed, eroded or restored at the drop of a Minister's order is a frightening experience . . . Whereas there is just as much racial discrimination in other parts of the world, including Britain and the United States, this is the only country where it is positively entrenched by law . . . While Uganda and Russia, for example, may perpetrate terrible things, neither Mr Amin nor Mr Brezhnev are claiming to do what they do in the name of Christian civilization. But Mr Vorster *is* . . . this is quite literally an excruciating country, excruciating in its beauty and its pathos.

John wrote a letter about South Africa to *The Daily Telegraph* (23 April 1975) when he returned to England. It ended:

> I am not optimistic, but I have been taught an immense amount about hope – humbled by the sheer courage and joy and humour of the people we met – Afrikaners, English, and Blacks of all hues, who go on going on without the iron entering into their souls, and without the cynicism and apathy and selfishness which so sour our political scene. I would gratefully go back any day – if I am ever asked!

John and Ruth were in fact determined to go back.

On 6 June 1975 Colin Peterson, the Secretary for Appointments to the Prime Minister and Ecclesiastical Secretary to the Lord Chancellor, visited Trinity, after being in touch with Lord Butler, in order to see John about his future. The time was ripe; for John had been at Trinity for six years and when he had gone there the suggestion had been that he should stay 'for a few years': to do his book on Christology, which he had, of course, done; and now his second large work at Trinity, *Redating the New Testament* was in the press. The time was ripe for a second reason. At Easter that year Oliver Tomkins had resigned the See of Bristol. It was one of the two diocesan bishoprics which still held some attraction for John – he had not lost the love for it he had gained as a curate. (The other diocese that drew him was Durham – the diocese of his heroes Lightfoot and Westcott; but that had become vacant in 1972, when John had hardly begun his time at Trinity, and was not to be vacant again until the year of his death.) It was not that John desperately desired to be a diocesan – far from it: he rarely gave the subject a thought. But it would have been 'nice to be asked' – and he never was. And certainly the many who cared for John – and the Church of England – were beginning to ask: 'When is John going to be offered a diocese?'

The time was ripe for a third reason. At the end of 1974 John had applied for the vacant chair at Cambridge: the Lady Margaret's Professorship of Divinity. By the time Colin Peterson came to see him John had 'dismissed the idea', expecting not to get it. And he was right; for that month Morna Hooker – whom he much admired – was announced as the successful candidate. A non-resident appointment had been brought in over the heads of the resident claimants like John. Whichever way one looks at it, it was failure. In the pang of the moment he must have wondered why they had denied him and asked for Morna. The answer was, in a sense, simple. As John's loyal friend Professor Moule has written:

> I don't think that John would rank as a 'learned' scholar. To the end, I doubt if he knew much Hebrew, let alone any other Semitic language. I don't think he was really intimate with the Hellenistic Judaism of Philo and Josephus. Nor (I think) did he read much patristic literature. He was not steeped, like an erudite New Testament scholar, in the literature of the period. What he did (besides being intimate with the Greek N.T. itself) was to read relevant bits of the sources *ad hoc.* He pursued the particular questions he was interested in through the secondary litera-ture until he had come to grips with the particular evidence this referred to – either at first hand, for himself, or with the help of the best experts. The result was that he generally got to the bottom of the evidence very thoroughly, though without a scholar's total immersion in it.

But whatever the reason John must have felt he had failed. He knew well that if he stayed he must now go on being dependent on Trinity – that was the financial face of his failure (not that Trinity was short of a penny!). He knew also he had disappointed not only himself but Trinity – not that anyone would say that to his face: it would be more likely to be said in subdued tones, Fellow to Fellow, as the port was passed in the Combination Room in John's absence, and behind the closed doors of the Master's Lodge. Had John been offered the vacant Chair he would have known he was needed in Cambridge – and wanted; and even the Diocese of Bristol might have beckoned in vain. The weeks went by, and the months: and John – rightly – dismissed any idea that he would be offered Bristol. (Eventually it was announced that Canon John Tinsley, then Professor of Theology at Leeds University, had been made the new bishop.)

But an incomparable – and acknowledged – sadness afflicted John that year. At the end of October 1975 his mother died in her ninety-sixth year. In her last years she had been cared for by the Deaconess Community of St Andrew at the Abbey House, Malmesbury. Ruth had been with her for her last fortnight and was with her at her death. There was no sorrow in John's life like that sorrow. He shared it openly with those who were near him at Trinity. Later, in a sermon in Trinity Chapel, he said: 'I remember so well the first time I dined in Hall after the death of my mother . . . I remember feeling, Pray God no one starts a conversation. I was just too full.'

As the year drew to its close, John wrote a careful letter to Lord Butler:

Dear Master
Thank you for your letter . . . I was in Canterbury before Christmas, where I gathered I was in the betting book for the new Dean (the present one having apparently announced his retirement for May). Whether I would accept it if offered, I simply don't know. It would mean assessing many things. . . But I confess that if I am going to move, this might well be the time and the place. At any rate nothing else has come up, or looks like coming up, either from the academic or the ecclesiastical side, that would seem preferable. At the end of the summer I shall have published the big book (on *Redating the New Testament*) on which I have been working and also got off a smaller, popular one. So it would be the moment to be turning to new things anyhow. And I am bound to admit that there is no other *place* that has the same emotional and spiritual pull

for me. I suppose that is not surprising since my father and grandfather were canons of Canterbury, and I was born and bred under the shadow of the Cathedral; but it was borne home again on me powerfully when we laid my Mother to rest there the other day.

I can't really imagine they will ask me – and I have no idea what the Archbishop has in mind. But I may have given the impression to Colin Peterson that I was in no hurry to move (which is true) and it would be a pity if the thing merely went by default on a misunderstanding. Since Harold Wilson approached you in the first instance I don't know whether you would think it appropriate (or counterproductive) to put in an enquiry. But I would certainly not wish to give an impression which would subsequently make it difficult to say no if it were offered. However, I am sure you are well experienced in handling these devious processes! It would be so much easier if these things were publicly advertised like academic posts. There is a large part of me that has no desire to move at all (Trinity gives me great freedom for which I am grateful), but another part which wonders if I shall be sufficiently stretched simply going on as I am for the next ten years.

At the front of *Redating the New Testament* John placed a dedication:

For my father
ARTHUR WILLIAM ROBINSON
who began at Cambridge just one hundred years ago
to learn from Lightfoot, Westcott and Hort,
whose wisdom and scholarship remain the fount
of so much in this book

and my mother
MARY BEATRICE ROBINSON
who died as it was being finished
and shared and cared to the end.

Remember that through your parents you were born;
What can you give back to them that equals their gift to you?
Ecclus. 7:28

All Souls Day 1975

Redating the New Testament was a not unworthy thank-offering for his mother and father. The reviews make that abundantly clear.

His book is a prodigious virtuoso exercise in inductive reasoning, and an object lesson in the nature of historical argument and historical knowledge. It is, I think, the finest of all his writings, and its energy is marvellous.

So wrote Don Cupitt in *The Listener*. Leslie Houlden wrote in *New Fire*:

> In fewer than four hundred pages, Bishop Robinson challenges almost all the judgements which teachers of the New Testament throughout the world commend to their pupils on the dating of the N.T. books: his reassessment has the simple effect of having them all complete before AD 70. The rumour of this revolutionary conclusion has already given the book notoriety and led some either to dismiss it out of hand or to lose patience with what is taken to be frivolous donnish antics . . . It is salutary to be reminded on how weak a basis many of the conventional datings rest. They are among the stock-in-trade of the subject which everyone knows to be questionable but generally treats as pretty firm. Many will profit from having to think afresh and to realise how little we truly know about the origin of those brief but powerful old books.

The Roman Catholic New Testamant scholar, Bishop B. C. Butler, wrote:

> I think Dr Robinson has convincingly shown that several of the radical positions about chronology – not to say authorship – of the New Testament books are open to very serious dispute.

Professor Moule thought it 'a brilliant tour de force'. *Time* for 21 March 1977 gave *Redating* a whole page. In the USA the 1977 National Religious Book Award was given to John for *Redating*. One reviewer wrote: 'It reads – and should be read – like a thriller, a detective mystery . . .'

Trinity was of course unmoved. The Master remarked at dinner one night: 'I see the Dean of Chapel has written a book saying that the whole of the New Testament was written before Jesus was born.'

John had reserved to the very end of his book a letter to him from the eighty-eight year old Professor C. H. Dodd, doyen of English New Testament scholarship. John had found it since completing his manuscript. The letter had evidently been written 'in response to a first intimation of my rethinking the date of the gospel of John, in which I must have adumbrated the implications as I see them for the chronology of the whole New Testament'. Some sentences of that letter should have a place in the biography of John:

> You are certainly justified in questioning the whole structure of the accepted 'critical' chronology of the NT writings, which avoids putting anything earlier than 70, so that none of them are available for anything like first-generation testimony. I should agree with you that much of this

late dating is quite arbitrary, even wanton, the offspring not of any argument that can be presented, but rather of the critic's prejudice that if he appears to assent to the traditional position of the early church he will be thought no better than a stick-in-the-mud. The whole business is due for radical re-examination.

It was David Edwards – the publisher of *Honest to God* – who found that *Redating* 'must raise the question whether it was not a misuse of his gifts to agree to become a bishop'. Certainly John's latest volume gave little support to the suggestion of Dr Paul Hammond that John was 'losing his touch' during his period at Trinity. He was *writing* as well, if not better than ever. The *succès d'estime* of *Redating* undoubtedly affirmed and gratified John. There were of course those who maintained that *Redating* was *merely* a *tour de force*, and that the outcome of scholarly debate would be that on many points certainly, on most points probably, and on almost all points possibly John would in due course be refuted. Small wonder that he saved and savoured his press-cuttings and reviews.

In February 1976 the former Archbishop, by then Lord Ramsey of Lambeth, spent a long weekend in Trinity talking to individuals and preaching. In a letter after his visit he wrote:

> I was very fascinated by the opportunity of conversing with so many members of a college both within and on the periphery of the Christian orbit, and could learn something of how they think and feel – so much integrity and so much of it in a godward direction – how can one not be thankful for that? I am glad you have been at Trinity in these last years, but I do understand your readiness to move in the very near future.

At the end of July that year it gave John much joy to join with the local Methodist minister at Brimington Common near Chesterfield in marrying Judith to Christopher Norton, whom she had met at Birmingham University where both of them were reading mathematics. Then in mid-August he went off for five weeks in Canada and the US – to the Conference of the Society for New Testament Studies at Duke University, North Carolina; to the Church of the Saviour, Washington, D.C.; to Kirkridge; to Riverside Church, New York; and to Al Shands in Louisville – among others.

John had written a kind of companion volume to *Redating* – a sort of *Redating* for the ordinary reader – and called it *Can we trust the New Testament?* – though the scope of this 'slim volume' was in fact wider than that of *Redating*. John *had* written; for the book had been written before *Redating*, and because of it John's 'marriage' with SCM Press – and they had been together now for twenty-five years! – had nearly come to grief. Without a word to SCM John had offered the book to Mowbrays, although he was still bound by contract to SCM. Dr Kathleen Bliss did some 'marriage counselling' and an 'Anglican compromise' was agreed: Mowbrays were to keep the book but it would be published after *Redating*. (For a while, 'Can we trust John Robinson?' was the question at SCM!) The incident with SCM is in fact not particularly surprising. From the time of *Honest to God* other publishers were clamouring – with promises of substantial advances. Each new book John wrote meant a kind of courtship ritual with SCM. John would say to John Bowden of SCM, 'I'm wondering who ought to publish this next book,' then they would have a good lunch and a long talk and reach agreement on the terms. Though the relationship between author and publisher was not particularly warm or deep – John said what he was going to write, and then wrote it as he wanted to – he remained to the end very loyal to SCM Press.

Can We Trust the New Testament? was in fact a masterly little book: a survey of various critical approaches to the New Testament made within the preceding half century, shot through with John's personal conviction. 'Charlie' Moule dropped John a postcard: '*Can We Trust* is absolutely splendid, and I'm going to give copies to lots of people.' The flavour of the book is best conveyed by two paragraphs in its last ten pages:

> If the resurrection story has a foot in *public* history (and to abandon that claim is to abandon something that has been central to the entire Christian tradition), then it must be open and vulnerable to the historian's scrutiny. Never let us suppose that we need not bother with his questions or that we are impervious to them. This is part of the risk of a religion of the Word made flesh – in Winston Churchill's phrase its 'soft underbelly'. And though the historian can neither give nor directly take away the faith, he can indirectly render the credibility-gap so wide that in fact men cease believing. My trust in the New Testament accepts that risk. That is why as a New Testament scholar I am convinced that it is important to be a good historian as well as a man of faith – and not to confuse the two by giving answers of faith where historical evidence alone is relevant. For *if* Jesus could really be shown to be the sort of man who went into hiding rather than face death, or just another nationalist or

freedom-fighter with a crime-sheet of violence, or the leader of a movement which rested in the last analysis on fraud, then I can think of other candidates in reply to Peter's question, 'Lord, to whom shall we go?' (John 6:68). The answers that history can give will never take us all the way – and at best they cannot be more than highly probable. Exactly what happened at the tomb, or anywhere else, we shall never know. All we can ask – and must require – for faith, for the response of Thomas, 'My Lord and my God!' is that the credibility-gap be not too wide. And that assurance, I am persuaded – or I would not remain a Christian – is what the history, after all the sifting of the best and most rigorous scholarship, can sustain.

[And the final paragraph of the book:]

A Christian has nothing to fear but the truth. For it alone could show that this movement is not of God (Acts 5:38f). But he also has nothing to fear in the truth. For to him the truth *is* Christ (John 14:6). It is large – larger than the world – and shall prevail. It is also a living, and a growing, reality. And therefore he is free, or should be free, to follow the truth *wherever* it leads. He has no advance information or inbuilt assurance precisely where it will lead. I know that I have been led through the study of the New Testament to conclusions, both negative and positive, that I did not expect. For instance, just what underlies the birth narratives, what were the relations between the movements of John the Baptist and Jesus, how and in what way did Jesus's own understanding of his role become modified by events, how did he think of the future, did he expect to return, what is most likely to have happened at his trial and resurrection, what is the relative priority for the portrait of Jesus of our different sources, especially of the Fourth Gospel, what pattern and time-scale of early church development emerges from the dating of our documents? – on these and many other things my own mind has changed and will doubtless continue to change. And my picture will not be quite the same as anyone else's – more radical at some points, more conservative at others. There is nothing fixed or final: our knowledge and our questions are constantly expanding and shifting. And who knows what new evidence may not suddenly be dug up? Yet out of all this my trust in the primary documents of the Christian faith has been strengthened rather than shaken. The scholarship does not give me the faith; but it increases my confidence that my faith is not misplaced. Yet it provides no copper-bottomed guarantee. For the Christian walks always in this life by trust and not by sight. And he is content to close his *Te Deum*, his most confident affirmation of faith, with the prayer of vulnerability: 'O Lord, in thee have I *trusted*: let me never be confounded.'

One sentence in *Can We Trust the New Testament?* revealed a new interest of John's: 'The empty tomb, even if it could be certified empty and the shroud produced (and I regard the famous Shroud of Turin as by no means to be dismissed out of hand), would finally prove nothing: the body could still have been removed from it.'

Few of John's actions led more people to think – and to say – John was concerned with the sensational, and to accuse him of gullibility, than his concern with the Shroud. But the evidence indicates a rather different attitude on John's part. On 30 July 1976 he wrote to Father Peter Rinaldi, head of the Holy Shroud Guild of the USA:

> You won't know me, though you may know me by name as the notorious bishop who wrote *Honest to God* and therefore about the last person to be a *believer* in the Shroud, if that is the right word! But for a long time I have been very much impressed by the evidence, and your book *The Man in the Shroud* confirmed my conviction that there is here something that cannot be easily explained away, and when I talk to scholars at Cambridge, I find a surprising agreement.
>
> The trouble is that first-hand scientific examination (as opposed to press reports) seems so hard to come by. I have tried in this country and failed, and it seems to me that so much of the material in English (I don't read Italian) is in America. I am shortly coming to your country again and should like to see what I can get hold of. My particular interest is from the point of view of the New Testament and of the Gospel of John in particular, which I am increasingly convinced contains early eye-witness evidence (and is indeed written by John, son of Zebedee).
>
> I am coming over for the meeting of the Society of New Testament Studies Conference at Duke University ... from August 16–19, and I wondered if you could possibly drop me a line there to let me know how and where I could get hold of the relevant literature, Father, and of any recent investigation – of which I only heard tell ... One of the things I would like to consider is an inter-disciplinary seminar of theologians, scientists and historians on it at Cambridge, but for this one needs things like academic monographs rather than press-reports and popularizations ...

By 1976 there was an interest in Britain in the Shroud among Catholics such as Group Captain Leonard Cheshire, V.C. Fr Rinaldi put John in touch with David Sox, an Episcopalian priest on the staff of the American School in London, whom John had already met. David was to become general secretary of the British Society for the Turin Shroud, which he and John helped to make ecumenical. John became an active member of the society and helped to plan a symposium for September 1977 at the Institute of Christian Studies, attached to All Saints, Margaret Street, in London, to coincide with a group of scientists going to Turin a week later with the proposal that in 1978 the Shroud should be Carbon-14 tested. (That year the four hundredth anniversary of the Shroud's presence in Turin would be celebrated.) To prepare for the delegation to Turin a gathering of scientists, scholars and clergy was held at Albuquerque, New Mexico in late March 1977. John and David Sox went to the meeting – flying there and back in three days. John gave a lecture on the complexity of the New Testament evidence on the grave clothes of Jesus. It was published in *Face to Face with the Turin Shroud* (edited by P. Jennings) and reprinted in John's *Twelve More New Testament Studies*. Only someone who has not read that lecture could say John was gullible. It is true that he believed there were

> aspects of this matter which we may no longer simply dismiss with what I have called 'the scepticism of the wise', let alone with 'the cynicism of the foolish'. We must come to terms and live with the new evidence, however disturbing to our presuppositions, scientific or religious. Indeed, it should help to teach us, like any other advance, that the more we know, the more we do not know . . . what we can allow it to do is to humble us and make us confess that God, in the words of my great Puritan namesake, John Robinson, 'hath yet more truth to break forth' from his holy Shroud.

The press in America made much of the fact that the *Honest to God* bishop was now interested in a relic. (And it is of course likely that John quite enjoyed that!) The *Church Times* published a notice that Bishop Robinson would be speaking 'on the day he returns from his discussions in the USA with NASA scientists on the Turin Shroud', on the subject 'Have We Really Got Jesus' Grave Clothes?' in St Francis Church, Friary Park, Wednesbury in the West Midlands.

At the 'Sindological' Congress in Turin in October 1978 John and David Sox pressed for Carbon-14 dating. It was only after repeated unsuccessful attempts to achieve that – and the obvious and telling reluctance of conservative clergy and Shroud enthusiasts – that John decided there was no point in his saying or doing any more on the subject. He would suspend not only judgment, but action. 'But nothing has shaken my conviction that the burden of proof still lies with those who believe it was an artefact to show how it was done.' David Sox –

who was undoubtedly the person closest to John where his interest in the Shroud was concerned – has written:

> It was just like John to get involved with something like the Shroud, because his mind was always open to any truth – no matter from what area it might come. I always felt he had a healthy attitude to the subject. On the one hand he would say he would like to see the faces of some Cambridge scholars if the relic received a Carbon-dating of the 1st Century! but his major interest was always intellectual. And why not? It is a fascinating article. Having an Anglican bishop involved in the subject was always appealing to the more 'believing' enthusiasts; but John would never have seen the Shroud as 'Exhibit A' for belief in the Resurrection – or anything like that.

It was of course difficult for those who had made up their minds that John was essentially iconoclastic to hear – and to bear – his insistence that the case for the Turin Shroud be heard before it was written off.

In February 1978 John applied for another vacant Chair: the Regius Professor of Divinity in Cambridge. He put in his application with little hope of success and was neither very surprised nor very disappointed when Henry Chadwick was appointed. Henry was the 'very model' of a Cambridge Regius Professor; he had been Regius Professor of Divinity in Oxford and Dean of Christ Church, after being Dean of Queens' College, Cambridge. But again there was the question: 'Why not John?' To some extent the reasons for his rejection for the Lady Margaret's Professorship again applied. But the questions were now more complex. Where Cambridge and John were concerned it was, at least in some quarters, a bit as it was with one of Henry Chadwick's predecessors as Dean of Christ Church:

> I do not love thee, Dr Fell;
>   The reason why I cannot tell,
> But this one thing I know full well:
>   I do not love thee, Dr Fell.

But in Courts and Combination Rooms Cambridge was not slow to provide reasons. 'Of course, dear John, whatever else he is, is *not* a philosopher' – said usually by someone who was himself no philosopher, and had never read John's thesis in philosophical theology 'Thou Who Art' – as Professors John Baillie, H. H. Farmer and Donald MacKinnon had done, and come to a different conclusion. (Nevertheless it must be said that John's friend Professor Charles

Davis felt bound to maintain that John had a 'weakness in philosophical or theoretical thought'.)

'Dear John: if only he'd stick to one subject' was another comment; or 'Dear John, if only he'd stop gadding about the globe'; and 'Brilliant intuition, of course . . . but New Testament scholarship is, I'm afraid, more than intuition: and, dear John . . .'

Such comments – or comments very much like them – abounded: unattributed and unattributable. They were mercilessly made from Olympian heights. John's ability to labour on, day after day, intensively – and at high speed – in support of his insights was virtually ignored. Of course, as 'Charlie' Moule said:

> John was sometimes inclined to overplay his hand, and once he had begun to entertain an explanation for some phenomenon or to construct some scheme that seemed to give coherence to an area of thought, was apt to pursue the project through to a tidy conclusion by force and without sufficient attention to the irreducible irregularities and without taking seriously enough the arguments against them.

But that could not be the heart of his critics' gravamen. It was of course exceptional if such comments were set down in writing. Owen Chadwick, Master of Selwyn College 1956–83, brother of Henry and a colleague of John's in the University for many years, was 'honest to John' in *The Sunday Times* of 18 March 1973. Reviewing *The Human Face of God* he wrote: 'His disadvantage is that he lacks all sense of beauty whether for prose, or poetry, or myth.' Lacks all sense of beauty? Had Owen never walked the Grantchester 'grind' with John; or to Haslingfield, Madingley or Wicken Fen? How could you write some of the prose John wrote – and he *did* write some splendid prose – and lack all sense of its beauty? How could you speak of the 'awful beauty of the Apocalypse' – as John did when lecturing on 'Interpreting the Book of Revelation' – and be dead to the beauty of myth? It is true John loved the more 'intellectual' poets – Gerard Manley Hopkins is a case in point – but 'lacks all sense of beauty in poetry'? But if Owen Chadwick thought that, he thought it. And in Cambridge: *Vox Chadwick* could be *Vox Dei.* And not only in Cambridge, but often in places where Regius Professors are made.

A more serious question may, however, lie behind the criticisms of John – and perhaps even behind his rejection as Regius: the 'threat' he posed to his critics and to Cambridge theology. For Cambridge cannot for ever go on maintaining that intimacy with the Hellenistic Judaism of Philo and Josephus, and so on, is *essential* for a professor of divinity. There are now other kinds of professors of theology – has Cambridge observed? – all round the globe. Perhaps John was right to believe that the doctrine of man is the right starting point for a contemporary theology: that it is *essential* to experience different social and cultural situations – Southwark, South and Latin America, South Africa, India – for the work of the theologian to be true: that 'context can alter content'; and to believe all this at the same time as he passionately pursued his work of technical New Testament scholarship. John was bound to be a threat to all those in Cambridge who cringed when he wrote in *Truth is Two-Eyed*: 'Another reason for turning East . . . is simply to learn, to be stretched by truth and patterns of life of which it is possible to remain wilfully ignorant by sitting in Cambridge – and we can no longer have the effortless superiority to presume like J. G. Frazer that one can write *The Golden Bough* without ever leaving Trinity Great Court.'

Dag Hammarskjöld had said: 'the road to holiness necessarily passes through the world of action'. For John the theologian, so did the road to a true theology.

John made his application for the Regius Professorship while he was on two terms sabbatical leave, which began at the end of September 1977: 'I strung together lecture-invitations, and my wife and I spent six and a half months going round the world – a month in South Africa, a month in Israel, a week in Iran, two months in India and Sri Lanka, a fortnight in Hong Kong and Japan, and two months in North America.' They arrived in South Africa on the day of Steve Biko's funeral and were there for the banning of the Christian Institute. On their second visit they would often be taking up where they had left off in 1975, meeting friends. Ruth was of course important to John on such a journey – interpreting him, protecting him, sometimes saving him from making gaffes or compensating for them, mending fences, and showing interest in domestic concerns while John concentrated more on people's ideas. John wrote in the front of the copy of *Truth is Two-Eyed* which he gave to her: 'To Ruth, my love, my companion on the journey and my other eye.' She played a full part in the discussions after talks and lectures, and saw a good deal of the work of the Black Sash movement – as she had done in 1975, International Women's Year. Her journal of the journey is often as revealing as John's:

Oct. 1st   We spent the afternoon with Helen Joseph. Despite a coronary last year she was as gay and courageous as ever. She is still 'listed', which means that no banned person is allowed to speak to her, so that when Winnie Mandela was banned and put under house arrest their only contact was to kneel side by side at a weekly Communion Service. She described Winnie as 'the daughter I never had', and they are very close . . .

Oct. 2nd Sunday   Johannes Rakale, the parish priest, came to fetch us for the service in Soweto at 10 a.m. . . . We had a tremendous welcome – warm hand-shakes and wide smiles from everyone. It was a large church and there were about 600 in the congregation, including lots of children who came up to be blessed by John after the service in what seemed an unending stream. The service, including baptisms, took two hours. Hymns and service were sung in several languages simultaneously and the sermon was translated into two African languages. During the 'Peace', when everyone moved around shaking hands, people were pushing towards me from all directions to reach my hand. It was wonderful to be one White person in such a crowd and welcomed with such delight. The White people in this country don't know what they're missing . . . In the evening, John preached in the Cathedral on 'hope as opposed to optimism' . . .

October 4th   Already, after only two days of being in close contact with Blacks and seeing things through their eyes, I feel overwhelmed by the seeming impossibility of the situation – so many thousands with the will to help themselves and discover ways of developing their own dignity and self-respect, and so much resistance baulking them at every turn . . .

October 5th   We had an exhilarating half-hour, meeting Desmond Tutu over lunch in a down-town hotel before he caught a plane back to Lesotho. He was brimming with vitality. Those who know him agree he is going to be a key figure in S. Africa . . .

October 7th   We visited Irene Mennel's 'bridging school' for Soweto students and talked to a group of disillusioned young people who were scathing about White liberalism . . .

October 14th   I spent the whole day on Table Mountain while John lectured, taking my lunch with me. John walked up to the Rhodes Memorial with me . . . On a spur of the mountain looking across to Robben Island I found a little cairn of stones placed on a rock on the side of the track. I built another nearby and wondered if the intention was the same.

As they travelled from place to place John was now able to use some of the material which would eventually form part of his Bampton Lectures on *The Priority of John*.

When John and Ruth landed in Jerusalem straight from South Africa it was with the uncanny feeling of coming down into the same situation (except that in Israel they found it was Arabs who were the 'second-class citizens'). John was lecturing to a course studying 'The Bible and the Holy Land: Past and Present'. It was his first visit there. For both John and Ruth Jerusalem was 'incredible', but what they valued most was the opportunity simply to walk about the countryside: along the lakeside in Galilee and the old cross-country road from Nazareth – where autumn crocuses were coming out – to Magdala. They visited Masada and Qumran and spent two nights on Mount Tabor and another two on the Mount of the Beatitudes.

John would be visiting Jerusalem again before *The Priority of John* took its final form, but already he was beginning to store in his memory the many personal observations which would eventually find a place in the book: 'There are today no active springs in Bethesda . . .', and so on.

Between their month in Israel and their month in India John and Ruth spent five days with the Bishop in Iran, Hassan Dehqani-Tafti, and his wife. The Iranian Revolution – in which the Bishop narrowly escaped assassination – his wife was wounded, saving his life, and his only son was murdered – was still two years away. The Bishop introduced them to the Persian poets and mystics – 'the only Bishop who has a weekly poetry reading!' – and on three mornings they left the house with him in the dark before 6 a.m. to climb the local mountain and see the sunrise, as the Bishop did regularly with a group of friends. They were also able to see something of the old Islamic centres of Isfahan and Shiraz and of the old Zoroastrian city of Persepolis.

From Iran John and Ruth went on to India. John was to deliver the Teape Lectures in Delhi, Calcutta and Madras. They are delivered annually, alternately in Delhi and Cambridge, and may cover any aspect of the frontier between Hinduism and Christianity. The Revd William Marshall Teape held in great regard his teacher Bishop Brooke Foss Westcott, then Regius Professor of Divinity at Cambridge, who founded the Cambridge Mission to Delhi. John wrote (in *Truth is Two-Eyed*):

> This was a field in which I could make no pretence to qualifications. My predecessors had been for the most part either distinguished Indian Christians visiting England or those from Britain whose study of comparative religion or missionary experience equipped them to make original contributions to the dialogue. I felt I could offer nothing distinctive. I had never been to the East and my theological education had been such that these concerns had remained peripheral to my reading and writing. But having been asked, I knew I must go, and going, stay long enough to learn and absorb as much as I could ... I have steeped myself in as much of the literature both from India and Western sources as I could lay my hands on or absorb in the time ... But this journey of the spirit has made me realise how 'one-eyed' the constraints of our western education and cultural conditioning have made us.

John admitted that:

> the invitation to turn East came as a call which secretly I had always funked. This was partly because, in Eliot's words, 'human kind cannot bear very much reality', and the prospect of treading the pavements of Calcutta among people for whom one was powerless (or unprepared) to do anything was a prospect that one did not naturally seek. But it was also because at a deeper level one would be shaken out of one's presuppositions and compelled to look at truth through a different glass of vision.

But John also confessed why as a Christian he felt impelled to 'turn East':

> That could be summed up in words which I found myself using more than once around Epiphany-tide in South India to describe the pilgrimage on which my wife and I were engaged: 'We have seen his star in the East and are come to worship him' (Matt. 2:2). It was not simply to understand Hinduism and Buddhism better, though that was an important objective; nor to be open to other light than that of Jesus as the Christ, though if one is humble and sensitive much comes; but, because we have seen *his* star in the East, to worship him, to shape his worth more wholly, more roundedly, than a one-eyed western approach has allowed. We came to expand, to deepen, our vision of the truth to be found in Jesus from the light which the East sheds on him.

John was glad to be able to play his part in the centenary of the Cambridge Mission to Delhi, but he was surprised to find that it was above all from Roman Catholic Christians that he learnt most in India:

> On the frontiers of Hindu and Buddhist dialogue and of spiritual and liturgical renewal it was the Jesuits and Benedictines who seemed to be setting the pace . . . psychologically and sociologically one can understand this, because they have the confidence born of long roots and widespread links. With a good deal of expendable ballast (very necessary in any church) they have the freedom and the courage to be radical [but] I would say that the most radical form of theological training I have seen anywhere, through immersing the students in workshops for the unemployed, industrial and agricultural projects and slum-living, came from the Tamil Nadu Seminary of the Church of South India at Madurai.

Besides their time in Delhi, John and Ruth had two days in the foothills of the Himalayas and a day in Bombay, and then they had to go South to Kerala, where they spent Christmas – and stayed in the house in which John's uncle Alfred had lived as a South Indian bishop, before he retired to Horspath Vicarage.

In Sri Lanka they were able to contemplate 'the massive tranquillity of the Buddha statues at Polonnaruwa', and John began his friendship with Lakshman Wickremesinghe, then Bishop of Kurunagala, with whom they stayed, which produced such a fruitful exchange in the next years, until Lakshman's untimely death six weeks before John's. Lakshman as much as anyone helped John to include Eastern perceptions in his theology and Christology.

Then it was back to South India – to Dom Bede Griffiths' contemplative ashram at Tannirpalli; to the Temple City of Madurai and the Tamil Nadu Seminary; to Madras for the second delivery of the Teape Lectures; to Pondicherry to the shrine of Aurobindo; to Bangalore, and finally to Calcutta, where John delivered the lectures a third time and visited the Oxford Mission to Calcutta and Mother Teresa's hospital.

John believed, as we have said, that he must experience 'different social and cultural situations' like Latin America and India – not least Calcutta. But it must also be said he was often very much the Englishman abroad – indeed the English public schoolboy-cum-Cambridge graduate abroad. 'Isn't this impossible!' was his constant cry to Ruth when things were not as efficient as he had come to expect, or as clean. He wrote home from India lamenting that he had been 'eating endless curry', and added: 'I must say there is singularly little variety – the only relief was a very good dinner at the British Embassy: I never thought I should yearn for English cooking!'

The international atmosphere of Hong Kong; the very different world and different beauty; the 'consumerism' and the change from rags to – at first sight – riches, meant that India quickly receded into a kind of 'improbable past'. Hong Kong was quickly followed by Kyoto and Tokyo. John lectured in both cities, but there was time for dialogue with Buddhists – and for a walk up to the black and bare base of Mount Fuji. And then it was Cathay Pacific to Vancouver; and John was on his old stamping ground for two months: California; Washington D.C.; Richmond, Virginia; Kirkridge; and Wheaton College, Massachusetts where he delivered the Teape Lectures material for the last time.

He had been able to use several of the university libraries to read and brood over the books that had been recommended to him in India, Sri Lanka and Japan, and then to develop the Teape Lectures into *Truth is Two-Eyed*. The footnotes to its pages and the bibliography reveal how much John had received as well as given: 'For both of us it was much more than a six-months safari. It was a voyage of exploration, keeping travelling on, in the hope that, with T. S. Eliot:

> the end of all our exploring
> Will be to arrive where we started
> And to know the place for the first time.'

They arrived where they started on 8 April 1978. The prophet had not been without honour for more than six months; now he was in his own country and his own College.

One of John's first duties at Trinity on his return was to prepare and conduct the memorial service for John Burnaby, the former Dean of Chapel and Regius Professor of Divinity. John had written from Princeton to his secretary: 'I am terribly sorry to hear of Burnaby's death – very sorry indeed.' Three other Fellows had died while John was away, and he had added: 'Everyone seems suddenly to be dying off in my absence.' It was a remark which, unbeknown to John, had been echoed in Trinity – as much in malice as in mirth – 'Fellows would wait till the Dean was away before they dared to die'!

In fact John took the greatest care over such obsequies. He conducted more than a score of memorial services in Chapel while he was Dean. He was aware what an important part the College clergy had to play at such a time in a society which held its Fellows in high regard and kept its aged members as its own responsibility. To find the right words – prayers, poems, lessons and music – for a devout theologian like Burnaby; for an agnostic classic like Andrew Gow, the friend and biographer of A. E. Housman; or for a physicist like Otto Frisch, who helped to construct the atomic bomb at Los Alamos – was no easy task; but John discharged this duty with diligence, sensitivity and skill. Of course much of such pastoral care was often known only to the recipients; though John once recalled how in 1974 the ninety-year-old F. A. Simpson had asked him as he lay dying: 'Just hold my hand.'

There was never any difficulty for John about 'settling down again'. He preached at the beginning of term on, of course, his 'Grand Tour', and for the Dean's Evening that term he had invited a particularly appropriate speaker, Dr Fritjof Capra, who besides his technical research papers on theoretical high-energy physics had written *The Tao of Physics*, correspondences between the theories of atomic and sub-atomic physics and the mystical traditions of the East. John enjoyed presiding at Dean's Evenings, whether his guest was the scientist Capra, or others distinguished in their own field, such as Alan Paton, Joyce Grenfell, Donald Swann, Monica Furlong and Tim Rice. Lent lunches, with a speaker selected from the Master and Fellows, also made an important contribution to the life of the College.

On 22 July 1978 Ruth drove John down to Canterbury for the beginning of the Lambeth Conference. John was a consultant to the Conference – to the group charged with confronting the question of the ordination of women – not to debate its pros and cons, for 'the unthinkable had already happened over considerable stretches of the Anglican Communion', but to confront the question: 'Can we live together with this challenge in integrity and truth?' John published his reflections on his experience as consultant in *The Roots of a Radical*:

> The group reflected a very fair cross-section of opinion and geographical distribution. I came to it with foreboding. But all I think would agree that we came out much more deeply united than we went in. This does not mean that we agreed, or even that we agreed to differ, but that there was a unity of the Spirit which not merely contained our differences but transformed them. And this was communicated not only to the large section on Ministry but to the plenary session of the Conference, where resolutions were carried by an overwhelming majority, with not a single bishop voting against (though three, I think, abstained), which were

nevertheless sensed on both sides to be creative and founded on positive theological principle and not simply on compromise. I believe the Anglican Communion was stronger and richer as a result of that vote, in marked contrast with the spirit of fear and partisanship and untheological bumbledom that have prevailed in the subsequent debates in the General Synod of the Church of England, not least in the refusal of the House of Clergy even to receive validly ordained women from other provinces, which I believe is patently schismatic.

When Lambeth was over John prepared *Truth is Two-Eyed* for the publishers and, never at a loss to 'turn an honest penny' – no doubt the result of a childhood in which every penny counted – decided to turn into a book the lectures on St Paul's Epistle to the Romans which he had given at Cambridge both in the 1950s and in the 1970s: 'now what the shops call "a discontinued line"'. He had 'vowed never to write a biblical commentary. For in a commentary you have to say something on everything, whether you have anything to say or not.' What John wanted to write was something between a commentary and a book designed for daily or group Bible study or for meditation, for the student or educated layman. 'Such a guide will set the historical context, draw attention to the points of interest and importance, and help him through the parts that are heavy going, so that he emerges, hopefully, with a sharpened appreciation of its contemporary relevance.' John rightly judged St Paul's Epistle to the Romans ('the "heaviest" of all his writings') eminently suitable for such treatment. *Wrestling with Romans*, as the title suggests, does not shrink from grappling with the hard issues. It recognizes that 'Paul's meaning can often be wrested only from a detailed application to his text and from a study at some depth of his big words'. John knew exactly the kind of people who would most value what he had written – former students, for instance, who were keeping up their reading but would probably tackle anything rather than Romans.

It was John serving the people in the Church he knew best:

A church where this wrestling is not being seriously attempted especially in the most educated generation of its history to date, will be impoverished in its capacity to transform the world rather than be conformed to it. 'I am not ashamed of the Gospel,' says Paul in this epistle. But there is mental as well as moral cowardice, a sheering off categories of thought, like those of justification and expiation, wrath and law, which are strange or even repellent to our world. Yet not to wrestle through them is to cut ourselves off from most of what makes Romans 8 perhaps the greatest chapter in the New Testament.

Wrestling with Romans, as we have said, crystallized a popular course of lectures. Although in Cambridge John lectured only intermittently (albeit more often in other parts of the known world) he was still week in, week out, a preacher. There are hundreds of unpublished Robinson sermons, each of them carefully crafted, most of them including biblical exposition. (Half a dozen of the sermons he preached in Trinity are included in *The Roots of a Radical*.)

One of his finest sermons was printed in *To God Be The Glory: Sermons in Honour of George Arthur Buttrick* (edited by Theodore A. Gill). Buttrick had reached his eightieth birthday after a notable ministry at New York's Madison Avenue Presbyterian Church, followed by many years at the Memorial Church of Harvard University and as Plummer Professor of Christian Morals. John would have carefully selected the sermon for Buttrick's commemoration. It was on 'Evil and the God of Love'. It wrestled with the problem of natural disaster – and with Romans: 'God who searches our inmost being knows what the Spirit means, because he pleads for God's people in God's own way; and in everything, as we know, he co-operates for good with those who love God' (Rom. 8:27–28 NEB):

> I remember having to write to a priest in my diocese whose seventeen-year-old son, on his way to school, was knocked off his bicycle by the rear end of a turning truck, and killed. His only boy was exactly the same age as my son, and I could hardly bear to think how I should have been feeling in similar circumstances . . . Whatever else was true, this was an accident, a ghastly accident, and the only conceivable culpability was either the driver's or the boy's or probably a bit of both. To bring in some intention on God's part in 'permitting' it, let alone 'visiting' it on this particular family, is, I believe, sheer blasphemy. And it's exactly the same with the accidents of nature – earthquakes, cancers, and the rest. The idea that there is any intention or plan about their incidence is, I am convinced, again sheer blasphemy . . .

There follows biblical exposition and wrestling, which includes the recognition that the pulpit is not the only place where wrestling with reality may result in fresh and true perception. 'Read, if you haven't *The Blood of the Lamb* written by Peter De Vries, that brilliant *New Yorker* humorist, about the death of his own daughter from leukaemia; or Camus' *The Plague* – though both are agonizing protests against the traditional Christian answer. But read, I think, above all, Petru Dumitriu's *Incognito* . . .'

A second, not uncharacteristic, example of John the preacher is his sermon at St Peter's, Eaton Square on 13 June 1979, the twenty-first anniversary of the founding of the Albany Trust. John was one of the Trust's founders. It had first met in Jacquetta Hawkes', and J. B. Priestley's flat in the Albany, Piccadilly, hence the name. John first of all outlined the history of the Trust, and then went on to what he believed remained to be done – the reform of discriminatory sexual law, the need for sex education, and the strengthening of counselling. As usual he pulled no punches in his illustrations: 'I vividly remember', he said (and he had joined the executive committee of the Homosexual Law Reform Society in 1960) 'attending a Gay Lib meeting in Cambridge. I have never met a more prejudiced and intolerant group, and some bitterly snide things were said about the Church. But how can you expect to be accepted, I asked, if you are as intolerant as those you condemn?' Then, biblical exegesis:

> According to the biblical myth, God said: 'Let us make man in our own image,' and 'male and female created he them'. God's own image is neither male nor female, nor both male and female; and in Christ there is neither male nor female in isolation or exclusion. The 'one new man' is always the Greek *anthropos*, the word for humanity, not *aner*, male. Liberation means being set free from the *captivity* of colour and gender and sexuality. So the only criterion of morality or of true life is the quality of relationship, of whatever 'colour', in the deepest fulfilment of love and self-giving. This is the 'glorious liberty of the children of God' from which *nothing*, no segregation, no inhibition, can separate. St Paul, who started perhaps as the least liberated character in the New Testament, found this in the 'love of Christ Jesus our Lord', in that 'mature humanity' into which we *all* have to grow, by the power of the one Spirit, through that which *every* joint supplies. Nothing short of that is true integration, and nothing short of that is true liberation.

Ten days after preaching to the Albany Trust John was on his way to New Zealand via Hawaii and Fiji. He addressed a gathering of fifty clergy and their wives in the Bishop's House, Hawaii – and was delighted with the 'necklace entirely composed of purple orchids' that they put round his neck. His next port (airport) of call was Fiji, for an all-day seminar for the Pacific Theological College in Suva. On 3 July he arrived in Auckland, New Zealand. The primary purpose of his visit was to deliver the Selwyn Lectures – named after George Augustus Selwyn 'the first far-seeing Bishop of New Zealand'. 'Since the invitation came from an Anglican foundation,' John wrote, 'I used them to explore my own roots and to reflect on the organic connection, as I see it, between the richness of the Anglican ethos in which I have been nurtured and the fruits of radical thinking and action to which it has led me. For of course the word 'radical' simply comes from the Latin *radix*, a root.'

John needed no new incitement to talk on the interrelation of 'root' and 'radical'. He had been doing it publicly since 1963, certainly, when he broadcast on the BBC 'On Being a Radical'. He had such a 'verbal' mind that once he had noted the connection he was unlikely to leave it alone. What is significant is the development of his concern with the connection. In 1963 he had related it more to political categories: to the reformist, the revolutionary and the radical. 'The revolutionary may be déraciné, but not the radical . . . the roots of the radical must go deep enough to provide the security from which to question even the fundamentals.' Now his concentration was not so much on the word 'radical' as on 'root'. Indeed it is as though the verbal connection between 'root' and 'radical' – and the alliteration was part of the verbal attraction – permitted him now to be preoccupied with his roots, allowed him, encouraged him to be, even absolved him from being, absorbed and obsessed with his roots; whereas earlier his roots permitted him, enabled him, 'provided the security' for him to be radical. The connection also enabled the radical in him to come to terms with the conservative. For the exploration of his roots was undoubtedly an exercise in conservation.

This concern with his roots was, again, not new. Far from it. His roots – and particularly the Robinson roots – had concerned him from childhood. Hamlet refers to the ghost of his father as 'this fellow in the cellarage'. At Arncliffe, John's Yorkshire home in his last years, the cellar was stacked with family papers, photographs and other memorabilia. It was as though John now needed to go down into the cellar to explore his unconscious, and his origins, in the manner appropriate to him.

There is a tough reality – sometimes an off-putting reality – about a real father. A child without a father needs father-figures, as John undoubtedly did. He hardly knew his father except through his mother's devoted memory. Father was as much fantasy to him as actuality. His first – almost his only – memories of father were of him behind the closed study door. Yet in his 'inherited blessing' was his security – security but also demand. 'Remember that through your parents you were born. What can you give back to them that equals their gift to you?' (Ecclus. 7:28) he had written in the dedication of *Redating*. 'Not for ourselves alone but for the whole world are we born' was the family motto. There was a compulsion in John to be the son of his father – the son of his *fathers*. The invitation to deliver the Selwyn Lectures under an Anglican foundation in New Zealand enabled him to gather his inheritance and take his journey into a far country: to that country in which Selwyn ceased to be a bishop (returning to be Bishop of Lichfield) when John's father was eleven.

The interpretation of the actions of others is hardly less dangerous than the interpretation of their dreams. But at this point it is important to set down some of the reasons why John may have wanted to write *The Roots of a Radical* – and give the Selwyn Lectures on that subject – at this precise point in his pilgrimage.

On 15 June 1979 – less than three weeks before he arrived in Auckland – he had celebrated his sixtieth birthday. Now that his father and mother were dead he was a 'leaf of the tree' but there was no longer a *tangible* connection with the root and the branch. His children had now all flown the nest and Ruth was living in Reigate while he lived, in term, at Trinity; and though she had shared most of the 'Grand Tour', much of his subsequent travelling – such as the journey to New Zealand and Australia – would now be undertaken on his own. The kind of travelling John did, twice round the world between September 1977 and September 1979, undoubtedly imparts to many 'jet-setters' a sense of rootlessness.

Although John had written to Lord Butler in 1975: 'There is a large part of me that has no desire to move at all'; he had also said, 'another part wonders if I shall be sufficiently stretched simply going on as I am for the next ten years'. Four years had gone by and although it is difficult to know just how much John was aware of the attitude of some of the Fellows of Trinity towards him, the 'prophet not without honour except in his own College' must surely have asked himself increasingly as the Trinity years went by – in a way he had no need to ask in his years at Southwark – 'Where do I really *belong*?' Finally his New Testament scholarship – *Redating*; *The Priority of John* – was leading him to conclusions which most of his fellow New Testament scholars regarded as 'conservative' – *radically* conservative. His scholarship was leading him to challenge the accepted 'establishment' of New Testament scholarship and was sending him back to his roots.

John gave his first lecture in New Zealand under the title, 'A Large Room' – 'Thou has set my feet in a large room' (Ps. 31:8), one of his father's favourite texts. It was reflections on 'my kind of Anglicanism' but less individualistic than that phrase – more 'the faith of our fathers', represented not least in the faith and ministry of his father and aunts and uncles. After the lecture John was asked 'what were the implications of what he was saying for those who could claim no "roots"?' The question came from one who was heard to say, 'It's all very well for him. But I am an orphan, and all I know about my parents is that they were descended from convicts in Australia.' John immediately recognized it was 'a question which demanded a careful reply'. He quoted (Matt. 3:9; Luke 3:8): 'God can make children for Abraham out of these stones'; adding, 'Stones have no roots at all!' Then he went on:

> Yet having said that as strongly as one can, it is also worth remembering all of us have roots. None of us was born yesterday. Indeed, Haley's *Roots* is precisely about the seemingly most rootless flotsam and jetsam on earth – slaves whose roots had been deliberately and cruelly severed and their very names changed so as to cut their links with the past.

It was a great gift of John's to listen intently to questions after his lectures and to answer them with care. Certainly in New Zealand where 'the most rootless persons are among the white *pakeha* majority', and where 'the Maoris, though borne across the sea from scattered islands over many generations, retain the strongest possible awareness of their genealogy', John was answering right.

John spent a month in New Zealand preaching and lecturing all over the North and South Islands. There were of course Robinsons to be visited – John's godson John and his brother, and their mother and father; Patrick, who was John's cousin and a grandson of both Charles and Frederick. Then he went to Australia for a fortnight to preach and lecture in Adelaide, Brisbane, Melbourne and Sydney: in Adelaide he visited the Oval where Cecilia had scored her century; and in Sydney he went to the Waverley Cemetery, to see the grave of aunt Caroline who had died of consumption in 1887 aged twenty-one. John had with him a photograph of the grave, which his father had visited with the Archbishop of Sydney, William Saumarez Smith, in 1894. John was glad to be 'following in father's footsteps', and it clearly meant much to him to make 'this pious pilgrimage'. As George Herbert wrote:

> Thy root is ever in its grave
> And thou must die.

In view of John's pre-occupation, the request from Oxford University Press – at Bishop George Appleton's instigation – that John should write a preface to a new edition of his father's *The Personal Life of the Clergy* could not have been more welcome to him. He signed the preface on 29 December 1979 ('my mother was born a hundred years ago on the day I sign this'). One major alteration was made to the book for the new edition: its title was changed to *The Personal Life of the Christian*.

John had read the book when he was on a retreat for Cambridge deans and chaplains conducted by 'Charlie' Moule at Hemingford Grey more than twenty years before, in December 1956. The letter he wrote to his mother then – and her reply – he tucked into his copy of this new edition of his father's book. He wrote:

> I am *conscious* of no direct connection or influence, and wonder how much there has been under the surface. How one wishes one had known and had been moulded by all the things one now most senses the lack of. As it is, one feels that any likenesses that have come out are almost coincidental, and you must notice the vast difference! Above all one is made aware what a great difference it would have made to have had the spiritual wisdom and maturity there, as one was working things out for oneself from scratch. Now one sees from afar things one wishes one had and could lay hold of, and realises how shallow and prayerless and unsimple one is! My only ray of hope is that I am still not as old as when his first book appeared and that one may yet have time to grow. But the fruiting and simplicity come of deeper roots . . .

It was in February 1980 that Buffy brought to the notice of Ruth and John the availability of a house in the remote village of Arncliffe in the Yorkshire Dales: 'a solid family house, overlooking the village green, with superb views of the fells on either side – there is no real shop, just one pub and a lovely old church'. 'Of course, Daddy is a slight problem,' wrote Buffy, 'but he won't be in Cambridge for ever, and while he is, what better place to spend the vacs?' Ruth was surprised when John took it seriously. Although it was further from Cambridge he felt it was important for Ruth to be happily placed, within reach of children and grandchildren in term time, and Buffy and Simon and their children were close by; and Stephen, who was a tree-surgeon in Clitheroe. Ruth had always had fantasies of one day living in the 'real' country of her youthful excursions from Liverpool. She and John had driven through Wharfedale on a tour of Trinity livings and had loved walking in the limestone countryside. They came up to look at the house in the Easter vacation and 'it immediately felt like our sort of home'. The children all loved it in a way they had never loved Fort Lodge at Reigate.

Leaving the Reigate garden was a wrench; but in November 1980 – 'during Term time, because I knew John loathed all the process of packing and unpacking' – Ruth moved in to Prospect House, and by the end of term – Simon and Buffy had worked on the house for weeks, doing necessary repairs and building work – everything was ready for John to 'come home'.

At the beginning of 1980 John did what he had done in 1960 and 1970: he gathered together a collection of papers representing what he called the 'spin off' of the decade. The focal point of the book was the set of three lectures on 'The Roots of a Radical', but he added six papers and six sermons. There was one paper that fastened on the important points in the continuing debate on Christology after 'The Myth of God Incarnate'. A second was on 'What is the Gospel?' which related it to, for instance, social realities like the Sri Lankan situation John had visited and the response of a Sinhalese Anglican priest, Yohan Devananda, who had founded a collective farm that would provide a meeting place for Buddhists, Christians and Marxists where the poor struggled for basic peasant land-rights, largely against British-dominated tea-planting interests. A third paper on 'Social Ethics and the Witness of the Church' was given at a conference on Christian Ecumenical Witness on Moral Issues organized by the Franciscan Friars of the Atonement at Westminster Cathedral in October 1976. A fourth was on 'The Place of Law in the Field of Sex' (the Beckly Lecture on a Methodist foundation in the field of Christian social ethics, given in July 1972). The fifth was on 'Christians and Violence'. The sixth was on 'Nuclear Power Options'. It was as careful a paper as John ever wrote. He knew of course it was outside his normal field and was not afraid that his critics would say so: 'Here more than anywhere factual details and technical judgments are inextricably involved in the moral and spiritual decisions . . . But it becomes increasingly obvious that the issues are far too important to be left to the specialist, let alone to the nuclear establishment . . .' At Trinity John had the great benefit of being able to consult such people as Sir Martin Ryle, Nobel Prize-winner and Astronomer Royal (who, alas, died seven weeks before John died). 'Nuclear power choices', John wrote, 'are *not* for the Christian the ultimate ones. Yet for our generation, they may be the penultimate. And this is where Bonhoeffer insisted the Christian ethic has to be lived and worked out: in the name of the ultimate to take with radical seriousness the things before the last.'

When Canon Maurice Wiles, Regius Professor of Divinity, Oxford reviewed *The Roots of a Radical* he wrote: 'John Robinson writes better than almost any theologian I know. He is a master of the telling phrase . . . He has things to say that need to be listened to, and the equally rare gift of saying them in a way which makes the listening a pleasure aesthetically – if not infrequently uncomfortable in other respects.' The aged Professor John Knox wrote:

> I have read *The Roots of a Radical* with greater *pleasure*, I think, than any other of your books I have read – I will not say, with greater profit, although that, too, may be true. The greater pleasure arises from the fact that this book is so revealing of yourself and that I can hear your voice so clearly in all of its pages.

That summer John was away a good deal. The University of Southern California, celebrating its centenary, had awarded him an honorary Doctor of Laws and asked him to give the Baccalaureate Address on that occasion. So at the beginning of June he flew over for the inside of a week to Los Angeles and Pasadena.

For the last fortnight of June John went with Ruth to Rome to the 'Romess' Conference for Anglicans and Roman Catholics, where – under the expert direction of Canon Bill Purdy – they visited many early Christian sites in and around Rome including the excavations beneath St Peter's; and attended a Papal Mass there. John gave a lecture on 'The Human Face of God Today' and a series on 'The Church in Rome in the First Century', during which he frequently referred to his *Redating the New Testament*. At the last night entertainment the Robinson contribution, to John's surprise, was a sketch by Ruth, wearing his cassock, of himself lecturing on 'my book, *Rewriting the New Testament*'! John and Ruth spent the following week staying in Perugia and Assisi and walking in the surrounding hills.

It was essential to John's work on *The Priority of John* that he should pay a second visit to Israel. He and Ruth set out on 20 March 1981. They were able to follow up their contacts with those closely concerned with the current situation: Arab Christians struggling to maintain or retrieve their human rights, and liberal Jewish writers. They also visited Bassam Shaka'a, mayor of Nablus, who had earlier been seriously wounded in an attempt to assassinate him. But the main purpose of their journey was to explore the geographical background to St John's Gospel. An illuminating afternoon was spent with Père Benoit of the École Biblique exploring the Pool of Bethesda area, and with Father Bargil Pixner in the excavated Essene quarter in the Mount Zion area of Jerusalem. In Galilee they were able to investigate and assess the possible sites of the Feeding of the Five Thousand; visit the excavations of first-century Capernaum; and, again with Fr Pixner, the pavement of the Roman Via Maris north of Bethsaida, and the ruins of, possibly, the 'seat of custom' where the road from Capernaum joined it. 'Fr Bargil Pixner and I sat among the barbed wire', wrote John, 'tracing the scene of the battle personally described by Josephus in *Vita* 399–406. "Follow the cowpats," said Fr Pixner, "and you won't hit a mine"!' On a memorable day out, under the guidance of Najib Khouri, who had earlier acted as interpreter to the American scholars interviewing the goat-herd who first discovered the Dead Sea Scrolls, they assessed possible sites for Aenon by Salim, where John and Jesus baptized; Sychar, where Jesus met the Woman at the Well; questioned Samaritan farmers about the time of the barley harvest; and visited again the lovely isolated valley of Ain Samniya, the biblical Ephraim, where Jesus retired with his disciples before his last entry into Jerusalem.

John and Ruth joined thousands of others for the Palm Sunday procession 1981, and the next evening were invited to share the re-enactment of a Passion Meal at the Jerusalem Centre for Biblical Studies. On the Wednesday in Holy Week they flew home, in time for John to preside at the Easter Communion at Arncliffe.

There had been a great deal of speculation in Littondale about the bishop who was coming to live in the village of Arncliffe. That he had written well-known books did not necessarily enhance his standing. He would have to prove himself. John of course knew this; though he probably underestimated the natural reserve and traditionalism of the Dales people. In Arncliffe church there was a tiny congregation, with people who were ready for change and people who were not. When

John arrived there had been no vicar for five years. The parish had been put in the charge of Canon Maurice Slaughter, Rural Dean of Skipton, who was already responsible for Bolton Abbey and Rylestone and had his hands full. John saw a need and rapidly moved in to help. The new Bishop of Bradford, Geoffrey Paul, who had spent much of his ministry in South India, quickly appointed John an Assistant Bishop. As Rowan Williams was to write in his memoir of Geoffrey Paul, *A Pattern of Faith*: 'Geoffrey rejoiced in the intellectual stimulus provided for him and for many others in the diocese; and John in turn was delighted to be asked to function as an Assistant Bishop in the Bradford Diocese, helping Geoffrey by performing various duties in the remoter bits of the Dales.'

John wrote in the local magazine that he was happy to be regarded as 'the curate of Littondale'. In the vacations of his first year in the Dales he visited all the villages, talking and learning, taking his job very seriously – as his card index of families shows. Many people who had no connection with the church were surprised and delighted to find him at their door, and even more surprised to find he was informal, a good listener, and interested in them for themselves. Others did not know quite what to make of him. Being John, he preached sermons prepared with as much thought and care as if he were preaching to a vast congregation in a cathedral.

With good intentions he arranged a meeting after the service one evening, simply to discuss what form future services should take. He said he had no desire to push one particular form. Those who wanted change said so; those who did not were silent. John obviously thought the suggested rearrangement was unanimous, which in a sense it was. But in such small communities the opponents of change are often reluctant openly and immediately to voice their opposition at meetings.

After the service on another occasion John discussed with the churchwarden whether there was room to bring forward the altar a little, so that he could celebrate 'facing the people'. 'Just get on the other end, and we'll see how it works,' he said. Though he was against the idea the churchwarden got on the other end; and the altar was moved forward a little. It stayed in its forward position a few weeks but when John returned to Cambridge it was quietly put back – to where it is now.

Ruth of course did what she could to strengthen the relations between John and the village. And John himself did his part – quite naturally and guilelessly. 'Will you take me out shooting with you one day?' John asked Michael Maude – who might have been squire of Arncliffe in other days. Michael was suspicious. He was not used to being asked a favour by a bishop – like a child asking to be taken out by his father – and he had not served in the Royal Inniskilling Dragoon Guards and the Foreign Office (and been land agent to an Oxford college) for nothing. 'I hope you haven't a bee in your bonnet about blood sports?' he asked John anxiously. John assured Michael he had not. Michael then had to approach the other members of the shoot with the request that the bishop should be allowed to come and watch the shooting. And, truth to tell, there was silence for a *very* long while after Michael had popped the question. Eventually they agreed; and on 1 October – 'the world's worst day; it never stopped raining' – John ascended above Arncliffe with Michael and his friends to the grouse moor. And also, truth to tell, at the end of the day Michael Maude was able to report that John was better at saying where the grouse were coming from, and when, than many 'Absolute Beginners' Michael had taken with him on previous occasions. There was the slight embarrassment that John tended to pick up not only Michael's birds but his neighbours', but he was not going to complain about that. Nor would he question John's accuracy when he declared that Michael had shot 49 per cent of the bag. After all, who was he to question the honesty of the Honest-to-God bishop?

One day John called at the Post Office at Litton where Brigie, Janet Taylor's sixteen-year old daughter, was ill – no one then knew just how ill. John asked her how she was, and she mentioned 'sciatica'. John said: 'Oh, well, I know all about back problems. You'll probably have that for the rest of your life'! It was not the best remark to a child already depressed at being ill for so long, and who in fact had terminal cancer. But John wrote to her mother a letter which 'warmed her', with the suggestion that 'faith means being open to anything'. Janet says of the service John specially arranged in the church:

> It meant that he was able to draw together, with Ruth's help, all the people who were desperate to help. He gave corporate expression to their concern for us all. None of us who shared in that service will ever forget it – there were many who would never normally go to church. It gave us a sense of the solidarity of the whole Dale behind us, and helped me to understand that peace and trust were more important than physical survival. There were moments when the absolute rightness of John's words almost stunned: 'We are here this morning . . . to go down,

as it were, to the water-table, to resources too deep for words or for tears.' It seemed to me that there was a great power of love released in that service, and John and Ruth were the channels.

John preached at Brigie's funeral on 5 December 1981. His address 'gave meaning and hope to what many must have seen as purposeless waste, and he did not mince words, referring openly to the cancer and its deadliness for the young. People said they had never heard a funeral address which was so fitting and right.' Janet has since written a book about Brigie's death (*Brigie: A Life 1965–1981*). 'One reason for writing it', she said, 'was to ensure that John's words and Ruth's would be preserved. They were too urgently needed to be lost.' Little did Janet – or John – or Ruth – know that in less than two years John would be preaching that sermon in much the same words in his last Evensong at Trinity, six weeks before he died.

In the spring of 1982 Britain was virtually at war with Argentina. John spoke on the BBC Radio 4 programme *Sunday* on May 2 and appeared that evening on BBC Television in a special Falklands *Newsnight* programme. They were in fact John's last appearances on radio and TV and there is no doubt he was glad to be asked to make them. It was like old times! It was possible for those at close quarters to him – as close as the High Table at Trinity – to be deceived and distracted by his almost schoolboy enthusiasm for what he was saying and doing, deriding his saying and doing it, and entirely to miss the seriousness beneath the surface and the importance and the quality of the contribution he was making. What John's attitude was, and the substance of what he said, he described later that year in the McAndrew Memorial Lecture in Christ Church Cathedral, Hamilton, Ontario:

> Over the past fifty years, successive Lambeth Conferences have reiter-ated the statement with almost tedious regularity that 'war as a method of settling international disputes is incompatible with the teaching of our Lord Jesus Christ' . . . Yet when it recently came to the crunch, and Britain *did* go to war to settle an international dispute arising out of the Argentinian occupation of the Falkland Islands, scarcely a voice of protest was raised from the official leadership of the churches (the Methodists and, as one would expect, the Quakers being honourable exceptions). The Bishop of London (and disappointingly Cardinal Hume) trotted out the old arguments for the 'just war', while the Archbishop of Canterbury took a long time to make, in the end, some

rather good noises about what happens when the price of it becomes too high. I found myself thrust upon the media, merely saying what Lambeth had said many times. I felt at first very isolated – until *all* the letters I got said with almost predictable regularity: Thank God someone has spoken up. Now I have been as used as any to what Jim Pike used to call 'negative fanmail', and its total absence on this occasion revealed to me an eerie vacuum. And the situation was made odder by the Pope, at the height of the Falklands Campaign and amid the unrestrained jingoism of the popular press, receiving rapturous applause for saying that war was 'totally unacceptable as a means of settling differences between nations' and 'belonged to the tragic past', with 'no place on the agenda of the future'.

[John went on to say:]

Until the day before yesterday the first thing you did in any international incident was to 'show the flag' or 'send in the Marines'. And Britain did that at Suez with disastrous results, and in the Falklands, with seeming success. The first instinctive response of Parliament was again to dispatch a 'task-force'. Of course, we were assured, it wasn't meant to be *used* (any more than 'the deterrent'). It was there to step up the pressure for a 'diplomatic solution'; but it soon became inevitable that it would be used and used quickly. For you couldn't have it bobbing around the South Atlantic all winter. So Mrs Thatcher won her war and a lot of (temporary) votes and 'liberated' the 1,800 Falkland Islanders (at a cost of many more casualties on both sides). But for what? We are as far away as ever from winning the peace; in fact a good deal further. For except in close co-operation with Argentina there is simply no viable future for the Islands. Meanwhile the economic and political strains, between north and south, east and west, have been exacerbated, and the only real beneficiaries are the manufacturers of Exocet missiles and the rest, whose order-books are bulging. A great opportunity was lost of showing the world a better way. As Kenneth Greet, the Secretary of the Methodist Conference in Britain, said at its summer meeting, 'When the task-force sailed to the Falklands the clock was turned back 50 years'.

John's fourteenth year at Trinity was now drawing near, and he could with confidence count on Trinity's generosity for another period of sabbatical leave. He felt he needed this to complete what would be in many ways his *magnum opus*, which when published would form a 400 page book. The offer of an appointment as Visiting Professor in the Department of Religious Studies of McMaster University, Hamilton, Ontario from 15 September to 15 December came at an opportune time. As well as working on his Bampton Lectures, John agreed to share some of his work with the students. McMaster, originally a Baptist foundation, is now a booming secular university of over ten thousand students, situated on the shores of Lake Ontario. The guest house John was allotted, in virtually a nature sanctuary, was ideal. It was 'all found' – including Eleanor Schoenfeld, the warm-hearted housekeeper who looked after him wonderfully.

He worked hard during the week. He enjoyed the work with the students, which was not exacting, and was pleased to 'come across much material I shouldn't have discovered at home'. He was able to serve the Church in Canada giving, as we have said, the McAndrew Memorial Lecture in Christ Church Cathedral, Hamilton, on 3 October, on the subject of 'The Church's Most Urgent Priority in Today's World'; John had no doubt what that was: nuclear peacemaking. A fortnight later he gave the annual Divinity Day lecture for McMaster's Divinity College on 'What Future for a Unique Christ?' On 28 October he lectured at the University of Waterloo, Ontario, in the Theatre of the Arts, on 'Religion in the Third Wave' – 'reflections on the state of the academic study of religion'. In November he gave a lecture at the University of Toronto and one at McGill University, Montreal, with his friend Professor Charles Davis as his host. The Suffragan Bishop of Niagara, John Bothwell, took him to ice hockey, and there was opportunity to meet Ted Scott, Primate of the Anglican Church in Canada.

Weekends were free, and John made the most of them, travelling into the United States, to New York City, Rochester (NY); and even to California, to Pasadena. He used every available minute of his midterm in November: *Cyrano de Bergerac* with Professor Rustum Roy at Niagara-on-the-Lake; then on to Rochester (NY); Kirkridge; Baltimore; Washington, D.C.; Fort Worth, Texas; and Louisville, Kentucky.

It is important for the undersanding of John himself as a person but also in estimating his significance that some record should be made of how people responded to him in the USA. His own simple statement: 'It is humbling to find how genuinely the people seem to want you to come and even to pay you to do it', conveys the truth of the matter. Half a dozen people whom John arranged to meet while he was spending his sabbatical term at McMaster can speak for dozens, indeed hundreds more.

The Revd Alex Methven has written:

> John was a model, a hero, one whose behaviour represented the Christlike living 'for others'.
>
> I had arrived at John's home in Blackheath the Sunday of the *Lady Chatterley* uproar. But we had a quiet tea together, with total concentration on my ministry and future, although a score or more reporters were hanging about in the driveway. When we left the house, his courtesy and patience with the reporters was evident. He drove me to St Michael's, Sydenham while he drove on to preach elsewhere. He picked me up again – the parish was mine. He was a real pastor. . . .
>
> I made a mistake returning here to the USA; but John never ceased to love and support me until that last year of his life. He never forgot to call when he was in the States, and visits to him in England were warmly received. I always tried to get together people he would enjoy meeting. His last visit will remain ever with me. I picked him up and delivered him to Washington Cathedral where he preached. I wish that every Episcopal priest had been there.
>
> We then left the Cathedral. He wanted to see the Viet Nam memorial, so we drove there and then walked to see the black gash of marble in the earth – which expresses what we both felt about the inhumanity of it all. We spent some time in silence, watching the people touch names, hold back, or shed tears. We walked away in a hushed atmosphere.
>
> Perhaps one of his greatest gifts to me was accepting me as I was and could become – always willing to ask, share, listen and learn, and in so doing gave immensely of himself.

The Revd Alfred R. Shands III has written:

> John Robinson is the theologian who continues to reach me the most thoroughly, and I would have to say that almost every word I speak or write about faith has been so deeply influenced by his point of view that I can't really tell where he leaves off and I begin. Sometimes I wonder if this is not because we both were products of the same times, and this is the point at which the clock stopped for me. Yet look though I do, I can't find anything better.
>
> Basically, I feel that the questions which he raised have yet to be fully explored, and that he was one of those highly prophetic figures who could see so far that it is taking a long time to catch up. Recently, I re-read most of his books, and was quite staggered by the amount of hot controversial subjects that he covered so well. This was certainly part of his power for our age.
>
> His appeal for Americans was most obviously related to the moment that he arrived on the American scene, when radicalism in politics and

social issues was current. His voice, with its theological affirmation of this world, gave depth and meaning to what was happening to us as a nation. He helped us to understand – and encouraged us to go even further than we dared – to take our own radicalism to its root depth. His energy and celebration of newness matched our own. Doubtless some of the impact he had was due to the fact that he was a bishop in the Church of England so heavily weighted on the side of conservatism. He stood in the revered American tradition of the maverick – the outsider who flaunts the establishment when the truth is being ignored. The motto of Virginia Theological Seminary, where he gave one of his early important lectures, is 'follow the truth, lead where it may, cost what it will . . .' a quote from an early 20th Century professor at the seminary. John showed us, sixty years later, what that motto meant. But there were other less obvious reasons why he reached us so deeply. America, easily the most religious of all western nations, is also the fountain-head of secularity. Rarely does either appear in its rawest forms outside this country – Oral Roberts and Las Vegas. The opposing values of these two phenomena have always created a sense of conflict and guilt in us, normally resolved by the ostrich position. John Robinson brought our head out of the sand and helped us to see that our secularity is only the gateway to a renewed sense of faith. Pure healing. The fact that he was above all a *biblical* theologian was very important – another American passion. There is among us an anti-European distrust of abstractions, but the truth of the Bible (though on the whole quite unknown to us) is something to be trusted. He normally related what he said to this yardstick. John Robinson seemed at home with American pluralism far more than most of us. He moved from the Baptist to the Presbyterian to the Episcopal Church with equal ease, setting us an example that we were not quite ready to follow in our own need for denominational labels.

Robert A. Raines, Director of Kirkridge, has written:

I came to know John as a Fulbright Scholar at Clare College 1953–54. I studied New Testament, and John was my tutor. He was wonderfully supportive to me, a young student; and he and Ruth were warmly hospitable to me and countless other students in their home. I remember the *agape* breakfasts after Eucharist, and the sense of friendship deepening in that year. Looking back, it amazes me how much of himself John gave me, and, of course, so many other students. Above all, he was a great and constant friend. One of the books he introduced to me in that year was the book of *Letters To His Friends* by his uncle Forbes. It was deeply true of John. He visited me at every church I served over the following years, and eventually here at Kirkridge.

One of his times at Kirkridge was in August, some time in the 1970s. He was lecturing to a crowd of people up at our Lodge. It was very hot, and everyone was wearing as little as possible. There was the illustrious Bishop Robinson, lecturing in his yellow swimming trunks! On many of his visits to me, he would ask for help in going to see his friend and colleague, John Knox – a journey of some 3 hours or more each way. What fidelity of friendship! John's fame and notoriety never turned his head regarding his friends. It astonished me in the early years to receive hand-written letters and notes from him from all over the world. Then I came to understand that he treated all his friends this way.

I sometimes felt that John's great heart reached out in friendship the way it did, perhaps partly to make up for some lack of intimacy, or perhaps some lack of warm appreciation from some of his colleagues in England. It occurred to me that John honored fidelity at the cost of intimacy. I marvel at his openness of mind, whether to people and ideas in India or Africa or the Shroud of Turin.

I loved John, and remain deeply grateful for his friendship and for his faith. He nourished, encouraged and befriended me in ways that deepened my humanity and Christianity. He has an honored place in my special cloud of witnesses.

The Revd Professor John Knox wrote:

He was one of the most brilliant and productive theological scholars of our time. More important than those and many other distinctions: he was a wonderfully good man – just and true, imaginatively generous, com-passionate, courageous, and as near to being pure in heart as, I believe, a man can be. I have known him well for more than thirty years, and have had no dearer friend.

Rustum Roy, Evan Pugh Professor of the Solid State, Pennsylvania State University, has written:

Over the years I had the great pleasure of coming to know John better and learning that behind the persona of the brilliant Cambridge don who was not given to much drawing room conversation was the roving mind of a true seeker after the new. He was always curious about my science and how a working research scientist could be so involved in ethics and theology – till I reminded him that his own curiosity was very scientific. We shared an interest in sex-ethics, and, sitting in our living room in 1966, we eventually named the book my wife and I had written – *Honest Sex*. And we often talked long into the evening about what the radically new *experiences* of sexuality would mean for the generations ahead.

John spent quite a bit of time on this side of the Atlantic the year before he died. And during that time I tried to summarize for him the frontiers where I felt he should be working. First, I did not think that he had taken seriously his own admonition that our images of God, and God-talk, really must go. He did make the turn to the East as he went to India, and his *Truth is Two-Eyed* was a very sensible synthesis. But perhaps he did not continue the promise, inherent in *Honest to God*, of attempting to re-define a Christian theology in a universal culture and language. In a way, I suppose the academic pull of Cantabrigian scholarship on the Gospel of John took him away from this task. Second, I do believe that he was *too* Anglican really to have a contemporary doctrine of the laity. He was simply not enough of a Quaker to understand house-churches and ecclesial base communities – which in a way were his most devoted followers. Third, he was fascinated by the challenge of science as *the* common religion of humankind but he knew that was 'not his bag'. He showed his fascination and genuine scientific curiosity in his intense interest in the Shroud of Turin. He even wrote a puff-piece for *Experimenting with Truth*, my Hibbert lectures in this field, but I know he was disappointed. He spoke knowledgeably of Arthur Peacocke and Alister Hardy, kept company with Brian Josephson and Fritjof Capra – feeling the importance of the whole area but not knowing how to get into it.

George Regas, Rector of All Saints Church, Pasadena, has written:

I met John Robinson on his first visit to the USA in 1955 in my final year at the Episcopal School of Theology, Cambridge, Mass. John had been invited by Harvard to do the Noble Lectures and to teach for a term at Harvard Divinity School. I was Dr George Buttrick's teaching assistant for his class on Homiletics, and I can still remember his words: 'John Robinson is the most creative and imaginative young theologian in the world today, and we want to give him a platform for provoking us into rethinking Christian doctrine.'

I took the courses John offered – one on the theology of the New Testament and the other on the Gospel of John. They were my most valued classes in my three years of seminary.

John stayed at E.T.S., and I drove him to Harvard on the days he taught. Unlike my American professors, he truly seemed interested in what I thought about life and American society and theology. He listened!

I wrote a paper for John on the eschatology of the Gospel of John which he liked very much, and said he would like me to come to Cambridge as a research student. I had two children and needed to put all this seminary education into practice. I was not really excited about doing three more years of graduate work. But John worked on me and shared with me a vision of theological scholarship that was enticing. I applied to Clare to work with Dr Robinson, and with his persuasive help I was accepted.

I spent a year at Clare with John 1956–7. My family and I lived in a garage apartment in Little Shelford. A month after I arrived in Cambridge, John had my wife and me to tea to meet Charles Moule and C. H. Dodd – two of the New Testament scholars I admired most. I was treated as though I really mattered; that I had convictions that counted; that I could be helpful to them, even though I was only 26 years of age.

In our tutorials John did two things with consistency. He pushed me to read all the literature I possibly could absorb – but then make my own interpretation. The search must be open-ended. Nothing closed off, tied down. No one had ever set my agenda so caringly.

My daughter Susan, then two years of age, was scratched in the eye by a neighbour's cat. My wife called Clare College. They couldn't find me. John Robinson went to our apartment and took my daughter to the hospital. When I got home that evening, John was there with my family. And I was just a student at Clare.

I returned earlier to the States than I had anticipated because of grievous illness. I was faced with surgery. John was thoroughly supportive as we talked our way through our decision as I lay for three weeks in a Cambridge hospital bed.

After my recovery from illness and surgery, my bishop sent me to be the priest-in-charge of a little mission in Pulaski, Tennessee, in the old South. It is notorious for being the place where the Ku Klux Klan was originally organized. I had 75 people in my congregation. In 1958 I arranged for John to come to Pulaski. In that Bible belt community we had invited everyone to come for the evening service where John would preach. It was raining, and I picked John up at the Nashville, Tennessee, airport. Coming back to Pulaski I was passing a large truck on the highway, and as I cut back into the lane in front of the truck my car went out of control and spun off the highway, through a fence, and came to a stop in the middle of a cow pasture. The doors had been thrown open, one torn off, and a fence post was resting across our laps.

We were shaken up badly but not hurt. John said, 'How can we get to Pulaski, George? We don't want to miss that service you've planned!' We left the car, walked across the field and finally convinced a passing car to drive us to Pulaski – for a handsome fee!

Over the three years I was in Pulaski I got discouraged with my work and the priesthood. Those were the beginning years of the civil rights movement and a ministry in the deep South was burdensome to my conscience. I often wrote to John. His response is still clearly remembered. 'Hold on, George. Don't give up. Hold on to hope. God must have something in store for us. Remember that fence post on our laps, and we are still alive. God must intend us to do something worthwhile with our lives.' Tongue in cheek or not – I took him to mean, stiffen up, go to work, accomplish something. This world is no place for a cry baby!

I was Rector of Grace Church, Nyack, New York, from 1960–67. John visited me several times and spoke in the church. I arranged for him to address a conference of 500 clergy in the Diocese of New York which was being held at the West Point Military Academy. John was amused and a little distressed that the Diocese was using this military setting for a clergy conference. The West Point technocrats had a most difficult time with the sound system, and the ability of the clergy to understand the Englishman was seriously impaired. It angered John. 'If the brainpower of West Point can't figure out how to manage a sound system, how can they ever figure out ways to defend America. I am apprehensive about the security of your great nation!'

John became the godfather of my son, Timothy, and took this role very seriously. He frequently wrote Tim over the years, always brought him gifts when he visited, was deeply concerned when Tim, at age 5, was ill in hospital and had surgery. He called us several times from London. John never did anything pretentiously. He just did it, offered it; and people did with his actions what they chose to do. We deeply appreciated them and loved him for them.

I became Rector of All Saints Church, Pasadena, California, in 1967.

Under John's encouragement I went back to work on my doctorate, part-time over the years, and completed it at the School of Theology at Claremont, California. John was proud of me! I frequently set up luncheon discussion events with John and some of the faculty at both the School of Theology at Claremont and Fuller Seminary in Pasadena. John often felt their criticism of his books was unfair, and took them on rather fiercely.

John came to All Saints at least ten times. He came over for two weeks as Scholar in Residence at the church in March 1973 and preached at the ordination of Mike McKee into the Baptist ministry in Los Angeles. Mike was joining my staff in an ecumenical ministry. He was also a volunteer policeman, and John went out with him on his beat one night to get to know him better.

John loved to hike on the mountain trails near Pasadena. It was on these walks that we talked a great deal about Panentheism in contra-distinction from Pantheism.

Probably the most remarkable part of the visit was his attack on

President Nixon. John had been speaking throughout the country and Pasadena was his last stop. He was very discouraged by what he had heard. This was just before all the most damaging news broke on Watergate. There were lots of Nixon defenders in March of 1973, especially in Pasadena. John spoke at the Rector's Forum and said he sensed a deep malaise in American life, a corruption of spirit, a profound lack of honesty in the body politic. Then he startled people by saying he doubted that anyone in the room would admit that they had voted for Nixon. Many shot up their hands in proud support of the President. He responded that they must not want to deal with the facts. America is in profound trouble. The President is not an honest man.

I had invited a reporter from the *Los Angeles Times* to cover the Forum. The next day it had a front page story on the 'gloomy Bishop'.

In June 1980 I introduced John to the work that All Saints Church and Leo Baeck Temple were doing on reversing the arms race. We had formed an Interfaith Center to Reverse the Arms Race with the office located at All Saints. I took John through the operation, had lunch with Rabbi Beerman and another Jewish friend, Harold Willens, talked long into the night about the work of reversing and ending the arms race as the quintessential task of the religious communities. John said I was right. He had not done as much as he should or wanted to do, and he would put his mind and heart to the task. When he returned to Cambridge, he wrote me, saying he had done an epilogue to his book, *The Roots of a Radical*, on the arms race.

I belong to a group of 25 Episcopal clergy from all over America, rectors of very large congregations. We meet for four days a year at the College of Preachers in Washington Cathedral. In May 1983 I asked John to come over and spend those four days with us as our theologian. He did, and we loved him. He took all of the books he had written, divided them into three headings, and just talked about what went into the writing of those books, what he was trying to accomplish, and where he felt they succeeded and failed. It was a richly fascinating and interesting time with this great man of the Church.

Within a month I received Ruth's letter and a note from John saying he had cancer of the pancreas. It was devastating news. I grieved for them. I flew to England in August. John was glad I had come. We reminisced, we walked, we talked about his options. I celebrated the Eucharist for him and gave him the laying-on-of-hands.

John, though shy in many ways, exhibited a warmth because he had the ability to share deeply in people's lives and sense what was happening. He had the capacity to sustain over long periods of time this type of caring. His perceptiveness was remarkable. He was the only person who ever said to me prior to my separation and divorce from Jane, my first wife, that he felt I was in trouble and things were in a bad way. I was too secretive with my problems. But even so, John was the only one to see through that and spend the energy to help me deal with it.

In the political, social, psychological and theological worlds, he had the ability to put his finger on the pulse beat. It is incredible how often he articulated a point of view, an interpretation, that was sorely needed but never heard – and his words were able, in astounding ways, to liberate people.

John loved America but he was a stern critic from his very first visit. His theology was never far from the political scene. His views jarred my Southern wife, and Jane often called him 'Red John'.

As a Bishop he never bought into the hierarchical rendition of truth. With all that is now happening in the Roman Catholic Church: with the censure of priests who dissent from the authoritative teachings of the Church, John's attitude of all truth is open-ended, and the final authority, Christ, and not the Bishops, and not the Church, is still so powerful a witness. The courage he had in never being afraid to challenge the teachings of the Church no matter what the cost will long be remembered.

His theology, his liturgy and his discipleship were never separated from the world. The final years of going deeply into psychology and the nuclear arms race were just new expressions of the inextricable union of theology and secular life.

It was 10 December when John arrived back in England. He went to Cambridge for forty-eight hours, then made his way back to Arncliffe. He was looking forward to a peaceful family Christmas and happy New Year.

Peace had been the subject of many of his recent sermons in Canada and the United States and it seemed 'obvious' that peace should also be the subject of his sermon that year at midnight on Christmas Eve in Arncliffe:

> Tonight, in a very few words, I want to concentrate on a deceptively simple word, from the angels' song, as the heart of the Christmas message – peace on earth, God's peace to men and women to whom his grace, his graciousness, has been shown (not 'goodwill towards men', as if it rests on our warm feelings, which are sadly fragile) . . .
>
> 1982 was a good year for war and the increase of Exocet missiles and the arms trade generally. But as it comes to an end there are signs of a rising consciousness throughout the world that we cannot go on like this . . .

I have just come back from three months in Canada and the US, and have been greatly impressed and heartened by the growing commitment of the Churches to peace as the single most urgent priority in today's world . . . I have brought back the draft of the RC Bishops' Pastoral Letter, 'The Challenge of Peace' . . . *How* we achieve this . . . Christians are sincerely divided and it is no subject for a sermon . . . the multi-lateralists and the unilateralists . . . I am profoundly convinced that both witnesses are needed . . .

On Tuesday night there was laid before the Arncliffe Parish Meeting the Craven Council's District War Plan – a thick volume now on view at the Post Office. Read it . . .

In the name of the Christian Gospel I believe that we must protest. We must insist that if our world is to be saved from unutterable destruction . . .

> Beneath the Angel-strain have rolled
> Two thousand years of wrong;
> And man, at war with man, hears not
> The love-song which they bring:
> Oh hush the noise, ye men of strife,
> And hear the angels sing!

What John said would have been warmly received in Great St Mary's, Cambridge, in St Martin-in-the-Fields – and in Washington Cathedral. In Arncliffe after the service 'the people murmured' – for a week. Then on New Year's Eve John, the pastor, visited the disco for the young people in the village hall, and decided he should also visit 'The Falcon', where the traditional New Year's Eve party was in full swing. His opening gambit across the bar: 'It's more peaceful here than in the Village Hall!' evoked the response, 'You can't open your mouth without talking about peace!' Then the suppressed anger at the sermon exploded, and it was quickly made clear that John's presence was neither welcome nor wanted. He returned home to Ruth visibly shaken, though he tried to make light of the sad event – and was touched when, later, one of those involved apologized to him 'for having had a drop too much'. Some who had not been in the pub deplored what had happened – though they had been equally antagonized by John's sermon.

From one angle, John had said nothing wrong. From his angle, he had only said what was right. But the Falklands war was a very sensitive and controversial issue in Littondale as elsewhere throughout the country and in Arncliffe there was clearly the question of pastoral wisdom and judgment. Did not the Gospel of John record that Another had said: 'I have many things to say unto you, but you cannot bear them now'? (John 16:12)

There was also the question of patience. Had John spoken too hastily? – he had not after all been long in Arncliffe. John's mother had written to him in 1956:

Things have come quickly and easily to you and in that there is danger – I have sometimes been anxious. I think the key word is *patience*. Do you remember the text your father had in his room – and it is now in mine: 'In your patience ye shall possess your souls'? He delighted in that especially in the slight mistranslation! I had the words put on the stone on his grave. I so remember when that book of Dick Sheppard's came out, *The Impatience of a Parson*, his vehement protest, how he said that 'the very first mark of an apostle, according to St Paul, is patience'.

But there is surely a patience *and* impatience appropriate to the apostle, pastor and prophet. There was a sense of urgency – surely not misplaced – about John's sermon on peace that Christmas night. If he had spoken too soon – let us say that he had – the question remained when, and where, and how, would it have been appropriate to speak? Some on that subject undoubtedly wanted him to 'hold his peace'. John the prophet, John the pastor, John the disciple could not do that.

Trinity had allowed John to have the Lent term in 1983 to complete his sabbatical. He spent much of January to March in Arncliffe working on *The Priority of John*. Ernest Blanchard was inducted as Vicar of Arncliffe and Kettlewell on 4 January but John still continued to help at the services. He went back to Cambridge for a few days at the end of January, not least to discuss the appointment of a Chaplain to succeed Ralph Godsall (now Vicar of Hebden Bridge in the Diocese of Wakefield). John had come back from North America – where he had met a number of women priests – believing that now there were women undergraduates at Trinity the time was ripe, if the right person could be found – and he thought he had found such a person – to have a woman priest as one of the Chaplains of Trinity. (A deaconess has since been appointed as Chaplain of Clare.) Trinity was all for 'equal opportunities' but very reluctant to appoint as a Chaplain someone who – since the Women Ordained Abroad Measure had not yet been published, let alone debated – would be unable to operate within the bounds of the Laws of the Church of England. It was not for Trinity to solve the Church of England's problems.

Since Brigie's death at Arncliffe a year earlier, her mother Janet had been much involved with helping George Knight, the Rector of Linton-in-Craven near Arncliffe, and his wife, whose only son Christopher, a recently married young man, had developed cancer. John and Ruth also visited, and as Christopher's condition deteriorated John was asked whether he would conduct a service of laying-on-of-hands and anointing. This took place around Christopher's bedside on 7 April, just before John's return to Cambridge. Janet and Ruth continued to visit, noting that *they* had been 'living with cancer' for quite a long time.

On 11 April John went to York as Assistant Bishop to attend the Bradford Clergy School and to chair the three lectures by Canon Rowan Williams (now Lady Margaret Professor of Divinity, Christ Church, Oxford).

John's fourteenth year in Trinity's employ was coming to an end. In that time not a single university lectureship at Cambridge in his field had become or looked likely to become vacant. Approaches had been made to him by other universities, but he did not pursue them: he clearly judged they could not offer more to him than his position at Trinity. John went back to Cambridge on 15 April for the weekend before the beginning of the Easter term, to take part in the College Retreat at St Francis House, Hemingford Grey. His six months sabbatical was ending.

John had no qualms about the pastoral care of the College in his absence. He always trusted his Chaplains. Ralph Godsall and Robert Atwell (who had become Chaplain of Trinity at Michaelmas 1982) came to know him very closely in his last months and years. It is important to have their assessment of him before we begin an account of his last term at Trinity – and of *his* living with cancer.

Ralph Godsall has written:

> I arrived at Trinity in the October of 1978 to renew a friendship with John which had begun almost 10 years earlier. At that time John had just returned to Cambridge from South London, and I had switched from Classics to Theology. The Dean of Queens', Henry Hart, a member of the Divinity School and University Lecturer in Old Testament, regarded the return of John with interest and mixed feelings. I remember that he chose John to be my New Testament supervisor, partly because of a common background in the Classics and partly because he sensed that I would respond more readily to a study of the New Testament

texts with someone whose knowledge of the subject was wider than Cambridge theology itself.

I remember the initial excitement of my first meeting with John in his rooms in Great Court. I regarded him as part bishop, part Fellow of Trinity (a College which filled me with awe), and part spokesman for the new Christian ethic. More than anything else I remember the careful way in which he drew out of me a love for the subject he taught. I left his supervisions with a deeper respect for the early traditions of the Christian faith than I had previously received elsewhere. He made the subject come alive. He was bold and exciting in his handling of the traditional material. He faced its problems with integrity and humility.

John also loved to talk, to tell me about his current concerns, and to introduce me to a world of theology which was wider than that I had previously known. Above all I remember two successful public occasions within the University at this time. The first was the series of four evening sermons at the University Church in the middle of the Lent Term 1969. John always rose to the big occasion, loved an audience, and rarely failed to deliver the goods. He was, I recall, a superb man of 'words', always finding a good contemporary image to bring to bear on his description of the essence of Christian belief. I began to feel it was a present and a future reality.

The other occasion was his Hulsean Lectures. Here too he managed to convey both a deep respect for the tradition he was exploring, whilst at the same time, trying to free a much older tradition from its more recent over-simplifications.

As a fairly traditional and narrow-minded undergraduate I think I can fairly say it was his academic work and his preaching which made Christianity an option for me at a time when I could so easily have become (like so many of my contemporaries have done) a rather superior atheist. In his early days back at Cambridge, John was providing a medium of expression (in a thoroughly conventional way) which challenged all comers to take the Christian faith seriously once more. He was undoubtedly the best known College Dean, and the one to whom we all wanted to listen.

When I returned to Cambridge in 1978 to work with John at Trinity, I was surprised to find that he no longer appealed to such a wide audience. He was still saying and exploring the same things, but somehow the situation had changed in the University, and John in some ways seemed a little washed up. I soon discovered that John relied a great deal on the friendship and loyalty of his Chaplains and on several of the younger dons.

Among the wider Fellowship of the College there was a reluctance to take John seriously and a refusal to acknowledge the study of theology as a necessary part of College life. John's relationship both with the University and with the College seemed distant and angular at times.

Yet in all my six years at Trinity I can never recall an occasion when John said anything harsh or cruel about anyone in the College. He loved it too much for that. He was immensely kind and generous with his time, especially to the older Fellows and their widows. He was a well-loved figure in the Porter's Lodge and often tried to help with the pastoral care of the College's domestic staff and their families. He was ever charitable, never (to my knowledge) lost his temper, and above all was completely honest and straightforward in his dealings. He was a man without guile or craft.

In the College Chapel John tried to maintain a mixed pattern of the traditional and the contemporary. He allowed his Chaplains the scope to experiment (even to turn the clocks back) with liturgy. He often expressed a sadness about the reluctance of the more musically highbrow to listen to more contemporary sounds. But he brought to the inner life of the College Chapel a quality of prayerfulness and unfussy reverence which no one could match. He often spoke in radical ways from the pulpit, partly because he liked to make his audience sit up, but mostly because he was concerned with the integrity of Christian truth, and had committed himself to follow wherever it led him, even inside Trinity itself.

John was always at his best away from High Table. He made a point of entertaining visitors (of whom there were a large number), undergraduates, graduates, younger Fellows and their wives on a regular basis. He liked nothing better than the intimate conversation of a small gathering of friends, especially if the friendship spanned the sexes, the continents, and the secular world. He loved to walk and talk. He liked to throw out ideas and have others bounce them back. John was always a passionate supporter of many movements and causes for change. He often criticized their tendencies to become myopic and muddle-headed. He was not afraid to resign from anything he no longer believed served the pursuit of truth as he had come to understand it. I recall his excitement at the advent of the SDP and his sadness months later when he decided to resign his membership.

John left countless opportunities for misunderstandings. His long absences from Cambridge were criticized. There were those who wanted him to adopt a more singular view of College life and to participate much more actively in its maintenance. John was often blind to such criticisms, partly because he was protected from them by his friends and partly because he simply never noticed them. He asked his

Chaplains to undertake many of his College duties, especially out of Term, because he knew he had to be elsewhere – at home with Ruth and their family, or 'on the road', looking for himself at 'the action', wherever it happened to be.

At the end, John became much more open. He accepted his cancer as a last stage of his acceptance and commitment to God. Trinity respected John in a very different way during the final period of his life. He will probably be remembered by more undergraduates and Fellows for his last Evensong sermon when he again rose to the occasion and spoke to a packed Chapel about God in the Cancer. But those few of us who knew him better than that will recall his last sermon at the College Communion just a week later when he joked about original sin and told stories about his family – for the first time in the hearing of many of us.

Robert Atwell has written:

'Which of my books have you read?' It was the second question fired across the Coton footpath that afternoon. Although I had been at Theological College in Cambridge, I was not a Cambridge graduate, and had consequently neither met John nor been taught by him. Having spent three years as a curate in a north London parish, I had been invited to be considered for the chaplaincy at Trinity. As was John's custom, the victims were dragged out – no matter how inclement the weather – to stride the path past the new Cavendish site, across the fields and motorway, to the village of Coton. As far as I could tell, this venture satisfied at least three things in John's mind: it appealed to his love of walking; it quietened his conscience, because it involved a modicum of exercise yet without distracting him from his beloved books for an inordinate amount of time; and thirdly, it helped him surmount his profound shyness, an obstacle not all ever discerned, and which few ever really traversed with skill or perception.

'Have you read *Honest to God*?' came the supplementary question to plug my silence. To my profound shame, I had to admit I had not – lose 10 points. What was worse, for the life of me I could not remember any of the other books of John's authorship – lose 10 more points, I thought. In retrospect I was able to recall *The Human Face of God*, *Twelve New Testament Studies*, and *The Body* – all of which I had read as an undergraduate and whose volumes still occupy a valued place on my bookshelves. In the white-heat of the moment, my poor memory failed to deliver the goods. The conversation – if so it may be termed, because it was difficult to get a word in edgeways at times – went from bad to worse to disastrous. No, I was not a particularly political animal; no, I had not seen the Turin Shroud; no, I was not a member of CND. My answers betrayed the awful reality that I was not a child of the 60s. 'Well, what are you interested in?' The rhetorical stance of the question and the incredulity of its tone suggested that the plenitude of interest lay within the confines of three topics only – beyond lay the desert of mediocrity or plain dullness. I lifted up my head in the semblance of a defiant gesture and proclaimed that the theatre, the cinema and music in general were my interests. It sounded weak and uninspiring even to my own ears, if not plain wet.

One hour later my troubled brow was being soothed by Philip Buckler, who, over a welcome cup of tea, inquired how my walk with John had gone. My gloom was apparent, and as I rehearsed the blow-by-blow account of my ordeal, he laughed. 'But he did all the talking,' I insisted. 'That means he likes you,' retorted Philip. 'The question is, do you like him?' I had to confess that I did. So began my friendship with John – because friendship it most certainly was, though one sadly that was to last but two and a half years. By the way, I got the job.

John was and is – I still find it remarkably difficult to use the past tense of him – undoubtedly one of the most irritating people with whom I have ever had the privilege of working. Indeed, I count it a privilege. I juxtapose privilege and irritation simply because I think we all felt a sense of awe about being with John, being party to his sharp mind, his gentle soul and generous heart, but at the same time had to cope with a certain extravagance of intellect. With John it was an idea-a-minute. They had the habit of falling at your feet, brick-shaped. Upon my arrival at Trinity in September 1981, it quickly became apparent to me that one of the prime tasks of the Chaplains was to interpret the Dean of Chapel to the College, and in some sense, when John got his wires crossed or was just preoccupied, the College to the Dean of Chapel. You found yourself saying things like 'Of course, when John said that, what he was really trying to say was . . .' John could be profoundly annoying at times, almost as if he were living in another world. Perhaps he was. What was also clear was that in spite of his shyness, John loved an audience and loved playing to the gallery. The temptation was irresistible.

I recall two incidents in particular, one when it was the outbreak of the Falklands War. John alone (I think) of the Anglican episcopate had ventured to vent his disapproval of Government policy and condemn the rampant jingoism of the tabloids. The media – always on the look-out for a spot of controversy – invited John into the fray. Would John appear on BBC 2 Sunday Newsnight? Would John appear? – how could they have ever doubted it? Later that evening on High Table, the first course having been served, John unable to contain either his manifest excitement or the melon set before him, hailed the Manciple who stood behind the Master's chair. 'Norman, could you serve me my next course immediately, because there's a car at Great Gate waiting to rush me to London where I'm appearing on Newsnight at 10.50 p.m.'. He couldn't resist the final bulletin, and those who remember the dulcet tones of John's voice will have little difficulty in imagining the volume, the clarity and range of his proclamation. For John it was the Sixties all over again. He was in the lime-light where he belonged. For the rest of us it was the usual odd blend of pride, embarrassment and amusement, as we swallowed a large gulp of Chateau de Barbe '78, pretending that we had not heard.

A second incident occurred not long after. Again the venue was the High Table and again it was Sunday night. By chance I found myself next to the Master. 'Is it true', he whispered, 'that the Dean has become a vegetarian?' I had to acknowledge that it was. 'Is it true that he had some sort of vision or something?' Unfortunately, it was. Unlike St Peter, whom we are told received a vision of a sailcloth let down from heaven containing all manner of animals, and heard the divine command to rise, kill and eat, thus it is claimed, nullifying Jewish food prohibitions; our beloved John had had the reverse dream, as it were. On three successive nights John had a dream about a whole pile of sheep carcasses in Arncliffe. Could this be divine intervention? (Was this the author of *Honest to God* I asked myself?) Henceforth, John declared to us all, no meat was to soil his lips. Ten days had lapsed since this episcopal announcement. I now followed the eyes of the Master. Further down the table sat JATR tucking into his roast beef.

John's fads lasted about as long as his enthusiasms; that's why one had to be careful. Yet for all that, they were an endless source of amusement. What I never discerned, nor ever shall now, was whether he realised what a source of fun he was. John himself had a wicked grin, his two canine teeth protruding, making him look like a cross between a flushed Trollopian figure and an ecclesiastical vampire. John's humour, however, unlike others' who sat with him on the High Table, never drew blood. There was no malice in John, no casual condemnation, no flippant dismissal of undergraduate or colleague; and, remarkably, no bitterness against the Church or the Establishment.

John was a worthy New Testament scholar. He was an excellent supervisor, as his pupils will testify. He was also a terrible singer. Standing next to him at the altar was sheer purgatory. He was, however, a first-class preacher. A Syrian monk once wrote: 'Put your mind into your heart and stand in the presence of God.' He wrote of prayer, but his words perfectly summarise John's attitude to preaching. Preaching for John was never a cerebral exercise but never crude sentimentality. He would never allow gaps to be fleshed out with devotional material. That was John the scholar. But he spoke with feeling and warmth and sometimes a passion that was surprising. John always had faith in the faithfulness of God. It never deserted him – even at the end.

8

Living with Cancer

It was in the course of the Easter term 1983 that it became apparent just how ill John was. After his sabbatical he had returned to Trinity with an enthusiasm and zest for life that left the Chaplains exhausted! But John had also returned with chronic indigestion. After Mattins he would always join the Chaplains in a quarter of an hour's silent meditation. On the first morning of term, 20 April, John surprised Ralph and Robert by lying prostrate on the Chapel floor. With the pain in his stomach it may have helped John's meditation; but it did little for Ralph's and Robert's. There was more mirth than meditation – while tragedy waited in the wings. John preached on 1 May on his hero Bishop George Bell, who had so profoundly affected the course of his life. On 2 May he went back to the United States for the last time – just for three days – to a conference for twenty-five Episcopal clergy at the College of Preachers in Washington, D.C., organized by his friend George Regas of Pasadena.

John saw his doctor, Tony Sills, on his return and was X-rayed in Addenbrooke's Hospital in Cambridge on 10 May. On the 16th he had the results. Thoughts of chronic hiatus hernia had now changed to the possibility of an ulcer, and Dr Sills prescribed accordingly. John went home to Arncliffe for mid-term and for Ruth's birthday, on 23 May. Ruth realized for the first time how persistent, especially at night, the pain was becoming, and John returned to Cambridge a day earlier than planned in order to see the doctor once more before the weekend.

On Tuesday morning, 31 May, Ruth drove to Cambridge for Mervyn Stockwood's seventieth birthday party that evening, and found on arrival that John had made a further surgery appointment for that afternoon. Tony Sills immediately detected signs of jaundice and, suspecting that the pancreas must be involved, arranged an interview with the surgeon Mr Everett for the next morning. John and Ruth enjoyed the conviviality of the birthday party in the evening, though the shadow of the next day's appointment hung over them. Their fears of a pancreatic tumour were then corroborated, though a final diagnosis had to wait on a scan at Addenbrooke's the following Friday.

'We walked back to the car, hands gripped tight and wordless,' Ruth wrote in her journal. That evening they drove out into the Cambridge countryside, the hedgerows lit by a golden sunset. The next day, Thursday, they drove to Little Gidding – which they had first visited together on 3 June 1944, a few months after they had first met. Now nearly forty years later they were able to 'kneel where prayer had been valid' and share in the midday Communion service for Corpus Christi in the secluded chapel. They had taken with them Eliot's poem and 'every phrase and every sentence' seemed to speak:

> We die with the dying:
> See, they depart, and we go with them . . .
>
> The moment of the rose and the moment of the yew-tree
> Are of equal duration . . .
>
> We shall not cease from exploration
> And the end of all our exploring
> Will be to arrive where we started
> And know the place for the first time . . .
>
> And all shall be well and
> All manner of thing shall be well.

An interview with Bill Everett on the Saturday following the scan confirmed the diagnosis. An exploratory operation would be necessary to see if the tumour could be removed; if this was impossible John could expect to live for six, or possibly nine, months.

On the Sunday morning John celebrated the Holy Communion in Trinity for the last time, supported – literally – on either arm by Ralph and Robert. At midday John and Ruth stood with the crowd in Great Court listening to the Choir singing madrigals from the tower of Great Gate, and in the evening attended Evensong in Chapel. John, standing alone to give the blessing at the end of the service, added two sentences from Dag Hammarskjöld: 'For all that has been – Thanks! To all that shall be – Yes!'

On Monday John went into Addenbrooke's for the operation next day. Ruth was with him on the Tuesday morning until he was taken to the theatre. She returned to John's rooms at Trinity to wait for Bill

Everett's promised call the moment he had finished operating. When it came he told her that the tumour was already too extensive to remove, but everything had been done to remove the pain and the cause of the jaundice. The six months prognosis stood. Ruth was in the ward when John was brought back and it was during that afternoon, while she was waiting for him to regain consciousness, that she wrote the first of the 'Letters to Their Friends' which would be such a help in the next months to those who could only share at a distance. John added his wavering signature to the letter the next day. He did not begin to come round until the evening, when his first question was of course whether the tumour had been removed, and Ruth told him what she had learnt earlier in the day. In their first letter they wrote:

> We are both so thankful that this has happened while John is still in Cambridge, where we have such expert skill and care immediately to hand and are supported by the love and support of so many friends. Above all we have appreciated the care and openness of Mr Everett, our surgeon, who has at every stage frankly explained to us what the situation is . . . From the world's point of view the prognosis is poor, but we feel that *we* are concerned not with duration but with the depth and quality of living which we intend to explore to the full. As to the future, though discarding any facile optimism, we are full of hope and very conscious that there are other resources to hand as well as medical, and that these latter may not have the last word.

John was in hospital for five weeks, much longer than expected, as a second operation was needed to remove adhesions. Trinity was marvellous. Ruth was allowed to live in John's rooms, where on return from the hospital each evening she was able to deal with the accumulated post and enquiries. John had been allocated a room to himself in the hospital, and thanks to a very co-operative Addenbrooke's staff Ruth was able during the day to help with the routine care of John from the time he awoke to the time he was settled for the night, and to relieve the nursing staff from attending to the continual stream of visitors. The drugs which John had been given were to relieve though not cure the cancer. He was told he would be given nothing that would make him feel awful or that would have disturbing side-effects.

John – typically! – decided to try and keep a journal while he was in hospital: 'something very different from a diary, which has always oppressed me. There you feel you have got to record something every day whether there is something worth saying or not . . . I would simply use the opportunity of setting down thoughts as they come.' They came! – via his tape-recorder and later typed; 74 pages of 400 words a page.

> I should have been far too exhausted to try and write a diary, but it is always possible to snatch a few minutes in bed at the end of the day or in some other space, to record fleeting impressions before they lose their spontaneity. As it is, I know from experience that what I put on tape always needs a good deal of editing.

They began on 1–2 June: 'Yesterday was the day when I was told that the most probable diagnosis would be that I had cancer of the pancreas. I confess that I hadn't the vaguest idea of where this organ was, let alone what it does . . .'

John's journal was obviously important to him. It was an extended soliloquy. Some of it can be published; most of it should not be; much of it could be regarded as a 'Letter to Intimate Friends'; quite a lot of it was simply for himself: a way of working things out. It was a means of communication – with all the resonances that word has of communing, company, things in common, sharing. Much of it was spoken into the tape-recorder in 'the slow watches of the night'. It was useful, not least, to occupy him. As John wrote: 'Several times, I find myself using the words, "Look thy last on all things lovely every hour."' He also wrote: 'I am not in the least afraid. In fact I am not quite sure what people mean by the fear of death.'

> *June 6th* [The evening before John's operation.] I end the day in good heart and at this moment await Peter Adams and Ralph and Ruth to come in for a brief service of laying-on-of-hands and Compline, which will be a nice close before I am subjected to more preparations.

> *June 8th* Well, here I am at the end of the day, after the operation, and I have been surprisingly perky . . . Ruth came in at 7 o'clock this morning and we had half-an-hour's quiet time . . . She has been in and out much of the day and has been wonderful . . .

> I always used to think the words in Bishop Ken's hymn: 'Live this day as 'twere thy last' rather morbid, but I now know what they mean: to count and enjoy every moment that is given you . . . One of the things that one of the letters said was that I must have a lot of anger. This has simply never occurred to me, and I can feel no resentment whatever . . .

> *June 11th* Alas, my absence from voting would have made no difference at all . . . The most appalling revelation of the Election is the total

unfairness of the electoral system. However, for Buffy's sake, I am delighted that Jack Straw got in at Blackburn with an increased majority. [Buffy had been up half the night at the count in Blackburn before coming down to Cambridge to see her father.]

June 15th I have had a wonderful birthday, with so many appreciative cards and letters, which makes one realise how much one has been loved. The climax was a birthday party which Alan Weeds had arranged, with champagne and two birthday cakes. All the nursing staff were asked in, and the rest were Trinity Fellows, Ralph and Ellen, Robert Atwell, Richard and Annette Marlow, Keith and Debby Carne. With all the doctors and nurses, it somewhat broke the rules that a patient was to have a maximum of two visitors! (Ruth's presence did not need to be mentioned.)

June 16th/17th [John recorded each visit, mostly with a comment or two. Some seemed to bring with them more than themselves.] Elizabeth Lampe – whose husband Geoffrey was diagnosed as having cancer about the time that he gave his Bampton Lectures, and died quite superbly, leaving an example to us all – was a splendid person to be able to share it all with, and full of hope.

The Master of Trinity and Lady Hodgkin, valued of course for themselves, really did 'represent' Trinity. John was clearly delighted to see the Archbishop of Canterbury, Robert Runcie, who 'spoke' of the Canterbury – and the Church of England – John loved. John told him that Bishop Lakshman Wickremesinghe (who died that October) had come to see him a fortnight before. John did *not* tell him that Lakshman had said he thought Robert Runcie had the potential to become a great archbishop, but he enjoyed passing on one of Lakshman's *mots*: 'Robert Runcie has the gift of saying the right thing at the right time: I shall be even more impressed when he says the right thing at the wrong time'!

On Sunday, 18 June John woke up at 5.45 a.m. trembling all over, his teeth chattering. He had had a very powerful dream. The houseman thought he should have his chest X-rayed.

June 20th My trouble yesterday morning, for which I was X-rayed, was diagnosed as a minor infection of one of the lungs. Since then I have been put on deep breathing and anti-biotics, which seem to have cleared it. The condition is known by the name of *rigor*, which I always only associated with *rigor mortis*, which I could hardly think was setting in yet. But two of my visitors yesterday – Bishop Leslie Brown, who had been in

South India and Africa, and Norman Anderson, who was in Cairo, both assured me that this was a regular thing with malaria – which fortunately also I have not got!

June 22nd [John was delighting in reading Owen Chadwick's 'Brilliant and brilliantly written' biography of Bishop Hensley Henson.] The chapter on his ten years as Canon of Westminster showed up Henson well . . . I was hoping that Henson's row with uncle Armitage would be given fuller coverage. He didn't say that in the end Armitage was sent down to Wells because relationships with the Chapter at Westminster, largely through his own autocracy, had become so strained, aided and abetted by Henson's spoiling for a fight whenever he could find one.

June 23rd 4.45 a.m.   I don't seem to have settled down to continuous sleep. I have woken up, quite comfortable, and at this early hour have been reflecting on something of what this has taught me about preparing for death. I suppose one's initial reaction is to feel that 'to make a good death' in the classical sense was to give up thoughts of and preoccupation with 'worldly things' and go into the full-time business of becoming a saint in the time available. That is to say one should concentrate on 'holy reading', trying to catch up on some of the great spiritual classics one has never read. At some time, of course, I should love to do this; but Bonhoeffer's distinction keeps coming back to me, that to be a Christian is not to be 'religious' in a particular way but to be a 'man' – in Christ. So, so far from being less interested in things that are going on around me in the world, whether it be at this moment politics or cricket, this doesn't seem distracting, but simply trying to live life better to the full. This is the sort of thing that encourages me about Eric James' remark when I said I was reading Owen Chadwick on Hensley Henson, 'Well, you've got your priorities right.' It also makes me feel less inadequate, even for the wrong reason, when at the end of my first year as Dean of Trinity I had to try and minister to Hugh Anderson, Norman Anderson's remarkable son, who had earlier that year been President of the Union, and of whom one could say as of practically no other undergraduate I have known, 'He'll be Prime Minister one day.' He was a great Socialist as well as a Christian, and it so happened that in the last few days before he died we had also just had a General Election. Because both he and I were interested in this – and frankly because I didn't know what else to say on a more 'spiritual' level – I discussed the consequences of this, though I knew he would never live to see them. I felt bad afterwards at the time – that I had let him down, as I should have been able to talk at a deeper level as a priest, which I hope in fact came through. But I am encouraged now perhaps to feel for him this was just the right priority, and we subsequently held one of the most moving memorial services I remember in

Chapel. The preacher was David Sheppard, who had recently gone to be Bishop of Woolwich. In fact, I think it is the only memorial service for an undergraduate we have had printed out in full like a Fellow's service, and the Chapel was packed. I remember choosing as the Lesson that remarkable passage from the Book of Wisdom, Ch. 4, which speaks of a young man (Hugh was only 21) fulfilling his time in a short number of years, and that wisdom did not consist in grey hairs.

June 28th Tonight I have begun to read through Brenda Kidman's *A Gentle Way with Cancer*, written in association with the BBC Television documentaries last March, about the work of the Bristol Cancer Help Centre, which much impressed me at the time ... One can't make a judgement on this or similar approaches (and obviously some are a great deal crankier than others) without having read and experienced a good deal wider. But I am a determined 'both-and' man and intend to take the best combination of advice and help from all sources ... But at least I am now preparing myself, with Ruth, for discussing the approach with Mr Everett and with Dr Wheeler ...

[John also discussed the book with Dr Sills and with Alan Weeds, who was Fellow of Trinity and Lecturer in Biochemistry, and with Stephen.]

I was astonished how Stephen was able to discuss with Ruth and the others the chemical and biological processes involved and what all the various elements did. Where he gets it all from I cannot imagine! At the same time he has been giving my *Redating the New Testament* an extremely thorough going-over, spotting very well all the places where one is skating on thin ice ...

July 2nd One of the positive thoughts I had yesterday was that, possibly, towards the end of August, when I would be due to check up with Dr Everett again anyhow, I should come down for the Society for New Testament Studies Conference, which this year is being held at Canterbury, which I should love to see again; then we might enquire whether it would be convenient for us to fly out to Bernhard and Bettina's chalet in Switzerland, which they have urged us to do, for, say, the last week of August, and then go on, possibly via Venice, to Florence. This was sparked off by the most beautiful card I have had yet – a detail, presumably from a crucifixion, of St John, by Giotto, in Florence, which I got from Lynne Rendell. The design and the colour are perfectly marvellous, and indeed it has occurred to me they might form the background to the dust-cover of *The Priority of John*. One of my ambitions would be to see the original, but Florence is a place I have never succeeded in getting to. We mentioned this to Catherine, who at once said that she has a painter friend who gave an open invitation to visit him in Florence . . . She would love to come on such a holiday with us. So this would be a marvellous bonus and something really positive to live for.

July 3rd   The day has been made by having Catherine here and also a visit from Janet Taylor from Arncliffe. She came bearing all sorts of kind messages and news from Littondale. She is such a nice person and so easy to be with. Tomorrow she goes to her publishers, Hodder and Stoughton, to check further about her book on *Brigie* . . . it all showed us how much we were genuinely missed up there and how concerned and kind everyone has been. It made all the difference . . .

July 4th   Ruth went on reading Harry Blamires' commentary on the *Four Quartets*, beginning where Catherine left off, with *East Coker*. Eliot's message really does speak to one's condition, and I was struck this afternoon by the point he made that the straight-line picture of middle-age gradually changing into the maturity of a 'calm unclouded ending' is simply not true to experience. Something suddenly happens like this which enables you to see the whole process shot through with a new meaning and value. It has indeed been a wonderful moment of illumination and deepening, both of love and faith. I don't think I have ever felt more at peace with myself . . . This has also brought home to me what a deep and strong support the form of faith was that went through *Honest to God* and the rest. It shows how wrong those were who thought this represented a questioning of the centre of my faith rather than a pushing out of the edges.

July 7th   I was reminding Ruth at Compline tonight of a remark I once made when we used to say Compline together each night when we were engaged, and wondered how either of us was going to be able to say the words of the prayer 'that when our bodies lie in the dust our souls may live with Thee' on the night of the other's funeral. I am sure we are mentally, if not emotionally, ready for it now whenever it should come. But Ruth, having now to expect to survive me, feels that the wrench is going to be quite physically tactile, when she is no longer able to kiss and touch me. But no one is better prepared for grieving and bereavement than she is, though it is going to be emotionally much more difficult for her. But thank God we have already an established home where she will be entirely happy to live and be alone, for no one has mastered the art of solitude, as opposed to loneliness, better than she. But it is going to take an extended living through, though each of us fully accepts it now as part of an entirely natural order of birth and generation and decay, which Eliot is so constantly stressing. We continued to read tonight into the beginning of the *Dry Salvages*. It is nice to feel that we can take our time and that there is no hurry. But equally I have no intention of thinking of death yet, and fully hope that all sorts of things are possible to prolong the quantity as well as the quality of life.

I listened to a tape earlier that David Watson, the evangelical charismatic leader had sent me at Mervyn's suggestion. I expected to find it rather embarrassing, and so played it to myself before Ruth arrived, so as to spare her. But in fact he came through remarkably well, as someone who had come in through CICCU, thanks to the instruction of David Sheppard, into a balanced and broad understanding. There was a scripturalism about it that I might have put in a different idiom, but nothing at all jarring, and he came through as such a nice and humble man. He has got cancer[1] at the age of 50, so naturally worries about death not for himself but more for his young wife and family. I was most grateful to listen to it, and may well ask him if he has any recommendations of a really good spiritual healer, who will not be a crank. For I fully believe that as well as the general work and prayer of the church as a healing community, there are remarkable individuals who have healing gifts – such as Conrad Skinner, the father of the subsequent Principal of Wesley House, who was an exact contemporary of mine at Jesus. If there were such a good person, I would gladly avail myself of him, as well as of the wave of prayer and intercession that I know is going out for me from the whole church. Once one has fully accepted that it may be the Lord's wish that one should die, then there are remissions and even cures to which one would be faithless not to be open if it turns out that there was still work that God wanted one spared to do. I still confess that I would love to see through the actual Bampton Lectures themselves next year, though nothing obviously of course depends on this.

July 8th   This is a red-letter day indeed. After a month and a day I feel just like being released from prison. I am now in the Evelyn Nursing Home, on the ground floor, with French windows leading directly out of my room into the most lovely fragrant gardens . . . There is really nothing else to say at the moment except an enormous thank-you, first for the treatment I received at Addenbrooke's, which was consummated for me this morning by celebrating the Eucharist in the day-room for three other members of the ward apart from Ruth and myself. Now a thank-you for this wonderful place – and such gorgeous weather to go with it.

July 9th   I have said to several people that I can hardly recollect a happier time in my whole life. In fact, if one has to die of something, I have come to the conclusion that there is a great deal to be said for dying of cancer, whenever it comes, though of course not if it is of a particularly

[1] Revd David Watson died 18 February 1984.

painful or distressing sort. For one has a long time to think about it and prepare and make one's dispositions with the family, and to get to know so many more people more intimately beforehand. I feel very privileged, and it is such a great liberation to know that one can do exactly what one feels one wants to do, without the burden of anything else.

July 10th   Hermann and Christine Bondi took the trouble to drive up all the way from Barnet this morning to see me. I regard him as a great scientist, communicator and humanist in every sense of the word, and it will be a delight to have them back in Cambridge when he finally takes up his appointment as the new Master of Churchill at the end of next academic year. He told us a splendid joke about God applying for a grant from a scientific institution to study the Origins of Creation. It was declined, on three grounds: first, that there was no visible evidence that he had done any work on the subject for a long time; secondly, because no one had been able to repeat his experiment; and thirdly, because the only records of it had not been published in any recognised scientific journal! . . .

I have found myself beginning to tick again in terms of throwing up all sorts of ideas, and indeed have written not only a draft Foreword to *The Priority of John*, but a possible Foreword to the English edition of the very good book I am reading on William Temple by the American, Charles Lowry, who came to visit me in Addenbrooke's. He has found it impossible to get an English publisher for it. It is really a rather moving personal portrait of Temple. Charles Lowry knew him well as a friend, and there are not too many of those left now.

July 11th   The first thing that Catherine spotted in the paper today was that Geoffrey Paul, Bishop of Bradford, died yesterday. He had written me a perfectly charming letter on hearing of my illness, and then himself had to go into hospital for a cyst near the spine, which in fact proved benign. After the operation he contracted an infection from which he never recovered, so that at the end they were not able to talk to him. The whole thing must have come as an appalling shock to Pam. I feel 'there, but for the grace of God, go I!' and realise how incredibly fortunate we have been to have all this warning and this marvellous time together.

Though Ruth does not know it, I have been working away from the early mornings and late evenings going through the slips or checking my manuscript to see what books I shall need before I leave Trinity at the end of the week, to take back to Arncliffe from the Faculty Library. I have already drawn up for Robert Atwell a long list from the University Library, which I hope he will be kind enough to search out and borrow for me. The rest I hope to be able to look after myself. So the old brain as well as the body is once again ticking well!

July 14th   A symbolic date to get out of prison! I have begun early, at
7 a.m., by reflecting in bed, after a good night, on the great feeling of
thanksgiving which I experience. I used the form of Thanksgiving after
Communion printed at the end of the Westcott House Compline Book,
which Ruth and I have used, and shall continue to use, at the close of
each day – with such joy and comfort.

After a week getting brown in the garden of the Evelyn Nursing Home,
and an afternoon with Catherine in the Botanic Garden – a place John
particularly loved – and a specially valued visit from Judith, now
expecting her second child, John went back to Trinity to prepare for his
return to Arncliffe, and gave up writing his journal.

To have kept such a journal at such a time was a remarkable
achievement. It does not diminish it to say that to those who knew him it
was entirely in character. One of the chief priorities of John was to 'get
things taped'. He, so to speak, subdued his experience through his
intellect, and – usually – his pen. It must not be imagined therefore that
in Addenbrooke's and the Evelyn an entirely different John had
emerged – witness a story of Catherine's:

> In his years at Trinity we had begun to discover each other. After many
> clearly painful years of watching me discard the opportunities of my
> university education (in which, incidentally, I only got a 2.2, which was
> shattering to him), he gradually accepted that I intended to follow a very
> different path from the one he had envisaged for me. At first he had
> assumed that after a few forays into community living, gardening and
> yoga, I would settle down into a respectable career. But the task he had
> unwittingly given me was to discover God, not through the intellect but
> through the heart – through feeling, through silence, through the body.
> He recognised in himself an inability to experience inner silence. For
> him, it was a vacuum, an absence of thought, and therefore a threat. In
> one of our early-morning times together in the hospital he asked me to
> help him to meditate. Thinking that perhaps he might 'connect' with a
> mantra, I began repeating some words, in time with our breathing. After
> a few minutes, he stopped me, and said: 'Do we have to go on with this?
> Once you've said it a few times you understand it'!

Stephen had come to help John with his packing up and was immediately called upon to accompany him to the Divinity Library. En
route John called on the travel agent for information about the
proposed trip to Florence and Switzerland, and returned having

booked the entire journey! It simply did not occur to him that he might not be feeling up to it six weeks later, without the daily intravenous feeding. There was no question then of resigning Trinity. He had a staff meeting with the Chaplains to plan the next term's events, leaving open when he himself would return.

On his arrival at Arncliffe he immediately arranged for a game of bridge the next day with Stephen and Michael Maude. John would in fact play many games of bridge with Michael in the weeks ahead, right up to his last days.

> Initially [wrote Michael] I did not take to John. He seemed rather aloof and austere and I could not persuade myself that I would ever have much in common with such a distinguished theologian. I also felt that I was just the sort of person of whom John would instinctively disapprove. I was wrong. With the passage of time and for whatever reasons we became close and good friends and I shall always be proud of and thankful for my friendship with him.

The next month was spent settling into the routine that suited John best. While he was at the Evelyn he had taken the first three-day chemotherapy course, which he was to continue at three-weekly intervals until the end. He found the early morning between six and eight the best time to work – he and Ruth would generally go for a short walk before breakfast. He refused to take pain-killers before lunch in case they hindered his working. He took a sleeping-pill and slept during the afternoon; then he and Ruth would go for another walk, often to a bend in the river, where he would sit on his canvas stool and enjoy the view. Sometimes he would swim in the waterfall pool – in those same yellow swimming trunks he had worn at Kirkridge (de-plored by the family for countless years!). By the evening the pain was too troublesome for much work. He would take his nightly morphine pill and go to bed early. During the day John took much pleasure in the sun-room they had recently added to the south wall of Prospect House and enjoyed reading there and talking to his visitors.

He had already finished *The Priority of John* when he went into hospital, and he had every confidence in 'Charlie' Moule and Chip Coakley who had generously promised to edit the book for publication. He knew he could rely on their meticulous care and judgment. But under the terms of the ancient Bampton foundation, what John had produced as a book had to be delivered from the pulpit of St Mary's,

Oxford as eight half-hour lecture-sermons. It was evident to John that after his two operations transforming the book was beyond his concentration. 'Charlie' Moule, in another marvellous gesture of friendship, agreed not only to deliver the lectures but to undertake the onerous task of writing them from John's material.

Meanwhile there were quite a number of items of unfinished agenda that John wanted to work at. The last thing he did before his cancer was diagnosed – after his return from the US – was the presidential address to the Cambridge Theological Society, on 12 May, which he called 'The Last Tabu: The Self-Consciousness of Jesus'. This and various other pieces, published and unpublished, led him to consider whether there might not be the material to hand for a collection of 'posthumous(?) essays', which he thought he would like to have some part in selecting. It surprised him to discover that there was probably sufficient material for two books. The first was a set of scholarly articles on the New Testament which would complement his *Twelve New Testament Studies* and should obviously be given the title *Twelve More New Testament Studies*. Since John alone could revise, and where necessary rewrite, these he decided to give them priority. Most of them required only limited work – with the aid of Jean Cunningham on her retirement from SCM Press, who actually wanted the tedious task of preparing the manuscript and making the index, not only for *The Priority of John* but also for the collection of Studies. There was every reason for getting on with them as quickly as possible and publishing them before the Bamptons; for this meant that John could refer to them as working papers for *The Priority of John*. Some had already appeared in print. But a number required extra work. This applied in particular to an old piece on 'Hosea and the Virgin Birth'. He also decided to re-cast in written form material on the Lord's Prayer which he had originally given in Cambridge as lectures, and he expanded what was merely to be a footnote in the Bamptons into a contribution under the title of 'The Fourth Gospel and the Church's Doctrine of the Trinity'.

Besides these more technical New Testament studies John found a number of pieces which fell more into the shape of the series of papers and addresses he had been publishing at ten-year intervals: *On Being the Church in the World* (1960); *Christian Freedom in a Permissive Society* (1970); and *The Roots of a Radical* (1980). The next collection was not due till 1990 but, 'only if need be', he would leave these to his literary executor to gather into a book, for which he suggested the title, *The End of All Our Exploring.* He was uncertain then whether that title should be followed by a question mark. There would be addresses on F. D. Maurice, J. B. Lightfoot, William Temple and C. H. Dodd; a paper he had done for the centenary of Rudolf Bultmann's birth; four lectures gathered into one on 'Interpreting the Book of Revelation'; several of the lectures he had delivered in Canada and the US on his sabbatical at McMaster University, on subjects such as the Arms Race, the Energy Crisis, 'What Future for a Unique Christ?'; and half a dozen Cambridge sermons.

In his limited working day before he tired he achieved a great deal; and, as he wrote, 'there is no doubt that it has helped to keep me going'.

In the weeks that had passed since John had entered Addenbrooke's he had depended hugely on Ruth. Whatever momentary fantasies she may have had when he claimed that 'there is nothing like knowing one has six months to live to make one recognize one's priorities', it became immediately clear that no priority could involve laying down his pen. He openly acknowledged his dependence on Ruth – and others: 'How does one get through this on one's own?' he said to her one day. During the last months his energies were too preoccupied in finishing his work for there to be much emotional capital for Ruth to put by. She of course regretted this – for both their sakes – and recognized what she was missing but did not resent it, for 'there is a curious grace available to us at these times which takes over. The only important thing for me was to enable him to live in the way that was right for him.'

When they wrote on 28 August their second 'Letter to Their Friends' they were able to say: 'We have seen a lot of the family and many friends from all over the world, as well as the neighbours in the Dale who kept everything going so marvellously in Ruth's absence and have continued to rally round with the most practical help.' John's brother Edward and his wife Wendy came over from Oxford. Geoffrey Paul's widow Pamela, and Rowan Williams and Jane, their daughter and son-in-law, were specially welcome visitors. John had received the laying-on-of-hands with prayer and Communion from John Petty, who had been with John for six years in the Woolwich episcopal area of South London and had moved to Lancashire; and from George Regas, John's former pupil, who flew from California specially to see him. When George enquired what Gospel John wanted him to use, John said 'tearfully and with a catch in his throat': 'Oh, use the story of the people letting the paralyzed man on a bed down through the roof to

Jesus for healing. I love that story now, because Jesus used the faith of others to heal the man. I need your faith.' John celebrated the Holy Communion in Arncliffe church and preached there for the last time; and lectured on 'Living with Cancer' at Scargill House. 'Charlie' Moule had much to discuss with him when he came for the day in mid-August, followed the next day by Eric James.

When Eric arrived in the late afternoon John was sitting in front of the television absorbed in the Kent v. Middlesex cricket match. They sat in silence for a couple of hours and more. Towards the end of the match the light began to fail, so that the television cameras could scarcely pick up the players out on the field. Suddenly John turned to Eric and with a wan smile – and with some of his old delight in discovering a living figure of speech that he had, so to speak, plucked from the air – said, 'My life is like a limited-over match, and the dusk is drawing on.' John had much to discuss with his 'literary executor'. He went through all the papers which might make the two posthumous books, and then, in Ruth's presence, told Eric it was his job to see that 'if anyone should want to write a biography of me, it's the right person who does it,' and added 'But Ruth and I want you to know that most of all we should like you to do it.'

At the time Eric did not take the idea very seriously that he should write John's biography (though he was moved and honoured by the invitation). But before Eric left the next day to return to London, John shyly produced two quarto pages on which he had written enigmatically: 'Where Three Ways Meet'; and underneath had listed all the major books he had written, divided into the 'three ways'. John had been doing some self-analysis (of his mind, not his psyche), apparently fairly recently (he had used the results at the College of Preachers in Washington that May), and wanted any future biographer to have the benefit of it. It is probably best simply set down as John wrote it:

WHERE THREE WAYS MEET

The way of theological exploration
Thou Who Art
In the End God
Honest to God
The Honest to God Debate
But That I Can't Believe!
Exploration into God

The Human Face of God
Truth is Two-Eyed
The way of biblical interrogation
The Body
Jesus and His Coming
Twelve New Testament Studies
Redating the New Testament
Can we Trust the New Testament?
Wrestling with Romans
The Priority of John
Twelve More New Testament Studies

The way of Social Responsibility
On Being the Church in the World
Liturgy Coming to Life
Christian Morals Today
The New Reformation?
Christian Freedom in a Permissive Society
The Difference in Being a Christian Today
The Roots of a Radical
The Church's Most Urgent Priority in Today's World

The Church and the Kingdom
Centre and Edges
Roots and Fruits
Both-and rather than Either-Or
Rooted in order to be radical
Paul to Romans . . .
Four Makers of Contemporary
    Theology: Pattern in writings
    and concerns
Fall into 3 classes
Three trajectories, constantly
    criss-crossing
A person where 3 ways meet
Lines on which all of us are
    travelling in our ministries
Must in different ways and
    different proportions hold
    them together
    if we are going to be
    whole in our response
Which first – arbitrary: no
    before or after in this trinity

1   *The way of theological exploration*
Constantly pushing out; questioning accepted doctrine; stripping away;
cutting to the heart; revisioning, re-interpreting; being stretched; never
resting content; pressing out from edges.

2   *The way of biblical interrogation*
Digging to roots; probing; compelling the Scriptures to give up their
message for us now; going behind received interpretations; refusing to
accept stock answers; return to source; centre; rooted to be radical.

3   *The way of social responsibility*
Responding to what God is saying to us through his world of people; the
call of the kingdom and the claims of love; reading the signs of the times;
forcing us out into the world.

All three journeys, trajectories, must illumine, challenge and correct
each other, driving us to the new questions. Constantly shifting kaleido-
scope; to be at the point of obedience which will differ for each one of us,
and from month to month and year to year.

Books waymarks reflecting my responses. Never left behind. Wouldn't
want to un-say anything I've written, but wouldn't want to say it like that
now. Return in new forms.

'Where Three Ways Meet' is of course a classical quotation referring to
the crossroads where Oedipus met and unwittingly slew his father.

It ought to be added that, probably some time after he had drawn up
this gnomic composition, John himself had written a series of additional comments not all of which are decipherable. Against *Truth is
Two-Eyed*, for example: 'Stretching. Uniqueness of Christ in a pluralis-
tic world. One-eyed defined, not confined – a bigger, not exclusive,
focus and first-fruits.' And against *Can We Trust the New Testament?*:
'Cynicism of Foolish; scepticism of wise; fundamentalism of fearful;
conservatism of the committed.' Several of his book titles had a cluster
of abbreviated comments alongside. It is not impossible that although
John was handing over these pages for a future biographer – and it is
obviously an important document for understanding how he saw
himself – it was conceived as the outline sketch of another fairly
autobiographical book which he hoped to have written had he lived: a
sequel to *The Roots of a Radical*.

At the end of July John had received a letter from his friend Max
Williman, the Old Catholic priest who married them in Switzerland,
who had himself undergone a successful operation for the removal of a

pancreatic tumour. Max suggested that John should see his surgeon, and a tentative appointment was made for September, when he and Ruth would be in Zurich. However a sensitive and courageous letter from John's own surgeon Bill Everett – writing 'as a Christian as well as a surgeon' – discouraged him, and John set the idea aside forthwith.

John and Ruth left Arncliffe on 21 August for their European holiday via Cambridge and Canterbury. The following day there were visits to his doctors and a further scan at Addenbrooke's, then they drove down to Selling near Canterbury, to spend the night with Nick and Anne Stacey.

> Ruth had warned us that John would be very tired and not at all hungry [wrote Anne] and when they arrived we learned that he had that morning been told by the consultant that the cancer had spread and he had only a few months left, so we were astonished that he ate quite a good supper and it was not until 10.30 that he said he would like to go to bed. It was an evening when it would have been easy to be sentimental or mawkish were it not for John's completely matter-of-fact manner, one of the warmest evenings I ever remember, with a wonderful full moon which rose over the orchard at the end of our garden. We had our supper outside by candle and moonlight, while John talked quite animatedly about all kinds of practical matters such as his investments and royalties and the financial provision he had made for Ruth, and reminiscing a little with Nick about the Woolwich days and some of the characters involved; never once did he betray what he must have known, that it was almost certainly the last time we would meet, though when I kissed him good-bye the next morning, he gave me an uncharacteristic little extra hug, which I took to be a sort of Adieu from this most undemonstrative of men.

Nick drove a silent John into Canterbury, to the International Conference of the Society of New Testament Studies at the University of Kent. (Ruth was staying with Cecilia at Tenterden and spent the time despatching the second 'Letter to Their Friends'.) John found it difficult to sit through the lectures at the conference and would spend much of the time resting. The main benefit for him was this last opportunity of seeing his theological colleagues from all round the globe and 'talking shop'.

One afternoon he was driven to the Precincts of the Cathedral, where he was able to recall and record on his camera his boyhood associations: the garden of No. 15 where he was born and the eastern crypt, which over the years had become a sort of Robinson family chapel. A memorial is there to Beatrice's father Dr Moore. It was there that Beatrice and Arthur were married. When in her later years Beatrice went each week to 'clean the Cathedral' it was the eastern crypt for which she made herself responsible and it was there that her coffin had rested during the night before she was buried. It was there also that John was baptized. John made this pilgrimage alone; for he now had another 'baptism to be baptized with'.

John joined Ruth at Cecilia's after the conference, and while there drove over to Sissinghurst for tea with Lord Coggan, former Archbishop of Canterbury, and his wife Jean. From Cecilia's they went to Gatwick, and so to Florence, where Catherine joined them. They stayed with Patrick Hamilton, who lived and worked there as an artist. Catherine's description of their holiday together in Italy should stand by itself:

> John's lasting impressions of Florence were largely negative. He always spoke of Florence in comparison with Switzerland, and it invariably came out worse. He was troubled by the constant noise of talking and scooters in the street below his bedroom, throughout the night; by the Italian habit of arguing and shouting, with all windows open in the adjoining courtyard; by the crowded and dangerous streets; by the dirt and smell. He was exasperated by the Latin temperament, which allowed museums to be shut without explanation, and the long-awaited visit to the sacristy in the Basilica of Santa Maria Novella, to see Giotto's fresco of St John, was a great disappointment, as the crucifix on which it was mounted was hung high up on an unlit wall, and almost impossible to see.
>
> The days were measured by the few hours in the morning when he was relatively free of pain and had sufficient energy to explore. There were some moments of intense and solitary attention, when he would sit on his stool, face to face with his imminent death: Michaelangelo's Pieta, the Dying Slaves, the Crucifixion frescos in the cells of San Marco. He did not talk about them.
>
> The evenings at Patrick Hamilton's house were happy and relaxed – listening to music, animatedly talking theology to Patrick while he sat for his portrait, reading the Office together before we went to bed. But apart from the few days together in Fiesole, when he was able to sleep and relax, Florence was a considerable strain.
>
> The contrast when we arrived in Switzerland was very marked. At once he felt at home, surrounded by order, cleanliness and predictability. At the centre of our whole trip was the visit to Max Williman, the priest

who had married John and Ruth in Zurich. He is a man who lives from
the heart, and he touched John's heart, in a way that no one else had
done, by his moving account of his own identical illness. Through it, he
learnt to give himself totally into God's hands, with a simplicity and
openness which released him from anxiety and fear. In his account he
apologised frequently for his being only a simple parish priest with no
learning. John would shake his head, close to tears, and urge him to go
on. He talked to me later about how much he had been affected by his
talk. Williman spoke from a conviction and a trust which went way
beyond intellect and ideas, and he held out a hand to John, showing him
what a total acceptance of God's will could mean.

The next morning we went to the church where he had married John
and Ruth. They knelt alone at the altar rail to exchange their wedding
rings once more – and I, a child of that marriage, felt the unquenchable
impulse of life to return to its source to bring forth new life out of death,
and I thought of that wonderful prayer of unconditional openness to the
generosity of God in the confession:

> forgive us all that is past; and grant that we may serve you in newness
> of life; to the glory of your name.

During the next days, staying with Bernhard and Bettina Mumm in
Château d'Oex, I felt very close to John in brief snatches of conversation
when we were alone on walks. We talked about marriage and relationship, and he talked of the burden he was placing on Ruth. All
through the months of his illness I felt that for him it was a solitary
journey, and not one that he was able to let Ruth share with him. Her
burden was to provide him with the physical and spiritual strength for
him to walk on alone, and perhaps he was more able to share occasional
moments of emotional closeness with me, than with her at this time.

There was an intensity in each day's events, sharing every experience
truly for the last time. John stood on the top of a mountain looking out
over the snow-capped peaks, the alpine meadows and the neat farms,
with the sounds of cowbells ringing in the cold clear air, and breathed
deeply. As we drove down again to the town, I thought of how that breath
and the wide mountain landscape would sustain him during the last
weeks of his journey.

The farewells with Bernhard and Bettina at the airport were brief and
quiet. He simply said goodbye, and walked through the ticket barrier,
and immediately immersed himself with practical details about where we
should sit – how we would get on to the plane. It was always as if he could
not bear very much reality, but surrounded himself with protective layers
of reason and thought through which his heart would find an occasional
chink, and catch him unawares. With me, during those weeks, he

searched out opportunities to let his heart speak, as if conscious of the chance slipping away.

On their return from Switzerland John and Ruth stayed a night with Shelagh Brown, a deaconess on the staff of St John's, Caterham, Surrey. Shelagh was writing a book, *Drawing near to the City*, in which different Christians speak about dying. She asked John if she could tape some of his thoughts for the book. In one paragraph John seemed to succeed in saying what he believed as simply and as cogently as in almost any other passage of his writings:

> For me the ultimate context in which life is lived is that of an I – Thou relationship with the Eternal Thou. That relationship is the umbilical cord of all that one is and all that one does. It seems to me that Jesus lived in the Abba, Father relationship, and that is the ground and basis of all one's being and of all the other relationships that one enters into. Each of these 'others' is a way through which this other relationship comes, both in grace and demand. One tries – inadequately – to respond to it, but if one is pressed back, then it seems to me that this is the final reality of life, in which and for which one is made. It is not something that begins and ends with what we call time, but it is the framework in which all things of space and time belong and are created and have their being. It is defined in Christ in terms of the love of God and fellowship and grace. It is the centre of everything and it is the context in which one tries to face everything else.

They drove back to Arncliffe via Cambridge, where John had a check-up with Bill Everett. John found it a relief after a month away to be home again and to settle into his work routine. He was very tired, and until he could be convinced that stronger pain-killers would not reduce his capacity to work, he was in a good deal of pain. His medical care was resumed by their local GP Ian Kinnish. In these last months they would depend much on his back-up support. Life was transformed when John began the routine of taking regular and adequate pain-killers from 6 a.m. throughout the day.

John particularly looked forward to Buffy's weekly visits and to Stephen helping him to check his references – especially the Greek ones! Other visitors during those weeks included Bishop Oliver Tomkins and Ursula, and Harry Williams, who came over from Mirfield. Maurice Slaughter invited John to take a confirmation in the twelfth-century Priory Church at Bolton Abbey. John knew it was his last, and Maurice tells how John, when he went into the pulpit, said with tears in his eyes: 'I feel that I've got something to say to you because I know that within a few weeks I am going to die – at any rate, my doctors tell me so.' And then he went on: 'All I've ever tried to do in my ministry is to extend the frontiers of Christian thinking. I've never doubted the essential heart of the Gospel.' When John arrived at the Priory that morning Maurice had wondered whether he would 'make it': at one point in the service he thought the whole congregation was going to 'express its emotion'. 'What is certain', he added, 'is that those who were confirmed that day will never forget the occasion.'

John and Ruth drove down to Cambridge on Sunday, 23 October for John to preach his last Evensong sermon in Trinity. He had 'phoned Eric James to ask him if he would come to Cambridge to sit next to him and take over the sermon if he could not get through it. Ruth sat the other side of him. Every seat in Chapel was full and undergraduates sat on the sanctuary steps. Ralph Godsall conducted the service and Robert Atwell led the intercessions. It is unusual to include in a biography the whole of a sermon, but each part of this particular sermon of John's was integral to the whole, and to omit it would be to remain silent where certainly John himself would want to speak at the end of his life. Yet it must be said that John often quoted Bishop Phillips Brooks' description of preaching as 'the communication of truth through personality'. Without the person of John therefore and all that manifestly that person had suffered and had learnt from that suffering, his words would have lacked much of their content and power.

LEARNING FROM CANCER

When I was last preaching here it was Trinity Sunday, and I knew I was going into Addenbrooke's the next day for an operation, which turned out to reveal an inoperable cancer. But I was determined not to give in and that I was going to keep my commitment to preach here tonight, if only to 'christen' this pulpit lectern that I wanted to bequeath as a belated thank-offering for what nearly 15 years in this place has meant to me. So I thought I would use this opportunity to reflect with you on something of what these past months have taught me at greater depth.

Two years ago I found myself having to speak at the funeral of a 16-year-old girl who died in our Yorkshire dale. I said stumblingly that God was to be found in the cancer as much as in the sunset. That I firmly believed, but it was an intellectual statement. Now I have had to ask if I can say it of myself, which is a much greater test.

When I said it from the pulpit, I gather it produced quite a shock-wave. I guess this was for two reasons.

1   Because I had mentioned the word openly in public – and even among Christians it is (or it was: for much has happened in the short time since) the great unmentionable. 'Human kind', said Eliot, 'cannot bear very much reality.' It is difficult for me to comprehend that there are people who just do not want to know whether they have got cancer. But above all, there is a conspiracy of silence ostensibly to protect others. We think they cannot face it, though in my experience they usually know deep down; and obviously it is critical how they can face other realities, and above all how they are told and who tells them (and of course whether they really need to know). But what we are much more likely to be doing is mutually protecting ourselves – and also that goes often (though less and less) for doctors. For we dare not face it in ourselves or talk about it at the levels of reality that we might open up.

But Christians above all are those who should be able to bear reality and show others how to bear it. Or what are we to say about the Cross, the central reality of our faith? From the beginning Ruth and I were determined to know the whole truth, which after all was first of all our truth and not someone else's. And my doctors have been marvellously open, telling us as they knew everything they knew, which they are the first to say is but the tip of the iceberg. And incidentally they say how much easier it makes it for them if they know this is what the patient wants. Moreover they are fully aware in a place like Cambridge University that too many people know too much (or have access to such knowledge) for them to get away with fudging anything! So from the beginning we were in the picture as it was confirmed.

That does not make it any less of a stunning shock, and the walk from the specialist's consulting room to our car seemed a very long one. But knowing is all-important to how one handles it. For as the recent TV programme 'Mind Over Cancer' has shown, the attitude one brings to it can be quite vital – though it is important not to give the impression that *all* depends on this, or that if you die it is because your attitude is wrong, any more than to suggest, as some Christians do, that if you are not cured it is because you have not enough faith. That just induces guilt. But it is equally important to say that 'cancer' need not mean death, nor to suggest that there is nothing you can do about it. In fact there are already numerous cancers that are not necessarily fatal. There are as many sorts of it as there are of 'flu or heart disease. To lump cancer together as a summary death-sentence is as unscientific as it is self-fulfilling. Whether we die of it or of something else is partly up to us. But all of us have to die of something; and by the end of the century, thanks to the elimination of so many other things, the great majority of us will die, in roughly equal proportions, either of cardio-vascular diseases, which still lead as killers but by preventive medicine are already dropping, or of cancer. And of course progress is constantly being made here too, though again there is unlikely to be a simple 'cure' for cancer any more than for the common cold.

2   The shock-wave was also no doubt due to my saying that *God* was in the cancer. As I made absolutely clear at the time, by this I did not mean that God was in it by intending or sending it. That would make him a very devil. Yet people are always seeing these things in terms of his deliberate purpose or the failure of it. Why does he *allow* it? they say, and they get angry with God. Or rather, they project their anger on to God. And to let the anger come out is no bad thing. For so often diseases of strain and depression are caused by suppressed anger and hatred of other people or of oneself. So it is healthy that it should come out – and God can take it.

The other question people ask in such circumstances is 'Why me?' (often with the implication, 'Why does he pick on me?') or 'What have I done to deserve it?' And this, deep down, is another good question to have out. 'Why have I got this? What is there in me that has brought it about?' To which the answer is for the most part, as in so much in this field, 'I don't know.' Certainly it is in my case. But the searching, probing and often uncomfortable questions it raises are very relevant, and can be an essential part of the healing. Sometimes there are direct environmental factors (such as smoking or asbestos or radiation) which we can recognise and, if we have the will, personal or social, do something about it – like diet in heart-disease or anxiety in duodenal ulcers. But usually it goes deeper and points inwards. The evidence mounts up that resentments, guilts, unresolved conflicts, unfinished agenda of all sorts, snarl up our lives, and find physical outlet. We do not love ourselves enough: we cannot or will not face ourselves, or accept ourselves. The appearance of a cancer or of anything else is a great opportunity, which we should be prepared to use. The Psalmists of old knew this secret, and recognized God in it. 'O Lord, thou hast searched me out, and known me . . . Try me, O God, and seek the ground of my heart; prove me, and examine my thoughts. Look well if there be any way of wickedness in me.' 'So teach us to number our days, that we may apply our hearts unto wisdom.' 'I will thank the Lord for giving me warning' (and pain is a beneficent warning. One of the features of my sort of cancer is that one usually gets no warning till it is too late). For God is to be found in the cancer as in everything else. If he is not, then he is not the God of the Psalmist who said, 'If I go down to hell, thou art there also', let alone of the Christian who knows God most deeply in the Cross. And I have discovered this experience to be one full of grace and truth. I cannot say how grateful I am for all the love and kindness and goodness it has disclosed, which I am sure were always there but which it has taken this to bring home. Above all I would say it is relationships, both within the family and outside, which it has deepened and opened up. It has provided an opportunity for this and for my being made aware of it which might otherwise never have occurred. It has been a time of giving and receiving grace upon grace.

People sometimes say of a coronary, 'What a wonderful way to go', and as a process of dying for the individual concerned it must be preferable to much else. But it usually gives you no warning, no chance of making up your account. Still less does it allow loved ones to prepare. And preparing for death is increasingly recognized as a vital part of the process of grieving, of bearing reality, and of being restored to wholeness of body, mind and soul, both as individuals and as families.

But how does one prepare for death, whether of other people or of oneself? It is something we seldom talk about these days. Obviously there is the elementary duty (urged in the Prayer Book) of making one's will and other dispositions, which is no more of a morbid occupation than taking out life-insurance. And there is the deeper level of seeking to round off one's account, of ordering one's priorities and what one wants to do in the time available. And notice such as this gives concentrates the mind wonderfully and makes one realise how much of one's time one wastes or kills. When I was told that I had six months, or perhaps nine, to live, the first reaction was naturally of shock – though I also felt liberated, because, as in limited-over cricket, at least one knew the target one had to beat (and this target was but an informed guess from the experience and resources of the medical profession, by which I had no intention of being confined). But my second reaction was: 'But six months is a long time. One can do a lot in that. How am I going to use it?'

The initial response is to give up doing things – and it certainly sifts out the inessentials. My reaction was to go through the diary cancelling engagements. But I soon realized that this was purely negative; and I remembered the remark of Geoffrey Lampe, recently Regius Professor of Divinity here at Cambridge, who showed us how anyone should die of cancer: 'I can't die: my diary is far too full.'

In fact 'preparing for death' is not the other-worldly pious exercise stamped upon our minds by Victorian sentimentality, turning away from the things of earth for the things of 'heaven'. Rather, for the Christian it is preparing for 'eternal life', which means real living, more abundant life, which is begun, continued, though not ended, *now*. And this means it is about quality of life not quantity. How long it goes on here is purely secondary. So preparing for eternity means learning to live, not just concentrating on keeping alive. It means living it *up*, becoming *more* concerned with contributing to and enjoying what matters most – giving the most to life and getting the most from it, while it is on offer. So that is why, among other things, we went to Florence, where we had never been before, and to Switzerland to stay with friends we had to disappoint earlier because I entered hospital instead. I am giving myself too, in the limited working day I have before I tire, to all sorts of writing I want to finish. And if one goes for quality of life this may be the best way to extend its quantity. Seek first the kingdom of heaven – and who knows what shall be added? Pursue the wholeness of body, mind and spirit, and physical cure may, though not necessarily will, be a bonus.

'Your Life in Their Hands' is the title of another TV documentary on doctors. At one level this is true, the level of physical survival (though it certainly is not the whole truth even of that). And my experience of the medical profession through all of this has been wholly positive. They have been superb in their skills and judgment and sensitivity – really listening rather than acting as gods who know the answers and treating you as the 'patient', the person simply on the receiving end. For the bigger men they are, and the more they know, the more they admit they don't know. Most of my month in hospital was spent simply in replumb-ing the stomach and getting it working again, and for this two operations proved necessary. In fact the cancer specialist did not arrive on the scene till towards the end, for there was nothing up to then that he could do. But when he did, he said: 'I know basically what your situation is; but before I say anything I want to hear how *you* feel about it.' How many professionals (and that includes not only doctors but lawyers and parsons) start like that? From the beginning I felt I was being asked to take my share of responsibility for my own health. And this was a point that came strongly through another series of BBC programmes this spring (and how fortunate we are compared with the TV of any other country I know!): 'A Gentle Way with Cancer?'. This was on the Bristol Cancer Help Centre, which is revealing and meeting an enormous need, and whose new building Prince Charles courageously opened the other day in the teeth of quite a bit of medical criticism. For this is alternative medicine, not opposing the profession and its techniques, but seeking to supplement them, at the dietary, psychological and spiritual levels (and the last level did not really come through the 'Mind Over Cancer' programme. Yet spirit over cancer is every bit as important). And at all points it is important to see these as complementary. For there are many approaches – orthodox and non-orthodox medicine, unexplained gifts of healing (which are no more necessarily connected with religion than are psychic powers) and prayer and faith-healing. I am convinced that one must be prepared, critically and siftingly (for one must test the spirits at every level), to start at all ends at once and I have been receiving the laying-on-of-hands from someone in whose approach I have great trust, which for me is a large part of faith (and I have deliberately not taken up others). In fact in everything I am a great both/and rather than either/or man. In the pursuit of truth I cannot believe that a one-eyed approach is ever sufficient. In the pursuit of peace I believe in both multilateralism and unilateralism. And in the pursuit of health this is even more obvious. For health *means* wholeness. It is concerned not simply with cure but with healing of the whole person in all his or her relationships. Hence the high-point of the Communion service, the gift of the bread of life and the cup of salvation, has traditionally been accompanied by the words, 'Preserve thy *body and soul* unto everlasting life', and it has ended with invoking 'the peace (the *shalom* or wholeness) of God which passes all understanding'.

Healing cannot be confined to any, or indeed every, level of human understanding or expectation. This is why too it shows up those twin deceivers pessimism and optimism as so shallow. In the course of nature, cancer-sufferers swing from one to the other more than most, as good days and bad days, remissions and recurrences, follow each other. But the Christian takes his stand not on optimism but on hope. This is based not on rosy prognosis (from the human point of view mine is bleak) but, as St Paul says, on suffering. For this, he says, trains us to endure, and endurance brings proof that we have stood the test, and this proof is the ground of hope – in the God who can bring resurrection out and through the other side of death. That is why he also says that though we carry death with us in our bodies (all of us) we never cease to be confident. His prayer is that 'always the greatness of Christ will shine out clearly in my person, whether through my life or through my death. For to me life is Christ, and death gain; but what if my living on in the body may serve some good purpose? Which then am I to choose? I cannot tell. I am torn two ways: what I should like' – he says more confidently than most of us could – 'is to depart and be with Christ, that is better by far; but for your sake there is greater need for me to stay on in the body'. According to my chronology he lived nearly ten years after writing those words: others would say it was shorter. But how little does it matter. He had passed beyond time and its calculations. He had risen with Christ.

After his sermon John was remarkably lively. He went into dinner in Hall and afterwards through to the Master's Lodge. The next ten days in Cambridge were very full, with visits from friends and references to be checked in the Faculty Library. He gave a sherry party for the theological students he had taught, and took part in a meeting of the 'Fringe Theology' group. He had organized a visit by the librarian of McMaster University, who spent several days looking through John's books and papers, with a view to their being catalogued and kept there. Eric James, who came to see John on the day before his return to Arncliffe, brought a different proposal. The Archbishop of Canterbury had long wanted to furnish a small room in Lambeth Palace, close by the Chapel, in which he and his successors might 'study to be quiet'. Cranmer's Parlour, much of it panelled in linenfold, overlooking the Chapel was ideal for the purpose. The Archbishop suggested that to have John's own theological library shelved in that room would be a wonderful resource, and proposed that John's papers, his published works, and his collection of books associated with them should be placed in Lambeth Palace Library itself, where they would be available to students. John was touched by the suggestion and gratefully accepted it.

One visit that meant much to him that week was from John Bowden and Jean Cunningham of the SCM Press, who brought with them the contract for *Twelve More New Testament Studies* for John to sign. They also brought the completed design for the cover of *The Priority of John*, incorporating the postcard of the Giotto St John. John was pleased actually to see what his book would look like. Ruth had the design framed for him while they were in Cambridge and he worked with it beside him in his study from then on.

They returned to Arncliffe early in November and John continued as before. Cecilia was able to be with him for several days, and Judith and her family came from Bristol. On 15 November, at tea-time, Maurice Slaughter came to visit John and anoint him. 'John looked at me', Maurice said, 'when I was preparing to anoint him, and with that wonderful quirk of humour that would break through at unexpected times said suddenly, "Magic again!"'

There was one further break for what proved to be the last trip to Cambridge in the latter half of the month, mainly for business purposes and collecting material for his own work. It was then that John, recognizing that he would not be able to return to Trinity the next term, announced his retirement as Dean of Chapel. Catherine came over from Norfolk on the Sunday evening to spend her day off with him – the last time they would spend together.

On 25 November, the day after John's final return to Arncliffe, Bishop Hugh Montefiore drove up from Birmingham and stayed the night. John enjoyed an evening talking with Hugh about their mutual concerns and putting the Church of England to rights. A happy and relaxed weekend, with Stephen at home, followed.

During the next week John posted off the corrected copy of *Twelve More New Testament Studies*, apart from the last chapter which he was still working on, and which Ruth gathered together from his desk the morning after he died.

On Thursday, 1 December, for the third time, John Petty made the journey from Manchester to lay hands on John. This time he asked Ruth to lay hands with him and suggested she continued to do so each day: 'The gift is in all of us,' said John Petty, 'but in most of us it is more or less blocked.' When John and Ruth talked it over that evening they saw it as a way of drawing together all the prayers that they knew were being made at that time: 'channelling and focusing' said John.

The end, when it came, was swift, almost casual, as death often is. In Ruth's words:

> We began the next morning, Friday 2nd, keeping a quiet time in our upstairs sitting room. It was a glorious morning, crisp and clear, and as usual we went for a walk before breakfast, a little way out of the village, with Jamie, our red setter. John sat on his canvas stool/stick in the pasture by the side of the beck, and asked me the tune of the Addison hymn, 'The Lord my pasture shall prepare', and we hummed it on the way home. He worked contentedly in the study for the rest of the morning until midday, when we sat in our sun-room with a drink of milk, reading the post. We had just decided to do his favourite walk along the river before lunch, when he began to be very ill, and had to go to bed. There was no reason to think this wasn't a temporary set-back, as there was no further sickness on Saturday or Sunday, though he was understandably weak and drowsy, and even the chest infection he showed signs of early on Sunday seemed to have abated by Monday morning . . . On Monday afternoon December 5th John was very ill again and this time we knew that he would only have a few days. Stephen and Buffy with the little granddaughters arrived very soon and Stephen was able to take on the lifting and keep him comfortable ('my gentle giant' John called him) and also received the precise whispered instructions about the wording and dating of the Preface to the posthumous essays! Scarlett and Sophie said good-night to Grandpa before they went to bed and Judith and Chris arrived later in the evening, with Tom, then three years old.

Catherine was setting out from Norfolk early the next morning. At 10 o'clock I settled John for the night . . . Later, after I was in bed, we said together the prayer we had used ever since we were first engaged, the Collect for what used to be Trinity IV: 'O God, the protector of all that trust in thee, without whom nothing is strong, nothing is holy: Increase and multiply upon us thy mercy; that, thou being our ruler and guide, we may so pass through things temporal, that we finally lose not the things eternal: Grant this, O heavenly Father, for Jesus Christ's sake.' John made one or two quiet comments about the family, and after about a quarter of an hour, at about ten to eleven, I asked him if he would like a sip of water. 'A little,' he said. He died as I raised his head to help him to swallow, though I didn't realise it immediately, so casually had it happened.

9

Time After

John had died six months to the day from the time his surgeon had spoken to him of 'six months'. On his first day in the Evelyn Nursing Home in July, he had written down his 'Directions for Funeral: I wish to be buried in a double grave with Ruth at Arncliffe.'

The day of the funeral, Friday, 9 December was wild and wet. The rain was torrential, and the becks and rivers in spate. Some had to drive through floods to reach Arncliffe, some were turned back. The full Trinity Choir, with their Director of Music Richard Marlow, had arrived the day before, and spent the night in their sleeping bags at 'The Falcon'.

John had been placed in his coffin wearing the cassock belonging to Bishop George Bell that Mrs Bell had given to him at his consecration. It was not possible for the Choir, with the elements raging, to walk ahead of the bier; instead they waited at the Church and sang for the congregation. As the bier was wheeled across the Green, it was flanked by Stephen, John's sons-in-law Simon and Chris, and Chip Coakley. Scarlett walked with Ruth immediately behind the bier, carrying a basket of rosemary Catherine had picked from the garden. Sophie trotted at Ruth's other side, giving the bier little protective taps and chatting amiably. Once the procession had reached the Church porch the coffin was covered with John's cope and his wooden crook and his mitre placed upon it. Maurice Slaughter said the Sentences; Ernest Blanchard conducted the Service in Church; Stephen read the Lesson: 1 Corinthians 15:20–26, 35–58; Ralph Godsall preached a memorable sermon. It was not the usual eulogy and encomium:

> John loved the cinema and I remember seeing with him one afternoon in Cambridge, *One Flew Over the Cuckoo's Nest*. It represented to John a splendid secular presentation of the Passion – of the free man who liberates others at the expense of himself being crucified by the system.

John knew something of this in his own life . . . He felt enlarged and not diminished by the Church he served and by the times in which he lived – even at the end. And so do we who have journeyed with him at different stages – albeit at least one step behind!

During the service there were three hymns: 'The Lord my pasture shall prepare', 'O Thou who camest from above' and 'Let all the world in every corner sing' – which seemed to gather into the service so many of John's friends in different parts of the world. The Choir sang the lovely anthem of Gustav Holst, 'The Evening Watch'; and as the coffin was carried out of the Church, Nunc Dimittis. The rain was still drenching down at the Burial. The rush of the river under the bridge all but drowned the words of committal, as Eric James spoke them at the graveside, and as Stephen, Simon, Chris and Chip lowered John into his grave. The Gloria the Choir sang had the rushing water as its orchestra. Scarlett handed sprigs of rosemary from her basket to all those gathered round the grave. 'And so', as Ruth wrote, 'my lovely impossible man was laid to rest.'

The fires and the hot soup at 'The Falcon' were welcome to the family and friends of John and Ruth who gathered there after the funeral on that December day.

During their Christmas visit after John's death Stephen and Catherine walked with Ruth up West Moor above Arncliffe, to search out a headstone for John's grave. They found one small enough to be moved and with a face flat enough to bear an inscription, then left it there till the ground of the grave was ready.

Later in January, Ruth and Stephen with Eric James went to Lambeth and talked to the Archbishop about his plans for John's books and papers.

At the end of the month, Ruth managed to get to Bristol in time to meet, a few hours after her birth, Vicki, the second child of Judith and Chris, and Ruth and John's latest grandchild.

With his 'Directions for Funeral' John had left:

Suggestions for Memorial Service
(NB   No one should be allowed to write their own memorial service – *cave F. A. Simpson*! – any more than their own obituary, or choose their successor.)

Among the Sentences: 'Lord, teach us to number our days that we may apply our hearts unto wisdom' (Psalm 90)

Another of praise and thanksgiving.
'Special Preface'. I suggest suggestions are solicited from Charlie
Moule, Eric James and Henry Chadwick, among others.

> *Psalm* 139 vv. 1–18, 23–4
>
> *Lesson.* Romans 8, NEB ('filleted'), 18–39.
> Beginning 'I reckon', vv. 18–19, 22–28, 31–2, 35, 37–9 (omitting
> the initial 'and').
>
> *Anthem* – open. Possibly Ridout's 'Thee God, I come from' as I love
> Hopkins.
>
> *Address* (short) by Eric James, since he has known me best in all my
> spheres of ministry.
>
> *Prayers* – usual – and open, though if a suitable one could be found,
> perhaps include one from my Father's collection, A. W. Robinson
> *Prayers New and Old* (There is a copy among my family's books in
> the left-hand shelves of my sitting room, or Ruth will have one at
> home), or possibly 'Remember, O Lord, what thou hast wrought in
> us' (translated 1928 Prayer Book by my uncle Armitage).
>
> Probably *after* the Donne prayer, the final 'In Paradisum' from Fauré's
> *Requiem*, which I first learnt to appreciate at Cecil Day-Lewis's memorial
> service in St Martin-in-the-Fields: (if the Choir can cope – how not?)
> PS   I forgot the hymns: Richard Baxter's 'He wants not friends who
> hath thy love' and Charles Wesley's 'O Thou who camest from above'.

And later there was a page more of 'further thoughts'! This was *not*
'writing his own Memorial Service': it was his suggestions for the
Memorial Service in Trinity; but it immediately became clear that there
would not be room in Trinity Chapel for all who wanted to attend such
a service, and that many in Southwark were asking for a Eucharist in
thanksgiving for John to be held in the Cathedral. The Bishop of
Southwark, Ronald Bowlby, readily agreed, and – knowing this would
delight Ruth – invited Mervyn Stockwood to preach the sermon, who
gladly accepted the invitation. This took place on 4 February 1984.

The Cathedral was crowded and included a coach-load of people
who remembered John – and Mervyn – in Bristol. As Mervyn said in
his sermon, 'I wonder how many curates would attract a coach-load 37
years after their departure?' The Moderator of the Free Church
Federal Council, Dr Kenneth Slack, read the Epistle from Romans 8;
John's successor as Bishop of Woolwich, David Sheppard, read the
Gospel, John 1:1–18; a reading from Eliot's *Little Gidding* was read by

Jill Balcon; the intercessions were led by Michael Marshall, then Bishop of Woolwich. The hymns were those John had suggested.

Mervyn's sermon held the congregation from the very first word to the last. He compared John with Barnabas. It was a sermon full of anecdote, humour – and personal testimony. 'It was John more than anybody who helped me to understand what it was to have a brother in Christ . . . In the forty years I knew John, I never heard him say a single uncharitable word, and he is the only man I have met in this world about whom I could say that.' It was also a hard hitting sermon:

> After he had left Woolwich and had been Dean of Trinity College, Cambridge for ten years, he told me he would like to return if possible to a full-time ministry in the Church of England. I approached the likely authorities in Church and State. I think that charity demands that the rest should be silence. Suffice it to say that John never once complained. John never expressed a word of self-pity. Why was John, this prophet and man of God, thus treated by the Church of England?

Ruth went from the Thanksgiving Eucharist in Southwark to Oxford, and next day to the first of the Bampton Lectures in St Mary's, Oxford where Professor Moule, with quiet and unassuming skill and scholarship, began the difficult task of interpreting the work of his friend and colleague to the learned congregation scattered among the pews before him.

The next week Ruth began in Cambridge the enormous task of clearing John's rooms – which the College generously made available to her until the end of May. She also sent out the third of the 'Letters to Their Friends' which had kept so many in touch with all that had been happening to John, and helped them, too, to 'learn from cancer'.

At the end of the week, on Saturday, 11 February, Trinity Chapel was as full for John's Memorial Service as Southwark Cathedral had been for the Thanksgiving Eucharist. They were quite different occasions, each with their own excellence. The Choir sang as an introit to the Memorial Service William Walton's setting of the words from the Song of Solomon: 'Set me as a seal upon thine heart'. Among the sentences was one from John Donne, which John had suggested: 'Whom God loves, he loves to the end: and not to their end, and to their death, but to his end, and his end is that he might love them more.' Then followed a 'Special Preface' read by Ralph Godsall – the kind of preface for which John had asked and which he had carefully composed for so many others:

We are here to thank God for JOHN ARTHUR THOMAS ROBINSON: for his deep exploration of Christian truth and foundations; for his eagerness to transcend barriers between the sacred and secular, East and West, rich and poor; for his singular gifts as a writer and teacher and his zest for life; for his love and honesty towards family and friends; and for the example of his courage, in life as in death, as seeing the unseen through Jesus Christ his Lord. Let us commend both him and those dear to him to the faithfulness of God.

The Choir then sang the Psalm of John's choice Psalm 139. One of the most moving moments followed the Psalm – the reading by the Master of Trinity, Sir Alan Hodgkin, OM, of a passage from *Le Milieu Divin* by Teilhard de Chardin, for which John had asked in his 'further thoughts'.

It was a joy to me, O God, in the midst of the struggle, to feel that in developing myself I was increasing the hold that You have upon me; it was a joy to me, too, under the inward thrust of life or amid the favourable play of events, to abandon myself to Your Providence. Now that I have found the joy of utilising all forms of growth to make You, or to let You, grow in me, grant that I may willingly consent to this last phase of communion in the course of which I shall possess You by diminishing in You.

After having perceived You as He who is 'a greater myself', grant, when my hour comes, that I may recognise You under the species of each alien or hostile force that seems bent upon destroying or uprooting me. When the signs of age begin to mark my body (and still more when they touch my mind); when the ill that is to diminish me or carry me off strikes from without or is born within me; when the painful moment comes in which I suddenly awaken to the fact that I am ill or growing old; and above all at that last moment when I feel I am losing hold of myself and am absolutely passive within the hands of the great unknown forces that have formed me; in all those dark moments, O God, grant that I may understand that it is You (provided only my faith is strong enough) who are painfully parting the fibres of my being in order to penetrate to the very marrow of my substance and bear me away within Yourself.

The more deeply and incurably the evil is encrusted in my flesh, the more it will be You that I am harbouring – You as a loving, active principle of purification and detachment. Vouchsafe, therefore, something more precious still than the grace for which all the faithful pray. It is not enough that I shall die while communicating. Teach me to treat my death as an act of communion.

The hymns were as in the Southwark Cathedral Eucharist. The Choir sang the Holst anthem they had sung at John's funeral. The prayers were led by Robert Atwell; most of them were those John had suggested with prayers also from Thomas Aquinas, Francis Bacon and Bishop Westcott. (During the prayers the ten-days-old Vicki announced her presence with one faint murmur.) Eric James's address was a shade longer than the 'Address (short)' that John's 'Suggestions' had implied, not least because he preached upon a passage, not just a text – from the translation of the Epistle to the Ephesians in John's uncle Armitage's unsurpassed commentary:

> 'He gave some, apostles; and some, prophets; and some, evangelists; and some, pastors and teachers; for the perfecting of the saints for the work of ministry; for the building of the Body of Christ; till we all come to the unity of the faith and of the knowledge of the Son of God; to a perfect man; to the measure of the stature of the fulness of Christ; that we be no longer children, tossed to and fro, and carried about with every wind of doctrine; by the sleight of men, by craftiness according to the wiles of error; but maintaining the truth in love, may grow up into Him in all things, which is the head, even Christ; from whom the whole body, fitly framed together and compacted by every joint of its supply, according to the effectual working in the measure of each several part, maketh the increase of the body, unto the building thereof in love'.

> I begin with that great passage for several reasons [said Eric] not least because that first phrase – 'He gave some, apostles; and some, prophets; and some, evangelists; and some pastors and teachers' – makes it immediately clear what a superlatively *gifted* man John was; for to him it was given to be an apostle, and a prophet, and an evangelist, and a pastor, and a teacher – and many other gifts that are not contained in that great passage. But I begin with that passage, primarily because it is in that context John's gifts, and indeed John's life, should be set; and it is in that context, certainly, John himself would have wanted them set. That passage is above all about our human relating in and to the transcendent purpose of God: the End of all our relating. And that was the subject which possessed and held John all his life.

Eric also said – in a sentence not unlike one in Mervyn Stockwood's sermon: 'Some of us will be for ever ashamed that the Church never invited John to be the brilliant diocesan scholar-bishop he had it in him to be – in the steps of his masters, Westcott and Lightfoot – or indeed to fill any further position of seniority in the Church.'

After the Memorial Service at Trinity Ruth went back to Oxford for the next Bampton, and then back to Cambridge; then back to Oxford – till the first four Bamptons had been delivered. The last four lectures were delivered on each of the Sundays in May. Ruth continued to pack up more boxes for Lambeth, until at last there were eighty-four boxes for kind young Trinity men to transport to London. On Saturday, 26 May, before driving to Oxford for the final Bampton Lecture, she handed in the keys of the emptied rooms in Nevile's Court at the Porter's Lodge. As she drove up the motorway from Oxford to Arncliffe for the last time the following afternoon it was her own life that lay ahead.

In July 1984 *Twelve More New Testament Studies* was published. It is very much a scholar's book – much of it closely related to *The Priority of John*. David Edwards reviewed it in the *Church Times*, drawing attention to the typical pieces of provocation the book contained for whoever chose to read it: 'The most indisputable fact about the birth of Jesus is that it occurred out of wedlock ... The only choice open to us is between a virgin birth and an illegitimate birth ... We shall never know, humanly speaking, who Jesus' father was.' In the book's final essay David Edwards finds a similarly stimulating passage: 'I have had the gravest uncertainty about many aspects of the traditional doctrine' of the Trinity, John wrote – partly because he was sure that in the first century 'Christian language about pre-existence was not referring to separate persons divine or heavenly', so that Christ is *not* 'God dressed up in human clothes, a heavenly being who takes on manhood' if we are to share the faith of the New Testament. 'This essay', John wrote in the last paragraph of the book, 'is but a contribution, from one angle, to the debate that lies ahead. Much honest rethinking will be required...' As David Edwards pointed out, in his penultimate book John arouses echoes of 'his famous paperback of 1963'.

What David did as scholar-journalist is what every good journalist does; in a book of formidable and solid scholarship he looked for the newsworthy, even sensational bits – the 'quotable quotes'. What needs to be emphasized however is what David as scholar also underlined: that this is a positive, careful book, the fruit of years of work and thought; the first article, for instance – on 'Hosea and the Virgin Birth' – sums up nearly forty years of a scholar's considered reflections upon an article he first wrote in 1948.

It was in the autumn of 1984 that Ruth asked her young farming neighbour to drive his Land-Rover to a spot on West Moor, near where John's gravestone was lying. Then, with Stephen, Simon and Buffy helping (and Scarlett and Sophie encouraging), the stone was moved, lifted into the Land-Rover, driven down to the lych-gate of Arncliffe Church, and carried to the grave. The children helped to dig the hole and Buffy mixed the cement and set the stone. (Afterwards Sophie, with spontaneous grace and a fine whimsical nonchalance, posed against it for a memorable photograph.)

Some months later while showing an exhibition of her batik paintings, Buffy saw the work of a fellow exhibitor, John Shaw, a young artist in stone, from York. Ruth asked him to come and see the headstone and design an inscription, on a circle of Welsh slate, which he completed and set into the stone the following autumn. Within the circle the words *John Arthur Thomas Robinson Born 15 June 1919 Died 5 December 1983* are set under a bishop's mitre. Within sight and sound of the river Skirfare – 'bright stream' – just over the Churchyard wall, John had been received into the Northern landscape. It is, as he asked, a 'double grave' with space for Ruth alongside. The next grave is that of Brigie – to whom John ministered and at whose funeral he preached. Each spring the Churchyard is a profusion of the snowdrops and daffodils in which John so delighted.

The Priority of John was published on 1 October 1985. That afternoon the Archbishop of Canterbury and Mrs Runcie welcomed Ruth and the children to tea at Lambeth Palace, together with Edward and Wendy, Celia, and Eric James. After tea they were taken to Cranmer's Parlour. The lower half of each wall had been shelved in keeping with the room, which had been furnished as a study; and John's books were now carefully arranged on the shelves. On the ledge that formed the top of the shelves on one side of the room stood the bronze head of John by the Polish sculptor Edward Ihnatowicz. Ruth and her family went from Lambeth Palace to the Jerusalem Chamber in Westminster Abbey, where the Dean and Chapter had gladly given permission for the SCM Press to welcome John's family and friends to a celebration of the publication. As the guests entered the Chamber – where many of the meetings of the translators both of the Authorized Version of the Bible and of the New English Bible had taken place – they passed the bust of a former Dean – uncle Armitage.

To produce *The Priority of John* – and it is a beautifully *produced* volume – after John's death, required the co-operation of several of his friends. John's former pupil Dr Chip Coakley had undertaken the huge work of editing, with Professor Moule as his consultant. John knew that it would mean 'checking endless unrewarding details'. Chip had come to Cambridge from the USA for a second BA and had let it be known that he planned at the end of it to return to the USA and study for the ordained ministry. John had said nothing either for or against this, but when Chip got a first-class degree John was very keen that he should seize the chance to stay in Cambridge and do research. He sketched out an area for a topic – the Fourth Gospel! – which Chip later abandoned – and wrote all the references he needed for grants. Chip was grateful for the interest John had taken in him in consequence of which he is now a lecturer at the University of Lancaster. Stella Haughton – 'my incredibly long-suffering secretary' as John called her – typed (and retyped) the manuscript, as she had typed all John's manuscripts for twenty years. Jean Cunningham copy-edited it – as she had *Twelve More New Testament Studies*. Jean had written to John in October 1983: 'I have always enjoyed working on your books chiefly for the interest of the material, but also for the felicity of the style; and I count it a great honour to have been asked to help at this stage and in these circumstances.' When John Bowden of the SCM Press told John that Jean would be seeing *The Priority of John* through the press, he had said: 'In that case I shall die content.' He totally trusted and was deeply grateful to all his friends who were to co-operate on *The Priority of John*. Stephen was glad to help Chip Coakley with the proofs. When this biography of John was finished, it was too soon for many reviews to have been published (though not too soon for the first hardback impression to have been sold – and for a reprinting in paperback 'to meet a strong demand', to have been ordered for spring 1987.)

An unsigned review in the *Expository Times* (October 1985) gives a particularly clear summary of the book:

> That John Robinson argued for a very early dating of all the books of the New Testament, is, of course, well known. 'Priority' however, as he uses it in this book is not synonymous with 'first'. He believes that 'all the Gospels were coming into being over a period more or less simultaneously, and at different stages their traditions and their redactions could well show signs of mutual influence. But the priority of John does not depend on which Gospel was begun or finished first. The priority of John means that 'we begin with what he has to tell us on its own merits

and ask how the others fit, historically and theologically into that, are illumined by it, and in turn illumine it'.

Having questioned the pre-suppositions on which the presumption of the posteriority of John has rested . . . Robinson states that he would argue for the priority of John in much the same way as he would argue for the priority of Mark – that it was not necessarily the first Gospel to be finished, nor that the tradition found in it is in its more original state, but that it stands both at the beginning and the end of the New Testament, starting from an eye-witness and containing a theology that leads us more deeply *into* the history rather than away from it . . . A major part of the book is devoted to an argument for the historicity of John's account . . . The upshot of the discussion is that Robinson holds that it is possible, accepting the priority of John, to recover the outline of the ministry of Jesus, and his third chapter has the title The Chronology of the Ministry . . . He claims that it is simply not true that the synoptic and Johannine pictures are so divergent as is assumed and that where there are differences it is John who is to be preferred. There is no reason to suppose that the early Christians were not interested in such things. Rather they took for granted a knowledge of the life of Jesus . . . He knocks the claim that there is evidence of anti-semitism in John's account of the trial of Jesus very hard indeed, asserting that such suggestions are grounded in a complete distortion of the evidence.

In *The Priority of John* it is made clear that the author thinks that the Gospel was written (or dictated) in Ephesus by John the son of Zebedee, the 'beloved disciple'. He thinks it possible that John's mother was the sister of the mother of Jesus. He considers it worthwhile to explore the geography of Palestine in relation to the Gospel.

The Priority of John was never intended to be a popular book. It is, as David Edwards wrote, 'a scholar talking with colleagues'. John nursed the hope that there might be a more popular book as a sequel. That was not, alas, to be written by himself, but there is every hope that in due time such a book will be written by John's skilful and unassuming editor, Dr Coakley.

Canon Leslie Houlden, Lecturer in New Testament Studies, King's College, London, in his review in the *Times Literary Supplement* (4 October 1985) wrote:

The book aptly conveys the essence of his doctrine on many matters that were central to his beliefs: the relation of history to concept in Christian understanding, the essential trustworthiness of the Gospels including that of John, the sufficiency of New Testament teaching (once it is properly understood) as the foundation for Christian belief. In that way, it is his fitting memorial and the moving achievement of a dying man who maintained to the end both his own vision of fundamental things and a capacity for fastidious judgment on innumerable detailed questions.

We now await the posthumous publication of John's essays: *The End of All Our Exploring?* and perhaps other books of his unpublished writings; for 'there are also many other things' which John wrote, the which, if they should be published every one . . . ! Studies of his work are beginning to be published. (*Bog dla nas* by Ks. Piotr Jackota; *God for us: an ecumenical dogmatic study of J. A. T. Robinson's Christology*, was published in Polish in 1986 by the Catholic University of Lublin.)

Certainly, as we have written, John deserves in his memory a theological study of distinction. Canon Houlden in his review of *The Priority of John* wrote:

> The public reputation of John Robinson, once Bishop of Woolwich, then Dean of Trinity College, Cambridge, was at its height in the sixties. On the theological scene, he seemed to epitomize the spirit of that period as well as anyone. Above all by writing *Honest to God* (1963), he became a symbol of radicalism, a disturber of religious peace, and a rocker of theological boats. As a bishop in South London, he helped to sum up a new mood of reform in the Church of England, in which the diocese of Southwark, under Mervyn Stockwood who appointed him, took the lead.
>
> Yet to see Robinson as *par excellence* the thrillingly shocking radical was a misconception. The essence of the man lay less in any consistent espousal of heterodox views and reformist policies in the church than in a constant independence of mind. He hunted with no pack for long but went his own way. His chief debts were not to the purveyors of novelty in his own day, but to figures in his past (mostly family or Cambridge) to whom his loyalty was assured. His books are liable to be as full of references to nineteenth-century scholars as to those more recent and are inclined to dig up names long forgotten by everybody else and never much attended to even in their own day. Those who have seen him as a late Victorian radical born out of due time are perhaps the most discerning. The many who failed to grasp these things about him were bewildered when, in *Redating the New Testament* (1976), he emerged as the champion of an unlikely and undeniably conservative cause – the dating of the New Testament books to the period before AD 70 and so the strengthening of their claim to historical accuracy. Both those who had once vilified but now (somewhat tentatively) embraced him, and those who saw with regret the spectacle of a radical turning reactionary as age crept on, had mistaken their man.

Robinson's work as a New Testament critic makes the independence and continuity, as well as the loyalty to past exemplars, perfectly plain. Nowhere do these features come forth more clearly than in his numerous writings on the Gospel of John, which span the greater part of his career in New Testament scholarship. That long germinating study finds its fruit in *The Priority of John.*

It is such comments that make it impossible not to ask the question why it was that John's so considerable pastoral, prophetic, scholastic and administrative gifts were not more fully used by the Church in his later years. John had argued that the Church should develop a system of care and deployment of the clergy which would be an example to the world at large when he argued for the implementation of the Paul and Morley Reports in the Sixties. But *Quis custodiet ipsos custodes?* Who were the shepherds keeping watch over John? The Archbishops? The Secretaries for Appointments? The Crown Appointments Commission? The Vacancy-in-See Committees? When possible appointments arose, did they consider and reject John – as the electing bodies in Cambridge had considered and rejected him – and choose other and better pastors, scholars or prophets?

Bishop Michael Ramsey, in a letter to Eric James dated 18 September 1984, wrote:

> I had no part in the move to Trinity, so far as I remember, other than sending a testimonial to the Master. There was no question of 'the Archbishop has had J.R. moved on'! Subsequently I had talk with 'R.A.B.', and we both said (independently) that it would be best if after a few years at Trinity, J.R. should go and be a Diocesan Bishop. I wish he had been a Diocesan . . .

Michael Ramsey thought the idea that John would have made a great scholar-bishop 'a good deal exaggerated'. He had resigned the Archbishopric of Canterbury in 1974. Lord Coggan, his successor, in a letter to Eric James, dated 4 September 1986, wrote: 'I do not recall John's name coming up for consideration as a Diocesan or Dean during my time at Canterbury . . . I do remember 'R.A.B.' Butler mentioning his name to me in a vague way when we dined next to one another once or twice in London, but not in connection with any specific appointment . . .' Lord Coggan resigned in 1980 and Robert Runcie was enthroned as Archbishop of Canterbury on 25 March 1980.

We know, and have recorded, that the Secretary for Appointments to the Prime Minister visited John on 6 June 1975 – after being in touch with Lord Butler. There is no evidence of any other similar meeting in John's meticulous diaries, or any item of correspondence indicating such a meeting. It is of course possible to maintain that a university appointment – even that of a suffragan bishop to be the Dean of Chapel of a Cambridge College – is a secular appointment, and that John of his own volition had 'stepped out of line'. But John always remained an Assistant Bishop, first of Southwark, then of Bradford. And we know that, having accepted his 'secular' appointment, the Secretary for Appointments visited him. We know that John confided in Lord Butler and wrote to him about one possible appointment – as Dean of Canterbury – and R.A.B. was as close as anyone to No. 10. Even that however might not be an unmixed blessing if R.A.B. had lost confidence in John – and there is some evidence to that effect. Remarks by R.A.B. about John are remembered – made no doubt half in jest – which are hardly of a kind to suggest a warm approach to a Secretary for Appointments. If Trinity had lost confidence in John and no longer felt it would get from him what it had hoped for when he was appointed, R.A.B. the politician would have been swift to sense it. As Master of Trinity he was treated very much as its monarch and mogul, and the Master's Lodge was his court; but he and Lady Butler kept their ears to the ground. He was of course no stranger to situations in which authority ditches today its bright hope of yesterday. However considerate and warm-hearted R.A.B. was personally, there is little evidence that he and his Dean of Chapel related closely, or that R.A.B. particularly appreciated John's gifts and worth and saw reason to fight for him. But R.A.B. ceased to be Master of Trinity in 1978.

Michael Ramsey has told us that he 'wished John had been a Diocesan'. Mervyn Stockwood has told us that he 'approached the likely authorities in Church and State' after John had been Dean of Trinity College, Cambridge for ten years, that is, in or after 1979.

It must be remembered that John was appointed a 'suffragan' bishop, which appointment was largely the choice of his Diocesan. But the method of appointing a diocesan bishop has greatly changed since (for instance) Mervyn Stockwood was appointed Bishop of Southwark. It is really a question of whether under the new system – the Crown Appointments Commission was established in February 1977 – someone with John's reputation is ever likely to gain the support of the majority of a Vacancy-in-See Committee, or the Crown Appointments Commission – let alone of a Prime Minister.

It has, of course, to be conceded that John's reputation includes his undeniable weaknesses – which the foregoing pages have not sought to conceal. One has written:

> His tragedy was, as is the nature of tragedy, that the greatest strengths of his nature had a 'kick back' from which he was the greatest sufferer. He was no more fond of the limelight than another man, no more anxious for people to listen to him or read his books. What he lacked was what most of us have studiously developed – the self-regard which enables us to cover up the less socially attractive traits of our human nature. Those who loved him knew this lack of self-regard to be a great gift – his refusal to take offence, the determination to pursue truth and justice whatever the risk to his own reputation, his care for the doubtfully acceptable. Those who knew him less were more likely to judge him at his face value and he was never one to recognise the need to save face. It could be said of him that those who knew him best loved him best; for them, occasional embarrassment on his account was a small price to pay for the blessing of such unaffected openness and generosity of spirit.

Two further questions must be asked: Why were John's weaknesses more apparent in his years at Trinity and Cambridge than in his years in South London? Few ever doubted in his Southwark days that John was a great suffragan bishop and had it in him some day to be a great diocesan bishop. It has to be said that John responded to situations and rose to occasions when his gifts were recognized, called upon and used. In his later years the Church of England showed few signs of doing that. And it is clear that in Trinity and Cambridge John's gifts were not fully recognized – though his weaknesses were – until all but too late.

The question also needs to be pressed: Should John have been a *diocesan* bishop? It is too often and too readily assumed that the gifts of a John Robinson are *best* used in this way.

Lord Beveridge called his autobiography *Power and Influence*. It was, he said:

> less of an autobiography for its own sake than an illustration of the theme set in the title . . . the chief alternative ways by which things get done in the world of affairs . . . Since I came to manhood, I have seldom been without influence. I have seldom had 'Government', that is power . . . Throughout my life I have poured out words remorselessly in books,

articles, memoranda, reports, records of travel, broadcasts, speeches and letters.

But does anyone doubt the importance of the *influence* of Beveridge in post-war Britain?

Could it not be that, as we have been reminded, as Dean of Trinity John had – thanks to Trinity's generosity – 'income, time for teaching, time for travelling' – time, we might add, for his 'Three Ways' of theological exploration, biblical interrogation and social responsibility? Could he have pursued all these ways as a *diocesan* bishop? Would *The Priority of John* have been produced if John had been a diocesan bishop? Should he have had power as well as influence? What was the priority *for* John? John was most likely to have made up his mind about that priority as he answered a specific invitation – as he did when he answered the invitation to be suffragan Bishop of Woolwich. The question remains: Did John's chief pastors consider extending to him such an invitation? Did they, after 1975, *discuss his future with him*? Lord Coggan (in his letter of 4 September 1986) writes:

> Speaking personally, I think John's creative and original gifts would have been – if not lost – seriously limited, if he had had the burden of a Diocese. A Deanery is another matter, but even Deans, in these days of diminished Chapters, are 'cumbered about with much serving'. His greatest gifts were, surely, academic; along those lines he made his greatest contribution. His time at Woolwich helped him to 'earth' those gifts and be a realist about the life of the Church. But, looking back, did not the combination of South London and Cambridge just about work out right for the best exercise of his many gifts?

The question how John's gifts should have been used is, of course, important. But the saying 'Man proposes but God disposes' is at least as old as Thomas à Kempis and *The Imitation of Christ*. Various proposals might have been made in John's last years which would have recognized, called upon and used his gifts. We now know they would have been brought to naught by what in fact finally called out from John his best gifts – paradoxically, a pancreatic tumour. And we know that John asked that at his Memorial Service the words of Teilhard de Chardin should be read: 'The more deeply and incurably the evil is encrusted in my flesh, the more it will be You that I am harbouring – You as a loving active principle of purification and detachment ...

Teach me to treat my death as an act of communion.' *In the End, God* was not simply the title of John's first book.

'Some there be which have no memorial.' John's memorial will be those whose lives he influenced and whom he taught. They will not forget him. His memorial will also be his own books – and books about him. And there are other memorials. There is the stone in the Churchyard at Arncliffe beside the Skirfare. And if you crossed a very different river, the Yamuna, east of Delhi, you would come to Seema-puri, just over the UP border at Shahidnagar, and the Deenabandhu School, set in lowly conditions. At the time of John's death, a memorial fund was set up, and as a result of his friends' contributions the Cambridge Mission to Delhi – the Brotherhood of the Ascension – was able to build a large class-room, part of the new extension to the School. A plaque suitably inscribed has been set in the wall outside the class-room door.

And if you went down the Thames ten miles, past Woolwich on the south bank you would come upon Thamesmead – the new town born in 1967. Already twenty thousand people have made a new life there. John had much to do with the beginning of the Thamesmead Christian Community and the ecumenical Team Ministry. In January 1987 a new junior school will be opened – the Bishop John Robinson Primary School.

This biography is of course also written 'In Memoriam' – one of John's father's books was a commentary on the great Tennyson poem of that title. Yet these pages have been written not only in memory of John but – to use the two words he himself at the end of his life caused to be inscribed on the pulpit-lectern he bequeathed to Trinity Chapel – *in eucharistia*, in thanksgiving.

Index